HOMEMADE MONEY

How to select, start, manage, market and multiply the profits of a business at home.

Barbara Brabec

BETTERWAY BOOKS

CINCINNATI, OHIO

Homemade Money. Copyright © 1994, 1997 by Barbara Brabec. Printed and bound in the United States of America. All rights reserved. No part of this book may be reproduced in any form or by any electronic or mechanical means including information storage and retrieval systems without permission in writing from the publisher, except by a reviewer, who may quote brief passages in a review. Published by Betterway Books, an imprint of F&W Publications, Inc., 1507 Dana Avenue, Cincinnati, Ohio 45207. (800) 289-0963. Revised fifth edition.

01   00   99   98   97   5   4   3   2   1

Library of Congress Cataloging-in-Publication Data

Brabec, Barbara.
   Homemade money / by Barbara Brabec. — Rev. 5th ed.
     p.   cm.
   Includes bibliographical references and index.
   ISBN 1-55870-466-3 (alk. paper)
   1. Home-based businesses—Management. I. Title.
HD62.7.B68   1997   IN PROCESS
658′.041—dc21   97-25552
                                              CIP

Edited by Perri Weinberg-Schenker
Interior and cover design by Paul Neff
Cover illustration by Gerard Mooney/SIS

The following page constitutes an extension of this copyright page.

Betterway Books are available for sales promotions, premiums and fund-raising use. Special editions or book excerpts can also be created to specification. For details, contact the Special Sales Manager, F&W Publications, 1507 Dana Avenue, Cincinnati, Ohio 45207.

··

DEDICATED TO THE MEMORY OF
WILLIAM J. SCHAUMBURG

Unlike his children, my father did not have the benefit of a good education. Yet he was smart enough to teach himself what he needed to know to make a living, first as a farmer and, later, as an auto mechanic and repairman who never met anything mechanical he couldn't figure out.

With little more than talent, determination and a belief in himself, he built his own home and garage business in a small farming community in Illinois, where he lived until he died in 1982.

As children, my two sisters and I did not realize that our father, by example, was quietly instilling in each of us his work ethic and entrepreneurial spirit, but as three entrepreneurial women, we certainly know it now.

This book is for him.

··

ACKNOWLEDGMENTS

I am indebted to the many business professionals who made special contributions to this edition of *Homemade Money*. In particular, I wish to thank tax attorney Julian Block and Mary Helen Sears, specialist in copyrights, patents and trademarks, for checking my manuscript for accuracy. The time and talent of these professionals, so generously contributed, have benefited all of us.

My thanks, too, to the countless home-business owners who, through the years, have shared their business experiences and expertise with me. So much of what I've learned has been gained from my readers, many of whom are quoted in this edition of the book.

Finally, a nod of gratitude to my husband, Harry (last on the list, as usual). Through the years, his help with the business has made all the difference in my ability to find extra time for writing, and his sense of humor has often made the difference between a good day and a bad one. I owe him more personal attention, vacation time and home-baked bread and cookies than I'll ever be able to deliver.

CONTENTS

PREFACE

MILLIONS OF AMERICANS AND CANA-
dians are generating income from an in-
credible variety of homebased activities. I
call it "homemade money," and this book
tells you how to get in on the action.

When the first edition of *Homemade
Money* was published in 1984, homebased
businesses were still a novelty to most
people. Those who did give consideration
to the idea were likely to be thinking only
in terms of doing something part time for
extra money. Few of us could have imagined in the early 1980s that millions of
people in the 1990s would be earning a
living from some form of homebased
work.

In the chapters that follow, you will
find immediate answers to thousands of
questions on how to start, operate and

stay in a business at home, be it a small, part-time endeavor for extra money, or a full-time entrepreneurial venture. *Homemade Money* is a reflection of my lifetime of business experience coupled with that of thousands of other professionals in my small business network, and it contains specific, how-to information on every topic related to the start-up, management and successful marketing of a homebased business. Trial-and-error experience may be a great way to learn, but it's expensive in terms of both time and money. There's no need for you to learn everything the hard way, because so many people are willing to share the benefit of their experience with you. This book is but one example.

Regardless of whether you're still dreaming about making money at home, just starting in business, or well under way, *Homemade Money* is designed to assist you at every stage of your business. Don't tackle this book with the idea that you need to absorb all of it in one sitting; rather, think of it as an idea stimulator and answer book you can turn to for help at every stage of your growing business. (The detailed index will be helpful in this regard.) Meanwhile, count on me for support as you embark on what could be the most interesting, frustrating, exciting, frightful, satisfying and fulfilling thing you will ever do: become your own boss.

THE WORK-AT-HOME INDUSTRY

1

BEFORE I GET TO THE MEAT OF THIS book—how to succeed as a self-employed individual working from home—I want you to have an understanding of the BIG work-at-home picture so you can see exactly how and where you fit into it. Actually, home-based businesses are just one segment of the huge and growing work-at-home industry, which also includes: (1) telecommuters; (2) "moonlighters" (people who work full time and run a part-time business on the side); (3) corporate employees who regularly bring work home from the office; (4) self-employed individuals who have a business base at home yet do not think of themselves as home-business owners because they perform services away from home.

When computer technology began to fuel the work-at-home industry in the

---

Home Free!

The Home has been dubbed "The New American Workplace," and that's probably not far from the truth. If the industry's unprecedented growth continues—and experts predict it will—the majority of Americans will work at home in the 21st century. Who was it that called homebased business a "fad" in the 1980s, anyway? None other than Megatrends *guru John Naisbitt. He now works at home.*
　　—Stephanie Barlow, Senior
　　　Writer, in an article for
　　　Entrepreneur magazine

Women Working at Home

The U.S. Department of Labor predicts that, by the turn of the century, women will account for one-half of the workforce and two-thirds of labor force growth. Other statistics indicate more than half of all mothers now work full time—and not always because they are seeking fulfillment. In these hard economic times, the extra income is likely to be needed. In one *New York Times* poll on women's issues, 83 percent of working mothers said they felt torn between the demands of their job and wanting to spend more time with their family. Such women are perfect candidates for a business at home.

mid-1980s, market research firms began to gather statistics for clients interested in marketing to this diverse group of homeworkers. Their findings became news because this was the first time anyone had made an effort to count the steadily growing number of people who were working at home. (See selected statistics in "A Brief History of the Work-at-Home Industry" at the end of this chapter.) If researchers are correct, we can expect to see continued growth in the work-at-home industry well into the twenty-first century. But whether the total number of home-based workers goes up or down between now and then, one thing seems certain: *Homebased businesses are here to stay.* They have become not only an important economic revitalization tool in both urban and rural areas—adding billions of dollars to the economy—but the lifestyle of choice for millions of Americans and Canadians.

In spite of all the statistics being bandied about today, no one knows for sure how many people work at home for others versus how many actually own part- or full-time businesses of their own. Surveys by government agencies do not always agree with those of various market research firms who are gathering data in different ways for different purposes. For example, one market research specialist told me his company's figures are based on an annual telephone survey of 2,500 consumer households, with telephone numbers generated randomly by computer. By comparison, the U.S. Labor Department gathers its data periodically from a changing database of 60,000 households. One of the reasons it is so hard to obtain a definitive count of the number of people working at home is different surveys of this population do not use the same definitions of homebased work, and homeworkers themselves aren't sure what they should be calling themselves. Are they "homebased employees," "part-time workers," "independent contractors," "homebased entrepreneurs," "home-office professionals," "home-business owners" or "self-employed individuals?" Adding to the confusion is the fact that writers and media people have coined a variety of new words to describe all these people. (See sidebar on page 5.)

Home Businesses Then and Now

Technology was certainly responsible for the tremendous growth we've seen in the work-at-home industry since the mid-1980s, but homebased enterprises have been part of the American culture since the days of the early American colonies when everyone worked at home—the baker, the silversmith, the candlestick maker, the weaver, blacksmith, doctor and so on. Bit by bit, we seem to be coming full circle as more and more people look upon their homeplace as workplace too.

My own home-business beginnings date back to the mid-

1960s when, like thousands of others, I got caught up in America's arts and crafts revolution. After ten years as a secretary in Chicago's Loop, I had great fun for several years selling my handcrafts at local shops and fairs, an experience my husband, Harry, thought I should write about. At his urging, and in spite of knowing nothing about the craft of writing, I began to create quarterly issues of a magazine we later would laughingly refer to as "a literary success and a financial flop." This second little entrepreneurial venture of mine survived only five years, which was more than long enough to make my husband wish he'd never told me to "get a hobby" back in the 1960s. Those three little words ultimately changed not only my life, but his. After five years of working full time at home, we had gained a clear understanding of how a home business impacts one's personal life. It all came to a head the day Harry said, "It's me or the magazine, kiddo, take your pick."

I didn't know it at the time, but twenty years before "home-based businesses" would become watchwords of America, I was gaining experience and contacts that would neatly position me as a pioneer and leader in the industry. People who worked at home during the 1960s and 1970s didn't broadcast the fact, and "entrepreneur" was a word few individuals could identify with, let alone spell. Yet, just like today's self-employed individuals, we attached a Schedule C Form to our annual income tax return to show income derived from sources other than a job. Common money-making activities of the day included mail-order businesses, independent sales of products such as Tupperware, Avon or Fuller Brush, freelance writing and publishing, and arts and crafts—activities that are more popular and profitable today than ever. As I see it, the only real difference between then and now is that now there are literally hundreds of different types of homebased businesses, and people at large are beginning to realize it's a special kind of achievement to be able to live by one's wits and build a successful business at home.

Like many others in the early 1980s, I took notice of but did not fully comprehend the concept Alvin Toffler advanced in his book, *The Third Wave*. He spoke about "commuting electronically between home and office," said there would be "new emphasis on home as the center of society," and predicted technology would be the spark for a revolution in the way people viewed work and play. What vision! In recent years, computer technology has dramatically changed our business and personal lives in ways few of us could have imagined, and we've only just seen the tip of the technological iceberg.

Computer technology, coupled with the unstable economic climate of the 1990s, has opened up unlimited opportunities for individuals to earn money from home, either as homebased employees, independent contractors or small business owners.

What Will You Call Yourself?

Here are some of the coined words being used to describe the current generation of "work-at-homers":

- Worksteaders
- Entrepreneurs
- Homepreneurs
- Kidpreneurs
- Ecopreneurs (those who are ecologically minded)
- Infopreneurs (those who sell information)
- Copreneurs (couples who work together)
- Propreneurs (corporate refugees and recent college graduates)
- Countrypreneurs (those who earn a living in the country)
- Electronic Cottagers (those who use computer technology)

Note: Some writers refer to businesses at home as "cottage industries." A true cottage industry, however, is a business with its management and marketing operations in one location, and production taking place in the homes of several individual workers. While some of today's homebased businesses are true cottage industries, it is not wise to broadcast this fact if one has hired independent contractors instead of employees. (See chapter six for details.)

Governmental Support for Homebased Businesses

In 1986, Iowa became the first state to host a major home business conference, and Kansas, Missouri, California, Ohio, Pennsylvania, Oklahoma and Indiana soon followed its lead. Oklahoma was the first state to form a statewide home-business association in 1990, quickly becoming a model for other states.

In 1989, British Columbia became the first Canadian province to aggressively support homebased businesses, when its Ministry of Regional and Economic Development established a business telephone hotline, published a self-study manual, and followed up with a provincial *Directory of Home-Based Businesses*. Canada's First National Conference/Tradeshow for Home-Based Business was held in British Columbia in 1992, shortly followed by the first government-sponsored seminar on homebased business in Alberta.

Around the world, an increasing number of European and Asian countries are also experiencing an entrepreneurial surge and looking to America for ideas they can adapt to their own needs. Years ago, it never dawned on me this book had a market outside the United States, but I recall the day someone changed my mind. At a home-business conference in Ohio where I was speaking, I met a woman from South Africa who said *Homemade Money* and my other books were exactly what she needed to help her in the cottage industry development work she was then doing. Today, my publicity mentions often generate foreign inquiries. No wonder, then, that I find myself hoping this new, expanded edition will find its way into the hands of readers around the world. Without question, the self-employment ideas and marketing concepts in this book have universal applications.

In both the United States and Canada, we have seen increased support from local, state and provincial governments, organizations and schools. These days, it is common to find business classes even in the smallest of communities. Often they are sponsored or supported by adult education centers, YMCAs, chambers of commerce, cooperative extensions, the Small Business Administration or SCORE (Service Corps of Retired Executives), or small business development centers at community colleges. There are now entrepreneurial courses in college, and, more and more, we see economic development people and government agencies working together to present educational business conferences to encourage entrepreneurism at all levels. In 1993, we began to see something new: home-office trade shows popping up in larger cities. As a speaker at many entrepreneurial events in the United States and Canada, I've had a ringside seat in the movement, and my contact with so many entrepreneurial-minded people through the years has given me unique perspective on the home-business industry in both countries.

Interesting Trends of the 1990s

By being a trend watcher, you can pick up on things that will give you ideas not only for new products and services you might sell, but new business and diversification ideas as well. The following trends are likely to continue through the turn of the century:

• Corporate "downsizing" continues to increase the demand for subcontractors (homebased entrepreneurs, moonlighters and self-employed people who consider themselves independent contractors).

• Married couples who work together, called "copreneurs" by some, may be the wave of America's business future, predicts World Future Society in its *Futurist* newsletter. The organization suggests it is only logical for corporations to hire such couples as a team.

• Home has become an important center of life where people are entertaining themselves inexpensively. Marketing consultant Ilise Benun says this suggests people will buy more pajamas and robes, books, videos, music, body oils and candles.

• The average age of Americans is inching up from thirty to the forties, and business owners need to keep this older audience in mind as they develop new products and services.

• More than 30 percent of American adults are now grandparents, and their number is rapidly growing. Since grandparents often have discretionary income and love to buy presents for their grandchildren, they represent a large niche market for craft and gift producers.

• A growing number of older Americans are hiring self-employed individuals to do jobs they no longer have the time or energy to do, such as home decorating, home repairs and yard work.

• We're seeing an increasing number of dual-earner and single-parent families, all of whom have special needs. They desire hassle-free products and services, and are often willing to pay more for something if its purchase will relieve stress or give them more free time.

• More dads are now becoming caregivers because mom is the only one who can find a job. This growing "dads-at-home" audience, which includes a growing number of homebased business owners, needs a variety of personal and business services that can be delivered by other homebased entrepreneurs.

• People are increasingly concerned about their personal safety and financial security, so entrepreneurs who can offer products or services to answer such needs will find a ready market.

• The environment remains a hot market niche. Because more health-conscious people now perceive the environment as a health issue, consumers are more interested in purchasing environmentally safe products for personal use—cleansers, air filters, water purifiers, etc. This spells opportunity for entrepreneurs interested in selling such products—or information about it.

In addition to the above business and marketing trends, there is an important overall homestyle trend in both the United States and Canada called "cocooning"—a term coined by author and trend-master Faith Popcorn (*The Popcorn Report*, Doubleday, 1991). Thanks to technology and the growing range of personal and business services available to us, we have less need to go out to do things—from shopping to getting an education to earning a living—thus finding ourselves "cocooning" within the comfort and safety of our homes, our fortress against the world.

Importance of Trends

"A trend is born when society makes a general movement toward or away from something," notes Erika Kotite, a regular contributor to *Entrepreneur* magazine. In one of her articles, she said a trend happens ". . . because of one big event, or as a result of many small events; it can happen overnight, or over a couple of centuries. Most trends are identified by marketing research experts who monitor the media, interview consumers, conduct surveys, look at past trends and then, make predictions. Trends . . . are tricky, and businesses of the next decade had better pay attention to them, because they are vital to maintaining a competitive edge."

—from *Entrepreneur* magazine.

The Restructuring of the Workforce

The growth of homebased businesses in both the United States and Canada has been greatly influenced not only by the economy but by technological advances that have totally eradicated millions of factory jobs and middle management positions. During the last sixteen months of the 1991-1992 recession, Fortune 500 companies released over 600,000 people through early retirement or layoffs. At that time, a spokesperson at a small business development center reported an increase in the start-up of homebased consulting businesses by corporate VPs in their fifties who had taken cash benefit packages as early retirement bribes and went on to work for their former employers as independent consultants.

In mid-1996, one researcher stated thirty-three thousand employees were losing their jobs every day in the United States. That's twelve million lost jobs in this one year alone. In a newsletter for entrepreneurs, futurist Watts Wacker said even more cutbacks were expected in 1997, but the upside of this economic upheaval was a growing entrepreneurial wave and way of thinking he believes will continue to grow for at least the next quarter century.

As Nick Sullivan said in an editorial for *Home Office Computing*, "The restructuring of America's workforce in the 1990s will be more dramatic than the retooling of American industrial plants in the 1980s."

By the end of the decade, Popcorn asserts, most homes will be as complete and self-sufficient as the Star Trek *Enterprise* ship, and we will hardly ever have to go out.

Who's Working at Home and Why

With job security a thing of the past, millions of people who once thought they would have a job for life are wondering if they're going to get the pink slip. Many still-employed corporate workers are taking steps to position themselves for self-sufficiency should the paycheck suddenly cease, and a growing number of ex-corporate employees are now working for their former employers as independent, homebased consultants.

Although job loss may continue to be an important factor in one's decision to start a business at home, various surveys through the years have revealed that most people start businesses of their own because they want to be boss. Others have indicated they

- Think they can make more money working for themselves.
- Are tired of their job.
- Want a new challenge.
- Desire a change of lifestyle.
- Want to spend more time with their families.

My daily mail suggests future homebased entrepreneurs will come from a diverse group of individuals, including the following:

- Dissatisfied job holders who lack any real advancement opportunities
- Happy job holders who simply need more money
- People from all walks of life who have lost their jobs
- Women who must work at home because of children or adults in their care
- Disabled people who cannot find employment in the traditional workplace
- Senior citizens who need supplemental income
- Hobbyists interested in profiting from leisure-time interests

As you embark on your road to extra income or self-sufficiency, remember this: Almost anyone can make extra money at home, but it takes a certain degree of skill, experience and knowledge to actually turn a homebased money-making venture into a *profitable business*. Be realistic about the amount of profit to be derived in the early years of a business because so much will depend on the amount of time and money you invest in it. Small business owners often tell me making lots of money is not nearly as important to them as making *enough* money for their particular needs. I agree. To me, the most important thing is I am doing exactly what I want to be doing, secure in the knowledge I'm spending my life in the most satisfying and profitable way possible. Too few people today are able to make such a statement. Like most people in the 1950s, I grew up with an employee mentality. I fell into self-employment quite by accident, and I'd be lying if I said that being my own boss is easy. It's not. But if I could do it all over again, I'd start ten years sooner. I hope the information in this book will enable you to share the same enjoyment, satisfaction and sense of pride I feel each morning as I get up to go to work . . . in the comfort and privacy of my home.

P.S. There's only one way to read this book: with marking pen in hand. Try a yellow highlighter pen and underline or otherwise mark all the information that's important to you. When you have finished the book, go back to the beginning and follow up on every mark you've made. The more marks, the more opportunities.

Comments From People Who Yearn to Earn at Home (From Barbara's Daily Mail)

- "Our money is extremely tight and I would like to get a home business going to supplement our income and afford me the luxury of being at home where my children need me."
- "My husband was forced to take an early retirement and nobody will hire him at his age of 54."
- "I am a burned-out registered nurse who would like to start something on my own in the health care field."
- "I am faced with that age-old question: What to do now that the kids are in school? I am frustrated with my present choices and wonder what I might do at home."
- "I am a new widow who has been sewing for people for years on a limited basis. Now I'm ready to work full time in making a career that will be as profitable as it is enjoyable."
- "Our financial situation is making it necessary for me to find employment. But because of my son's health, working outside home is impossible."
- "Daily I disguise myself as a legal secretary and put up with a multitude of egos and personalities. How I ache to join the ranks of homebased entrepreneurs!"

A Brief History of the Work-at-Home Industry

No one can say with certainty exactly how many homebased businesses there are, but the following reports from authoritative sources through the years provide an interesting history of the industry's growth and an idea of what its size may be at the turn of the century.

1981.
The U.S. Labor Department predicts that within the next ten to fifteen years, about 40 to 50 percent of the American workforce will be working at home. Contributing to this trend, they say, are inflation, higher gas costs and the burgeoning computer industry.

1982.
The U.S. Chamber of Commerce reports fifteen million businesses in the United States have filed IRS report Schedule C (sole proprietor), and ten million of these taxpayers listed home addresses for their business. "Many of those businesses are operated by women," it states.

1984.
An AT&T survey indicates ten million American households are engaged in a business; 60 percent of these home-workers are between 25-44, most of them young males. AT&T estimates more than half these businesses are full-time operations providing the bulk of the household income.

1985.
Family Circle publishes the results of its home-business survey taken of 14,000 readers who answered a home-business questionnaire. Fifty-three percent report they are making money at home, most of it on a part-time basis.

1986.
The White House Conference on Small Business places the concerns of homebased business high on its list of issues, and the SBA's Office of Advocacy predicts self-employment will grow more rapidly in the next fifteen years than it has in the last fifteen years. By 2000, small firms are expected to be producing a major share of the nation's goods and services.

1987.
The U.S. Small Business Administration (SBA) indicates there are now more than fourteen million U.S. home-based businesses, and its Office of Advocacy reports husband-wife businesses have been the fastest growing business segment in the United States from 1980-1987, up 92 percent. Five years ago, it was common for a wife to start a business that would eventually become successful enough for the husband to join. Today, many husbands are losing jobs or burning out, and they're starting businesses that are later joined by wives who quit outside jobs, the report concludes.

In Canada, where the home-business industry is still pretty much an underground movement, Wendy Priesnitz in Ontario is working to build support for home-business entrepreneurs through her newsletter, *The Home Business Advocate*. She says, in Ontario, 69.5 percent of women starting new businesses plan to operate from their homes. She also notes the average amount of money invested in the start-up of new home-based businesses is less than $10,000, with 60 percent of these ventures being started on less than $5,000.

1988.
The second annual Work-at-Home Survey conducted by market research firm LINK Resources (New York) reveals at least 23 million Americans now work at home; 9.2 million as selfemployed individuals and 14.1 million as corporate workers.

1989.
A report from the New York-based market research firm FIND/SVP states the number of individuals who take work home with them and the number of work-at-home households are expected to accelerate in the coming years. They add that the emergence of the home office will not be felt in its full force until 1993, when the home-office product integration is expected.

1990.
Oklahoma becomes the first state to form a statewide home-business association.

This year's annual Work-at-Home survey from LINK Resources confirms the growth of the home-office trend. Says research specialist Tom Miller, "We're seeing a 22 percent increase in homeworkers this year."

Although Miller cannot say how many of these homeworkers are homebased business owners, he says there is a strong trend toward moonlighting. "Close to half of all corporate homeworkers may also be producing sideline income from their own part-time businesses," he says. "The expansion of freelance workers and moonlighters suggests, as employees become skilled in the use of information products, they also become more entrepreneurial."

1991.
GTE Telephone Operations predicts, by the year 2020, a full 30 percent of the nation's workforce may be telecommuting. GTE defines "work-at-home employees" as "anyone who works at home eight or more hours weekly, or operates a small business from the home." These workers, says GTE, are likely to be married, with mi-

nor children, and largely in the "Baby Boomer" age of 35-45, well educated, with an average household income of $42,000.

LINK Resources' 1991 survey reveals a 12 percent increase in the number of homeworkers. True self-employment (where the primary source of income is based on home business activity) has grown by 600,000 households—a 6 percent increase since 1990. Altogether, 11.8 million Americans fit the self-employed description, according to Tom Miller, director of research.

1992.

After Oklahoma, Nebraska becomes the second state to form a statewide home-business association.

In May, Canada's First National Home Business Conference is presented in New Westminster. This is also the first year in which meaningful statistics on the Canadian home-business industry are available. In *The B.C. Home Business Report*, editor Ted James reports many displaced Canadian workers are now creating their own jobs at home as successful entrepreneurs, and a newly released study (*Home Enterprise: Canadians and Home-Based Work*) indicates one in four of all Canadian households is operating some form of home business. "This represents over two million homes," says James. "Almost 50 percent of home workers are self-employed business owners. Of the remainder, 14 percent are *substituters* (employees who spend the workday at home), and 39 percent are *supplementers* (employees who bring work home). By the end of the decade, homework is expected to account for 40 percent of all employment."

More specifically, the Minister of Economic Development, Small Business and Trade states in British Columbia there are presently 130,000 homebased businesses, with 12,000 to 15,000 new businesses being started in the home each year. Other facts turned up by Canadian researchers reveal about half of home-based businesses (HBBs) provide services, with the remainder being manufacturers (many craft businesses) and wholesalers.

In the United States, LINK's 1992 annual survey indicates a 9.4 percent growth rate, bringing the total of part- and full-time homeworkers in the United States to 39.0 million. The SBA's 1992 stats indicate there are approximately 20 million small businesses, 15 million of which are sole proprietorships with no employees. Women continue to start businesses at nearly twice the rate of men, the SBA reports, adding if this trend continues, women will own nearly 40 percent of all businesses by the year 2000.

1993.

LINK's 1993 annual survey reveals slower but continued growth in the industry, with the total number of full- and part-time homeworkers now set at 41.1 million.

1994.

To bring attention to the benefits and realities of the homebased industry, the American Association of Home-Based Businesses (AAHBB) launches the first annual National Home-Based Business Week in October. California becomes the first state in the nation to declare its own "Home Based Business Week."

Missouri is the third state to form a statewide home-business association. Home-business history is also made this year when the Oklahoma Cooperative Extension Service sponsors a first-of-its-kind national conference for home-business educators. Nearly two hundred concerned individuals attend to hear leaders from all areas of the industry share their experience.

On a dark note, 1994 is the year we see an explosion of home-business opportunity scams. Con artists are now cooking up hundreds of new money-making schemes and worthless business ideas that can be sold to an unsuspecting populace by mail, on the Internet and through high-powered sales spiels at hundreds of so-called home-business "conferences" across the country.

1995.

In mid-1995, in an unprecedented federal and state assault on the growing national epidemic of business opportunity scams preying on would-be entrepreneurs, the FTC files suit against a hundred swindlers who have been peddling phony business opportunities. They estimate such scams are now costing consumers well over $100 million a year.

1996.

This year, an increasing number of homebased entrepreneurs begin to explore their marketing options on the Internet and World Wide Web. Many self-employed individuals are also benefiting from membership in one or more of the national organizations formed in the past two years. These organizations offer a wide range of business services, publications, discounts on equipment and supplies and affordable group insurance programs.

LINK's latest research indicates the number of telecommuters has decreased while the number of home-based entrepreneurs has increased. By 1997, they predict the size of the work-at-home universe will be 51.3 million homeworkers, of which approximately 30 million will be part- and full-time self-employed individuals.

HOMEWORK MYTHS, SCAMS AND UN-PROFITABLE IDEAS

2

WHEN PEOPLE ASK IF YOU WANT the good news or the bad news first, what do you say? As a positive-thinking person, I like to get the bad news out of the way first so I can concentrate on the good. This chapter, admittedly a burst-your-bubbles collection of information, could be thought of as bad news by some, but the good news is all this "bad news" is likely to save you a great deal of time, money and frustration. I know you'll thank me later for bringing all this information to your attention at the beginning.

Although millions of people now work at home, "homework" is not that easy for the average individual to get. This chapter addresses some misconceptions people have about making money at home while also warning against common work-at-home scams, mail-order schemes, activities that violate postal laws, and so-called "opportunities" that are simply unprofitable. Finally, I'm going to help you stay out of legal and financial trouble by telling you about a number of things you cannot do as a business because they are in direct violation of copyright or licensing laws.

Chain Letters

All chain letters (like pyramid schemes) are illegal, but we continue to receive them in our daily mail because postal authorities simply can't keep up with all the con artists out there. Some people think they are getting around the illegality of chain letters by saying they are offering a "mass merchandising mail-order program," or simply a hobby or recipe exchange. But since some states have laws against pyramid schemes of any kind—even when no money is changing hands—a no-money recipe or hobby chain letter may be as illegal in your state as one that asks you to send money. Often, you will be asked to order a report costing between four and ten dollars that will not only prove to be worthless, but is likely to put your name on a mail list being investigated by the U.S. Postal Inspection Service. "Chain letters are illegal," inspectors say, "and they don't work." If you participate in a chain letter promotion, you may be in violation of federal and state laws, so the smartest thing you can do is give the chain letters you receive to your local postmaster.

But what about chain letters that say, "This letter is entirely legal"? Just remember, con artists are used to lying and they're difficult to stop. As fast as postal inspectors put one out of business, a new one sets up shop somewhere else. Once when I called the Postal Inspector's Office about a particular scam making the rounds, I was informed that each letter mailed was considered one count, and the penalty for mail-order fraud is up to five years in prison for each count. Ouch! It doesn't pay to mess with the U.S. Postal Service.

Work-at-Home Misconceptions

Myth: All you need to make money at home is a typewriter or computer.

Whenever you see an ad stating, "Homeworkers in Demand! $500 Weekly Possible," ignore it. More than likely, the free information you will get will be an ad for a directory of worthless addresses or other material describing expensive "career manuals."

Many people with typing or secretarial skills believe all they need to start making money at home is a list of companies who hire people like them. Alas, there is no magic list, and although you may find work-at-home directories in print, a careful reading

Junk Mail

As one of Canada's best-known home-business advocates, Wendy Priesnitz receives the same kind of junk mail that regularly fills Barbara's mailbox: get-rich-quick schemes sent by people from all over the country.

"It's interesting how these things never have a return address," says Wendy, who shares this example of a scheme that's as common in Canada as in the United States:

"Newspapers reported that three Toronto men had been arrested and charged with conducting an illegal scheme and pyramid selling. The letter they were mailing apparently told prospective participants to send away for four reports at $5 each. But police said the reports, entitled *How to Make $250,000 Through Multi-Level Sales*, *Major Corporations and Multi-Level Sales*, *Sources for the Best Mailing Lists*, and *Evaluating Multi-Level Sales Plans*, simply outlined how the reader could begin his or her own scheme by sending out the same letter. Metro police said they had also received complaints about this scheme from people in Calgary and Nova Scotia. One officer was quoted in the paper as saying, 'If it sounds too good to be true it probably is.'"

of listings will reveal what companies are really looking for are capable *self-employed individuals* or *freelance business professionals* who are interested in working as independent contractors. I was astonished when a prison inmate wrote to ask how he could find gainful employment by mail doing typing. He had the equipment and skills, so he figured he could do the work. Maybe so; but who do you suppose would send a typing job to a prison inmate? Some common sense is called for here. If you are a qualified typist or word processor, your best bet for getting "homework" is to call on businesses in your area to let them know you are an experienced professional who's interested in working on a part-time basis as an independent contractor.

Myth: If you have great computer skills, you can work at home for some corporation.

In truth, telecommuting opportunities are available only to a small segment of the population. You can't just say, "I have a computer—give me some homework." To do computer-related work at home, you usually begin by first being employed by the company in question. Then you hope the company will be receptive to the idea of your doing work at home that for years has been done in the office. While a growing number of companies are using telecommuters, others have been reluctant to try such a program. In short, telecommuting opportunities do not exist for the average individual looking for computer-related work to do at home . . . *but self-employed individuals with computer expertise* will find many opportunities to make money at home, as this book will show.

Myth: There are many opportunities to work at home doing knitting, sewing or assembling products for companies.

Certain manufacturing plants—not many—may have a limited amount of contract work available to individuals who live near enough to pick up and deliver finished materials on a daily basis. Training may be required or offered. If you don't have such a manufacturer in your backyard, don't waste your money on a directory that promises to lead you to such companies. Typical product assembly work may include packaging material in plastic bags, adding tags, inserting pins into promotional badges, adding buckles to belts, or hand-wrapping fishing rods. Sewing and craft work may include mending sweaters, stitching shoe parts, making ski masks, neckties, tote bags or T-shirts, trimming threads on commercially woven placemats, or putting in coat linings. Good work for a few, perhaps, but awfully boring to most. There may also be limited opportunities for craftworkers who can do machine knitting, sewing or figurine painting, but if you have such skills, you would be better off starting a small business of your own.

Make-Money-at-Home Ads

In a free country, people can place ads for anything they wish, provided it does not violate postal laws. But con artists in both the United States and Canada pay no attention to such laws, and magazine publishers generally accept all the ads they can get. Publication of an ad, however, does not mean a publisher has endorsed the advertiser in any way. It remains the reader's responsibility to use common sense in deciding whether to send money to an advertiser.

"Opportunity classifieds" appear in many magazines, and it's not unusual to find the same ad in several publications at once. Readers may be asked to send from twenty-five cents to a dollar to receive information. So far, you're not out much. But what most people receive next are instructions to send larger sums of money for start-up kits, "secret information," or books of questionable value. This is where you must become especially cautious. Don't be too eager to believe snappy advertising copy implying you can get rich without a considerable investment of time or money. It if were this simple, we'd all be on easy street. You may be too smart to fall for most of the slick "business opportunity" advertisements that promise easy money for little work and no skill or experience, but you may not be aware of all the work-at-home schemes and mail-order ripoffs I am about to describe. In addition to these specific examples, there are hundreds of variations of each scheme. No matter how they are described or what riches are promised, always remember the old adage, "If it sounds too good to be true, it probably is."

Myth: You can get rich quick with no effort at all.

You've seen the full-page ads—sometimes they're two pages long—with headlines proclaiming you can get rich sooner than you think, or "Secret money-making system revealed!" or "Just mail two letters . . . and make $15,000 in one month." The convincing copy in such ads often tells the sad tale of a man or woman who, on the verge of bankruptcy, suddenly discovers the secret to wealth, and now, out of the goodness of his or her heart, is going to share it with *you*. How lucky can you get! To prove just how profitable these ideas are, the ads often include a list of their bank deposits for the past twelve months, along with a statement from their accountant swearing it's true. I don't doubt it. Thousands of suckers are sending such advertisers ten or twenty dollars for an information product that probably costs less than a buck. These promoters have discovered the secret to wealth all right—they've learned how to pick the pockets of gullible opportunity seekers.

I fell for one of these ads several years ago (and it's still running today). The picture of a lovely woman and the promise

Author Fights Back

After losing $30,000 on a scam, Graham M. Mott shared his experience and all his research on scams and cons in a self-published book the opportunity magazines won't mention for fear of losing advertisers. He calls himself a "scambuster" and he's on the warpath against the thousands of con artists out there today. His research indicates scams cost us between $40 and $50 billion each year.

"Scams are like wildfire, totally out of control with no rain in sight," says Mott in his book, *Scams, Swindles and Rip-Offs—Personal Stories, Power Lessons*. (See chapter sixteen.) "We all want to believe scams only happen to others, but virtually everyone is a potential prospect for a scam," he says. "Many times the prime candidates to be ripped off are those who have been involved in a previous scam. Hoping to recoup their losses, people take unnecessary risks. Most losses are in the range of a few dollars to a few thousand dollars. Since legal aid can cost more in time, money and emotional strain than is worthwhile, few people report the smaller losses; losing larger sums of money can be so embarrassing to people that their embarrassment and shame far outweighs their desire to do anything about the loss."

of "two volumes—a complete set of my ideas and systems" made me part with $20 for which I received two skimpy little books on how to get rich in mail order—information I found completely worthless. Like many others, I justified this expenditure by charging it to "research" (or perhaps we should call it "live and learn"). Whenever you read an ad that speaks in vague terms about what you're going to get for your money (besides the promoter's "secrets") and never quite explains exactly what you'll have to do to earn the promised income, don't bite. An order is likely to bring you only a worthless book on mail order or some other "plan" of little interest to you. Remember that *no one* ever shares their "secrets of success" in a full-page ad "out of the goodness of their heart." They're in it strictly for the money.

Myth: You can make money selling handmade products made from kits.

Beware of ads that begin, "$341.04 weekly possible making baby bibs at home!" or, "Make our kitchen aprons for fun and profit—$344.08 weekly!" Such advertisers say all you have to do is buy their supplies and materials, make products to their specifications, and they'll buy everything you make. Don't believe it! There is *no market* for products that come in "supply kits" offered in opportunity ads. Since this is a scam thousands fall for every year, it deserves extra attention here. These people—mostly mothers who want to stay home with the kids and make money too—are quick to believe the magazine ads that say it's easy to make money selling craft items—such as baby bibs, potholders, aprons, jewelry, Christmas ornaments, pillows and the like. The promoters of such schemes will guarantee your complete satisfaction and a full refund of your money, but they simply won't do this. They may offer to buy all the products you make, but they won't, and their reason will be that your work does not meet their standards. And it never will, because they have no intention of ever buying anything from anyone. These advertisers are simply out to sell you cheap product kits. But you don't have to take my word for it. Just listen to what some of my readers (all women) have reported:

- "I figured because you see handmade items advertised in virtually every catalogue there must be an abundance of work-at-home opportunities," writes Dorothy in Illinois. "I pored through craft magazines and began writing for free information. After receiving a number of responses, I narrowed these down by type and pay and then called the Better Business Bureau in each respective area. A couple of them said they had no information on companies in question, but the Better Business Bureau in San Francisco did say one company on my list was a member of the BBB (although this was not to be taken as an endorsement). I congratulated myself on being smart enough to check them out before sending a money order for $47.90 for the cost of their kit, directions and rush handling.

"Two weeks later my anxiously awaited package arrived. What a disappointment! I had settled on an ornaments kit because I don't sew very well. What I received was a couple of bags of beads, some fishing wire, and some complicated instructions for an ugly little thing that looked sort of like a wreath with about 8 dangling columns hanging from it. I returned the kit immediately, requesting the return of [my investment] minus the $11.90 I had agreed to in the initial mailing to cover 'shipping, handling and inspection' (although the mailing costs had been only $1.45). I decided this was their gimmick: They send out an ugly little complicated kit. Their customer is disappointed and sends it back, which still gives the company $7.50 off each respondent and an extra $2.95 if they are excited enough to request rush handling."

• Virginia, in Missouri, reported she kept the jewelry kit she ordered and sent the completed products for payment, only to be told they were unacceptable. "I spent three months trying to get it right and finally gave up," she said.

• Cathy, in Florida, had made pillows for gifts for years, so she bit on the ad that promised her money from pillows. After receiving her $50 kit and sending the finished pillows back to the company, she was astonished to learn her work was considered borderline. "My friends told me I'd been taken, that these companies do this just to get the kit money," she wrote. "I still defended my work by saying I had only a couple of pillows that did not meet their standards, and when I got them back I would just fix those and send them all back. Since I have worked in quality control myself, I was very surprised to see that not one of my 'mistakes' was marked in any way—which made rework impossible. That was when I knew my friends were right."

• Nancy, in Michigan, went so far as to file a complaint with her local BBB only to find many others were in the same boat. "We were asked to complete all types of legal papers against the company," she said, adding that the State Attorney General's office was investigating the matter.

As Dorothy pointed out, an unfortunate side effect to such scams is once you respond to one ad, your name is automatically added to every "sucker list" in the country. "Not a day goes by," says Dorothy, "that I don't receive work-at-home opportunity ads or 'you have won . . .' garbage in the mail. I've turned many of the chain letters and other offers over to the Postmaster, but the sheer volume of such mail finally wears you down to the point you just throw it away."

Myth: You can make good money stuffing envelopes or mailing circulars.

According to the U.S. Postal Inspection Service, the most common work-at-home frauds involve stuffing envelopes at home and/or mailing circulars. In one of its consumer booklets the Service says: "The Postal Inspection Service knows of NO work-at-home promotion that ever produces income as alleged. A homework scheme promoter will . . . take your money and give you little or nothing in return except heartbreak and grief."

Ads for such offers may speak of a "revolutionary home-mailing program" that will pay up to $300 a day. A typical statement in such ads is "we could never possibly reach the *millions* of people who need this information, so we're willing to let you help us." Of course the copy sounds believable—it's written by pros. If you fall for this type of scam, you'll probably end up paying from $10-$40 for a package of literature that includes the same sales letter you got originally, along with instructions on how to put an ad in the paper. Then when people write to you, you try to sell them the same thing you just fell for. Not a good way to build a reputation for yourself, is it? As the Council of Better Business Bureaus, Inc. confirms in one of its consumer pamphlets, "Most of the ads are simply lures by the advertisers to sell information on how to set up your own business or conduct the same scheme as the advertiser's."

In short, the only ones making money in this business are the ones who create the programs and circulars other people use. The reality of mail-order marketing is it's tough to get even a one-half percent response to a circular mailing, and if it's poorly printed and offers questionable products or information, it's likely to be completely ignored by recipients.

Myth: You can build a profitable mail-order business using a promoter's ads, catalogs and products.

As you will learn in a later chapter, I believe in mail order, and I'm always quick to encourage individuals to market their own products and services by mail. But mail-order novices not interested in selling their own products should avoid promoters who offer them the chance to build a mail-order business using their ads, catalogs and products. How-to booklets and reports of questionable value (some have been circulating for over twenty years) are commonly promoted in this way. Although these business promotions are not illegal, they are bound to be unprofitable. What promoters neglect to tell interested prospects is, although they supply the ad copy to sell such products, the dealer must place and pay for all the ads. The promoter may supply the mail-order catalogs, but dealers must pay for them, as well as the postage to mail them, plus buy their own mailing lists as well. What mail-order beginners do not realize is catalog mailings may yield only a ½ to 1 percent order response—which is only 5-10 orders for every 1,000 pieces mailed. And that's if the list is good; if it's bad, it's entirely possible to get only one or two orders, or none.

Similar "opportunities" offer people the chance to sell a line of inexpensive imports or novelty items. Promoters say the beauty of this kind of business is that you need not buy products outright or stock inventory—simply send all orders to them for fulfillment. While such companies may indeed be legitimate, most of them are making their money first on the sale of catalogs (sold at highly inflated prices) and second from the sale of mailing lists unlikely to result in orders. (Often these are nothing more than names of other opportunity seekers.) The only time such a mail-order endeavor might be profitable, in my opinion, is if the entrepreneur already has an established prospect or customer list likely to be interested in such items. As the Council of Better Business Bureaus cautions, and which I can affirm, "Building a solid, profitable mail-order business is a demanding, full-time task. Few inexperienced individuals can learn enough about the business before their capital or patience runs out."

Myth: You can make money compiling mailing lists.

The ad may read, "We'll pay you fifty cents for each name and address you compile. If you have a pen and can write down a name and address, you can do this to make money." Or maybe the headline says, "Don't throw away your order envelopes—trade them for cash!" In checking out one of these schemes, here's what I learned.

In this scheme, you compile names by placing certain classified ads that the company provides. When you get responses to the ad, you forward the names to the company, and you will actually be paid fifty cents for generating this valuable sales lead for them. Meanwhile, the company will send "your" prospects a brochure or catalog that describes one of several money-making plans they offer (all legal). For example, you might place an ad telling people how to make money mailing letters, and what they would receive from the company would be information on how to order a manual that will tell them how to make up to $1,000 a day just for mailing letters. It may be described as "the opportunity of a lifetime" but is probably nothing more than a common mail-order guide. So your participation in such a program only helps to push the snowball downhill, setting up other suckers for yet another get-rich scheme. Legal, yes, but what do you suppose the chances are for financial success?

Remember this: *Your* name will be on those classified ads, and if people are upset with the material they receive as a result of contact with you, who do you think is going to get the flack? My good name means too much to me to use it in this fashion.

Scams on the Internet

You may find cyberspace exciting, but it's also an industry running amok, with no rules or regulations or anyone in control. In addition to being wary of greedy, though not necessarily dishonest, entrepreneurs whose prices for Web services are out of line, you must also be wary of shady opportunists. You can be sure the same con artists who have previously used the mail and telephone to prey on unsuspecting consumers were among the first to get on the Internet and World Wide Web.

Gambling and pornography are running rampant and have only recently begun to be noticed by legal authorities. In 1996, the U.S. Postal Inspection Service joined other federal law enforcement agencies in monitoring computer online services for fraud and direct marketing scams. Although some operators have been closed down, many charlatans continue to separate people from their money with a fancy-looking webpage and unsubstantiated claims about the profitability of their "hot" money-making or investment opportunity. Beware!

Even if you really do not care about using your name to promote someone else's products, do you really believe you'd make money here? A classified ad might cost $25-$50 or more. At $50, you'd have to bring in 100 prospects just to break even. So the company is spending a mere fifty cents each for its prospect names while *you* foot its advertising bill and get absolutely nothing in the bargain. While you're wasting your time and money on its ads, the company is keeping a tight rein on its cash flow and profiting from the sale of its expensive manuals.

Here's another variation of this scheme. A mailer from a promoter stated I would be paid six cents for every new name I could generate for them. On closer investigation, I learned they will buy only the names of people who have responded to opportunity or money-making ads. The promoter compiles such names into new opportunity-seeker mail lists, which he will sell back to the very people who responded to such ads in the first place. (Examples: those who do circular mailings, push multilevel marketing programs [MLM], or peddle useless information.) Now do you begin to see why your mailbox suddenly fills up with junk mail as soon as you bite on that first opportunity ad or chain letter invitation?

Myth: You can get paid for reading books.

Legitimate book publishers either have their own in-house proofreaders or easy access to professionals in their area. They don't need inexperienced people off the street. Some unethical directory publishers may include the names and addresses of publishers in their useless work-at-home directories, but book publishers have not authorized such listings.

Another variation of this scam is when you are asked to buy a book that gives all the inside secrets of this "plan" for "only $29.95." Still another variation is that you will be offered the opportunity to "be trained as a proofreader" at home for some imaginary editorial or publishing service. After paying a nonrefundable fee for this worthless "education," you'll be told you haven't passed the aptitude test. That's because there was never any real work in the first place.

Thanks to an increased awareness program by the U.S. Postal Service, more and more consumers are notifying the Inspection Service of suspicious advertising, and thousands of phony work-at-home operations have been put out of business as a result. Ask your Postmaster for a free brochure on this topic and for information on how to report questionable work-at-home promotions you receive in the future. (Canadians may also wish to report questionable promotions to their federal government's Department of Consumer and Corporate Affairs.)

Myth: You can make a million in MLM (multilevel marketing).

In a word, no. See chapter four for a detailed discussion of your true financial opportunities in the MLM industry, which has always been plagued by "scam operators" who ask for large, up-front amounts of money and promise prospects they will get rich quick for doing little or no work.

You and the Copyright Law

The average person does not understand the copyright law and thus often breaks it unknowingly, sometimes only to his or her embarrassment, other times at some cost on the wrong end of a lawsuit. As a businessperson, however, you cannot afford to be ignorant of this federal law. The following information is vital to this book's readers because some of you may consider starting a business based on the intellectual property of others—property is protected by copyright law.

Since whole books have been written on this very complex subject, I am limiting this discussion to information that will help you avoid violating the rights of others. (In chapter six, "An A-to-Z 'Crash Course' in Business Basics," you'll find detailed information on how to use copyrights to protect your own intellectual property.) I have a good working knowledge of U.S. copyright law, but I will not attempt to discuss Canadian copyright law here. Although similar, it is not the same, so Canadian readers should use the following information only as a guideline to situations they ought to investigate in their country. The following information does not constitute legal advice, but it has been checked for accuracy by Mary Helen Sears, an attorney in Washington, DC, whose practice is mainly devoted to patents, copyrights, trademarks and related matters. Any suggestions she made were incorporated into my material. Following are answers to questions I've been asked most often in the past:

Q: What does a copyright protect?
A: The U.S. Copyright Law (enacted in 1790 and amended a number of times, most recently by acts in 1978 and 1989) protects the rights of creators of intellectual property in seven broad categories that include literary, musical and dramatic works; pantomimes and choreographic works; pictorial, graphic and sculptural works; motion pictures and other audiovisual works; and sound recordings. Although ideas themselves may not be protected, a copyright does protect the *expression* of an idea. For example, four people could paint a picture of the same scene (the idea), and all four could copyright their original creations (their individual expression of the idea). Things that cannot be copyrighted include inventions, names, titles, short phrases,

methods and systems. (They may qualify for a trademark or patent, however, topics which are discussed in chapter six.)

Q: How can I tell if something is protected by copyright?
A: To investigate the copyright status of a work today, you can (1) examine a copy of the work to see if a copyright notice is present; (2) make a search of the Copyright Office catalogs and other records; or (3) ask the Copyright Office to make a search.

Note: The last edition called attention to a movement in Congress to abolish the requirement that one must register a copyright in order to be able to sue for infringement. Though much discussed, this had not become law as of September 1, 1996, and whether Congress will succumb remains to be seen. If this does become law, it will be almost impossible for anyone to investigate the copyright status of a work, and we will all have to presume everything is copyrighted.

Since a notice of copyright is no longer required by law; however, one cannot automatically assume a work is unprotected by copyright simply because a notice of copyright (the word *copyright* or the symbol ©) is absent. In fact, under current law, copyright protection exists from the moment a work is created. To illustrate: If you give a speech, you own your words the moment they fall from your lips, and you're the only one who has the right to put those words into written form or on an audiotape for purpose of profit. Everything you draw or write on paper, even a letter to your mother, is your property the moment it appears on paper, and no one else has the right to use or sell it without your permission. That is one reason why you need not be concerned about sending articles or book manuscripts to magazine editors and book publishers without registering the copyright first. In addition to the fact that editors and publishers usually are ethical people who do not steal from writers, it is automatically understood that you are the owner of that material *until such time as you decide to sell or convey its copyright to someone else.* (See also point 3 in the following list of money-making ideas that violate the copyright law.)

Q: What about material in the public domain? Isn't that safe to use?
A: Yes, you can use material in the public domain, which means material on which the copyright has expired *or has not been claimed.* Some people believe anything published before 1910 is automatically in the public domain. Not true. Copyright duration before the 1978 Act varied greatly and many copyrights were renewable. It can be risky to use any material that appears to be in the public domain, simply because someone else may have obtained rights by putting it into new form, and claimed a copyright on that new form. Dover Publications, for instance, has reor-

ganized and reformulated many books that were once in the public domain and obtained copyrights for their own new forms. Thus, in all cases, if you plan to use previously published and copyrighted material for your own profit, you would be wise to obtain a legal opinion from an attorney who specializes in copyright law.

Q: How would you define "copyright infringement" and what are the penalties for same?
A: This is a complex area I will only touch on here, but here's a good rule of thumb: A copyright is infringed whenever one violates the exclusive rights covered by copyright. In both the United States and Canada, it requires only "substantial similarity" to establish infringement, and the penalties may be especially harsh when such infringement affects the profits of the original author or creator while resulting in profit to the user. In addition to legal fees, copyright damages may be $100,000 or more in the United States and up to a million dollars and imprisonment in Canada, a country that takes copyright matters very seriously. By heeding the warnings below, and double-checking questionable situations with an attorney *who is knowledgeable about copyright law in your country*, you should be able to avoid this legal problem.

Ten Money-making Ideas That Violate Copyright Law

1. Do not copy, for purposes of resale either as a design or a finished product, the designs on handcrafted products or commercial gift items. All commercial manufacturers and most professional craft designers/sellers protect their work by copyrights or design patents.

It is all too common today for a person to copy commercial designs or buy a pattern to make products for sale. Sometimes such buyers will modify the design or pattern a little bit, thinking this will suddenly make it their own. In spite of what you may have heard, it is *not* all right merely to "change one thing" or use a different color or material. Merely changing the way a design is used does not alter the fact that it is a copy. A work does not have to be identical to the original to be a copy, but only has to repeat a "substantial part" of it, according to the Copyright Office. Unless you can legally define the words "substantial part," you should avoid altering commercial patterns and designs for sale as your own "original designs."

The illegal use by consumers of copyrighted patterns and designs is known as "pattern piracy" in the crafts industry, and it is a matter of growing concern today as an increasing number of craft and hobby consumers unknowingly break copyright laws

A Little Copyright Story

A woman decided to modify a pattern she had purchased and offer it for sale in a crafts magazine. She called the advertising department of that magazine and told them she wanted to advertise a pattern that was based on someone else's design. "It's OK as long as you've made a few changes," she was advised.

So the woman took her savings to pay for the ad, and upon publication, a friend of the original designer saw the ad and sent her a copy. Whereupon the original designer contacted her lawyer, who in turn informed the advertiser she had infringed on a copyrighted pattern and must stop selling it immediately. Furthermore, all proceeds from the ad had to be directed to the original designer.

Moral of the story: To be safe, be original. And *never* take advice on important matters unless the person giving the advice is an authority on the topic.

How One Designer Handled Infringement of Her Copyright

While conducting one of her "Designer Sweatshirts" classes at a shop, Mary Mulari noticed a packet of information and designs for sale on the topic of decorating sweatshirts, also the subject of her first book, *Designer Sweatshirts*. Since Mary keeps a close eye on what her competition is doing, she purchased the packet.

"It was a shock to recognize my own diagrams, illustrations and designs, as well as my text only slightly reworded," she wrote. "This was clearly an infringement of my copyright; my information and drawings had been stolen and now were being offered by another company at a price much lower than my own book."

Mary found an attorney who informed the company publishing the packet that the designer was aware of their unlawful use of her materials and that they had to cease selling their packet or face a trial.

"The first response from the company was to pay me royalties," said Mary. "From that point, we were able to work out an agreement that includes royalties, their payment of my attorney's fees, and written information in each packet crediting me for the information and listing my name and address. A court trial was avoided."

This experience taught Mary the importance of keeping in touch with the marketplace and with other publications, as well as the value of registering a copyright. Her story also illustrates how infringements are discovered, and why it can be costly to steal the creative work of another individual.

and thus affect the profits of craftspeople, designers, writers, publishers and manufacturers. As a result, many creators have instigated lawsuits or are considering them.

How can you stay out of trouble here? Generally speaking, you may not encounter problems if you sell your "borrowed designs" only to individuals at a church bazaar or home party or through your local consignment shop, *but you must never "go commercial" (enter the wholesale marketplace) with products that use someone else's patterns or designs*. Some designers sell all rights to a publisher, while others sell only "first rights" (which means they have retained the exclusive right to sell finished products or kits made from their own patterns and designs). When you see a design you like in a book or magazine, you have no way of knowing whether the designer or the publisher owns the copyright, but if you see something you'd really like to produce in quantity, you have nothing to lose by writing to the designer (in care of the publisher) to see if you might get permission to make multiples of the item for sale. Sometimes this permission will be granted without charge; other times, a fee or royalty may be part of the deal.

2. Do not make for sale any reproductions of copyrighted characters such as Snoopy, Raggedy Ann and Andy, the Sesame Street gang, or Walt Disney characters unless you have *written permission* from the copyright holders to do so.

Anyone who uses such designs without permission, and without paying mightily for the privilege, is asking for trouble. Yes, we have all seen handmade products bearing such designs, but with few exceptions, these crafters are in violation of the copyright law and just begging for a lawsuit. For example, the sale of licensed Disney merchandise is a multimillion dollar industry, and the corporation is aggressive in its efforts to protect its rights. They have sued many retailers for selling items with copyrighted Disney characters on them (and the craftspeople who make such items are just one step behind the retailers).

Commercial patterns or kits of such characters—which have been offered to buyers by licensed manufacturers—are designed for personal use only. Unless a magazine, book or pattern specifically warns against reproduction for profit, however, the innocent person who makes handmade items for sale in the local craft shop or church bazaar won't likely be held liable in a court of law.

3. Do not make reproductions of any kind of any picture, photograph, painting or other piece of artwork you may have purchased.

Many people think their purchase of a particular object gives them the right to reuse the design or image on that object. This is not true. The creator of that object owns the copyright, *and that copyright can be conveyed to another person only in*

writing, or by other transfers that occur by operation of law.
If you buy a painting from an artist, all you own is the physical
piece of art. The artist still owns the *image* of that artwork, and
only he or she has the right to copy it as prints, postcards, greeting cards, calendars and the like, *or grant the right to copy to
someone else in the form of a license.* (See "Licensing" in chapter six.)

4. Do not photocopy—for sale or trade—any pattern, article
or other printed material from any book, magazine, newsletter,
etc., because such use denies the creator the profit from a copy
that might have been sold. (Even when there is no copyright
notice, you must assume such work is copyrighted.)

5. Do not photocopy any part of any copyrighted publication—particularly books and manuals—for use as a teaching aid
unless you plan to use it only once, or are teaching a charity
group without charge. And the amount of material copied must
be "reasonable." Never, for example, make several copies of an
entire book (as some teachers have done) for use in a classroom
setting.

6. Do not reprint and offer for sale any previously published
material still protected by the copyright law (not in public domain), even though such material may no longer be available
from the original publisher. That publisher, or the creator, still
owns the copyright to that material, whether he or she wants to
do anything with it or not.

7. Do not duplicate records, cassettes or tape recordings,
videotaped television shows or computer software for sale or
trade. Sound recordings, audiovisual works and software are fully
protected by copyright laws.

8. Do not copy and republish recipes from books or magazines exactly as they have appeared. A group of previously published recipes can be republished in new form, however, provided
you make changes, such as (1) the recipe's title, (2) the order
in which ingredients are used, or the amounts of ingredients
used, and (3) the way the instructions are written on how to put
the recipe together.

9. Do not use poems or poetry written by other people without their written permission. Novice self-publishers often use the
work of well-known poets in their newsletters, magazines, booklets, or on greeting cards or calendars, etc. But the use of an
entire poem is a flagrant violation of the copyright law because
it represents the use of a whole work of an individual creator
who is receiving no financial benefit from such usage. Giving
credit to the creator is not enough. The use of one or two lines
of a poem, or a paragraph or two from a book or other publication
may be considered "fair use," according to the copyright law, but
some publishers are now asking that even such limited usage be
cleared with them beforehand. The same rules apply to all words

in general. Never "lift" material from books, magazines, newsletters, etc. for inclusion in your own articles, books or speeches *without giving full credit to the creator*. Even then, you must be concerned with the amount of material that is quoted and whether it falls into the "fair use" area of copyright law mentioned above. When in doubt, always request permission from the writer or publisher in question.

10. Finally, a special note for computer users who work with scanners or drawing programs to create illustrations: *Do not* alter original line artwork or commercial art illustrations for your own use. Thanks to affordable computer technology, high-tech copyright infringement has reached epidemic proportions. Many people, ill-informed about the copyright law, believe they can simply scan in someone else's images, change this or that, then claim the illustration as their own because it's now in their computer. *This is not true.* While some "borrowing" with credit to the artist may fall under the "fair use" doctrine of the copyright law, it would be dangerous for the average person to do this. (Remember what I said about the definition of "substantial" in point 1.)

As you have seen, the Copyright Law is complex and nothing to mess with. Your library will have books on this topic, should you wish to pursue it, and the Copyright Office itself offers a wide selection of explanatory circulars, free on request. (See chapter sixteen.) In the end, my best advice to you is . . . to be safe, *be original*.

The Celebrity Rights Act

I'm closing this "bad news chapter" with a few words about a little-known law business beginners should pay serious attention to. Your state may or may not have a *Celebrity Rights Act*, but that will not protect you from a lawsuit if you are caught selling unlicensed products and services that fall under the provisions of this law.

It specifically prohibits any person or company—without permission—from (1) producing a product; (2) advertising a product; or (3) providing a service that in any way *utilizes the name, voice, signature, photograph or likeness of a deceased person during a period lasting fifty years after his or her death.*

How does this law affect product makers and service providers? I recall a crocheter who designed a Marilyn Monroe Doll for sale to her mail-order customers. If she's still selling this particular doll or its pattern, she's inviting legal trouble, and if you're an entertainer who plans to dress up as Mae West or Charlie Chaplin and do imitations for profit . . . don't.

My husband has a handpainted plaster bust of W.C. Fields

hanging in his office. The company that made it and the retailer who sold it may have violated the celebrity rights law without knowing it. Such replicas cannot be made without special permission from the estate of W.C. Fields. Note that the Celebrity Rights Act affects not only the manufacturer or creator of an unlicensed product or service, but distributors and retailers as well. All can be sued, according to the owner of Roger Richman Productions, Inc., the Beverly Hills agency that represents the heirs and estates of such personalities as Marilyn Monroe, W.C. Fields, the Marx Brothers, Abbott and Costello, Mae West and others.

Not all states need a special law about this because there simply aren't enough celebrities in some states to warrant it. Regardless of whether there is a state law or not, you may be sure that somewhere there is an attorney or agency looking out for the rights of deceased personalities. Here's an alphabetical list of commercial uses affected by this act: advertising, animation, apparel, barware, calendars, ceramics, collectibles, dolls, domestics, figurines, games, gifts, handcrafts, jewelry, lithographs, look-alike services, mirrors, mugs, office supplies, party goods, photographs, premiums, prints, promotions, publishing, records, reproductions, sound-alikes, souvenirs, stationery, syndication, textiles, timepieces, toys, T-shirts, videocassettes, wax museums, wall decor, and all other general uses mentioned above.

The following are uses excepted from the bill: plays, books, magazines, newspapers, musical compositions, films, radio or television programs, political and newsworthy material, single and original works of fine arts and certain advertisements. In the event you want to obtain a license to use a particular personality's characterization in some way, Richman suggests you contact the Screen Actor's Guild or the Academy of Motion Picture Arts and Sciences in Los Angeles.

ASSESSING YOUR SITUATION

3

WHETHER YOU'RE A HOMEMAKER about to launch a part-time business on a shoestring or a corporate executive who's thinking about investing your life savings into a full-blown entrepreneurial venture, you need to assess your personal situation before you begin to work at home. The first part of this chapter is for nervous beginners who wonder whether they've got what it takes for success and what they are letting themselves in for when they start a business at home. Readers who are comfortable with the idea of being their own boss and confident of their business abilities may wish to skip to the midchapter section, "Home Business Pros and Cons."

Are You a Good Home-Business Candidate?

Before you launch a business at home, you need a clear understanding of yourself, your capabilities *and* your limitations. You must know your strengths so you can build on them, your weaknesses so you can shore them up.

Find out if you're a good home-business candidate by taking the following "test." There are no right or wrong answers, of course; I just want you to do a little thinking about your strengths and weaknesses. After you have answered the questions, ask a family member or a close friend to answer them with you in mind. If there is disagreement, it could be that you're trying to fool yourself, or you haven't let other people see the real you.

Yes No

☐ ☐ I'm not afraid to make decisions, even though they may be wrong.

☐ ☐ I can take criticism and rejection.

☐ ☐ I enjoy taking charge of things and seeing them through to the end.

☐ ☐ I'm an organized worker.

☐ ☐ I'm an independent, self-confident person.

☐ ☐ I get along well with most people.

☐ ☐ I like to work, and I'm willing to work hard for something I want, even if financial rewards come slowly.

☐ ☐ I'm willing to do a lot of self-studying, research and planning to make my home-business dream a reality.

As you may have guessed by now, the more "yes" answers you have, the more likely a home-business candidate you are. Having a couple of "no" answers doesn't mean you have to give up your business dream, but it could be a sign of trouble to come.

For instance, the person who is afraid to make decisions will certainly encounter difficulty the first time a major business decision has to be made. The person who cannot take criticism and rejection may crumble the first time a customer says "no" to a sales pitch. People who are reluctant to take charge, or unwilling to accept responsibility, should not subject themselves to the stress of managing a home business. On the other hand, all of these problems might be overcome if one were to join forces with a partner who does have these desired business qualities.

If you answered "no" to the questions about being organized, having confidence, or getting along well with others, this is an indication that you would benefit from some self-help books on these topics. With time and effort, anyone can learn the secrets

Partners

Pam and I each had four years' experience in our own businesses when we became partners. I was coming from finished handcraft manufacturing, and Pam had been designing for magazines and manufacturers. Since our goal was to publish a line of craft patterns, we soon discovered the two experiences meshed wonderfully.

Pam enjoys technical writing and layout, while I enjoy promoting products and people. We also found our creativity blossoming. An idea no longer became one creation, but hundreds. Also, the support of another person helped both our egos.

This is not to say we've not encountered difficulties. We both were used to doing things our own way—compromise was in order. We both have personality quirks that require patience from the poor soul being subjected to it. But all of these things have been treated so far with a big dose of humor. In many ways, our partnership has been like a marriage. To respect and trust the other individual is the key. It is working for us.

—Beth Morrow, partner of Pamela Noel, Pecan Street Designs

of organization, develop a greater degree of self-confidence, and improve working relationships with other people.

I do hope you answered "yes" to the last two questions because a home business definitely requires concentrated effort, time and energy, to say nothing of the three *P*s: Patience, Perseverance and Planning. From experience, I can assure you that your home business, whatever its kind or nature, will take twice the amount of time and energy of any salaried job you may have held in the past, and unless you are extremely lucky, it will also take longer than you think to make a profit from your endeavor. Therefore, be patient in your financial success expectations. Allow at least two years and as many as five, depending on your type of business, the time, energy and money you give it, and the skills and experience you bring to it.

Above all, remember that a successful home business requires *planning*—in detail and *on paper*. "People don't plan to fail," goes an old saying, "they fail to plan." Trying to build a business without any kind of plan is like riding an exercise bike: You do a lot of pedaling, but you don't get anywhere.

Why Businesses May Fail

Through the years, I've communicated with thousands of people who are engaged in a variety of part-time homebased, money-making activities. Many of these people do not consider themselves to be "in business," and those who do often lack business expertise and marketing know-how. Furthermore, many of these money-making activities are underground operations as far as the Internal Revenue Service (or Revenue Canada) is concerned. While some people may think they are pulling a fast one on tax collectors, they are more likely cheating only themselves. That's because there are numerous personal and financial advantages in bringing a home business to the surface, and this book explains them to you, along with a lot of other things you may be surprised to learn.

Since no one knows how many homebased businesses there are, it's clear we have no way of knowing how many of these businesses will eventually fail. My research, however, confirms there is tremendous coming-and-going in this industry. Many newcomers, at first excited by the idea of working at home, soon become disenchanted when they realize a homebased business means commitment and *hard work*. Since such activities were never really businesses in the first place, it's hard to think of them as business failures when they cease. But if I had to guess, I'd say that at least half of all "wannabes" won't last long enough to become a real business. *Yet this is no reason for you not to try!* You may be among the successes, and even if you're not, I can guarantee your entrepreneurial experiment will teach you wonderful things about yourself you will never learn otherwise.

Some homebased businesses fail not because they are unprofitable or unsuccessful, but simply because of some uncontrollable event in the owner's life that makes cessation of the activity necessary. A marriage, a divorce, a death, a birth, loss of one's home to a fire, hurricane, flood, a sudden illness—all these events and more can have a great impact on your business plans and the overall business-failure rate of homebased entrepreneurs.

The good news is, if you reach the stage where you are really in business and keep putting time and effort into your endeavor, your odds for success may be as high as 95 percent. One reason today's business beginners have a greater chance for success is because so many others have gone before them, sharing their experience and knowledge in books, magazines, newsletters and success tapes. Today's small business owners also have the advantage of computer technology, which makes it possible for them to operate much like Fortune 500 companies. In addition, a wealth of help is available from government sources, community colleges, and other learning centers, plus individual teachers and advisers like me. (See chapter sixteen of this book for some of the best general sources of small business information, along with guidelines on how to find all the specific business management and marketing help you'll need as you continue to grow.)

If you do not possess business management and marketing skills and feel you cannot acquire them through self-study, one option is to work with someone who does have a "head for business," such as a family member or friend who can be your business partner. "Do what you do best and hire out the rest" is excellent business advice, but it's expensive to hire outside business services, which is why I've put so much detail into this book. You may be surprised by how much you can do on your own with a little time and effort. When you do need outside help, I hope you will support the home-business industry by hiring another homebased business to help you. Many communities now have helpful directories of homebased professionals or organized networking groups where such contacts can be made. You can also connect with such professionals by joining a home-business organization or reading entrepreneurial magazines on your newsstand.

Good advice is always helpful, but don't let other people tell you how to run your business. There is much to be said for following the dictates of your heart, trusting your intuition and gut instincts, and marching to a different drummer. I didn't become a leader in my field by imitating the actions of my competitors, and many times in the past it would have been a mistake for me to take the advice others gave me, particularly that of my husband, who rarely agrees with the way I do things. (Fortunately,

A head for business—that's not something inherited, or something shared by only the talented few, it's something you can acquire, and it's essential.

—Colette Wolff, author, designer, owner of Platypus Publications

he leaves me alone to make my own mistakes.) As you develop your own business ideas, I urge you to read, study *and carefully weigh* the advice and experience of others while also remembering your way just might be as good as or better than anyone else's.

Many people who think they do not possess the necessary talent and skill to start and operate a successful business are often surprised to discover their true abilities and potential for success once they get going. Thus, what you may be doing best a year or two from now, when compared to the things you now do best, will no doubt amaze you. Once you have started your business, I wager you'll soon be saying, "I can't believe I'm actually doing this. I had no idea I was capable of such things."

Identifying Special Skills and Talents

Here's a little assignment to help you identify your many talents and skills. Title three sheets of paper as follows:

1. Special Skills and Talents
2. Work Experience
3. Practical Know-How

Include education, hobbies, abilities, volunteer activities, job experience, favorite home activities, extracurricular or social activities, etc. For example: Do you have good communication skills? Do you enjoy using the telephone . . . meeting people . . . speaking in public? Do you have writing ability . . . a flair for design or decorating . . . skill as a cook . . . a fundraiser . . . a tour guide? Can you type . . . operate business machines . . . use computers? Do you have a "green thumb?" Are you good with children . . . animals . . . older adults? Do you sew . . . do stitchery . . . make handcrafts? Do you have teaching experience . . . accounting or bookkeeping skills . . . legal training . . . managerial ability? Any experience in sales? Are you an organizational wizard . . . a "take charge" person . . . a creative thinker . . . a problem solver? Are you especially knowledgeable about one thing in particular? Is your background unique? Are you a Jack or Jill of all trades? What do you do that others might like to do? You've got the idea, I'm sure. And you probably have more skills and talents than you realize.

In addition to giving you an ego boost, this little exercise will automatically suggest new business ideas. Keep your worksheets handy as you continue to read this book. Add to your list each time you are reminded of something else you know or do well. By the time you have finished, I guarantee you'll be impressed, particularly if you're a homemaker who has thought of herself for years primarily as a wife and mother.

This book is not for women only, of course, but my daily mail suggests more women than men own businesses at home or want to start them. (Women have always outnumbered men at all the home-business conferences I've attended.) The SBA's research also shows that, over the past decade, women have been starting businesses at twice the rate of men. (Canadian statistics show women are starting their own businesses at *three* times the rate of men.) Mothers still represent one of the largest categories of would-be home-business owners. Since the very job of homemaking tends to release a woman's creative abilities, it is not surprising so many home businesses are closely allied to homemaking arts such as cooking, sewing, child care, needlecrafts, handcrafts, music, art, gardening, interior decorating and pet care. Often out of need, boredom or accidental discovery, the idea for a home business just sneaks up on a woman, and before she knows it, she's making money.

Why People Avoid "Business"

My daily mail has also shown me this fact: the homemaker who suddenly starts to make extra money at home seldom feels like a businesswoman, and she may never feel as though she's "in business," even though she may continue to make money at home for years.

This reluctance to look upon your money-making activity as a business tends to be common among women in general and is particularly prevalent among the thousands of men and women who sell art, crafts and other handmade items at fairs throughout North America each year. Yes, money is being made from such homebased enterprises, but little *profit* is being realized by the majority of these people. That's because so many of them are part-time hobby sellers who lack business expertise and an understanding of the crafts or giftware marketplace. Unfortunately, their failure to look upon their endeavor as a business makes profit almost impossible to attain.

Success in a home business begins with the right attitude: a *money-oriented mindset for success.* You have to want money to make it, and you must desire success to attain it. Without a professional, businesslike attitude about what you're doing, you are destined to remain small-time forever. If that's what you want, OK. But I'm betting that what you really want is more than "pin money" or even part-time income—and you can get it *if you're willing to work for it.*

I once read about a woman whose business was baking bread on Saturdays. By working twelve hours on that one day, she said she could turn out as many as sixty loaves that she could sell locally for seventy cents each. After deducting her expenses, she said she netted $35, and she seemed happy with that money. I'm

A Special Message for Women

Observers have noted that the ability to focus on a task in both its large and small dimensions, despite distractions and limited resources, is characteristic of women's role in the home and is also needed for entrepreneurial success. The displaced homemaker, who is frequently turning to entrepreneurship, is finding that experience gained nurturing a family is useful in nurturing a business. In addition, many observers comment that women entrepreneurs show a greater willingness than male entrepreneurs to admit ignorance, to seek help, and to do their homework. Many entrepreneurial women need only business training and equal opportunity to be successful.

—from an Annual Report to the President's Interagency Committee on Women's Business Enterprise

"Pin Money"

Did you know that pins were once so expensive that only the wealthy could afford them? And so rare they were offered for sale for only two days at the beginning of each year?

At that time, husbands would dig down deep to come up with as much extra money as possible so their wives could go out and buy this expensive luxury item. Thus the expression "pin money."

sure she wasn't counting as expenses the gas or electricity she was using, or her car expenses in delivering the product, so in truth her profit was even less.

If this woman had the desire to expand her business instead of just making a few dollars on the side, she could have done it. But like thousands of other people who have feelings of insecurity, this woman clearly had her mind set on staying small, for reasons we can only guess. I've often wondered if she ever raised her prices. Probably not. People with this kind of mindset are often afraid to raise prices for fear of not selling at all. Their logic is simply that $35 is better than nothing at all, even though they end up working for less than minimum wage.

Why are so many people so hesitant to approach their home-based, money-making activity as a business? The simple answer is . . . *fear*. The very word "business" seems to scare some people half to death, particularly women who have never held outside jobs. And a certain number of men and women alike are apt to shun the idea of a business by saying, "Who, me? Nah, I just want to make a little extra money." In reality, some of these people are not ambitious enough to build a real business. Others are afraid they would fail if they tried, and still others are afraid of success.

Why People Fear Success

Why do people fear success, of all things? *Because it signals change.* For example, if a home business were suddenly to "take off," it might necessitate, among other things, out-of-town business trips to find buyers or participate in trade shows and the hiring of employees or sales representatives, not to mention a large investment of time and money. Women working at home may be especially fearful of success when it involves such things, and with good reason. They know that if a home business were to become successful, the whole family lifestyle would have to change. Since many families are reluctant to accept change in any form, this is not a concern to regard lightly.

Where marriages and home businesses are concerned, one has to consider the generation gap as well as individual personalities. Older, longer-married couples may have more problems in this area than younger, more enlightened couples who have been socialized with a different image of "wifely responsibilities." It's not at all unusual these days to hear about men who are planning to quit salaried jobs so they can work full time at home on businesses their wives started.

Many women have told me it would have been impossible to build their home businesses without the full cooperation and support of their husbands. I heartily agree. If a man is unsupportive and is going to use the home business as an excuse to criticize the way his wife runs the home, she's going to experience stress with a capital *S*, and not every woman can handle it. Some women need to ask themselves this disturbing question: "If my business succeeds, will my marriage survive?"

Sometimes a husband may see his wife's emerging successful business as a threat to his own place in her life. More than anything, I think, a woman's desire to give to her family is the one thing that ultimately holds her back from great financial success. Many women have told me their family simply must come first, and they must be careful to keep their business small for that reason, even though greater profits would come with growth.

But sometimes sudden growth comes anyway. If you're a married woman, and your new business takes off like a shot, could your husband accept the fact you might end up making more money than he ever did? Divorce, of course, is not unknown in home-business land. One woman at a conference told me how her overwhelming passion for crafts had changed her life, led her to a soft sculpture shop of her own, and ultimately a divorce. She said things got so bad that at one point her husband picked up a piece of lint from the carpet and sarcastically asked, "Can I throw this out, or do you plan to *make something with it*?"

Fortunately, far more marriages seem to thrive on the entrepreneurial lifestyle than dissolve in divorce. Many of my readers have reported that working together as a couple has enriched both marital and personal lives. As home businesses of all kinds continue to be recognized as a vital economic force in North America, we'll see more and more couples striving for a full-time, self-supporting business of their own. If such couples are wise, they will work together from the very beginning, each assuming a certain responsibility for the business as well as for the home and family.

Is Something Holding You Back?

People have a lot of reasons for not doing something about their dreams and ambitions. Here are some of the more common excuses, and my rebuttal to them. Check the ones you have been using lately. (If none apply to you—my congratulations!)

☐ **But my job leaves me with no time for my home-business idea.**

You need to change your attitude about time. Everyone has the same number of hours to spend each day. As someone once said, "Some people count time; others make time count." Many people automatically "find time" by not doing certain things they used to do—things that no longer seem important after the business is begun. After all, what's more important: being able to say you

People are always blaming their cir-
cumstances. I don't believe in circum-
stances. The people who get on in this
world are the people who get up and
look for the circumstances they want,
and, if they can't find them, make
them.

— George Bernard Shaw

have just shipped a big order or completed a profitable job, or that you have the best-looking lawn or cleanest house in town?

☐ But I have no money to start or expand a business.

Many home businesses can be started with a small amount of cash, and there are ways to generate capital even when one has no collateral for a bank loan. (See "Business Loans and Other Money Sources" in chapter six.)

☐ But there's no room in my home to set up an office or workroom.

I know people who run home businesses in house trailers, apartments, even RVs. You have to let your home know who's boss. Don't let it dictate the way you live in it. Make room for what you want to do by changing the way you live. To get started, turn the dining room table into a temporary worktable by covering a board with fabric and laying it on top. (At day's end, store the board against the wall, turning it into a decorative accessory.) Claim any drawers you can find, and lay siege to at least one closet. Consider the use of a room divider to turn one large room into two, and take a serious look at the back porch, the garage, the basement. You have space somewhere. The trick is in learning to use it efficiently. Books and magazines will give you ideas.

☐ But my family won't support my efforts.

You may be surprised by the support you'll receive once you have started and shown your family how serious you are about what you are doing.

☐ But I'm always being interrupted in anything I do at home.

And you'll continue to be interrupted until you "lay down the law." Tell family and friends that you must work, and you cannot be disturbed at certain times of the day. Establish a work schedule for yourself—even if it is only two hours a day—and stick to it.

☐ But I'm too old to start a business.

Regardless of your age, if you feel you want to start a business, I encourage you to try. It takes only a good money-making idea and the ambition to see it through. Talk to older people you know who operate home businesses. Some of their ambition is bound to rub off on you.

☐ But I'm handicapped.

If you have a physical handicap, gain the courage you need by reading books and magazines written especially for handicapped people. (Ask your library for a list of them.) Also discuss your ideas and dreams with friends and professionals who might be able to help you. A home business may allow you to carve out an exciting life for yourself.

☐ **But I don't have a good education.**

In a home business, a formal education is not nearly as important as the education you can give yourself. If you can read and are willing to study, you can learn what you need to know. Increase your education by taking special courses and attending workshops and seminars related to your interests. Join appropriate organizations and network with others who share your dreams.

☐ **But I'm scared because I don't know anything about business.**

The education you give yourself will dispel many of your fears. This book is a good beginning. Think of it as a college course in home-business basics. The more you learn, the less frightened you will be.

The most common excuse, besides fear, is the natural worry that one will not have enough time or money to do the job right. Yet many people with full-time jobs and growing families have managed to find the time to start a business at home, and just as many have started on the proverbial shoestring.

As I see it, there is no "right amount" of money required for a home business except that you *do need enough for your particular needs.* (Those needs can be determined by preparing a written business plan, which you will learn how to do in chapter seven.) A major benefit of starting with only a small amount of money is that you automatically limit your financial risks. Small expenditures mean small mistakes, and the lack of money can actually be a benefit because it will force you to think more creatively.

As for time, the lack-of-time excuse can be merely a cover-up for one's fear of the unknown. Regardless of your situation, I urge you never to let lack of time stop you from trying to achieve the things that are important to you. My own experience leads me to believe that we only find time for special things by simply beginning. Then, mysteriously, the needed time materializes in direct reversal of Parkinson's Law (i.e., that work expands to fill the time available). In this case, it is time that expands to make room for all the things we want to do.

Home Business Pros and Cons

Advantages

There are many special benefits to having a business at home:

- If you have been a caregiver, you can continue in that role, whether it's for kids, a sick or disabled spouse, or aging parents.

The Cowards Never Started

In many ways, home-business entrepreneurs are like the pilgrims who came to America on the *Mayflower.* Some have the courage of their convictions, others don't:

"It was alright to talk about it. They made plans. They had a moment's vision, a fleeting dream. But in the end, some lack in their moral fiber, some gnawing, nibbling fear held them back. They never started . . . they stayed where they were. They dropped back. They failed somehow to release within themselves that power which lies in every individual, and is released only when he starts forward in a straight line for the object about which he has dreamed. The man who never starts, never feels that sense of power."

—From *The Cowards Never Started*, by Ray Dickinson. ©1933 by Franklin Publishing Co. Inc.

Couples in Business

The main ingredients in a couples-working relationship are love and co-operation. These values must never be neglected. You can discuss something and argue a point and be bull-headed and generally go through all kinds of emotions that seem to get deeper and deeper into the hypnosis of conflict, but . . . if you keep the goal that you will not sacrifice your love for each other, and that you are dedicated to resolving any issue or conflict, you can always work it out. Nothing could or should be allowed to go unfiltered by these two values.

> —Connie and Timothy Long, partners in North Star Toys since 1980

How to Work Together and Stay Married

- Each of you should do what you do best and don't tell the other one how.
- Both of you should also do what you hate worst.
- Do not talk about business during meals and after 8:00 P.M.
- Get away from the house for separate or together "fun" activities.
- Build friendships with people who can give you "warm fuzzies" and the support your partner or clients might not give you.
- Set your priorities straight: Faith, Family and Financial Gain.

> —Patricia LeBlanc, a dairy farm wife and owner of Hazen Road Quiltworks

- If you're handicapped, a home business may be a perfect solution to your special employment problems.
- If you're older and without employment but not yet eligible for social security, a homebased business can be a wonderful bridge, giving you not only personal satisfaction but income that otherwise might not be possible. (Of course, many people already on social security are finding a homebased business not only provides extra income, but a way of staying active and involved in life.)
- Whether young or old, male or female, as a self-employed individual you are in control of your own time and working hours. (Of course it goes without saying you'll push yourself relentlessly, but at least you'll be the one doing the pushing, and where stress is concerned, that makes all the difference.)
- In your own office at home, you have the luxury of enjoying a smoke-free environment if you don't smoke or smoking when you feel like it if you do. You can also choose your own kind of background music or work in silence if you prefer.
- The high overhead costs that kill so many new businesses are low, sometimes nonexistent, when your home becomes your place of business. Also, when you're at home all day, you dramatically cut the chances of being burglarized.
- By working at home, you automatically save money on clothes, lunches out, transportation expenses, and day care costs.
- You don't have to earn as much when you work at home because a homebased business enables you to shelter a sizable chunk of your gross income from taxes through home office deductions and other strategies outlined in chapter six.

A homebased business offers intangible benefits as well. Although some marriages have crumbled under the stress of doing business at home, many couples have told me their marriages and relationships with their children have been greatly strengthened from working together on a family business. Parents who have found the courage to leave unsatisfactory jobs to strike out on their own from home base have suddenly discovered the joy of being available for their family in ways that were never possible before.

A business that does reasonably well can greatly increase one's self-confidence and make one aware of special talents and abilities previously undiscovered. Women, in particular, have often told me how their businesses have increased their self-esteem and feelings of worth.

And all of us who work at home share a smug satisfaction about being able to stay at home when others have to face gridlock on the expressway or risk their lives driving in blizzards, heavy rain or fog. We're grateful we no longer have to face other commuters on trains or buses, or fight for a seat in the restaurant at lunchtime. We're happy to be able to work in the most comfortable clothes and to know the office is just a few steps away. If this isn't a terrific way to live, I don't know what is.

Yes, it's true that homebased business owners put in awfully long work weeks, especially in the first few years of their business. But in the end, we decide when to start and stop. No boss is telling us what to do, and this adds to the quality of life.

Disadvantages

Curiously, the same things that make a business at home most satisfactory are also the ones that cause problems. For example:

• You're in control of your own time and working hours, but you'll soon find you tend to be self-exploiting in that there is no one to tell you when to quit and go home. (Business owners in my network have reported they often work as many as eighty hours per week.)

• You may have total privacy from the world in your own home, but not from your family. Your children or spouse may intrude into your daily work schedule, and household responsibilities have a way of perpetually interrupting productivity. (It's difficult for the average homemaker to find large blocks of time for serious work. Most are lucky to find even twenty scattered hours a week for their business.) Even without children, interruptions are the norm. Houses naturally demand attention when things go wrong, and spouses don't like to be taken for granted. The "Honey, I know you're busy but . . ." line is especially annoying to me, but it's something I had to adjust to. As my husband put it. "When the day comes that your business comes before me, look out!"

On the Lighter Side:

As soon as you start a business at home, you will never again have enough time to do everything you want to do. As someone once said, "If it weren't for the last minute, nothing would ever get done." You'll stop polishing your copper-bottom pots, forgotten food will turn green in the refrigerator, and you'll soon adopt the attitude, "If I can't see it, I don't need to clean it." Gourmet cooking will quickly fall by the wayside, and if you have been preparing fantastic meals for years prior to starting a business, the oven is not the only thing that's going to heat up when you start throwing quickie meals on the table. A homebased business will also curtail your social life. Either you'll be working in the evenings or on weekends, or you'll simply be too tired to think about entertaining guests, let alone cleaning house for them.

Fired Into Action!

- **Loses job, becomes self-employed artist.** After ten years as a publications director for a government contractor, Philip Sularz was laid off. Putting his twenty-five years' experience as an artist-illustrator to work, he created a limited edition offset print of a small Soo Line Railroad steam locomotive. This was the start of his homebased activity. Now he has developed a full-time design studio with a growing mail-order ink and pencil portrait line of homes, animals and individuals.

- **Laid off, buys franchise.** After four years with McDonnell Douglas, Kathy Axcell was laid off from her job. "I purchased an existing 'Molly Maid' franchise that had employees and over two hundred customers," she says. "In a short while I had expanded the business by 20 percent, and growth continues today."

- **Laid off, now does antique shows.** When Claire Bishop, a librarian for twenty-two years, was laid off, she went to work full time at an activity that until then had been part time only. Now she sells rubber stamps, fantasy sculptures, jewelry and dollhouse accessories through shows within a three-hundred-mile radius of her home. "This business is a great way to make extra money, to give yourself an edge in case of unemployment, to meet new people, to use as an excuse to travel, and to test the market for new shows."

- **Unemployed, now cutting it up in her own pattern business.** Carrol Davis has been sewing since childhood and has been selling her work for years. "A new business was born out of my desperation to work solely from home after joining the ranks of

(continues on page 41)

Before long, you'll find yourself identifying with the Tupperware rep who shared this insight on housekeeping: "When I can write my name in the dust on my coffee table, it proves one thing: that I'm literate."

Overcoming the Fear of Failure

If fear is the main thing holding you back from starting a business, ask yourself what's the worst thing that could happen if you tried? Failure? Of course. But failure can be a beneficial experience because it teaches you what *not* to do the next time around.

I certainly have had my own share of failures. In fact, my first home business was profitable only in terms of experience, knowledge and friendships gained (not a bad bargain at that). There was very little financial profit, so when the business ended, I felt like a failure. But only for a short while. Then I began to realize the important lessons failure had taught me. In looking back, I now see that failure in one area is often a necessary step to success in another.

"Failure does not take something out of you; failure builds a lot of necessary character and personality qualities into you," says a success expert. "You are not weaker because you fail, you are tougher, stronger, more determined—and much wiser."

Since the very act of beginning involves the unknown, most of us have a tendency to shy away from it. Yet we cannot make gains either as individuals or business owners if we do not constantly explore unknown territory and test our new ideas and theories. If you have a business idea in mind at this time but are being held back for one reason or another, use this time to sharpen old skills, acquire new ones, and gain an education in business basics. As Ben Franklin put it, "An investment in knowledge pays the best dividends." Starting a business right now may not be nearly as important in the long run as being able to do it well when the time is right. Each new thing learned will broaden your economic base, each new skill acquired and sharpened will increase your income potential. Everything you do to develop your skills and business expertise will be like depositing money in a special savings account. Invest in yourself! You'll never find a more worthy investment.

Taking a Chance on Yourself

If you're out of work and without interesting job prospects, you have little to lose by launching a homebased business now. (See nearby sidebar for a motivational boost.)

If you have a strong desire to be self-employed, but are being held back because of a full-time job, you may have considered quitting and "going for it." While I would not recommend this to everyone, sometimes it is the best solution. Sometimes a person really does have a profitable idea, the necessary skills, the right experience, the right market, and enough money to take the risk, plus the necessary confidence and determination to succeed in business. In that case, it may be now or never.

In my case, it was also "put your money where your mouth is." After the publication of my first book in 1979, I began to receive a lot of mail from readers who had interesting questions and useful information to share. A couple of years later, when I started a newsletter to communicate with these people, I began with the simple notion that this would be a little sideline business, in addition to my full-time job. At that time, I was general manager of a small book publishing company, and it wasn't long before I realized I could not do justice to both tasks at once. Something else began to bother me, too. Here I was, sitting high and dry with the security of a good-paying job, telling other people they ought to start a business at home. It soon occurred to me I wouldn't have much credibility if I didn't practice what I preached. So, in June 1982, I took courage in hand and quit my job. It was a simple quote in *Reader's Digest* that finally moved me to action:

Progress always involves risks. You can't steal second and keep your foot on first.
—Frederick B. Wilcox

It is sometimes necessary to take personal and financial risks to get what you want. I took the risk and it paid off. It might for you, too. *But don't quit your full-time job to start a full-time home business unless you're absolutely sure you understand the risk involved.* Stealing second is only part of the game. The question is, Can you make it to home plate before your money runs out?

This book presents a clear picture of the home-business industry, your opportunities in it, and what you must do to achieve success as a self-employed individual. Understand from the start that doubt comes with the territory. With my husband between jobs at the time I started my business and expressing concern that I was foolish to give up a good job to go out on my own, I had to overcome my feelings of doubt about whether I was doing the right thing. I worried about whether I was going to lose the money I'd borrowed from personal savings, which had been earmarked for a down payment on a house. Although confident on one hand, I was scared to death on the other. The memories of my own start-up thus prompt me to caution you to never risk more than you can afford to lose, be it time, money, confidence or ego.

the unemployed," she says. "Now I would like to develop a flexible schedule that will allow me to take care of my parents."

• **Laid off, turns hobby into retirement business.** Donna J. Newton was laid off from her clerical job in 1981. Back then, she decided that with a lot of hard work she could combine both her hobby and her journalism talents from younger days. She envisioned publishing a newspaper and forming an unorganized fellowship of collectors of Scottie dog memorabilia. Now her *Scottie Sampler* serves over 900 collectors and dealers, and Wee Scots, Inc., provides a nice supplement to the Newtons' retirement income.

"Self-Employed Individuals" vs. "Entrepreneurs"

Have you ever taken one of those entrepreneurial quizzes to see if you've got what it takes for success? If you have, and got high marks, congratulations. But if your score was disappointing, don't take it to heart. Some of these tests are not all they're cracked up to be, and while they're meant to be helpful, in some cases they tend to discourage good people with a lot of potential.

Although I've been profitably self-employed for most of my life, I've never felt comfortable with the entrepreneur label. A while back, when a highly rated entrepreneurial quiz was making the rounds, I took the test just for the fun of it. As an internationally known author, speaker, publisher and home-business expert, I figured I'd score high. Imagine my surprise when the test revealed I was "unlikely to succeed."

This information was both amusing to me and useful because it gave me interesting perspective on the difference between classic entrepreneurs and self-employed individuals like myself. While I have many entrepreneurial traits, there are two I lack, which set my score back: First, I tend to be inflexible, and second, I care too much about the feelings of others. The classic entrepreneur, you see, operates in a flexible and spontaneous style, but like so many others who have started businesses at home, I am more comfortable with a *planned, predetermined way of life*, both at home and in business. I set guidelines and timetables for my business, and I don't like to leave things up in the air. Without question, I am less willing to change course in a venture after it is under way, and once I make up my mind on an issue, I'm not easily swayed from my opinion. (Mother always said I was bullheaded, just like my father.)

These qualities set me—and thousands of other successfully self-employed individuals—apart from the classic entrepreneur, who typically has *an impersonal, logical approach to business*. Unlike typical entrepreneurs, homebased business owners tend to be caring individuals who are truly concerned about the needs of others, and their commitment to providing worthwhile services is important to their success.

The test I took did confirm that I'm a "go-getter" who understands the importance of finishing tasks thoroughly and on time and that I'm disciplined and have learned the secrets of managing my time effectively. (Stated philosophically, this means each day we are faced with many situations in which we must choose between self-discipline and self-gratification. The choice is not always easy.) A cautionary note on my test said, "Because of your nature, you may have to temper your desire to do everything yourself—make an effort to delegate responsibility." (Oh, if only it were that simple—as you may soon learn for yourself.)

My major entrepreneurial weakness is that I still have difficulty with my "outer sphere adaptability." In other words, like most people, I prefer to work in my own "comfort zone." Although I couldn't have attained my present position as a leader in my field without stepping outside my sphere on occasions, this is not to say I've felt comfortable doing it. As your business grows, you, too, will find many opportunities outside your immediate comfort zone of friends, contacts and resources, and you'll have to explore new territory, too, whether you call yourself an entrepreneur, freelancer, self-employed individual, or plain vanilla "home-business owner." So get used to feeling uncomfortable. It's a natural part of being in business for yourself.

Or as the well-known quilt designer and author Jean Ray Laury says: "If you are being pulled out of your comfort zone, out of your area of competence, you are being challenged. Anything that challenges tends to push us to the extremes of our abilities . . . and that's when we discover things about ourselves."

WHICH HOME BUSINESS FOR YOU?

4

THE INFORMATION IN THIS CHAPTER is designed not only to spark new business ideas but also to help those already in business evaluate the long-term profitability of current endeavors.

If you're still looking for that first great home-business idea, my first tip is that you should take money-making idea books with a grain of salt. Some of the "profitable" ideas in such books are good only for laughs.

My husband, Harry, who works full time with me on the business and handles much of our daily mail, often writes funny notes to me in the margins of letters or advertising material. There was this flyer promoting a book of home-business ideas that read:

"Selling dust from your vacuum cleaner is just ONE of the unusual money-making ideas in this book!"

In the margin, in red ink—and with lots of exclamation points—Harry wrote: "BUY THIS!!! We have a fortune under our feet and don't know it!!!"

Some of the make-money-at-home idea books currently in print provide an enthusiastic but haphazard listing of hundreds of home business ideas such as "Decorate cakes!", "Restore antiques!", "Sell your crafts!" or "Start a typing service!" One that really made me chuckle was "Be a rowboat maker! Make a mold and manufacture fiber glass rowboats." Sounds easy, doesn't it? Unfortunately, only the right person, in the right place, with the right kind of experience, know-how, and marketing expertise— to say nothing of sufficient business capital—could succeed in a rowboat-building business.

A good business-idea book will include information on start-up costs, skills or equipment required, advantages and disadvantages of each type of business, and an indication of profit potential. In just one chapter, I can't begin to give you that kind of detailed information, but this is something Paul and Sarah Edwards have done in their book, *The Best Home Businesses for the '90's.* Like me, the Edwardses also question the profitability of the ingenious ideas in some business-idea books. "The fact that something is a clever idea that could be done at home doesn't mean people can make money doing it," they emphasize. Their book describes seventy carefully researched business opportunities (most of them service-oriented, and many dependent on computer technology) they feel offer the best possibilty of financial success in the 1990s.

Other practical business ideas in tune with the times will be found in newsstand magazines such as *Entrepreneur* and *Income Opportunities.* The only problem here is many of the franchise and service businesses featured in such magazines require large, up-front cash investments or equipment purchases many people can't afford. While this chapter includes perspective on homebased franchises, my primary aim is to help people with limited funds start low-investment, "from scratch" businesses that utilize existing skills, knowledge and experience.

"I wish I could discover or devise a magic formula for combining all my talents and interests into one tremendously successful package," someone once said to me. That's the trick, all right, and I believe each of us can create some magic in our lives through a combination of concentrated self-study, patience, determination and perseverance.

"Perseverance," said Longfellow, "is a key element of success. If you only knock long enough at the gate, you are sure to wake up somebody." Right now, I'm the one who's knocking on your gate, trying to wake you up to the many home-business possibilities awaiting you.

The Sources of Ideas

. . . Some of my best business ideas came out of sheer desperation when my back was against the wall. Remember: the most impressive plants can grow out of manure piles.

—Investment advisor Howard Ruff, in an interview for *Business Age*

Big ideas come from the unconscious. But your unconscious has to be well informed, or your idea will be irrelevant. Stuff your conscious mind with information. Then unhook your rational thought process. If the telephone line from your unconscious is open, a big idea wells up within you.

—David Ogilvy, founder, Ogilvy and Mather

To get a sound, profitable idea, we have to learn to look past the end of our nose. We have to obliterate our preconceptions and prejudices. Look around. Observe what is successful. Then, start brainstorming. Ask yourself a thousand questions and try to answer them. Ideas do not hide from us. They are everywhere we go, in everything we do. They are not beyond reach. But some of us are mentally blind.

—John Sheehan, writer

Two Basic Kinds of Businesses

In spite of the hundreds of individual things you might think of that could bring in extra income, there are just two kinds of businesses after all: those that are *product-oriented* and those that are *service-oriented*. Let's analyze them, two by two.

• Product-oriented businesses fall into two categories, as indicated on the "Product-Oriented Businesses" chart on page 47: (1) products that are self-created or manufactured; and (2) products that are made by others and either purchased for resale or sold for others on a direct-sales or drop-ship basis. (Drop-ship means you solicit orders, then send them with appropriate payment to a publisher or manufacturer who ships the order directly to your customer.)

• Service-oriented businesses also fall into two main categories: (1) Services performed *at* home (work generally performed at home after sale of service); and (2) services performed *from* home (some or all work performed away from home after sale of service). These at-home and from-home services are sold to two primary markets, as indicated on the "Service-Oriented Businesses" chart on page 48: (1) individuals at home; and (2) people in the business community (including business professionals, companies, shops, stores, organizations and institutions).

Because many services can be adapted for sale to both business and consumer markets, there is some overlapping here. I believe, however, the true profit potential of any service business can best be analyzed by viewing it from this marketing standpoint: *Simply ask yourself which market you are most qualified to serve and best able to reach.* The same logic can be applied to product businesses, too.

"There is no new thing under the sun," according to the Bible, but every product or service in the world can be changed, improved, presented or sold in a new way or simply offered to a different audience. That's what makes business so exciting and your money-making opportunities so many and varied.

Take a look at the charts that follow, and try to relate what you see there to the self-profile you recorded on your skills/talents/experience worksheet from chapter three. (If you haven't completed this little exercise yet, do it soon because these worksheets will be helpful to you in brainstorming for money-making ideas.)

If you already know what you want to do and have established certain goals for yourself, you have taken an important first step toward success. Just hang on to the mental picture you have of your idea and begin to develop it. And be sure to call on your subconscious mind for help, because it will never fail to obey

Product-Oriented Businesses

Self-Created *(or Manufactured)* Products	Products Made by Others *(Manufacturers or Publishers)*	
Made for sale at retail, wholesale or on consignment. Involves inventory.	Purchased wholesale and resold (at retail or wholesale). Involves inventory.	Generally purchased for resale in direct-sales situations or on drop-ship basis. May or may not involve inventory.

Product Examples

Books/directories Kits (craft, hobby) Crafts* Patterns and Fine art and prints designs Food products Periodicals Furniture Reports and infor- Garments mation sheets Greeting cards/ or booklets notes Rubber stamps Herbs, plants Tools, equipment Household items *The crafts category is so broad as to be almost indescribable. Basically, it includes anything made of wood, metal, clay, glass, fiber, fabric, and all materials in between and covers such specific items as gifts, decorative accessories, miniatures, toys, dolls, novelties, jewelry, clothing, sewing, weaving, needlework and so on.	Advertising specialties (items imprinted with ad messages) Antiques and collectibles Books and booklets Calendars and posters Craft supplies and materials/kits Crafts and needlework (finished products) Flea market goods Food products Housewares Imported gifts and novelties Jewelry Nutritional products Office supplies Perfume Stationery and note cards	Cleaning supplies Cookware Cosmetics Craft and hobby kits Diet/health products Giftware Greeting cards Housewares How-to books Jewelry Lingerie Perfume Toys

How and Where Product Sales Are Generally Made

(See chapter ten for detailed marketing idea charts.)

There are only two ways to get a product to the ultimate consumer: directly or indirectly. Retailing is *direct* selling; wholesaling is *indirect* selling.

Retail Sales

• *Direct selling* to consumers on a face-to-face basis—at fairs, shows, bazaars, flea markets, home parties, network marketing, person-to-person sales and in-home demonstrations.

• *Indirect selling* to targeted consumer markets—through direct-mail or telephone promotions, special distribution programs and media advertising.

Consignment Sales

Neither fish nor fowl, consignment selling is simply an alternative marketing method for people who can't or don't wish to sell at wholesale.

Wholesale Sales

• *Indirect selling* to consumers—through retail shops and stores, mail-order dealers or distributors and other wholesalers, by means of sales calls, trade shows, sales representatives, direct-mail promotions, special distribution programs and trade advertising.

Service-Oriented Businesses
Generally sold locally, in person; some also sold and performed by mail.

The listings below are merely examples—no attempt has been made to list every possible service one might sell. (See also "Country Businesses" idea chart in this chapter.)

"At Home" Services

Sold to Individuals

Auditing services (utility, tax bills)
Beautician
Calligrapher
Child care
Class instructor (cooking, sewing, crafts)
Consultation (career, weddings, fashion, business, art, beauty, diet)
Custom design (crafts, gifts, gift baskets)
Dressmaker or tailor
Food specialist (party food preparation, special diets, menu planning, party cakes)
Mechanic or small engine repair (where zoning laws permit)
Pet care (kennel, grooming, training, dog walking)
Repairs/restoration specialist (art, antiques, furniture)
Tax preparer
Taxidermist
Teacher or coach (piano, voice, special education, drama, speech, art, sewing, etc.)
Telephone salesperson
Therapist
Writer (family memoirs, résumés)

Sold to Business Community

Accountant
Ad consultant or agency
Agent (literary, sales, booking entertainment, insurance)
Artist/crafts designer (architectural commissions, interior design)
Artist/graphic designer (brochures, catalogs, books, printed materials, signs)
Bookkeeper
Calligrapher (diplomas, scrolls, certificates, etc.)
Clipping service
Computer programmer or other services
Consulting (by phone or mail)
Counselor (investments, social services)
Financial advisor/planner
Medical services (billing, transcriptions)
Printing consultant or broker
Publicist
Research services
Secretary/word processing (legal, academic, business)
Tax preparer
Writer (copywriting, press releases, resumes, newsletters, ghost writer)

"From Home" Services

Sold to Individuals

Appraisal services (real estate, antiques, jewelry)
Auctioneer
Babysitter
Caterer
Chauffeur
Chimney sweep
Computer training
Construction services/building repair
Escort (children, the elderly)
Hairdresser/barber (house calls, shut-ins, hospital patients)
Home services provider (plumber, carpenter, painter, etc.)
Insurance agent
Interior decorator/designer
Landscape/gardener
Maid or butler
Medical insurance claims processing
Mover (furniture, equipment)
Party entertainer (singer, instrumentalist, magician, puppeteer, clown)
Party planner/coordinator
Personal shopper or delivery service (gifts, groceries, meals, medicine)
Photographer or videotape services (people, events, possessions for insurance records)
Private teacher/tutor (math, music, horseback riding, swimming)
Repair services (large appliances, electronic equipment, home repair)
Sitter (house, pets, people)
Snow removal service
Studio instructor (dance, exercise, music, etc.)

Sold to Business Community

Consulting
Coordinator (special events, projects)
Courier/messenger (bonded)
Craft demonstator (trade shows)
Efficiency/organizational expert
Entertainer (supper clubs, organizations, private groups)
General contractor
Human resource development consultant
Instructor (sports, drama, dance)
Janitor (offices)
Model
Photographer (specialized—medical, horticultural, etc.)
Plant or floral service (flowers/plants delivered and maintained)
Producer (cultural events, shows, plays)
Sales representative/agent
Speaker (seminars, workshops, keynote addresses)
Stenographer/secretary
Tour guide (museums, parks, sightseeing buses)
Translator

any clear and emphatic order you give it. (I have my subconscious mind so well trained I can give it a problem to solve at bedtime and wake up in the morning with an answer. With a little practice, you should be able to do the same. If you need a little help in this area, read a book on the power of the subconscious mind.)

Keeping Technology in Mind

I'm sure you realize the role technology is now playing in both our personal and business lives. Computers and recent technological advances continue to affect not only the way millions of people live and work, but the types of new businesses being started and the methods being used to market them. That's why it's so important for you to plan any new business with an eye to what's happening where technology is concerned. It's true that many homebased businesses can be successfully launched without a computer, but sooner or later you must become "computer literate" and add this technology to your business if you hope to stay abreast of your competition or merely in control of your business. (We'll see more about the role of computers in homebased businesses in chapter thirteen.)

By 1999, it is expected that 70 percent of all households will have personal computers. "Nothing has changed the face of the American economy as dramatically as the computer has during the past few decades," says business writer Scott Matulis in *Entrepreneur* magazine. "And in the future, the computer will have an even greater effect on the business world." He cites Bureau of Labor Statistics that predict a hot future for computer programmers, systems analysts, service technicians, and computer console and equipment operators—all services that could be offered by a self-employed individual based at home.

In spite of all the computers, robots, lasers and digital technology in our lives, however, there will always be a demand for business and creative skills only human beings can perform. Although you may ultimately need a computer to manage your business, this does not mean you have to offer a computer-related service or product to make money at home. In fact, John Naisbitt, author of *Megatrends*, believes the more high tech our lives become, the more we will need to balance this situation with what he calls a "high touch" counterpart. This suggests a continuing demand for personal services of all kinds in areas that call for increased human contact. I also interpret this to mean there will be a continuing demand for high-quality handcrafts and other finely made goods that will satisfy people's nostalgic longings for "the good old days."

Creative people may well have an edge in our high-tech future, according to Ric Tombari, a professor of management at California State University. In the above-mentioned article for

Selling to DINKs

A broad range of personal service businesses are in evidence, targeted at what one marketer calls "DINKs" (double-income, no-kid couples) who have money to spend on extras. Examples of such businesses are shopping services, home decorating and interior design, personal image services, lawn and garden management, pet care, party planning, gourmet foods, etc.

Remember: There will always be people who have money to buy the products and services of small businesses. What they may lack most of all is time, so they willingly pay others to do for them what their own time won't allow. Small enterprises can give the kind of customer service larger businesses can't afford to provide, and it is this very thing that often ensures success.

Give Good Service

"Make sure your business provides something that is truly beneficial to others," says resort owner Kyle Staples, "because the amount of money you will earn is proportional to how many people benefit from your efforts."

"Before you start a business, decide what type of people you most like to help and what you most like to do," says photographer Martha M. Oskvig. "My business keeps growing as I keep serving the needs of others."

Entrepreneur, he indicates creative individuals will make up the majority of future entrepreneurs. "Because creative people are less structured and better able to consider and accept new ideas, they will have an easier time charting a course through the constantly changing business world," he says.

Change Is Part of the Picture

From my viewpoint, the most successful homebased businesses today are those built around a good idea backed by a lifetime of acquired skills, working experience and common-sense knowledge—coupled, of course, with a commitment to the concepts of business and marketing (which we'll get to later). Whether you are already in business or still groping for a profitable idea, I can guarantee your feelings about your chances for success are going to run hot and cold as you read each succeeding chapter of this book. That's because everything in life—including business—is connected to something else, and whenever one thing changes, a lot of other things change, too. Thus your "business picture" is going to shift each time you gain new knowledge or perspective, and it will continue to shift throughout the life of your business as you acquire new information and gain entrepreneurial experience and business contacts. Throughout this book, you will find examples of how home-business owners think, operate and market themselves and their businesses. These examples will automatically trigger new ideas on how you might change, improve or redirect your own plans.

Remember, too, your choice of a business and your chances for success in it will be strongly influenced by such changeable factors as your personal lifestyle, financial situation, age, amount of business experience or education, your level of ambition, your professional attitude, your health and the amount of support you receive from family and friends.

Your choice of both business and marketing methods will also be affected by where you live (urban or rural area) and by the economy in your particular area (affluent or economically depressed). At this very moment, things are changing in the economy that could affect the marketability of your present business or budding idea. A new technological advance could just as easily render it obsolete as increase its potential a hundredfold. And just as some businesses are made extinct by technology, the social and economic changes now occurring will prompt a need for many new kinds of businesses.

Implant these thoughts in your mind as you launch a new enterprise or become more deeply involved in your present venture: *Nothing stays the same. Remain flexible. Go with the flow.*

Read, Listen and Observe

Many good business (and marketing) ideas will come to you as you read how-to books and business periodicals. (And believe me when I say you *must* find time to keep up with your reading if you hope to succeed in business.) Other ideas abound in daily newspapers and on radio and television. Still others will come as you begin to circulate in the business community, join organizations, attend workshops, seminars and trade shows or network with other business owners. Many people have gotten their best ideas just by watching what others do, then figuring out a way to do the same thing better.

In studying my reader mail, I have often noted the frequency of phrases such as "I read," "I saw" and "I realized." The following examples illustrate how profitable business ideas are generated merely through an increased awareness of and receptiveness to what's happening in one's day-to-day life:

• Lisa Kanarek, Everything's Organized: "I started my business because I had gone as far as I could in my position as a sales promotion director. *I read* about a woman in New Jersey who was a professional organizer and I thought, 'I can do that!' I quit my job, started my business, and have had the opportunity, on a daily basis, to use the skills I have acquired in previous jobs."

• Bette Laswell, BDL Homeware: "I started my business because the people who run the personal computer industry are technology buffs, and *I saw* an opening for a 'people-person' who had strong computer skills, but didn't feel the need to show them off to the user."

• Peggy Bartz, Classic Expectations: "When one of my customers became pregnant, she begged me to make her maternity wardrobe because of the lack of executive-looking maternity wear in ready-to-wear. I agreed, and after hearing the comments of her fellow office workers and talking to other pregnant executives, *I realized* there was an untapped market waiting for me."

Find a Need and Fill It

Home-business novices typically begin with little money and a strong belief that if they deliver a quality product or service and work very hard, they'll succeed in business. While this is important, it's only part of the picture. More than likely, the difference between financial success or failure will depend on management and marketing skills—your clever approach to the marketplace . . . the way the business idea is publicized or advertised . . . the way a product is packaged, presented or delivered . . . or the pizzazz with which a service is performed.

As more companies cut back on secretarial help, there is a continuing need for outside service providers in this area, notes the owner of a word processing service.

The owner of a personal shopping service says, "With fewer employees, those who still have jobs are often asked to work overtime, which means they have less time than ever for the kind of work I can do for them. They're reluctant to say, 'No, I can't come in on Saturday,' for fear of losing their job, so they hire me to shop for them."

JoAnna Lund's Success Story 1997 Update

Beginning part-time in 1991, working at her dining room table, JoAnna Lund launched a newsletter that promoted her common-sense approach to healthy living (see right). Within five years, her newsletter was probably the largest subscription food newsletter in America, her several recipe books had close to half a million copies in print, and she had a contract with Putnam for two new cookbooks a year. She now has the same publisher and editor as Graham Kerr.

JoAnna first diversified her business by launching a talk radio program on WOC-AM in Davenport, Iowa with husband Cliff as cohost, and later introduced her own line of herbs and spices. Then she opened a Kitchen Cafe and Health Wagon Catering service in Davenport and began to publish a new series of 64-page "cookbooklets." In the fall of 1996, she began production on a Public Television series tentatively titled "Help Yourself with JoAnna Lund," produced by the same company that created the Graham Kerr Show.

JoAnna now has 25 employees and her business is housed in a 10,000 square-foot building. Until a year ago, husband Cliff had never touched a printing press, but he now handles all the mechanics of getting JoAnna's booklets printed. In a recent newsletter editorial, JoAnna gave all credit for her success to God, saying: "I firmly believe that everything is in God's hands and timing, from the expanding of my business to the shrinking of my hips. I do my part by praying and doing. The rest is up to God. By trusting in the Lord, I've become a walking billboard for change, personally and professionally."

Before you actually launch or expand a business, spend time checking out the market for your new product or service. (See chapter eight.) When in doubt, follow the rule, "find a need and fill it." Unless you want to spend all your time educating your market, don't offer a product or service so new or unusual people can't understand why they need it. Offering a product you love to make, but no one wants to buy, is also foolish. (This is the pit into which so many craft producers fall. They create to satisfy themselves, forgetting it is the customer who must be satisfied first.)

How many times have you or a friend said, "If only I had someone to do (such-and-so) for me"? Maybe you're the person who ought to be doing this job, or maybe you can develop a salable solution to the problem that will enable others to get the job done easier, better, faster or cheaper. Often, in solving problems for yourself, you accidentally stumble onto a good idea for a business.

Since it is easier to sell a product or service for which a need already exists, look for problems that are being created because the right product or service *doesn't* exist, then challenge yourself to provide it. "Great opportunity has often come dressed as something missing, and great rewards are given to those who find a way to provide what's missing to others," says motivational writer Barbara J. Winter.

JoAnna Lund can identify with that statement. After shedding 125 pounds by using low-fat, low-sugar recipes she developed herself, she realized a lot of other people had the same problem she had just solved. Encouraged by a friend, she gathered her recipes into a book called *Healthy Exchanges*, borrowed money to print a thousand copies, and sold them in a few weeks. In her first eighteen months, from marketing efforts only in the state of Iowa, JoAnna sold over 42,000 books through radio publicity and local workshops. Clearly on to something hot, she quickly launched a companion newsletter to keep her fans loaded with new recipes, and within fifteen months had captured 11,000 subscribers from her book-buyers database. It was at this point that she began to promote beyond her own state and publish a second book called—you guessed it—*The Best of the Healthy Exchanges Newsletter*.

JoAnna says her success is due to the fact that she is "just a common person with a common problem solved with common sense," but she adds that her business would not exist if she had not first achieved a major goal: to lose weight. After grossing $300,000 in her first year of business, JoAnna encouraged her husband, Clifford, to quit his truck-driving job and join her in the business. Before he knew it, he was cohost of her "Healthy Exchanges" radio show.

Since I first interviewed JoAnna in 1993, her business has

expanded far beyond the boundaries of the homebased business she once envisioned. (See sidebar at left.)

Do What You Love

If you start a business you don't enjoy, you'll be tempted to throw in the towel the minute things get rough—which is a given with any new business. Thus, in choosing a business, don't just go with the idea that seems to offer the most money. When I was still struggling for survival in my business, I interviewed an enthusiastic Mary Kay salesperson who was making five times the money I was then generating. "Why don't you get involved in this program? You could make a fortune!" she insisted.

Why not? Because I've never been interested in cosmetics, I wouldn't enjoy giving facials, I don't like direct selling, and I certainly wouldn't want to spend my evenings throwing home parties—not for any amount of money. It took me a while to achieve my biggest goals and reach the level of income I was striving for, but even when the money wasn't there, I loved my work, and I've long been content in the knowledge that I'm doing the kind of work best suited to my lifestyle, personality, experience and skills. That kind of contentment is what I wish for all of you who are striving for a more satisfactory way to earn a living. *If we must spend a third of our lives working, then let it be at something we truly enjoy doing!* Or as entrepreneur and author Harvey Mackay puts it, "Find something you love to do and you'll never have to work a day in your life."

Of course, many self-employed individuals have an entirely different view of work than their 9-to-5 counterparts. Perhaps you've heard this old joke: An entrepreneur will happily work sixteen hours a day for himself just to avoid working eight hours for someone else. Entrepreneurs may sleep only six hours and work most of the remaining eighteen, rarely having time to squeeze in anything that remotely resembles relaxation, but when I talk to such people, I often hear, "but I don't mind because I really love what I'm doing." One couple put it this way: "Although we work longer hours than we ever did in our lives, it doesn't feel like work because we enjoy it and because it's something we've chosen to do. It's a lifestyle more than work. It's hard to define as *work*. We just don't think of it that way."

Pleasure from a homebased business is often greatest when one is able to turn a passionate hobby or leisure-time interest into business. Bruce Fife once worked as a clown and juggler on the side but found he loved it so much he wanted to do it full time. That desire led him to something he enjoyed even more: writing and publishing books. His best-selling book, *Creative Clowning*, has been adopted by many clown schools and colleges as a textbook on clowning.

Creativity

Creativity is just doing what other people don't do.
　　—Hal Riney, creator of the Bartles & Jaymes television ads

You have two choices in life: you can dissolve into the mainstream, or you can be distinct. To be distinct, you must be different; you must strive to be what no one else but you can be.
　　—Alan Ashley Pitt

Terror is a great foundation for creativity.
　　—Actor Rod Steiger, discussing a difficult role he once played opposite Marlon Brando

Country Businesses Idea Checklist

Certain businesses do better in rural areas than others. The following types of businesses appear to be most popular with farm families and others living in rural communities. If you have an interesting type of country business not on this list, please tell Barbara about it.

Food Businesses

Baked goods (breads, pies, cookies, cakes; for local restaurants, stores, individual customers)
Cake baking (birthdays, weddings, anniversaries)
Candy making
Catering (using local commercial kitchen facilities)
Chemical-free beef
Culinary herbs (fresh or dried)
Deer farming
Gourmet foods (sauces, seasonings, soup mixes, flavored popcorn)
Jams, jellies, juices, wines
Maple syrup and related products
Soy nut snacks
Yogurt and specialty cheeses

Special Farm Crops

Birdseed
Christmas trees
Commercial food production (raspberries, strawberries, blueberries, seedless grapes, miniature vegetables, mushrooms, nuts, honey, fruit trees, sweet corn, other fresh market vegetables)
Fish (catfish, salmon, trout)
Flowers (fresh or seeds) and ornamentals
Popcorn
Poultry and eggs
Sod/turf
Special grains
Sprouting seeds (mung beans)

Services for Farmers

Auctioneering
Bookkeeping/taxes
Consulting (crops, animals, equipment)
Dairy service (for vacationing families)
Excavating
Grain bin insulation
Repair services (home appliances; farm machinery, implements)
Restoration services (antique furniture; old farm equipment)
Rose arbors and yard accessories

Small Business Services

Accounting
Burglary alarms/systems
Computer services
Consulting (any area of expertise)
Fertilizer service (lawns, golf courses)
Financial planner
Insurance
Marketing services (varied)
Secretarial/word processing

Popular Arts and Crafts Businesses

Corn shuck crafts
Custom artwork (portraits of children, pets, horses, farmhouses)
Custom leatherwork (chaps, saddle bags, bridles)
Doll and toy making
Farm-theme handcrafts (cows, pigs, horses, chickens, geese, bunnies, duck decoys, nature items, dried miniature corn, haybales, grapevine baskets and wreaths, corn shuck crafts)
Feather pillows
Handcrafted products of wool, fur and hide
Quiltmaking, needlework and sewing businesses
Teaching art and crafts
Woodcarving

Other Country Businesses

Bait shop/worm production
Bed and breakfast inns
Campground areas
Carpentry/repair service
Cross-country skiing
Dog kennel (grooming, showing, obedience classes)
Farm tours
Greenhouse
Gun dogs (boarding kennels; training)
Home parties (all types of products)
Hunting guide
Hunting lease operation (pheasant, quail, other game birds)
Intermediate care for elderly
Petting zoos
Self-publishing (cookbooks, patterns, how-to booklets)
Sheep farming (selling sheep's milk, cheese, fleece, yarn, gift items)
Upholstery and furniture repair
Vegetable stand
Videotaping services

Harry S. Ross launched Soitenly Stooges in the fall of 1989 with a catalog of new and older Three Stooges memorabilia— T-shirts, hats, ornaments, clocks, lithos, photos, books, videos, games, buttons and more. "I've been a Stooge fanatic my entire life," says Harry, who was married in a Stooges shirt and tie. (He ended up in the newspaper when he proposed to Nancy wearing a gorilla suit and holding a bunch of bananas.) Nancy has her own profession, but she helps Harry with business on occasion. At Harry's first Stooge Festival in Akron, Ohio, over 2,000 pies were thrown during "The World's Largest Pie Fight."

When Tim Long lost his teaching job, he turned his wood-working skills into a new career as a cabinetmaker and trim carpenter. He made his first toy when a friend needed a birthday gift for a child. He began making toys for his own children, and before long, both Tim and his wife, Connie, were working together to create products for sale.

"We've been creating quality wooden toys and puzzles since 1980," says Tim, who emphasizes that the main ingredients in a couples-working relationship are love and cooperation. The Longs are not formally trained in their business activities but say they have good common sense. "We find out what we need to know by reading about it or asking someone for help."

Once, when Tim was being interviewed for an article and was asked if a hobby still can be fun after it becomes a job, he replied, "It's a blast. As soon as it stops being fun we're going to stop doing it and look for something else."

Build on What You Know and Do Best

In trying to find the home-business idea that's right for you, look for marketable products or services compatible with your work background or business contacts, or those that tie into your professional or personal fields of interest. If you already have a good understanding of the field you'd like to enter as a business owner, it will be much easier to market your business.

My research shows a close connection between previous work experience and successful home-business start-up. Consider Doug Fletcher. As a registered nurse for over four years, he saw the positive effects of humor on recovering patients. "I also saw the stress and burnout nurses experience," he told me. It was this insight that led him to launch a magazine, *Journal of Nursing Jocularity*.

"It took hundreds of hours to research, two jobs and countless hours at my computer, but now the dream is real," Doug told me after he had been publishing for about a year. With a host of contributing editors and a circulation of 16,000, Doug is now able to spend all his time on the magazine and related projects,

Dramatic Life Experience Sparks Business Idea

As a girl of eleven, Kathleen A. Hopwood was kidnapped, but she escaped. Then during her teens and early twenties, she was almost a victim of sexual assault several times. "This potential victimization prompted me to train in the martial arts," she says.

Having seen hundreds of women who wanted self-defense skills but didn't have the time to devote to a long-term martial arts class, Kathleen figured there had to be a way to distill the essence of martial arts training into short-term seminars that could get across the main concepts and skills of being able to defend oneself. By taking the simplest approach to the physical techniques, combined with the findings of current sexual assault prevention research, Kathleen developed programs to fit women's needs and time constraints. Since 1989, she has been developing a seminar business, offering comprehensive programs in crime prevention and self-protection.

"There aren't many women in this field," says Kathleen, "It takes fortitude to get the appropriate training, develop programs and sell the concept to the general population. Our programs, however, are breaking new ground in the field of employee training, and we continue to help people avoid becoming victims."

Consulting

This is the information age. The fastest growing business in the decade of the '90s will be packaging and selling information through consulting, speaking, training and products. Economic opportunities for consultants, professional practitioners, trainers, speakers and information product developers/marketers are unprecedented. Nominal capital investment is required to profit in these businesses. My annual surveys reveal the average annual income for consultants in the '90s is just under $100,000. Daily billing rates average in excess of $1,000 a day.

—Howard Shenson, author of *Shenson on Consulting—Success Strategies From the Consultant's Consultant*

Consultants . . . raise to an art form the dissemination of biased information. Their handling of collected data invariably has two results. They find a way to have the finished report coincide with the opinion of the person who hired them. Secondarily, they usually find a way to make the final report become an entree to their being asked back for more consultations.

—from *Infomaniacs—A Brown Paper Bag View of Information Interaction in Corporate America*, by Joseph S. Casciato and Robert M. Vass

including an annual "Humor Skills for the Health Professional" conference.

Like JoAnna, Doug found a need and filled it, and with laughter, he has a product that's hard to beat. "Laughter is more powerful than any pill, more potent than any IV drip, more healing than any doctor," he says. "Laughter keeps us sane. It makes us alive. It resuscitates the dying soul."

Yvonne Conway is another example of one who turned her professional skills into a successful business. Using her experience as a licensed beautician, she launched "My Line," a mobile beauty service that offers haircuts, permanents, shampoo sets, hair coloring, manicures and pedicures. (Her motto, "This hairdresser will come to your home, office, or jail," got her quite a bit of publicity.) The demand for such services in her area was so great that her son, Craig, launched a similar service called Haircuts on Wheels, Inc.

Yvonne's clients are mostly elderly or confined, while Craig serves young families and professionals. "Convenience is the key word," says Yvonne. "Tight schedules, poor health, or just plain snob appeal makes mobile services viable in any and all realms of society."

After seven years in business, Yvonne expanded her business base with the publication of *Mobile Hair and Beauty Services—Your Guide to Profits on Wheels*, a comprehensive how-to manual that is helping others follow in her footsteps. She followed up with a second book on how to launch mobile businesses in other fields, illustrating once again how one thing always leads to another.

The Advice Business

In chapter twelve, you will find information about five business activities commonly used to diversify or expand an existing business: writing, publishing, speaking, teaching and consulting. However, many people like me have built full-time businesses out of a combination of all five of these activities, which neatly fall into one category called "The Advice Business," one of the hottest home-business bets around. There are great opportunities for profit in this field, and many good books to help you realize your potential and find your niche as an adviser, information-provider or consultant.

A combination of entrepreneurial drive and white-collar layoffs has dramatically increased the number of consultants who are selling expertise in all fields. Part of the reason is a growing desire among professionals to be their own boss. Others move to consulting when a company cuts its work force. As companies cut back, the need for consultants may increase. Instead of hiring permanent employees, consultants can be hired for shorter periods of time.

To become a consultant in any field, you first must have special knowledge about that field, and a market willing to pay for it. Don't think consulting is limited only to laid-off executives. Anyone who knows something other people want to know probably can offer that knowledge through consulting. Artists and craftspeople could well find themselves advising museum curators on lost arts and crafts. A homemaker-turned-entrepreneur may be an expert in organizing a home, planning a wedding or working with children. As an experienced home-business owner, you will find many opportunities to consult with beginners in this field in areas of advertising, marketing, publicity, communications or sales. Pick any field you can think of, and you will find consultants specializing in it. There are even consultants who teach people to become consultants.

As jobs become more specialized, professions often require the individual to specialize within a specialty, notes Herman Holtz, author of *How to Succeed as an Independent Consultant*. Today's complex, technological society means more specialists will be needed to handle specific jobs. "But it does you no good to have the skills of a consultant unless you also know how to market them," adds Holtz, whose book contains practical guidelines on how to do this.

Holtz—a man who has been called "the guru's guru"—is the author of several other books on the advice business, a field he says is wide open to professionals, technicians, managers and individual entrepreneurs of all kinds. He points out that advice is not a regulated business, and anyone can sell advice in any form (except for advice in some regulated or licensed professions). "And even in these fields," says Holtz, "one is free to sell general advice to the public at large (rather than to individuals) because it is then *information*."

This is an important point, Holtz emphasizes. "Any layperson is free to write, lecture and otherwise render advice in general for fees as long as the advice or information is general and not offered to an individual. For example, you may write or lecture about legal matters in the abstract, but unless you are a licensed attorney, you may not counsel a person in legal matters for a fee."

If you think you have to be an expert in order to sell your advice, you're wrong, says Holtz. "In many cases, simple access to, or even the ability to gain access to, useful information is ample underpinning for selling advice profitably," Holtz says, adding that consulting is not a business or a profession, but a way of doing business or practicing a profession. "Ergo, anyone with a marketable skill *of any kind* is in a position to become a consultant, teaching others to do what he or she does, solving

Coach and Marketing Consultant

Prior to starting her consulting practice in 1989, Jan Cook Reicher was vice president of marketing/development with a real estate developer and director of marketing for a commercial general contractor. Now she is a business coach and marketing consultant to women business owners, senior managers, family business members and independent contractors. She has developed expertise in coaching leaders, organizational assessment, research, planning and implementation and maintenance of plans. Clients retain her for long-term consulting as well as for short-term project development and coordination. She also conducts seminars and workshops on topics related to marketing and networking.

Jan's clients include the retail, consulting, real estate, construction, architecture, senior care, entertainment, legal, marketing, art and financial industries.

"Laid-off employees often become consultants who enlist their former employers as clients," says Jan, pointing to a benefit consultants should emphasize: "From a business standpoint, this may provide the ideal alternative to valuable personnel who can no longer be supported full time in the belt-tightening 1990s."

others' problems, and/or doing for others on a temporary, permanent, or semipermanent basis."

If you plan to educate yourself to all the possibilities on how to sell your intellectual know-how, you also need to study the books of Jeffrey Lant, who is known internationally as "the unabashed promoter" (also the title of his successful publicity book). In *Money Talks*, Lant discusses how to profit from the lucrative world of talk with workshops, seminars, lectures, institutes, conferences and more. Says Lant, "If you know something and can open your mouth, this book is for you." In all of his books, Lant zeros in on what advisers of every kind need to know to profit from what he calls "the remarkable transformation of the American economy" and to launch profitable advice and consulting practices in any field.

"The trick to building a practice in its early stages," says Lant "is to find a specific service which produces for the client a disproportionate benefit compared to your fee and to leverage each individual success to get further clients." And don't be sheepish about your fees, he adds. "Your ability to deliver success to your clients, a disproportionate benefit compared to fee, entitles you to raise your prices. A client is not merely paying for your current time, but all the years, the effort, the intense mental concentration, the innovation, the creativity, and patient practice and determination it took you to get to this point." (He adds that it's a pity so many client prospects fail to understand this, but he counters with the kind of information you can use to get the message across.)

Lant's books, all of which he publishes and markets himself, enjoy excellent sales in spite of their high cover price. "That's as it should be," he says. "I believe that we who assist other people, who do good, should do well in the process. Keep this belief as your credo and you, too, will do well."

I'll buy that.

Newsletter Publishing

A press release in late 1992 stated the following: "With the age of desktop publishing, newsletters are inheriting the earth. There are already over 100 million issues of newsletters published yearly in the North American continent. Anyone can publish a newsletter, but not everyone knows the elements of newsletter design."

Design is only part of it. While a newsletter can become a profitable sideline or full-time business, it takes skill, time and money to make it pay. Whether it is profitable or not depends, first, upon the market for it, and second, upon the creator's ability to write well enough to hold the interest of his or her audience. Good writing alone isn't enough, of course; the information imparted must also be sound and needed by many people.

According to the Newsletter Association of America, the definition of a newsletter is "a specialized information publication which is supported by subscription sales and doesn't contain advertising." But there are many newsletters that do contain advertising (usually classified ads only), and not all newsletters are published on a paid subscription basis. (Many are used strictly as promotional tools.)

The one thing all newsletters have in common is specialized information that appeals to a specific audience of readers. If you can identify a universe of at least 20,000-30,000 possible subscribers, and you have a way to communicate with them, you may be able to make a go of a newsletter. Conventional wisdom says, however, that you will be lucky to get as much as 10 percent of this universe as subscribers; and once you have them, the challenge is to keep them. This isn't easy, even when you have a terrific newsletter. Even the most skilled publishers are lucky to get a 60-65 percent renewal rate, according to Frederick D. Goss, author of *Success in Newsletter Publishing*, and second-year renewal rates are not likely to go higher than 70-78 percent. If you cannot keep at least half of your first year's subscribers, something is definitely wrong with either the editorial content of your newsletter or your promotional or renewal efforts. Or maybe you're just trying to sell the right information to the wrong market.

As you will learn in chapter ten, you have to send mailings to a lot of people to get even a few orders. The same thing is true of newsletter subscriptions, which are best obtained through direct mailings and the two-step advertising method. Considering these expenses, each new subscriber may cost you $10 or more to obtain, so first-year profits usually are nonexistent. And if you're going to lose 35-50 percent of your subscribers every year, you can see that you have to hustle just to stay even. For that reason, a lot of novice newsletter publishers quit about the middle of their second year. Those who survive consider themselves lucky if they can reach the 2,000 circulation mark.

One newsletter directory publisher says an estimated 5,000 subscription newsletters are in existence, but it's anyone's guess as to how many nonsubscription (promotional) newsletters are currently circulating or how many amateur newsletter publishers there are who never get listed in newsletter directories. (I have seen estimates of 100,000 or more.) Most subscription newsletters deal with finance, investing and business in one form or another. Periodicals in this category are often quite expensive, from around a hundred dollars per year to more than a thousand, depending on the type of information being presented and, more important, the expert who is presenting it. Many other newsletters are produced by "kitchen table entrepreneurs," freelance writers, and other professionals who serve a small but select readership. Here, subscription rates may be as little as $6/year or as much as $96/year. Very little is known about just how profitable most of these newsletter publishing ventures are.

A lot of people think newsletters are a quick way to make money, but having published a newsletter for fifteen years, I can assure you this is not true. Clearly there is more to subscription-newsletter publishing than buying a computer, designing a good-looking publication, and filling it with interesting writing. I can't count the dozens of new periodicals that have crossed my desk in the past decade, only to disappear a few issues later. It takes a serious commitment to marketing to survive, not to mention a loyal following of readers who will renew year after year, and an unlimited well from which to draw new prospects to replace the hundreds who will drop their subscriptions sooner or later. Or, as Barbara Winter, publisher of *Winning Ways News*, puts it: "Publishing a newsletter is a lot like being an engineer on a train: At every stop people get on and others get off."

Mail Order/Direct Mail

Not everyone understands that mail order is not a type of business, but simply an effective way to market a wide variety of products and services. But since so many people think in terms of starting "a little mail-order business," the topic needs attention here.

Today, the mail-order industry is referred to as the direct mail or direct response industry. Most people learn this business the hard way—through trial and error—but beginners could save themselves a lot of money and heartache if they would only study some of the classic how-to mail-order books on this topic before placing ads, renting mail lists, or creating printed materials (topics discussed elsewhere in this book). With determination and a willingness to learn the rules of the game, the average person can master the principles of marketing by mail. But remember this: For every astonishing mail-order success story, there are thousands of stories of failure. Unless you have a lot of money to invest up-front, it will take time to achieve financial success in a traditional mail-order business that involves the purchase of goods for resale through a catalog.

On the other hand . . . if you have even one terrific product, can reach your targeted market through inexpensive classified ads and publicity, and have ideas for related items you could add to your line, I would be the first to encourage you to get involved in a mail-order business. After all, I started in 1980 with just one product (my first book), and in those days it sold for just $8.95. But I soon followed with a newsletter and special reports, wrote and published other books, and diversified with workshops and other speaking engagements; before long I was generating enough income for a good living.

The beauty of a mail-order business is that you can control its size and dollar volume by increasing or decreasing the number of ads or mailings that bring in business. The curse of a mail-order business is that, if you don't have employees, you can never get away for more than ten days at a time, because the mail just keeps coming and someone has to fill all those orders.

As with any endeavor, a mail-order business will grow in direct proportion to the amount of time, money and effort invested in it. Good products and prompt service are important keys to success. The following are characteristics of a good mail-order product:

1. It is a product not readily available elsewhere, either in retail stores or from other mail-order firms. The more exclusive the product, the better.
2. It will appeal not to a wide universe of buyers, but to some special-interest group of individuals, often a relatively narrow market large companies are not interested in because profits aren't great enough. (Sales that would be "peanuts" to them might represent a substantial amount of money to you.)
3. It is an item in which people will not quickly lose interest.
4. It is an item people can use, appreciate and understand, one that offers a benefit of one kind or another.
5. It is easy to describe in writing.
6. It photographs well and looks good when pictured in a catalog.
7. It is easy and inexpensive to pack and ship for arrival in customers' hands in undamaged condition. (Postage should cost no more than 10 percent of the retail price.)
8. It is small, so many items can be stored in a minimum amount of space.
9. It retails for less than $25 and has a profit margin of 65 to 70 percent.
10. It is a product of high quality. (While you always can sell a bad product, the customer who bought it won't buy from you again. This is vitally important, since the real profits in mail order come from repeat sales to satisfied customers.)

Note: As I mentioned in chapter two, be wary of trying to launch a mail-order business using catalogs offered by companies who want you to sell their product lines, such as novelty items, gifts and opportunity manuals. Many of these products are questionable at best, and some catalog companies make their money on the sale of mail lists and catalogs, not on the sale of products. If you have a good audience for such products, you would be much better off finding your

Observation Leads to Mail-Order Business

While selling title insurance at a trade show for realtors, Larry Furlong noticed a guy across the way who had a long line of people all day. What he was doing to promote the same kind of product Larry was selling was laminating business cards as luggage tags.

"I began to think about this idea in terms of what else could be done with business cards," says Larry, "and eventually hit on the idea of magnets so they wouldn't get lost." Larry spent a lot of time on the "detective process," trying to turn his idea into reality. He began by talking to people in related businesses who gave him raw material ideas, then tracked down the special materials he needed.

"I then turned my own business card into a giveaway item that helped me sell insurance," says Larry. "But before long, a lot of other business people wanted the same product, and I found I had created a demand for a product that didn't even have a pricing structure yet. Some people wanted us to make business cards into magnets, and others wanted our kits to make their own. We gave them both options."

Larry proceeded to develop the product as a mail-order item available to any company who wanted to create magnetic business cards as a giveaway item. His list of satisfied customers continues to grow, and Larry no longer has to sell insurance to earn a living.

Two-Family Craft Business

Many successful craft businesses involve the whole family, including relatives who may help with craft production. In Rexburg, Idaho, a single company—The Carousel Man—provides the livelihood of two families, Sherrell and Brenda Anderson and Ross and Andrea Clark.

The Carousel Man is the only carousel production shop west of Ohio. The company produces do-it-yourself carousel horse carving kits and also carves full-size, museum-quality carousel horses, finished or ready to paint. Say the Andersons: "We enjoy this business and have been surprised at how our involvement in it has fostered growth in other areas of our lives. We are doing what others spend their whole careers working to achieve; i.e., working at something we love, providing a valuable service, being our own bosses, and being able to live in a rural area where crime is low and the standard of living is high. We have enough money to live on and time to indulge our hobbies (amateur acting). What more could one ask of life?"

own wholesale sources for high-quality merchandise that could be sold on a drop-ship basis until you reach the point where you can purchase inventory.

There are many good manufacturers and publishers who will work with you on this basis. For example, all of my books are available to mail-order dealers who want to list them in their catalogs, as well as to teachers and seminar leaders who want to offer them to students. When you work with a "drop shipper," you operate risk-free, needing no cash up front for inventory. You simply solicit orders and send them with a shipping label and payment (you retain your share of the profit, usually 40 to 50 percent) to the publisher or manufacturer who ships for you.

Arts and Crafts Businesses

Many people view arts and crafts businesses as nickel-and-dime ventures, and rightly so, given the millions of hobby sellers out there these days. But this industry also includes thousands of highly successful men and women who earn a living doing what they love to do most: working with their creative hands and minds. While a hobby crafts business may be lucky to net a thousand dollars a year, professionals in this industry are generating gross incomes of between $30,000 and $250,000.

"Arts and crafts" are a multibillion-dollar industry that offers many opportunities to creative individuals who are willing to approach the sale of handcrafts and related products and services *as a business*. Selling handcrafts at weekend fairs and in a shop or two is a good way for a crafts hobbyist to make a few extra dollars while having lots of fun, but to earn a good part- or full-time living in this field, you must make a serious commitment to the idea of business and master the management and marketing principles explained in this book.

There may be as many as 20,000 arts and crafts fairs annually in the United States that attract hobby sellers and professionals alike. There are dozens of wholesale markets for production sellers, including handcraft fairs, gift shows and catalogs. Hundreds of magazines, newsletters, newspapers and books also serve this industry.

As the author of *Creative Cash* (one of the most popular crafts marketing books ever published), I have thousands of arts-and-crafts success stories on file. I've often noted that the most successful people in this industry are those who have designed a complete business package that includes a variety of products and services. Some product makers do custom-design work for individuals, architects or corporations, while others build solid lines for sale through their own mail-order catalog or a variety of wholesale outlets. Many then diversify their businesses through writing, publishing, designing and consulting.

Cindy Groom Harry is an excellent example of what can happen when a person takes creative skills seriously. After years of "crafting," Cindy discovered her special design talents and went on to sell many original projects to craft magazines. In 1989, she resigned her teaching job to pursue designing and consulting for manufacturers full time. Now she serves a variety of corporate clients including Black & Decker, Inc., Hunt Manufacturing, Rubbermaid, Fiskars Manufacturing Corp. (scissors) and the Dial Corp.

"We help manufacturers introduce their products into the craft industry," says Cindy. "We create designs, write instruction sheets for making those designs, and then help companies with their marketing and sales plans."

Cindy was one of the first designers in the industry to see the importance of working with manufacturers on a consulting basis, and it was her membership in the Society of Craft Designers years ago that helped her build a network of designers and sparked the ideas that ultimately led to her successful home-based business, Designs and Consultation. Cindy, who lives in Ireton, Iowa, a small town of 600 people, now contributes to the economy of her community by employing a dozen designers, instruction writers and office staff. Three-fourths of these people work from home, thanks to computers and fax machines.

MLM/Network Marketing

I have become known for always leveling with my readers—showing both the good and bad sides of any picture. While it is not my intention to tar the MLM (multilevel marketing) industry with a negative brush, neither will I join those who promote MLM as the greatest thing to ever come down the pike.

While many people have made good money in the MLM industry, thousands more have "bought the promise and have nothing but full garages and empty wallets to show for it," says Reiva Lesonsky, editor in chief of *Entrepreneur* magazine. Small-business magazines rarely promote MLM programs because there has been so much controversy about them, but the MLM community is adequately served by its own opportunity publications, which announce new programs and emphasize how to succeed in this industry.

Joe Molnar is now involved in a program that promises to yield a good profit for the ten hours a week he is currently working it, but Joe says he was one of those who got "scammed" the first time around. He lost nearly $2,000 when he got suckered by a promoter who asked for a large up-front investment and never fulfilled his promises. "The most important thing I learned," says Joe, "was that no reputable MLM company will

Crafty Country Businesses

• Often, the idea for a successful sideline business is right under your nose—especially if you live on a farm or in the country. Near Eureka, Illinois, Joy Crouch and her husband Dennis own The Sheep Station, raising sheep and selling both lambs and wool. But Joy has expanded their income greatly with her successful mail-order catalog of "sheep gift items." In addition to obvious items such as sheepskin slippers, she also sells "Lamb Chop Puppets," "Thank Ewe Notes," Sheep X-ING signs, a lamb cookbook, handcarved leather belt buckles ornamented with sheep heads, and T-shirts and sheep caps—101 items in all. (Only a short while ago, there were just 64 items in their line. "If we can incorporate a sheep into a product, we'll try it," says Joy.)

• Marcia McDonough and Jill Jefferies—who live in what they call "the extremely rural community" of Mathias, West Virginia—became partners in 1981 when they began to manufacture a varied line of character doll ornaments with heads hand-carved from the burrs of teasel plants—a weed that grows plentifully along West Virginia's country roads. Their business, Teazle Enterprises, now has enough customers to keep a dozen people working part-time in their homes.

One secret to their sales success is that they have located specialty stores that appreciate Appalachian crafts, finding them in such unlikely places as California. Working through a sales rep, they also have found an international market for their products in several Far Eastern countries.

ever ask for a lot of money up front. They may require a member-ship fee of from $25-$100, however, which will include a manual or videotape that explains the program in detail."

Joe suggests you "run like hell" if you are approached by a company who promises you'll earn fast money for almost no work at all. And be wary of any company that offers you "hot prospect names," because all you're likely to get is a worthless list of oppor-tunity seekers.

In promoting their programs, new MLM programs often point to the success of such established direct sales companies as Tupperware, Amway, Shaklee and Mary Kay Cosmetics to prove how well the MLM concept works. But the big corporations in this industry no longer want to be thought of as MLM compa-nies, because this industry has had more than its share of bad apples through the years and is still fighting a bad reputation.

"That's why so many now refer to themselves as *direct sales companies* that offer *network marketing* opportunities," says Cyndi Monroe. Cyndi, who is a wife and mother, says this type of business is just perfect for her. "It meets a need I have in my life now, and it meets it better than anything else out there."

Although people involved in MLM run "homebased busi-nesses," they do not think of themselves as "home-business own-ers" because they sell the products of other companies. "Actu-ally," says Cyndi, "I think of myself as a homebased professional network marketer." Although selling is a big part of what MLM distributors do, Cyndi says few of them are salespeople. "People who are strictly sales-oriented will fail in network marketing," she explains. "You can't be successful in a program unless you use and believe in a product, and you must also be willing to teach and train others how to build their own business—in other words, duplicate your efforts."

Cyndi and friend Bebe Wenig got into network marketing when they were running an exercise salon. After searching for a good weight maintenance program, they found a product that worked for them, and they enthusiastically sold it with success for three years, building a network of one thousand distributors. Cyndi and her partner (and all their satisfied "downliners") are now offering what they feel is a much better line of nutritional meal replacement products with a much broader market. Unlike most MLM distributors, Cyndi and Bebe expect to be involved in this particular program for a long time. "A solid MLM program must be based not on how far *you* can go, but how many you can bring with you when you climb the ladder of success," says Cyndi. "Thus, if you are not willing to teach and train, you cannot be a successful network marketer."

Like Cyndi, Joe Molnar doesn't look at network marketing as "a selling business" but rather one of sharing. "My view of

MLM is that it is not selling in the traditional sense; it's sharing your enthusiasm for a product with other people," he says. Joe, a social worker, has benefited by using the health enhancement product he sells, and he has "shared" it with friends, neighbors, and some of his fellow workers. He seconds Cyndi in saying network marketing is "a wonderful business for me, with high profits and no overhead."

Actually, MLM selling is similar to mail-order selling in that it is not really a business at all, but merely a way of marketing products. New companies in this industry do not market through regular retail outlets, but through individual distributors, and the kind of products most often sold this way tend to serve niche markets larger companies are not interested in. The most successful MLM products seem to be household products, personal care items, and particularly herbal and vitamin products, some of them imported from other countries. Often, these new products will benefit from a demonstration or explanation on how to use them for best results.

Many people believe MLM selling is about getting other people to sign up under a distributor and do all the work. But anyone entering MLM with this idea in mind is going to fail. The only way to succeed in this business is to find a good product you're excited about and make it available to other people who will also get excited about it. If they also want to sell it to *their* friends, you will profit by bringing them into the program as a "downliner."

Charles Possick, author of *Mail Order Multi-Level Marketing Techniques*, believes as many as ten million families in the United States may be involved in MLM selling. "For 98 percent of them, one of the best bonuses of an MLM distributorship is the fact they can buy products at wholesale prices," he says. (A large family, for example, who wants to add vitamin supplements to their diet could save a small fortune by joining an MLM program that offered the products they needed.)

Like all businesses, MLM companies come and go; 90 percent of them are likely to fail within ten years. This automatically affects the distributors who were handling their products. So when a company goes under, the MLM sellers who were promoting its products naturally start looking for new products they can get excited about, and they may sell them indefinitely, or only until they find something they like better. Thus there is a lot of coming and going in this industry, and many, many companies promoting to all known MLM sellers, trying to convince them to stop selling what they're presently selling and to start selling their product. "But this is OK," says Charles. "Being able to pick and choose is what freedom is all about."

Note: My legal rights were violated in 1992 when an MLM entrepreneur in Minnesota began to use this book's title as

MLM Legal Aspects

Attorney Jeffrey A. Babener, Portland, Oregon, who has lectured and published extensively on multilevel marketing law, suggests all MLM entrepreneurs study a company carefully before joining a new program. "Because of the abuses of the 'rotten apples' of the industry, multilevel marketing has become a closely scrutinized and regulated industry. Over the years, it has come perilously close to extinction as a result of prosecution by regulators who claimed the industry promoted pyramid schemes under the guise of legitimate marketing. Regulations regarding multilevel marketing companies in the United States are a constantly changing patchwork of overlapping laws that lack uniformity and vary from state to state.

"The basic thrust of these statutes is that marketing plans are prohibited that require an investment or purchase by sales representatives for the right to recruit others for economic gain. Under these statutes, multilevel marketing companies must be bona fide retail organizations that market bona fide products to the ultimate consumer. Inventory loading and 'headhunting,' or remuneration for the mere act of recruiting others, are prohibited," Babener emphasizes.

the name of his business and MLM "opportunity" magazine. I coined the "Homemade Money" phrase in 1984, and this name has automatically acquired trademark status because of its long-time use in connection with my name. The use of my book's title by an MLM company was detrimental to my business because I have a reputation as a provider of high-quality business information. Using legal means at my disposal, I finally resolved this problem.

The brochure advertising the "Homemade Money" MLM opportunity emphasized the five-get-five-get-five concept that so many MLM promoters use and that is so misleading. It read as follows:

If everyone in your downline sold 5 monthly subscriptions, your organization could look like this:

1	....	5
2	....	25
3	....	125
4	....	625
5	....	3,125
6	....	15,625

When you multiply 15,625 subscribers, times a $50 commission, times twice a year, you get $1,562,500.

To understand why this illustration doesn't hold water, consider these remarks by Leonard W. Clements, publisher of *Market Wave*, a business analysis newsletter focusing on the MLM industry:

First, there is a high attrition rate in MLM, so we must assume 90 percent of your people will drop out. But the above numbers assume all 15,625 people will get into the program before even one gets out, then all 90 percent will drop out at once. If you are going to assume a 90 percent drop out rate, you must assume it from the beginning. In other words, four or perhaps all five of your original first level people are going to drop out! In truth, you may have to sponsor twenty people to find five that will go out and sponsor five others. And they will have to do the same.

Although I personally have a total lack of interest in network marketing, I can understand its appeal. I caution you, however, never to believe the kind of MLM hype in the above illustration. You're as unlikely to make a million in MLM as you are in any other business, but through hard work and attention to business and marketing details, you might find this kind of homebased business *profitable*, and just right for you.

Direct Selling

Over four million people are now involved in direct selling as a full-fledged career or a profitable second job, and over 80 percent of them are women who have learned that direct selling fits nicely into their family lifestyle.

In years gone by, it was common to see salesmen going door-to-door to sell such products as encyclopedias, vacuum cleaners, cookware and Fuller Brush products. But door-to-door selling is now a thing of the past, and the saleswomen who have replaced most of the salesmen do their selling in the safety and comfort of other women's homes. It's called "party plan selling," and it's one of the most successful types of marketing ever invented. It works anywhere, even in the smallest rural community, and anyone can learn to do it.

Any commercial product line, including jewelry, cosmetics, cleaning products, kitchenware, lingerie, toys and gifts, will sell this way, and many individual craft producers have also found party plan selling to be a terrific way to sell handcrafted merchandise and craft and needlework kits.

The party plan concept is simple: You arrange for parties to be held by friends or relatives who, in turn, suggest the names of other friends and relatives who might like to hold a party. A host or hostess at each party supplies refreshments and earns points according to the sales volume of the party and the number of additional parties booked. The salesperson plans the presentation, supplies any necessary game or door prizes, and displays wares for sale. Orders are taken, but merchandise is not delivered until later. This job falls to the host/hostess, who also must collect payment for the seller. (A deposit, especially on custom-designed or personalized items, is recommended to discourage later cancellations.)

Like the MLM companies discussed above, direct sales companies also encourage their distributors to recruit party hostesses, bringing them into the dealer network and generating income on another level.

Twyla Menzies is a good example of the profit potential when one becomes involved in the sale of good products offered by reputable companies. When she joined Mary Kay Cosmetics as a beauty consultant in 1981, she had no idea of the possibilities. "I was only interested in making the same $200/week I was then earning at my job," she said. "I soon discovered I could earn that much with only 6-8 hours a week in Mary Kay."

After attending her first annual Mary Kay seminar, Twyla learned if she would hold three beauty shows a week, consistently, and spend some time on the phone, there was no limit to her sales possibilities. She stepped up her activities to three

Direct Sales Opportunities

Many companies, such as Lady Remington, Shaklee, Watkins, Avon, Tupperware, Discovery Toys, and Mary Kay Cosmetics, are eager to work with sales-oriented people who want to build profitable part- or full-time businesses. (You'll find their ads in many consumer and business magazines on the newsstand.) In deciding which products to sell, be sure to compare the offers of several companies, noting the following especially:

1. Start-up costs
2. Cost of promotional catalogs, brochures, delivery bags, etc.
3. Whether you have to pay for merchandise in advance of receiving payment from your party customers.
4. Local competition (Ask companies for the names of dealers in your area.)

Homebased Franchises

In 1992, nearly 5,000 prospective investors in search of a franchise contacted The Hayes Group, Inc., a marketing and francise development firm in Ft. Washington, Pennsylvania. Fifty-two percent of these people were interested in investing less than $20,000 in a franchise, according to a news release from the company.

"The main factor prompting people to consider a franchise investment was the economy," says John P. Hayes, president of The Hayes Group. "One of every eight people who contacted us was unemployed, or was about to lose a job, and they wanted to find a franchise business immediately. Another 10 percent said they expected to be unemployed within six months to a year. In addition, many of the prospective investors noted they were unhappy with their corporate lifestyles and hoped to become their own boss through franchising."

Hayes says homebased businesses will continue to be popular. "Sixty-eight percent of our prospects said they sought a home-based business that provided a commercial or residential service. Many people want to work from home . . . and these businesses are generally less expensive to start up."

(continues on page 69)

shows per week and obtained directorship nine months later.

"As a Mary Kay director, I receive a 10-13 percent director's check on every member of my unit in addition to my 12 percent commission check on those people I have personally recruited. My income is not limited to what I, alone, can produce," she says, adding that this type of business is great if you have a family. "I have always been able to schedule my work around my two children," she says.

Although large profits are certainly possible in direct-sales companies such as Mary Kay, few sellers get rich quick. Like all other businesses, the amount a person can earn is directly tied to the amount of time and effort expended. The majority of Mary Kay consultants earn less than $30,000 annually in commissions or prizes, but Twyla is one of the exceptions. "Mary Kay has more women making over $50,000 a year than any other direct sales company," she says. In singing the praises of this company, Twyla said it was one of the first direct sales organizations to offer a family retirement program, and it has a good group health insurance program as well.

Now into her second decade with Mary Kay, Twyla has so far won two pink Buick Regals, three pink Cadillacs, has twice taken the cash option plan ($350/month for two years), and her sales unit continues to sell at least $300,000 in products each year.

Franchises

In the United States, franchising currently employs over eight million people in more than sixty major industries. Sales from franchise businesses are expected to top a *trillion* dollars in 1994, and by the turn of the century, franchising is expected to be the dominant way of bringing a new product to market.

The franchise industry is experiencing aggressive growth in both the United States and Canada, and there are now a growing number of franchises suitable for operation from home base. Start-up costs generally range between $10,000 and $40,000.

"Starting fresh with a new business certainly permits you the most freedom, since you are not restricted by what has gone before and are not regulated by someone else's rules," says the U.S. Department of Labor in one of its informational booklets. "On the other hand, there are distinct advantages to buying an established franchise.

"Here, the purchaser or franchisee receives the right to operate a business under the leadership of a well-known distributor or manufacturer. In return for a fee and royalty payments, the franchisee has immediate access to a proven product, a consumer image, publicity and goodwill. In many instances, the franchisor provides the goods as well as the training and techniques for conducting the operation. If the franchise is a sound one, the likelihood of success in one's own business is increased."

The disadvantages of a franchise are that you, the franchisee, have to conform to someone else's standards; sell only their product at their price; share in their distributor problems, even though they are not of your doing; possibly end up with management that is unresponsive to your needs; and, of course, share the profits.

Before buying a franchise, the U.S. Department of Labor suggests you visit other franchises, the Better Business Bureau and the chamber of commerce to investigate a company's reputation and track record. Consult an attorney before signing a contract since your agreement will regulate key items such as exclusivity, inventory, royalty rates, purchase requirements and investment obligations.

I would advise you to consider whether or not you might be able to start a business similar to some of the franchise packages. A couple of women who attended one of my workshops told me they had long debated about buying a $17,000 housecleaning franchise. They finally decided they knew as much about housecleaning as anyone and could learn the rest on their own. They launched their own cleaning business and did very well with it. Sure, they had to do a lot of business research, acquire their own industrial cleaning equipment, find their own wholesale sources for cleaning supplies, and develop their own special work methods, marketing techniques, advertising materials and so on—things that are usually provided in a franchisor's package—but they saved $17,000 and got to keep all the profits they generated.

Not everyone has entrepreneurial abilities, which is why franchise packages were originally developed. On the other hand, a lot of people have abilities they don't realize until they begin a business of their own. And with this book in hand—which gives you the equivalent of a master's degree in Homebased Business—you may be able to save your nest egg and create your own successful business package without the help of a franchisor.

As I see it, when you buy a franchise, you are paying someone else to do your homework. If you have the money and can afford it, great. But if you have more time than money, consider trying it yourself. Remember: An investment in a franchise does not automatically guarantee there is a market for the product or service being offered. The job of finding and selling all those customers is still going to be your responsibility. Further, with a franchise business, somewhere along the line you might want to move your business in a new direction, expand to a new area, or simply change the image you're projecting to the public . . . but you won't be able to do this because such things are controlled by the franchisor.

The company offers these examples of entrepreneurs who left corporate jobs to build successful homebased franchise businesses:

- Nancy Gentry left her job as a personnel assistant with a government agency to operate a Citizens Against Crime franchise out of her home. She now gives regular workshops and promotes safety-related products.
- Brent and Joanne Lewis left high-powered positions in the automobile industry to establish a mini-blinds franchise, which they operate out of their home.
- Ernest Edricks, who used to own a dental lab, now owns and operates with wife Carolyn a homebased franchise of United Coupon Corporation, which specializes in sending money-saving offers to consumers.

Importing

Considering importing products to sell by mail? Unless you have found a source of supply on your own by visiting a foreign country, you will need to connect with agencies that can provide the names of firms that export products. Each country has a consulate office in the United States, many of which are located in New York City, Chicago or Washington, DC.

If you are importing raw materials, you may be able to deal with individual firms in other countries. But if you are interested in importing handmade goods, you probably will have to work through special marketing organizations for each country. For example, all goods from Poland must be channeled through Cepelia in New York City, handmade items from Greece are marketed through the National Organization of Hellenic Handicrafts and so on. Each country's consulate office will put you in touch with the specific marketing contacts you'll need.

When merchandise from a foreign country arrives in this country, it must go through customs, so consult a customs broker in advance of ordering any goods. You can clear only a certain dollar value of shipments through customs yourself, and this may affect the quantity of merchandise you order at one time. In addition to customs regulations, there are state and local requirements about licensing and the payment of sales tax. Check with your state treasury department about this.

Canadian Readers: Wendy Priesnitz, a business writer and publisher in Ontario, says "franchise laws in most provinces (with the possible exception of Alberta) give little or no protection to franchise purchasers (franchisees). And while the risk is lower in terms of business failure, it is not eliminated by any means."

Wendy emphasizes the importance of shopping around, asking questions, doing research and using a lawyer. "Also contact your provincial consumer and small business ministries for any publications and advice they might have available."

Other Business Ideas

Additional home-business ideas that are dependent on computer technology are discussed in chapter thirteen, including desktop publishing, graphic design, word processing and business services. In chapter sixteen, you will find references to many special-interest books, periodicals and organizations. Some are directed to a broad business-oriented audience while others are targeted to niche groups such as craft producers, artists, inventors, direct sellers, mail-order entrepreneurs, designers, photographers, etc. A little research in your library will lead you to many other resources on your favorite business idea.

Summary

"You can stop looking for the perfect business plan—it doesn't exist," says Georganne Fiumara, founder of Mothers Home Business Network. "Businesses, like babies, are born with unlimited possibilities but must evolve through trial and error."

"Don't be afraid to try something you really want to do," says writer and self-publisher John Cali. "I hesitated for years to get into something I really loved because I was afraid I'd fail. Then a good friend told me the only way to know if you can fly is to jump off a cliff. So I jumped off the highest cliff I could find. Much to my surprise, I found I could fly."

As you now realize, no one can tell you what business you ought to start because there simply are too many variables in the picture. You must make this decision yourself. In selecting a business to run with, you may be concerned that, even after all your deliberation, you've made the wrong decision. That's a definite possibility, but you're not going to know for sure until you begin, and since nothing new and exiting is going to happen until you *do* begin, don't dillydally too long in the dreaming stage. Or, as Georganne puts it, "Don't wait for all the pieces to fall into place before you begin to work. Ideas evolve and tend to take on a life of their own once you set them free."

All business beginners have to go through the process of matching their capabilities to the needs of the marketplace. This takes time, so be patient. You may have to operate your business for a year or more just to know if you're going in the right direction. In fact, actual experience may be the only way to determine this. "Most successful entrepreneurs now have a product or service quite different from what they started out with, because they rarely got it right the first time," says investment guru Howard Ruff. "They just never gave up until they figured it out."

Reg Rygus, author and publisher of *The Idea Generator*, says every business begins with an idea, grows, and is sustained because of ideas, and will die for the lack of them. "Everyone has the potential to be an idea generator and to profit from their ideas," says Reg, "but many people let others' expectations of them govern their lives and they stifle their own dreams in the process. Life is too short to live it wishing you were doing something else. Regret for what we didn't do often looms larger in old age than regret for what we did do."

Reg explains the correlation between intelligence, creativity, idea generating and innovation like this: "*Intelligence* is a storehouse or womb for knowledge. *Creativity* is the process by which ideas are generated, formulated and birthed. *Innovation* is the process by which these ideas are transformed and implemented into real, practical and useful products or services."

He adds that people who don't exercise their creativity forfeit their independence and security. "They are captive to outdated means of thinking and problem solving and outmoded methods of doing things. They are bound to a job because of the money, and the failure to develop their creative ability locks them into mediocrity."

I know this book will spur your creative thinking process, but more than that, I hope it will give you the courage you need to reach out for the kind of personal satisfaction and independence that can be yours as a self-employed individual working at home.

You are not yet far enough along in this book to realize what a *powerful success tool* you are now holding. It has already changed the lives of thousands of its readers, and thousands more will benefit from this new, expanded edition. If you will only *act on your good ideas*, and use this book as the "success bible" it is, in a little while you, too, may be thanking me all the way to the bank.

Stimulate Your Subconscious!

By reading more, listening closer and paying keen attention to what's going on around you, you will be methodically packing your brain with the kind of stimuli that could lead to a "brilliant brainstorm" when you least expect it.

As you begin the idea generation process, your main goal should be to get your brain vibrating with ideas, on both a conscious and subconscious level. Your mind is like a giant computer—the more input you give it, the more you'll get back. Throughout your entire life, your subconscious mind has been gathering all kinds of information, impressions and ideas, storing them for possible future use. You know a lot more than you think you know, and now is the time to retrieve some of these data for your financial profit. By constantly stimulating your mind with new information and ideas, you will automatically release some of what's already hiding in there on a subconscious level.

POSITIONING YOURSELF FOR SUCCESS

5

The will to prepare to win is more important than the will to win. Preparing usually means doing those kinds of things failures don't like to do. It means studying and learning. It means reading books, going to seminars. It means not being afraid to corner experts and ask foolish questions.
　　—Robert G. Allen, from an
　　article in *Creating Wealth*

WHEN THEY WORK AT HOME, THE British call it "fiddling." Here in North America a lot of people earning money at home are just fiddling, too. They may put in long, hard hours on a money-making activity, yet fail to generate a true profit. Some people simply don't know what to do to make more money; others know, yet are reluctant to do anything about it. Some people fear failure; others fear success. Still others simply have their minds set on staying small. But even small, part-time businesses can generate a fair amount of capital and profit if they are properly managed and promoted.

If you'd like to make more money from your small business endeavor, the first thing you need to do is *stop fiddling around*. It's a trap to think small. If you think small, you'll stay small. But if you dare to think big, you have at least a chance of making it big, financially speaking. That's why I encourage you to E-X-P-A-N-D your thinking, S-T-R-E-T-C-H your capabilities, and R-E-A-C-H farther than you have reached before. Accept the fact that you know more than you think you know, and you can do more than you may now believe possible.

To Be Legal or Not—That Is the Question

To successfully position yourself and your business for success, you must develop a professional attitude about business. In case you missed it earlier, I'll say it again because so many beginners need reminding:

Success in a home business begins with the right attitude: a money-oriented mindset for success. You have to want money to make it, and you must desire success to attain it. Without a professional, businesslike attitude, you are destined to remain small-time forever.

Do you operate an underground business or think of your income as "money under the table"? This is not only an unprofessional attitude but a self-defeating trap. No business can grow if it remains hidden; it needs visibility to survive and prosper. But why should you be legal, especially when so many others are obviously "getting away with it"? Even if you think the chances are pretty good you will not be caught, I think it boils down to whether you want to be an honest or a dishonest individual. Do you prefer the feelings of pride and accomplishment that are the rewards for honest actions, or shall you live instead with Fear and Guilt, companions to Dishonesty? As ordinary people, we have enough feelings of guilt in our everyday lives without having to worry about the fact that we're cheating on our taxes and could get caught, publicly embarrassed and punished at any moment. I recall one woman who told me she finally was going to "go legal" simply because she was beginning to wake up in the middle of the night in a cold sweat, convinced the IRS would soon be knocking on her door. Surely no amount of taxes saved could be worth this kind of anxiety.

What too few people realize is that self-employed individuals qualify for many breaks that substantially lower their taxes. You see, once you are "in business," and not just "fiddling around," you'll find you are entitled to many tax deductions that can offset a sizable portion of your annual gross income. In fact, in the early years of a business, it is quite likely that you will end up with a business loss, at least on paper, which can be used to offset income from salaries and other sources, and thus cut taxes.

"Taxes are the price we pay for a government that guarantees us the freedom to earn enough money to pay our taxes,"

Setting Goals

You must choose your goals within the perimeters of reality—and even then, you must calculate the cost in hard work and effort. Then you must decide if the prize would truly be worth the effort you would have to expend. Don't set impossible goals. And when you do achieve one, set another realistic goal quickly. Be prepared to pay the price for each goal achieved.
  —Jerry Buchanan,
  TOWERS Club USA, Inc.

someone once said. Once you begin business operations, it will not seem at all unusual to the IRS (or Revenue Canada) that you need to buy office equipment, a computer or a new car to advance your business. Lo and behold, a large percentage of such costs can immediately be offset against receipts or written off (depreciated) over a specified number of years. Once you qualify for the home office deduction, you become entitled to deduct a comparable percentage of your regular living expenses, from rent or mortgage interest to utilities, repairs and maintenance on your home. Another way to get legal tax deductions is to hire your spouse or children. (These topics are discussed at length in chapter six.)

Who but a fool (and a dishonest fool at that) would continue to hide his or her income and give up all these delicious and perfectly legal tax deductions to which a legitimate home-business owner is entitled? Besides, if you're trying to prove your credit worthiness—possibly to get a business loan or a home mortgage—you will want your gross income (and net profit) to be as high as possible.

Developing a Mindset for Business and Financial Success

Success experts remind us we can't achieve any goal until that goal is clearly pictured in our mind, so it's important for you to define success before you reach for it. Some people equate success only in terms of dollars, saying, "I want to make lots of money," or "I want to create/make/invent something I can sell for thousands of dollars in mail-order catalogs/exclusive shops/ chain stores." Such financial goals, however, are neither realistic nor clear-cut, which makes them unachievable. If you set such goals, you will only become discouraged when you don't reach them. So remember this rhyme: *To be achievable, a goal must be believable and conceivable.*

In the beginning, home-business owners need a series of small gains and achievements to keep them going, so it's important to set realistic dollar goals for yourself. For instance, a first year's goal might be: "I'm not going to lose more than $1,000 this year." (A paper loss, we hope.) In that case, you'd feel good at year's end if you lost only $500 because you would have achieved—even exceeded—your goal. Once you've met or bettered your first-year objective, raise your financial goal the second year to break even or perhaps make a small profit.

Remember, it often takes two years just to work out the kinks in a home business—to refine and improve products or services, test new theories, set up efficient office systems and procedures, locate necessary suppliers, and establish basic marketing channels. By the third year, things will begin to fall into place, and a true profit might be realized for the first time. (I say "true profit" because it's not fair to you or your business to say you've made a profit if you've worked all year without a salary, as most home business owners do for two or three years. The employees and all other expenses get paid first, then the owner.)

It's not businesslike, either, to ignore the overhead costs of your business that fall into the area of "home expenses"—such as the rent or mortgage payment, electric or gas bill, and telephone bill. Whether these costs increase as a result of your business is not really the point. What you need to consider is this: If you build your business on a no-overhead principle, what will happen if you become successful to the point where you must move to outside quarters? In all probability you will not have set your prices high enough to cover the now-unavoidable overhead costs, and you will have to do some fancy figuring to get out of this trap without losing your customers or clients, who by now will be accustomed to your low prices.

"Profit" is another good word for you to define as you develop your mindset for success. It is not always synonymous with cash, of course. New businesses can lose money for several years in a row yet still be extremely profitable to their owners. For instance, a profitable year might mean valuable business contacts, acquired knowledge and experience, a new understanding of your strengths and weaknesses, or the discovery of a new marketing channel that will pay off big the following year. It can also mean you have made money, but you put it into a retirement plan or simply reinvested every dime into the business, perhaps in the form of equipment, larger inventories, new employees, a computer and so on.

Even a failed sideline venture can be profitable if it points the way to a better idea that will work, or if it reveals something important in your character that encourages you to go forth in a new direction. Again, failure has its redeeming qualities, and you will always learn something from it.

Setting Up Your Office or Workplace

Whether you allow customers or clients into your home office or not, you need to give special consideration to where you will work. Ideally, your office will be located away from main family activity, such as downstairs in a family room, or a spare bedroom that doesn't have a lot of traffic. In one of her columns, Erma Bombeck once advised readers never to locate their office outside a bathroom door: "We're talking freeway traffic here, plus outbursts of steam, singing and gargling," she warned.

Since whole books have been written on how to set up an office at home, I will emphasize here only the importance of

---

A Four-Step Plan for Success

When we began our literary agency, my husband and I sat down and individually did two things: (1) we made a list of all the things we wanted from life—dreaming up everything we could think of, which was quite enjoyable; and (2) we listed what we saw as our own and our spouse's strengths—every kind of positive thing we could think of.

Then we shared our lists with each other and really had a good time evaluating them. Our third step was to write out our joint goals: business, physical, spiritual, mental, financial, social, home and family. Only then did we write our business plan (step 4). All of this material went into what we call our "gold book," which is a three-ring binder that really is metallic gold in color. At the end of the book, we have an appendix of "axioms," which are inspirational quotes we've gathered from all over.

So, early in our marriage and our business partnership, we made clearly stated goals by analyzing our wishes and desires, ranked these according to their importance, and formulated concrete plans to achieve these goals, both personal and business. We believe in supporting each other in achieving our true potential, and are partners in everything we do.

—Barbara J. Doyen,
Doyen Literary Services, Inc.

The Professional Homebased Business

This letter to Barbara illustrates a problem many new homebased businesses share:

We are trying to get into the graphics/screen printing business. We put a small display ad in a local publication but haven't had much success with it. We don't get many calls, and of those we do get, half are requesting services we don't do, and the other half wants to come to our store office.

In our city, customers aren't permitted to come to the homes of homebased business owners to receive any services. Usually if someone requests a service and asks where we're located, I tell them we can come to them. They ask why, so I tell them, and usually get the reply, "Well, I'll call you back later," which of course they never do. Customers seem to think that those who work from their homes are not as professional and don't do work as good as those working out of stores. Any ideas on how to overcome this problem?

In this couple's case, the problem seemed not to lie in where they were doing business, but *how* they were trying to do it. Their letter was handprinted in capital letters on plain white paper, suggesting they had no stationery or sales brochure. If buyers are hesitant to do business with someone who works at home, the lack of professional printed materials will only add to their unease. This couple was advised to work on their professional image and hone their marketing skills.

creating a space that's entirely your own, one that's both comfortable and pleasant. When I launched my present business in 1981, my office was a small pantry off the kitchen with floor-to-ceiling shelves on both sides and a board across to hold my typewriter. It got pretty hot in the summertime, not to mention claustrophobic. I was greatly hampered by the fact that this particular house had no other suitable place to work, and with my business supplies and files scattered in three closets, one corner of the bedroom, and the basement, I was constantly irritated by the time I wasted running back and forth from one place to the other. How my productivity and satisfaction level increased when we moved, and I was finally able to have an entire room to myself! As time passed, I bought new furniture, good chairs, and added atmosphere with nice carpeting, good lighting, lovely plants and fine art. The nicer my office has become, the more productive I've become, and I'm also less stressed because I'm so satisfied with my surroundings. I can't think of a better place to put your early business profits than into your office, studio or other workspace—and your first investment should be a good chair and lighting.

Other considerations in setting up your office have to do with the purchase of equipment, from telephones and answering machines to typewriters, computers, fax machines, copiers and so on. Again, whole books have been written on this topic, and since the main thrust of this book is business and marketing, I will leave it to you to read selected titles in this subject category.

Projecting a Professional Image

A professional image does not just happen. You have to create it, then carefully maintain it throughout the life of your business. It involves everything from your business name and logo, to good-looking printed and promotional materials, to efficient communications and services.

You have *two* professional images, says Sylvia Ann Blishak, author of *Improving Your Company Image—A Do-It-Yourself Guide* (Crisp Publications). "Your invisible image is the one that people hear. Your visible image is your business stationery, order blanks, invoice, business card and brochures. Being aware of both the visible and invisible images you're projecting, and updating them periodically to make sure you're communicating information that fits the changing nature of your products or services, is an excellent way to appeal to customers, and to make them feel comfortable and confident about dealing with you."

One problem many homebased workers have is getting family or friends to accept the fact they truly are in business and not just playing around with a hobby. If this is your problem, you need a strategy to combat this hobbyist image, and it must begin with your own attitude about yourself and your business. The way you conduct your business influences the way people think of you.

Begin by setting up some ground rules. If your friends and neighbors are used to dropping by for coffee and conversation, tell them how much you're going to miss this contact with them, but ask them to kindly respect your business hours in the future. Emphasize that you are not just "fiddling around," but have started a business, and you need undisturbed periods of time in which to work. Tell them what you are doing and ask them to help you by spreading the word to prospective customers or clients. In the future, arrange to visit friends in the evening or on the weekend.

If you plan to see customers or clients in your home, be sure it is neatly maintained at all times, and greet people like the well-groomed professional they expect to see. Don't apologize for working at home. Instead, stress this benefit: *You provide a quality product or service at a more reasonable price because you are a homebased business without a retailer's overhead expenses—and customer service is your specialty.* (Be careful never to say your prices are cheaper. The fact that you work at home is no excuse for lowering prices. Even when your prices are the same as a retail competitor, your pricing edge is the fact that you are able to give your customers more individual attention and personal service than the average retailer can.)

If you have young children, keep them away from the phone. The last thing you want is a child yelling into the ear of a prospective client, "It's for you, Mommy!" The one I especially dislike is the precocious youngster who answers the phone and then insists on knowing your life history before he'll go fetch mom or dad, or the child who picks up the phone, then leaves it off the hook without calling the person you want. If your children could ruin the business illusion you are trying to create, a separate business phone or answering machine should be considered.

Many home-business owners complain they lack credibility in the eyes of prospective buyers. One said he had added "References Provided" to his business card after a prospect told him flat out that she would never buy from anyone who worked at home, let alone from a garage, as this person was doing. "Would it help to join a trade organization?" he asked. It might. Some people are impressed by such things. But membership alone is not going to give anyone instant credibility—that's something that comes with time. You can speed the process by acting on the advice that follows.

Are You for Real?

Many self-employed people lose credibility because they don't behave like the professionals they would like to be.

"Real" business people have business cards so they have a way of giving a contact an easy and legible record of name, business, address and phone.

"Real" business people answer mail within a reasonable time on business stationery that has the business name, address and telephone number. They type correspondence, and use correct grammar and spelling.

"Real" businesspeople are aware that time is money. They don't expect others to spend time giving them free advice. And if they do receive help, they reciprocate later with a contact, reprint of a helpful article, or at least a thank-you note.

If you're "for real," then let everyone know it. Behave like the professional businessperson you want to be.

—Millie Delahunty, consultant and home economist

Selecting a Business Name

Your business name should tell customers or clients something about you, your product, publication or service. Don't name your business until you know exactly what you're going to do, and remember that any name you choose may automatically position you badly or beautifully in the eyes of prospective customers or clients. (See the marketing chapters for more about this topic.)

Many small business owners like to use their own name, and this can be a good strategy if you are known and respected in your community or in a particular field of endeavor. Your name on a business service, such as Brown's Catering or Thomas Smith Photography, will automatically conjure a certain image in the minds of those who know you. I'll never forget the advice a businessman gave me years ago. "Don't sell your products," he told me, "sell your good name. Once people know and accept you, they'll also accept your products or services." This message came home to me the day a fellow sent me a fan letter saying, "When is your next book coming out? I'll read anything you write."

Some people are able to cleverly tie their last name into a phrase that catches one's interest. For example, Linda Highley named her business *Highley Decorative*, while Trish, Tom and Chris Powers called their enterprise *The Powers That Be*. Pat Cody went a step further by incorporating her last name into the middle of her business name and using excellent graphics to illustrate it:

calico·dysigns

She says this name is general enough to cover all her business activities, which include design sales to magazines, wearable and fiber art consignment sales and books.

Many people have fun playing with words, using their names in conjunction with such ordinary words as "original" and "primary," such as Jane Nichols, who named her business *Orijanels*, and Mary Prima, who settled on *PriMary Reflections*. Names like these are much more likely to be remembered than common names such as *Jane's Originals* or *Reflections by Mary*. Instead of using their own names, some people merely use initials, such as *C & S Associates*. While this may have meaning for the owners and even look great in a business logo, it will mean nothing to customers, and it won't give them a clue as to what the business is about—which only makes your marketing job harder. Some people deliberately misspell words in order to make them go together with their names, but it's wise to avoid a name like *Kathy's Klever Kreations* if you are trying to buy supplies and materials from craft wholesalers. Many will not sell to hobby businesses, and a name like this is a dead giveaway. Having a business letterhead and sales tax number may make no difference. (This is what I meant earlier about how a name can position you poorly in the minds of others.)

Julie Felzien's business name, *The Mad Tatter*, is a good example of how to tie a name to a literary work so people think they've heard of you before. Elayne Bloom's gift basket business, *Hound of the Basketvilles*, is another example. And look what some folks in Texas have done with their name, spotted in a business periodical: *The Greatest Little Storehouse in Texas*. Brings an immediate smile and a desire to go there, doesn't it?

You probably realize you cannot use the words "Limited," "Ltd.," or "Inc." unless you are an incorporated business. But I tip my hat to the people who named their business *Desktop, Ink.* This name not only is appropriate, but it sounds like an incorporated business without being one.

Two things you might avoid in a business name are long names and words that are difficult to pronounce or remember. And consider *not* using the word "enterprises." So many beginners now use this word as part of their business name that it has become synonymous with amateur or homebased operations.

In summary, your business name should not be selected in haste because your financial future could depend on it. Try to pick a name that won't tie you down if you later decide to branch out into other areas. And if you already have named your business and now realize you made a poor choice, change it. The cost of the printed materials you may have to throw out will be insignificant when compared to the probable increase in business a more appropriate name will generate. Times change, and we must change, too, or be left behind.

Robert Compton, a Vermont potter, illustrates my point. When he first began to sell, he operated as *The Mad River Potter*, a folksy name that suited the times. As his work improved, however, and his prices increased, he realized the need for a more professional-sounding name, one that would offer customers more psychological security. By changing his name to *Robert Compton Ltd.*, he enhanced his professional image, which enabled him to raise prices, which increased profits.

When Bruce David launched his first business, he was marketing his writing and PR services. "I felt if it was worth writing, it was worth printing," he said, "so I named my business *Worthprinting, Inc.* The only trouble with this name was that people thought I was a printing company. When I became more involved with marketing and the publication of a marketing newsletter, I changed my name to *Worthpromoting, Inc.*, which successfully repositioned my business to attract the kind of clients I wanted."

(See chapter six for information on how to register and protect your business name and logo.)

Designing Printed Materials

One way to make your business look successful, even when it's not, is to have classy printed materials—a well-designed business card, a good letterhead and matching envelopes printed on quality stock and a brochure. It's nice, but not necessary, to have your card match your letterhead.

As your business grows, you will need a number of other printed materials to add to your professional image and, of course, to promote and sell your products or services. You will need inexpensive flyers from time to time, a good brochure or catalog, price lists, order forms, press releases, postcards and so forth. Since few small businesses have much of a budget for printing, they often learn to create their own camera-ready art, thus saving a great deal of money.

If you don't feel you can design your own printed materials, discuss your needs with a graphic artist (check with the art department of your local high school or college), or call printers in your area. Now that so many small businesses and print shops have computerized typesetting and graphic arts software, classy printing can be designed almost with the flick of a finger. Even better, if you have a computer and laser printer, you can create a wonderful variety of professionally printed items by ordering from Paper Direct's catalog of colorful papers and predesigned envelopes, letterheads and brochures. All you have to do is "drop in the type." (Their ads appear in all the computer magazines.)

If you can use a computer, but just don't have one yet, check out local print shops or service centers, such as the franchised Kinko's Copy Centers, which offer do-it-yourself services that include the use of their computers and software and whatever assistance you may need. Some entrepreneurs use these centers almost like a temporary office at night or on weekends. (Most Kinko's are open twenty-four hours a day.) Or, if you don't want to do it yourself, you can turn in copy on disk with a sketch of what you want, specify the fonts and design elements you like, then turn the job over to an expert.

Many beginners in business fail to grasp the direct relationship between good printing and more sales. Some will try to get

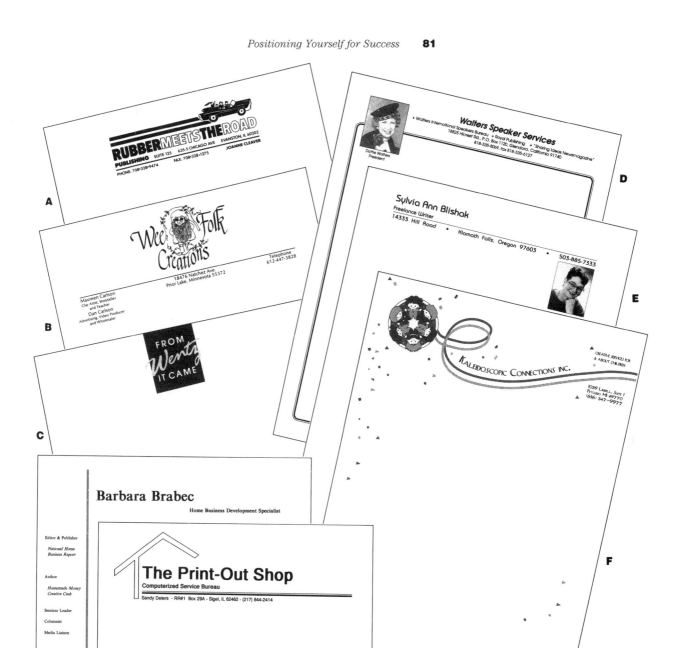

These sample letterheads illustrate a variety of ways to design business stationery: (1) with business logo and address at top; (2) with right-or left-hand motifs and use of photographs; (3) with business logo at top and address centered at bottom of page; and (4) all-around box, or horizontal or vertical lines (and copy) for design emphasis.

These letterheads also illustrate different uses of paper and ink colors. (A) is blue ink on white; (B) is brown ink on tan; (C) is navy blue ink with "Wentz" printed in pink over the blue box on white stock; (D) is maroon on ivory; (E) is black ink with red for name; (F) is pink, purple and turquoise on white, with specks of color scattered along the left and right edges; and (G) and (H) letterheads are computer-generated.

by for a while with typewritten copy and hand-drawn illustrations when, for just a few dollars more, they could have professionally printed materials. I understand where such people are coming from, because I once was there myself. Beginning with only an IBM Selectric typewriter and unable to afford typeset brochures, my only professional investment initially was in stationery. For my direct-mail pieces, I "made do" with changeable type balls and press-on letters. I was satisfied with my brochures, considering what I had to work with—even smug at times, because each mail piece brought me orders. It's easy to justify your actions when there is no other choice at the time, so I operated like this for quite a while. When I finally began to sell with a professionally designed typeset brochure, however, I saw a dramatic difference in both the number and size of orders, which more than paid for the extra cost of printing and better paper. I promptly kicked myself for waiting so long to improve my professional image.

Small craft businesses have an edge over many other homebased businesses in that they're often dealing with prospects who don't mind a simple, homemade look. Generally speaking, however, it's tough for any homebased business to succeed if its professional image isn't comparable to that of competitors. No matter how professional you may be in your business dealings, you must be concerned with *the buying attitudes of prospective customers*. A few will always buy, regardless of a seller's image, simply because they really want or need the advertised product or service. But to survive in business, you must eventually *sell* all those other prospects whose interest has only been piqued. If such prospects are also being solicited by the competition, a buying decision is likely to rest on the professionalism of one's marketing approach and printed materials.

While there is nothing wrong with taking a simple approach to selling and marketing—and nothing wrong with hand-drawn, hand-printed brochures, for that matter (some sensational examples have crossed my desk over the years), there is no excuse for *photocopying* a flyer or brochure on cheap white paper when for only pennies more you can have as few as a hundred copies printed on quality paper at any good quick-print shop.

When it comes to a choice between price and quality, only you can decide what's essential for your business. Just remember that your customer is likely to judge you, your product and your service on the quality of your printed materials. Superior printing isn't always necessary for promotional flyers, price lists and certain other printed materials such as inner-office forms and order blanks. But your brochure or catalog—the piece that really carries your business—*that* has to look not just good, but great. So should your stationery, business cards, and catalog sheets for wholesale buyers. (You don't apologize for your products or your service; neither should you have to apologize for the printed materials that describe them.) If my experience and that of my readers is any indication, I can guarantee that the cost of better brochures and other promotional printed materials will always be offset by greater sales and profits, providing one has a salable product or service to begin with.

Here are some additional thoughts on designing business cards and brochures:

Business Cards

An originally designed card (which may not cost any more than a standard raised-letter business card) can speak volumes about you and the quality of your business, product or service. The kind and color of card stock you select, the ink, the artwork—all these things convey to your customer or client an image of you and your business. Just make sure you convey the image you want them to have.

Standard-sized cards are most likely to be saved in regular business card files, but odd-sized cards have their place, particularly when they serve a purpose. Some people use oversized cards so they can print a map on the back to direct customers to their out-of-the-way business. (I recall one craft shop owner who got his business cards paid for by tying the location of his crafts gallery to that of a hotel in his area.) Others suggest their card can double as a bookmark, or they add special information on the back to turn the card into a promotional "freebie." (See chapter eleven.)

Folded cards may also be appropriate and impressive, especially if you want to include more than the usual amount of information about you or your business. In fact, this kind of card can be an effective minibrochure. Now that photo cards have become more affordable, many small businesses are using them with great success. Photo cards may include your own picture, or one or more of your products—which makes them especially valuable to crafts sellers who lack color flyers. Such cards are an excellent visual marketing tool—a minibillboard—likely to be kept longer than regular business cards. Printed messages may be included on the front or back or on both.

In preparing the information for your card, remember to include your name as well as the business name, plus a line that describes your business specialty, your products or your service. Some people use a logo or add a motto. I still recall the line on a chimney sweep's card: "Satisfaction guaranteed or double your soot back!" If you list your telephone number, don't forget to include the area code. Also add the zip code to your address. Not everyone who ends up with your card will live in your area. (See examples of interesting business cards and letterheads contributed by people in my home-business network. Don't copy them,

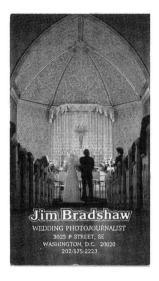

These full-color business cards speak highly of the owners' professionalism.

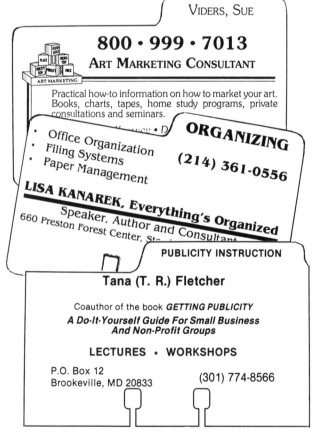

A vertically designed card sometimes works better than a horizontal card. The "Soft-Hearted" card above is printed red and black ink on ivory; the "Flytes of Fancy" card is blue ink on blue-grey stock.

Above: Rotary cards are good promotional tools—affordable and readily available from your local printer. They can also be printed on a laser printer using special stock available from PaperDirect, Lyndhurst, New Jersey.

Left: These cards utilize metallic ink for design emphasis. The *S* and the squiggle at bottom-right are printed in purple ink over black ink on white textured stock; the other card is enhanced by a silver background.

Jerry L. Anthony
Photography

- craft & fine arts
- product photography
- graphic design
- printed advertising materials

Sharon Richwine
graphic design & printing coordinator

114 E. Kelso Road   Columbus, Ohio 43202   614-267-8909

Samples of horizontally designed cards from the author's collection.

SHAWN (GUS) VITALE
Sound Engineer

P.A. AND LIGHT RENTALS
AUDIO CONSULTANTS

(301) 967-7267

(415) 886-0591

Teri Donat
Training & Development

Ez 4 U COMPUTERS

P.O. Box 452, San Lorenzo, CA 94580

FAX MARKETING

MAIL
ORDER   &   BUSINESS
SERVICES

460 Carrollton Drive
Frederick, MD. 21701

Roger Davis
(301) 695-7018

(510)
655-4296

NINA FELDMAN CONNECTIONS

Referrals to over 150 Bay Area
computer and office professionals

- Word processing & desktop publishing
- Graphic design & typesetting
- Tape transcription
- Computer troubleshooting & repair
- Temporary placement

. . . and many more computer and office support services
Call for free consultation
6407 Irwin Court, Oakland, CA 94609

Left and right: These copy-intensive cards clearly describe the range of professional services offered.

CINDY GROOM HARRY
DESIGNS AND CONSULTATION

Phone/FAX: 712-278-2340
Hwy. K-30 NW
Ireton, IA 51027

• Craft Industry Consultation
• Original Craft Designs   • Commercial and Graphic Arts
• Complete Instructions   • Fine Arts
• Line Illustrations   • Lecturing and Instruction
• Member of The Society of Craft Designers
• Craft Marketing Connections, Inc. — VP Design/PR

SUZANN THOMPSON
DESIGNER WRITER TEACHER
KNITTING, CROCHET, & CRAFTS

2704 DEL CURTO RD
AUSTIN TX 78704
(512) 441 8769
(800) 768 8838

Bonner Bears & Friends

Collectable Handcrafted Bears by Jan Bonner
P.O. Box 839 • Worthington, Ohio 43085-0839 • 614-436-1571

1990 - $99,430   1989 - $75,513

SAMPLE - SALES COMPARISON
WINDY DAWN MARKETING

WINDY DAWN MARKETING

JUNE DAWN WINDBLAD
132 Carroll Street
New Westminster, B.C. V3L 4E4
PHONE: (604) 521-2571

COLOR GRAPHICS PRESENTATIONS

Left and right: The design of this unusual fold-over card utilized four different software programs: CorelDRAW!, Quattro Pro, Lotus 123 and Harvard Graphics. It serves as a mini-brochure and example of the kind of computer work this company can do for its clients.

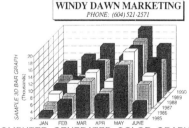

WINDY DAWN MARKETING
PHONE: (604) 521-2571

SAMPLE 3D BAR GRAPH

COMPUTER GENERATED COLOR GRAPHICS

☐ Financial Presentations   ☐ On-Screen Computer Shows
☐ Desktop Publishing   ☐ Manuals and Booklets
☐ Customized Spreadsheets   ☐ Ibico Binding
☐ Graphs and Charts   ☐ Newsletters, Flyers and Ads
☐ Slides and Overheads   ☐ Software Sales and Installation
☐ Word Processing   ☐ Banners for All Occasions
☐ Business Card Design   ☐ Stationery Design
☒ Color and Black and White Scanning and Format Conversion
☒ OCR Scanning and Document Conversion
☒ Beginning and Advanced Computer Software Training Programs
☒ Computer Consulting - System and Software Upgrades

POWERFUL...PERSUASIVE

Standard Printer's Folds

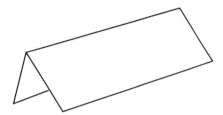

1. Single Fold

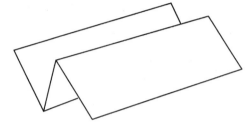

2. Accordion fold

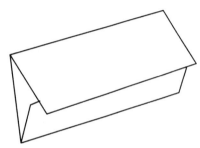

3. Standard letter fold

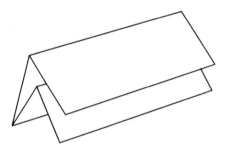

4. Double parallel fold

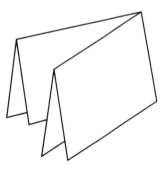

5. French fold

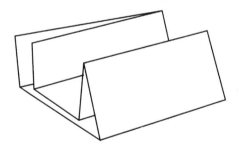

6. Gate fold

These illustrations will give you ideas on how to create simple brochures or mail pieces that can be printed on paper of any kind or on card stock (useful if you need a reply postcard incorporated into the piece). Do a little experimenting with blank sheets of paper of various sizes to create a brochure that's just right for your needs.

If you can use at least 5,000 brochures, you might want to check with specialty printers who advertise in direct-mail publications about getting a brochure that includes a tear-off reply envelope.

Three-panel format (also known as standard letter fold)

BROCHURE DESIGN IDEAS: Samples of three-panel and four-panel brochures used by home-business owners in the author's network.

Four-panel format (also known as double parallel fold)

Suggested stock: paper or card stock, 6⅛"-8½" × 11"

BUSINESS REPLY SIDE	BACK COVER	FRONT COVER
PAGE 5	PAGE 6	PAGE 1

Side 1 of artwork

Suggested stock: paper or card stock, 6⅛"-8½" × 14"

BUSINESS REPLY SIDE	ILLUSTRA-TION AND COPY AREA	BACK COVER	FRONT COVER
PAGE 7	PAGE 6	PAGE 8	PAGE 1

ILLUSTRATIONS AND COPY AREA		ORDER FORM
PAGE 2	PAGE 3	PAGE 4

Side 2 of artwork

ILLUSTRATIONS AND COPY AREA			ORDER FORM
PAGE 2	PAGE 3	PAGE 4	PAGE 5

but do use them for inspiration in designing your own original stationery.)

Brochures

See the illustrations showing the standard printer's folds for brochures and how to place copy for maximum effect. Basically, you want your brochure to be a handy reminder of what you offer customers or clients. It should focus on the benefits of your product or service, include some customer testimonials, and convey your overall professionalism. Paper does make a difference. Select a paper that matches the mood of whatever you're selling. There are soft, velvety papers, dozens of different kinds of textured stock, papers in light colors, bright colors, *electric* colors! Feel the paper . . . let it speak to you. Your customers and prospects will take notice.

The right color has much to do with order response. For example, older buyers who have difficulty in reading may automatically toss mailers that are printed with black ink on red or dark blue paper, not to mention type that is too small to read. While men may hate pink, women tend to love it. When I changed the color of one of my standard follow-up mailers from a sedate ivory to a shocking yellow, I received an amazing 8 percent order response when 3 percent would have been the norm. I'll never use ivory for this group of prospects again. Experiment, experiment!

Including your picture on the brochure could also make a difference in the response you get. Silvana Clark, who offers innovative presentations for seminars, workshops and banquets, says the inclusion of a picture of her dressed in a safari suit made a big difference in getting jobs. "I frequently get calls from people who say the picture on my brochure makes me look like an entertaining speaker. Spending the extra money to get good quality paper has made me proud to leave my brochure with groups I speak for."

I, too, believe the use of my photo in my brochures and other sales pieces has increased response because people have often commented that "my smiling face" made them feel comfortable about ordering from me, even though they'd never heard of me before. I also use line drawings of myself on other items such as promotional newsletters and follow-up postcards to prospects who earlier received my mailings.

Artists will generally do a line drawing for from $35-$75, but here's how to do your own: Take a smooth piece of clear plastic that will accept ink, insert a head-shot photo of yourself, then carefully trace the picture onto the plastic overlay using a fine-point black pen. Then, using a photocopy machine that offers reduction/enlargement capabilities, create the number and size of line drawings needed. Product sellers could do the same thing to create illustrations of certain products. (One craftsman says he takes close-up slides of his products, then projects them onto white paper hung on a wall so he can trace the image.)

If you've done all the writing, typing or typesetting and proofreading of your brochure copy, get someone else to proof the piece before printing. I've learned from experience that it's impossible for the creator of such work to spot all the errors in it because the mind tends to see what it knows is supposed to be there, whether it's there or not.

Finally, be sure to check the weight of a sample piece before printing to make sure it can be mailed at the rate you desire (brochures under one ounce, for instance). Also make sure the size of your mail piece is standard, according to postal regulations, or you may incur a penalty charge on each piece mailed.

Working With Printers

There are printers . . . and there are *printers*. When you find the latter, you've found a helpful companion for your business.

A good printer will take the time to help you with your printing problems and will answer your questions because the more you know, the easier his or her job will be. Also, the better your camera-ready artwork, the better the finished job, and the happier you'll be.

If you live in a rural area with no printer anywhere for miles around, or if you're just not satisfied with your present printer, there are specialty printers across the country who can work with you by mail. (You'll find them by reading books on mail order or self-publishing.) Sometimes you need a specialty printer instead of an offset printer like the quick-print shops now found in even the smallest of towns. Some printers specialize in printing envelopes, or package inserts, or business forms and stationery, and often these specialty printers will give you the best job for your money. Their ads will be found in trade publications serving the mail-order/direct-response industry.

It's always a good idea to get quotes from more than one printer and samples of their work, too. The type of machinery they have dictates the prices they can give. For example, my local printer does my postcards and self-mailers, but he can't begin to compete, pricewise, with the printer in Minnesota who prints my quarterly periodical and mail-order catalog, and neither of these printers can compete with the printer in Michigan who does all my book printing. In requesting a quote for any print job, put your specifications in writing, and ask for quotes on different stocks and weights of paper. Sometimes paper alone can double or triple the cost of a job, and sometimes it also throws the weight of your printed piece into a different postage bracket.

Do You Really Need a Brochure?

Just because someone says, "send me your brochure," doesn't mean that's what you have to send. What they really mean is, "I want to know more about your business. Send me some information." Don't let the fact that you don't have an official "brochure" prevent you from getting that important information to your potential clients in a timely manner.

Brochures are valuable because they give your prospects something tangible in your absence and can convey stability or reliability. But the creation of a brochure is often a long and expensive process and, depending on the nature of your business, may be unnecessary. Letters and postcards are viable options that offer you flexibility and are considerably more cost-efficient.

—Ilise Benun,
self-promotion specialist

Thoughts on Success

While the annals of entrepreneurship may be filled with success stories, few business owners achieve their exalted status overnight. For most, the journey is strewn with bumps, detours, and more ups and downs than even the most ardent of roller-coaster riders can endure. But entrepreneurs are a hardy lot, persevering—sometimes beyond all reason—propelled by what drives them most: the pursuit of their own personal Holy Grail.

　　—Rieva Lesonsky, editor in chief, *Entrepreneur* magazine

There is no business entity or individual . . . that 'has it made.' There is no business so successful and secure that there isn't the chance of a big surprise just around the corner. Success is a thing of the past, not the future, because you can never be sure what's coming. About all you can predict is that things will change and there will be surprises.

　　—from the *Printer's Ink* newsletter, published by Thomson-Shore, Inc., Dexter, Michigan

Using colored stock will normally add 15 to 20 percent to the cost of any print job. Each color of ink used in addition to the basic color (usually black) adds to your cost, too, because the press has to be washed after each color is used.

Ask for quotes on different quantities, too, such as 500, 1,000 and 2,500 for small press runs, and 5,000, 7,500 and 10,000 for larger runs. It's the first 500 copies that cost the most, due to the printer's expenses in preparing negatives and plates and setting up the presses. After that, the primary expense will be paper and press time only, which is nominal in comparison to other costs mentioned. Don't make the mistake, however, of ordering more printing than you can use on the notion that you're saving money.

The least expensive printing done by "quick printers" involves paper masters, which are good for one-time runs only. For a few dollars more, you can get metal plates that can be put back on press for a later rerun, thus saving some money on the reprint job. If you've paid for metal plates, the corresponding negatives belong to you. The printer will be happy to store them for possible future use, but be certain to stipulate whether you want them back or not, should there be a limit on the length of time such materials are retained for customers. (Or maybe you'll just decide to change printers and take the negatives with you.)

Always put your printing instructions in writing and retain a copy for yourself. All kinds of things can go wrong in a print shop, and if the error is the printer's, you will want to be able to show it with your written instructions. Good printers will always do a job over at no charge if they've made the mistake. For everyone's protection, especially yours, ask to see a "blue line" before final plates are made for a long press run. Better to find typographic errors and other problems at this point than to end up with 5,000 catalogs that have something wrong with them. (And this kind of thing has happened to all of us at one time or another.)

The Whole Ball of Wax

This chapter has discussed the relationship between success and your mental attitude about business while illustrating how the right business name and printed materials can position you for greater success. In following chapters, you'll learn more about positioning as it relates to the marketing of products and services. As you continue to learn, remember it will take time for everything to gel into a cohesive whole.

After he had been in business for a year, Steve Martin, owner of Groceries to You, a Chicago-based delivery service, confessed that his first year was *hard*. "There were many times when I had to fight depression and cope with the usual problems of too little time and money, to say nothing of trying to keep my old car working as it was being used more and more to haul groceries."

Although Steve had been receiving publicity steadily since he began, along with a constant flow of interested prospects, it was still difficult to sell people on his service. Part of the reason was that he was blazing a trail when he launched his business—it was the only service of its kind in his area. But Steve, thirty-nine, had such faith in his dream that he gave up his job to work full time on his business. In looking back, he summed it up this way: "The whole ball of wax doesn't come at one time. Wax drips and builds . . . and you've got to keep relighting the candle to keep the wax building."

Steve's persistence in following up with prospects, his salesmanship, his personality, his professionalism, his commitment to the idea of *service*—all these things were building while he was struggling so hard that first year. *His ball of wax was slowly taking shape.* By year's end, he no longer had merely a dream, he had a *vision of success*.

"I can't put my finger on it," he told me, "but something has happened recently to turn things around. All of a sudden I'm getting an increase in calls from people who have heard about my service, and I'm signing up new customers every week. My bank account looks better all the time, and I know now that I'm going to make it."

Many others have shared similar stories with me through the years, so take heart, those of you who are just beginning, those who are fearful of the unknown, or those who struggle against opposition from friends and family. It's not easy to build a business, but even when it's hard, it's satisfying. Even when it's financially unprofitable, it's rewarding. Take comfort in the fact that you are not alone.

A BOOK-WITHIN-A-BOOK

. . . .

CONTENTS: A-to-Z Business Basics

AN A-TO-Z "CRASH COURSE" IN BUSINESS BASICS

6

THIS HANDY BOOK-WITHIN-A-BOOK will enable you to find answers to questions or business problems quickly, as they arise. It presents reliable information from experts in my small business network while also incorporating both the shared experiences of my readers and lessons I've learned from a lifetime of business experience.

Information is presented in logical topic categories listed alphabetically (see the preceding table of contents), but since different aspects of some of these topics are also discussed in other chapters, be sure to check the index to make sure you have all the information you need on any given subject.

Also see chapter sixteen, which includes a list of books, periodicals and organizations related to specific business and legal topics discussed in this chapter. There you will also find addresses of government agencies in the United States and Canada that will provide a wide variety of additional small business information on request.

For your added assurance, the following individuals, each a specialist in his or her own field, have read the material related to their field and verified the information's accuracy at the time of this edition's printing. Any changes they suggested were incorporated into the text.

• Julian Block, author of *Julian Block's Tax Avoidance Secrets*, is a former IRS agent and nationally known authority on tax-saving methods. He practices law in Larchmont, New York.

• Bernard Kamoroff, CPA, is the author of *Small-Time Operator* and owner of Bell Springs Publishing in Laytonville, California. He lectures occasionally at the University of California.

• Mary Helen Sears has been in private law practice in Washington, DC, since 1961. The M.H. Sears firm is mainly devoted to patents, copyrights, trademarks and related matters.

One of my experts—my insurance specialist—chose to remain anonymous because he felt his errors and omissions insurance would not cover giving general insurance advice in a book. He did read all my material, however, advising me on topics that needed clarification; thus his expertise has been incorporated into the book and is much appreciated. Another business expert, who also preferred anonymity, read and approved all the material on independent contractors and labor laws.

Each of the above experts approved the copy in this chapter with the understanding that some information could be incorrect or out-of-date by the time this edition of *Homemade Money* saw print. (State and federal laws discussed in this book could change at any time.) As I see it, this in no way detracts from the value of the information you are about to receive because (1) it serves to familiarize you with important areas of concern for homebased business owners, and (2) it gives you enough information to enable you to ask the right questions when you meet with your own tax adviser, accountant or other professional. I do ask, however, that you read and accept all the technical and legal information in this chapter with the proverbial grain of salt, and remember to double-check it with your own professional adviser before making an important business decision based on this information.

Someone once suggested that it might be better for me to omit all discussion of taxes, in particular, because tax laws change so often and so quickly. Yet to do so would be lax, in my opinion, since a general understanding of this area is critical to the financial success of any business—homebased businesses in particular. If I did not at least acquaint my readers with these topics, some of them might never take the necessary steps to learn more about them.

Note: The Fifth Edition of *Homemade Money* was published in 1994. Prior to the 1997 reprinting of this edition, information throughout the book was updated. This edition now includes tax changes from the Small Business, Health Insurance and Welfare Reform Acts of 1996.

A Note to Canadian Readers

New to this edition of the book is information for Canadian business owners. Because I regularly read several Canadian home-business newsletters and magazines, I have gained a general understanding of Canadian laws and regulations. If I am aware of special similarities or differences between U.S. and Canadian laws or regulations, I've included a note to this effect. When no reference to Canada is made, readers should generally assume the information at hand relates to U.S. businesses only.

Although many U.S. and Canadian laws are similar, they are not the same, so Canadians are advised to use the information in this chapter primarily to gain business perspective and to form intelligent questions about specific Canadian laws and regulations likely to affect their own businesses.

Accountant
(See also Bookkeeping)

Many business novices hire accountants when they actually need bookkeepers. Although accountants know how to do bookkeeping, they are not bookkeepers. Their primary function is to analyze your books and prepare tax returns based on the figures in them. In the process, however, they often perform other important jobs as well. In truth, a good accountant can be something of a management consultant for you, helping you understand your total financial picture and make wise decisions in all areas of your business.

For instance, an accountant can give you advice on whether to purchase equipment, hire employees vs. independent contractors, take on a partner, or incorporate your business. If you need a business loan, an accountant can prepare the necessary financial reports in a way that will show your business in the most favorable light. He or she can also help you plan strategic financial moves that will save or defer taxes each year and represent you should the IRS audit your return. And when you do reach the point of hiring employees, even if it's just your spouse or children, an accountant will take the hassle out of all those aggravating government tax forms and quarterly reports and perhaps save you tax dollars as well.

Contrary to the usual advice given to all new business people, an accountant is not needed at the beginning of a business *if* the business is small and you are capable of setting up the necessary record-keeping system to operate it. But unless you happen to be thoroughly acquainted with the tax code, you'll need an accountant, or at least a highly qualified tax preparer, when tax time rolls around. Be sure to look for someone who is thoroughly familiar with the many special deductions to which a home-business owner is entitled. Not every accountant is comfortable in this area.

Avoid accountants who handle only corporate work. You want someone who understands *small* business. Pick an accountant the way you would select a doctor or lawyer; ask around. Get recommendations from other business owners like yourself, as well as from your banker or lawyer if you have one. Before you make a decision, ask whether you can come in for a short, no-charge discussion of how he or she can help you in your business. Don't hesitate to ask the accountant to furnish the names of clients who are in financial brackets and occupations similar to yours, and be sure to ask about the firm's fee structure since there are several ways to bill for services.

Certified Public Accountant (CPA)

Not all accountants are certified. A CPA is licensed by the state after passing an exam given by the American Institute of Certified Public Accountants on completion of four years of college and one to two years on-the-job training. In view of this extra education, CPAs charge more than noncertified accountants and are more likely to specialize in larger businesses. Although you may prefer to use a CPA, the average small home business does not require one. More important than the title is the fact that the accountant you pick should have knowledge of your particular occupation or type of business and be willing to work with you.

Tax Preparers

Tax preparers generally work only with the figures a taxpayer gives them. As a rule, they are not trained to handle the more complicated tax reports of home-business owners. Unless you are knowledgeable about every business deduction to which you're entitled and can prepare all the necessary figures for your annual tax return, you'll be wise to use an accountant, not a tax preparer. (You'll probably save more money in taxes than you'll spend for the accountant's fee, which is tax deductible, just like your payment for this book.)

Enrolled Agents

An enrolled agent is one who is approved by the Internal Revenue Service to represent taxpayers before the IRS. Such agents have completed a comprehensive IRS-administered examination in federal taxation and related subjects and must complete a minimum number of credit hours each year of continuing education. Enrolled agents may work as independent consultants or practice in a firm that includes both CPAs and lawyers engaged in tax preparation. Their cost may be higher than a national tax service but less than a CPA. To find an enrolled agent near you, call the National Association of Enrolled Agents in Rockville, Maryland.

Attorney/Lawyer

How to Get Along Without One for a While

Contrary to popular belief, you do not need a lawyer to start a simple home business. Many small businesses have never used a lawyer and never intend to. Of course, if you need someone to hold your hand through the start-up process, a lawyer will be happy to do it, while giving you a big bill for fast answers to your questions. With this book in hand, you're getting the same thing for a lot less money.

As your business grows and various legal questions come to mind, you'll often be able to answer them yourself through a study of books and periodicals like those described in chapter sixteen. Your library has others.

When You Really Need Them

There are certain times when you should hire a lawyer, even if you're strapped for funds, because the alternative might cost far more than your legal fees. To cite an obvious example, if you lack a good understanding of the kind of legal language normally found in contracts, it could be an expensive mistake to sign one without the advice of legal counsel. Of particular concern should be long-term agreements, such as partnerships, cooperatives, exclusive dealer or distributor agreements, licensing or franchise arrangements and royalty contracts. And *never* purchase property or buy a business without the guidance of a lawyer who will make sure you're not placing yourself in an uncomfortable legal or tax situation. (Of course, your accountant or CPA can also advise you on tax matters. Not all lawyers are tax experts, just as not all tax lawyers are authorities on contract law.)

Do you need a lawyer to incorporate your business? Legally, no; for peace of mind, yes. Books in the library may give you the how-to steps to setting up your own corporation, but the time

Tip:

Never assume an accountant, CPA or tax preparer knows it all or never makes a mistake. When pushed by many clients who are trying to meet the tax deadline, even the best of them can get overtired and make mistakes you can catch by carefully double-checking every figure on your return.

Tip:

Time is money in a lawyer's office, so you'll save a lot of both if you go prepared. First check available legal self-help guides to gain a better understanding of your situation or problem. Then, in the shortest time possible, you'll be able to clearly explain it to your lawyer, and get answers you couldn't find on your own.

you spend trying to figure everything out will take valuable time away from your business. If you can afford to incorporate, you ought to be able to afford an attorney to take care of the matter for you.

At times, your business may require the help of an attorney who specializes in a particular field, such as taxes, patents, copyrights or trademarks. You do not need an attorney to get a copyright, however. (Some business novices have told me they've paid attorneys $100 to do something they could easily have done themselves for just $20—fill out a form. See Copyrights elsewhere in this chapter.)

How to Shop for One

As with accountants, you shop for a lawyer by asking for recommendations from friends or business acquaintances, including your accountant or banker. If you have neither, ask for a recommendation from any other business professional you know and whose advice you trust, including your doctor, dentist or minister. What you should be looking for is a good, low-cost attorney with some experience in business law. When you think you've found one, be sure to ask about his or her fee structure before you go in for a visit. In fact, ask if a free, initial consultation is offered.

When you find an affordable attorney you like—and one you'd like to consult with more often—discuss a retainer arrangement. On this basis, you might get a lot more advice for your money. For instance, in return for a small up-front retainer, many good, low-cost attorneys will agree to meet with a client a couple times a year, answer quick questions on the telephone throughout the year, and even throw in the preparation of a short legal document. It doesn't hurt to ask. If you're refused, keep shopping. (Beginning lawyers are just like new home-business owners: They need all the business they can get.)

Note: Artists and craftspeople who need advice but cannot afford it should contact the Volunteer Lawyers for the Arts (address in chapter sixteen). This organization, which has branches in many states, is dedicated to providing free legal assistance to artists and arts organizations in all creative fields.

Bad Checks
(See also Collection Techniques)

How to Avoid Them

If you have a mail-order business and you receive a check that looks suspicious, remember that you have thirty days' time in which to ship the order without violating FTC rules. Thus, you may wish to deposit the check, wait a couple of weeks (if a check is going to bounce, you'll know it by then), and then ship the order. Some mail-order businesses follow this procedure as a matter of general practice, viewing all personal checks as suspicious, a practice I do not recommend. In nearly twenty-five years of selling by mail, I've rarely received more than two or three bad checks a year, and these usually clear when deposited a second time.

Checks bounce for a lot of reasons. Once, when I got a bad check for $62 from a buyer in California, I called her to see what she planned to do about this problem. She had the best excuse I've ever heard: *Her bank had been bombed!*

If a check is large, and you're doubtful about it for any reason, you can also call the bank that issued the check and ask if there are sufficient funds in the account to cover it. (While this does not ensure that other checks won't be presented before yours, it will relieve your concern to get a "yes" answer.) In taking checks from buyers at consumer fairs or shows, try to *feel* a transaction as it is being made. That uncomfortable sale will most likely be the one that results in a bad check, says one of my readers. "In those situations where you feel uncomfortable, ask more questions of the customer and get complete information. In addition to identification, obtain the individual's place of employment and phone." Also look closely at the picture on a buyer's driver's license and jot down the license number on the check.

What else might merit your attention? The SBA recommends never accepting checks that are undated, postdated or more than thirty days old, adding that checks should be written and signed legibly in ink, with no erasures or written-over amounts. I do not like checks with signatures I can't decipher, nor those without a printed address or sequence number, although such checks are common and certainly legal. (Experts say checks with sequence numbers below 300 are more likely to bounce than those with higher numbers.)

Collection Strategies for Bounced Checks

Checks may bounce because of nonsufficient funds (NSF), a closed account, or no account (evidence of fraud). Most checks returned because of nonsufficient funds will clear the second time you deposit them. A check can only be redeposited once, however, so if it's for a large amount, you may want to telephone the person who wrote it to make sure there will be sufficient funds to cover it the second time around.

If the check bounces again, you may elect to send a *certified letter* notifying the recipient that you intend to put the matter

Tip:

An ex-con gone straight once appeared on television with tips on how to avoid bad checks. He said that real checks are perforated on at least one side while phony checks are usually smooth on all four sides. He also suggested checking the routing number in the lower left-hand corner, adding that real checks have a magnetic ink that doesn't reflect light. This number on a phony check will look shiny and slightly raised because of the copying process used. If you're really suspicious about a check, dampen your finger and rub it across the background color on the front of the check. If it starts to run, look out!

Tip:

Check to see if your state has a "Bad Check Law." In my state of Illinois, for example, any person who writes a NSF check can be sued in small claims court for three times the amount of the check plus the face value of the check. Being able to quote your state's law to a delinquent account would add weight to your demands for payment.

into the hands of an attorney if payment has not been received within the time you specify. (You may not have an attorney, but the recipient of your letter won't know this. A well-typed letter on good stationery will add considerable strength to your demand for payment.)

Another option for collecting on a bounced check is to take it to your bank and ask them to try to collect for you. There may be a small fee for this. Normally, the bank sends the bounced check back to the originating bank with instructions to pay you as soon as funds have been deposited to the account. However, if a deposit isn't made during this holding period—usually a month—you're out of luck.

Hang onto the bad check as proof of the customer's indebtedness to you. If you believe there has been intent to defraud, and the check is for a substantial amount, you may wish to send a copy of the returned check, along with notes about your efforts to collect the money, to the district attorney's office, or perhaps simply to your local police department. When you get a bad check from an out-of-state customer, your police department may be able to work with the police in your customer's city to get action. They can't actually collect the money, but since it's a crime to write a bad check, police intervention might throw a good scare into your customer.

Banking

(See also Bad Checks; Business Loans and Other Money Sources; Credit/Credit Cards)

Business Checking Account

Do *not* use your personal checking account to conduct the transactions of your business. A separate business checking account is essential for accurate record keeping and substantiation of business deductions for tax purposes. You can save money if you select your business bank with care because each financial institution has a different way of charging for services. Call several banks and savings and loans in your area and prepare a worksheet that answers the following questions, then fictionalize a typical month's banking activity. You'll be amazed by the wide variation in monthly bank charges.

- Is there a charge for *each deposit made*?
- Is there a charge for *each check deposited*? (Some banks make a charge for each deposit, while others charge for each out-of-state check deposited—very costly for mail order businesses.)
- Is there a charge for *each check written*, or are checks purchased in quantity for a flat fee?

- Is there a charge for *bounced checks*? (Some banks charge up to twenty dollars per check.)
- Is *interest* paid on the checking account balance?
- Does the financial institution offer (a) a business line of credit; (b) small business loans; and (c) merchant credit card services (see below)? Not all do.

Check Writing and Banking Tips

1. If your checking account pays interest, hang on to your money as long as possible. Bills paid later in the week take longer to clear because of the weekend.
2. Never type checks using a self-correcting typewriter ribbon because this kind of ink can be lifted off the paper. In the wrong hands, a check could be written for a larger amount.
3. When writing the dollar amount of a check, always place figures close to the printed dollar sign on the check to make it impossible for anyone to add another figure between your figure and the dollar sign. *Example*:

   $9.85 (Correct) $ 9.85 (Dangerous)
4. When spelling out the dollar amount on the second line of a check, take the same kind of precaution, filling the entire line. *Example*:

   Nine and 85/100————————————————Dollars

5. If you receive a check with a different numeral and written dollar amount, your bank will generally accept the amount that is written, rather than the amount shown as a figure. This fact may help you decide whether to return the check for rewriting (and risk losing the order) or just let it go through as is.
6. If you receive an unsigned check, it's best to return it for signature. Although it may be possible to collect an unsigned check, the process is complicated.

Merchant Credit Card Service

Many homebased business owners have complained about the difficulty they've encountered in trying to get a merchant credit card service so they could offer their customers a charge card service. One reader sent a list of businesses considered high-risk by her particular bank. It included mail/telephone-order merchants, insurance agents, self-improvement courses, homebased businesses, limousine services, travel agencies and house party plans . . . right along with massage parlors, used car dealers and phone sex merchants.

In one of her small business seminars in California, Sylvia Landman invited her banker and the bank's merchant sales rep

Tip:

When your money just won't stretch far enough, certain bills should be paid first to keep your credit history clean. Banks, finance companies, and major credit card companies generally report to credit agencies right away, so pay them first. Gas credit charges and American Express may not report late payments until an account is several months overdue. The same is true of doctor and dentist bills, utilities, rent or mortgage payments. If you can't make a business loan payment, or the full mortgage payment, ask the bank if you can pay just the interest for one month.

Tip:

If you are unable to get merchant status through a local bank, you now have two other ways to acquire it: through an independent sales organization (ISO), or through membership in one of the many professional organizations that now serve the home-business community.

Since hucksters everywhere are preying on homebased entrepreneurs today, you must be particularly cautious when dealing with an ISO. Some may take your application fee and disappear. Others may not deliver the terminal and forms that have been paid for. One of the best known and most stable ISOs is Cardservice International, founded in 1988 and sold through individual sales representatives (network marketing). Their service and leasing fees are very high, however. You can probably save a great deal of money by joining a home-business organization that offers merchant card services as a benefit of membership. Several are listed in chapter sixteen.

to be guests in her class. In fielding questions from her class, she learned why so many fledgling business owners fail to qualify. "Banks prefer storefronts to homebased businesses," she says, "and they also prefer to deal with clients with whom they have a long-term banking relationship. A business must be legal within the community, be at least one year old, and be prepared to provide the various documents a bank wants to see: credit and bank references, résumés, sales figures, proof of the legal structure of your business, tax returns, your promotional printed materials and more."

Bartering

If you trade services or products for personal use, the IRS code requires that the value of that trade be declared as taxable income. This is a tricky area. Best to check with a qualified tax adviser.

Better Business Bureau

You can give your business added credibility by registering it with your local Better Business Bureau. (Registration is not the same as membership.) As long as you have a license for your business, they will be happy to register your company. All that's involved is the completion of a simple questionnaire, to which you may wish to attach copies of customer testimonials, your promotional literature, and any favorable publicity you've received. Then, if people should inquire about you, the BBB can say, "Yes, they're registered; we've had no complaints about them." A good reference, indeed. However, be advised there are *no* tangible benefits to be derived from registration with your local BBB, and even members receive only a plaque for their office wall and occasional written reports on companies they might want to deal with.

In fact, the BBB seems paranoid about anyone even *mentioning* its name, and *no one* can legally say, to promote their business or give it added credibility, that they are a member or even registered. The BBB symbol and name are registered trademarks owned solely by the Council of Better Business Bureaus, Inc., and no one can legally use its name in promotional or printed materials. To quote the BBB, they "cannot lend credibility to an individual firm as they neither recommend nor deprecate any product, service or company."

So, although customers who call the BBB for information about your business may *think* you more credible by the mere fact that you are registered, the BBB denies that such registration adds to your credibility. Although a consumer may get a favorable reply about you from the BBB (meaning no complaints on file), the BBB denies this is any kind of "reference" or "recommendation." Therefore, even if home-business owners would be accepted for membership, they would derive questionable benefits at best. But since it costs nothing to *register* with your local BBB, and it may result in favorable information being passed on to customers in your area, do consider this action. *Just don't tell anyone you've done it.*

Bonded Service

Bonding is a form of insurance you buy to give your customers peace of mind—assurance that you are trustworthy and reliable and that they're fully protected against loss. Bonding companies are listed in the yellow pages. Call one of them for more information about procedures and costs. Some services can be sold more easily if they're bonded, such as housesitting or vacation services where you would have access into someone's home during his or her absence. Another example would be a delivery service that normally handles valuable documents or expensive objects—jewelry, art, etc., or possibly a photographer who is taking pictures for insurance purposes.

Bookkeeping

Someone once said "the difference between an accountant and a bookkeeper is a sizable figure." The primary job of a bookkeeper is to post all business transactions to a company's journals and ledgers. Some small business owners consult with bookkeepers for help in setting up their books, while others hire them to do all their bookkeeping. However, Bernard Kamoroff, a CPA and author of *Small Time Operator*, says all business owners should keep their own books for at least a year, just to learn how to read and use the books once they've been posted.

Many home businesses use single-entry bookkeeping systems, which keep paperwork, figurework and headaches to a minimum while still providing all the information needed to properly manage a business and prepare tax returns. Others do their bookkeeping on computer, using one of the many accounting packages now available. For a sole proprietorship, however, a simple system consisting of a business checkbook, a cash receipts journal, a cash disbursements journal and a petty cash fund is quite sufficient. (Note that the IRS prescribes no specific accounting records, documents or systems. They merely require that taxpayers maintain a set of records adequate enough to prepare an accurate tax return. Since the burden of proof lies with the taxpayer, make sure your records reflect *all* income and expenses.)

An important first consideration in setting up your bookkeeping system is whether you will operate on a cash or accrual basis.

Cash Method

Used by some small businesses. All income is taxable in the year it's received, and expenses are generally deductible when paid, with some important exceptions an accountant can explain. Under current law, the cash method of accounting may not be used by (1) corporations (other than S corporations); (2) partnerships having a corporation (other than an S corporation) as a partner; and (3) businesses with inventories. (All sales-plus-inventory businesses and all service businesses stocking parts must use accrual for inventory.)

Accrual Method

Tax must be paid on earned income, whether it has been collected or not; expenses may be deducted when they have been incurred, whether they have been paid or not.

"Hybrid System"

A mix of the above types of accounting systems. For example, a small business might use the accrual system for inventory purchases and the cash method to record all income and expenses. An accountant will help you decide which method is best for you. (Some businesses are required by law to use the accrual accounting method.)

Business Expenses/Deductions

(See also Business Use of Home and Personal Property and related chart.)

Tax evasion can lead to a stay in the slammer; tax *avoidance*, however, is the right of every American and Canadian taxpayer. If you operate a business at home, a wide variety of expenses become deductible, provided you can show they are *ordinary, necessary and somehow connected with the operation and potential profit of your business*. A nearby chart gives you a master checklist of deductible expenses available to business owners. Note that the list includes some expenses (marked with a footnote reference) that are deductible only in certain instances:

1. Legal and accounting fees. As a general rule, you are not entitled to a deduction for legal and accounting advice you obtain *before* you start a business. This is considered an organizational expense. Therefore, it would be tax-advantageous if you were to legally establish your business *before* you hired any legal or accounting professionals. (The same rule applies to start-up expenses and research and development costs.)

Business Deductions Checklist for Home-Business Owners

Note: With few (if any) exceptions, these deductions are applicable to both U.S. and Canadian taxpayers. (According to the Canadian Income Tax Act, all money spent "for the purpose of gaining or producing income" can be deducted from your business and full-time employment income.) Since tax laws are constantly changing, however, one should annually verify the legality of all business deductions with an accountant or other tax authority.

Many home-business owners tend to overlook some of these deductions. Remember, these are *in addition to* deductible expenses on the checklist on page 114, and the deductions normally allowed on your personal income tax report.

- ☐ Accounting or bookkeeping services
- ☐ Advertising expenses
- ☐ Bad debts/bounced checks[1]
- ☐ Books and periodicals related to business
- ☐ Briefcase or samples case
- ☐ Business development expenses[2]
- ☐ Business gifts
- ☐ Christmas cards for business associates
- ☐ Cleaning services (office, business, uniforms, equipment)
- ☐ Commissions (sales reps, agents, other sellers)
- ☐ Consulting fees
- ☐ Conventions and trade show expenses
- ☐ Delivery charges
- ☐ Donations (charitable or business-related)
- ☐ Educational expenses (business seminars, workshops, classes, handbooks, manuals)
- ☐ Entertainment, business-related (must be carefully documented)[3]

- ☐ Equipment lease costs
- ☐ Equipment purchases (may be depreciated or expensed)
- ☐ Freight and shipping charges
- ☐ Insurance premiums (product liability, special riders on homeowner's policy, computer insurance, etc.)
- ☐ Interest on business loans or late tax payments
- ☐ IRA or Keogh account deposits[4]
- ☐ Labor costs (independent contractors)
- ☐ Legal and professional fees[2]
- ☐ Licenses and permits
- ☐ Mail list development and maintenance
- ☐ Maintenance contracts on office equipment, and other repairs
- ☐ Membership fees or dues in business-related organizations
- ☐ Office furnishings (depreciated or expensed)
- ☐ Office supplies
- ☐ Postage
- ☐ Product displays, exhibiting expenses

- ☐ Professional services (artists, designers, copywriters, etc.)
- ☐ Refunds to customers
- ☐ Research and development (R&D) expense[2]
- ☐ Safe deposit box (if it holds documents related to production of income or business documents, computer back-up disks, etc.)
- ☐ Sales commissions
- ☐ Stationery and printing
- ☐ Subscriptions to business periodicals
- ☐ Supplies and materials
- ☐ Tax preparer's fee
- ☐ Tools of your trade
- ☐ Travel expenses connected with business (meals and lodging for overnight stays, plus airfare, train, bus, taxi, auto expense, tips and tolls)[5]
- ☐ Uniforms or special costumes used only in trade or profession
- ☐ Union dues (related to home-based business or profession)
- ☐ Wages to employees, including those paid to spouse or children

Footnotes

1. Bad debts and checks are not deductible if cash method of accounting is used.

2. Start-up expenses are deductible only when one is already in business; major expenditures should be deferred until that point.

3. Deductions for entertainment are a touchy area; ask an accountant for help in taking such deductions because they could trigger an audit.

4. Under current law, deductions for IRAs are primarily limited to those who do not participate in the pension plans of their employers.

5. Deduction for business-related meals and travel expenses is currently limited to 50 percent. Spousal travel deductions are now allowed only when the spouse is an employee of the company.

Tip:

Here's a year-end tax strategy to remember: IRS considers that payment has been made on the date of a credit card transaction, not when one actually pays the bill. Thus, business items charged to credit cards are deductible in the year of purchase even when a balance remains on the credit card. The only catch is you must use a third-party credit card such as MasterCard or Visa—not a card issued by the company who supplies the deductible goods or services, such as a department store purchase on that store's credit card.

2. Bad debts or bounced checks. If you use the accrual method to report income, you are entitled to a deduction for bad debts (bounced checks and other uncollectible accounts) because they were previously counted as reportable income. If you use the cash method, however, you cannot deduct an uncollectible account because the payment was not previously counted as reportable income.

3. Previously nondeductible until they were sold, trademarks (as well as copyrights and patents) can now be deducted over a fifteen-year period.

Not everything one spends in connection with a business can be "expended," or deducted, at the time the money is spent. Some purchases must be depreciated over a specified number of years; others, such as inventory purchases (anything bought for resale), are expensed only when actually sold. (Example: You buy $1,000 worth of inventory but sell only $700 in the year of purchase; you deduct $700 of inventory costs and carry the remaining $300 worth of inventory to the next year's tax report.)

Business assets, such as equipment, office furnishings and other major purchases connected with your business, are generally expensed through depreciation, a complicated tax area that may require professional help. Depreciation must be taken in the year in which it is sustained. You cannot deduct in any one year the allowable depreciation you failed to take in a prior year. Business owners have another option, however, called "expensing." In 1997, U.S. business owners may completely write off up to $18,000 worth of new equipment that would normally be depreciated—an excellent strategy to use in years when your income takes a jump while regular expenses remain the same. The amount you can expense each year will increase in $500 increments each year until the year 2000, then jump to $24,000 for two years and increase once more in 2003 to a maximum of $25,000. Ask your accountant to help you decide whether expensing or depreciation is best for you in any given year.

Business Forms

Standard business forms can be purchased in office supply stores or ordered by mail from many companies. Here are six forms used by most businesses:

Sales Order Form

Needed when dealing with wholesale buyers. If you do not wish to use a sales order book, simply write an order on your business letterhead, making a copy for the buyer. Some buyers, of course, will give you their own purchase order. Make sure it is signed by the buyer, and that he or she agrees to all your terms and conditions as stated on your price list.

Purchase Order

You may receive purchase orders as well as send them. A purchase order received from a shop or store should be acknowledged either with immediate shipment of the order, or by an order confirmation that indicates when later shipment may be expected. When you use a purchase order for your own suppliers, it signifies you are a businessperson, not a hobby business, which is why the use of this form may help you in getting wholesale prices or credit. Purchase order forms are also helpful inner-office records that enable you to keep track of incoming supplies, invoices that must be paid, and the volume of business you are giving each of your suppliers.

Price List

Do not place retail and wholesale prices on the same sheet, but print individual price sheets for each, adding them to your sales brochure. Your wholesale price list should state your conditions for new customers (your need for credit references or check with first order, etc.), your guarantee (if one is offered), and your shipping charge policy. (Some sellers charge the actual postage or shipping costs incurred, while others work on a certain percentage of the order—such as 5 percent—which few buyers would question. The latter charge probably would help offset your overhead costs in packing orders.)

Packing List

Product buyers need some kind of checklist when they are unpacking a shipment. The packing list serves this purpose by describing the contents of each box or carton in the shipment. The packing list must agree in description and number with the information shown on the invoice, which is why some standard invoice forms include a packing list as one of the copies in the form. Obviously, this saves time by eliminating the typing of a second business form.

Invoice

Standard invoice forms are available in three-, four- or five-part sets but many business owners now create their own computer-generated invoices. An invoice should include the following information: seller's name and address; buyer's name and address; ship-to address (if different from sold-to address); date of

Tip:

Banks rarely lend money on purchase orders since they are always subject to cancellation, but unpaid invoices for goods and services already rendered are collateral that can be assigned to a bank for a loan.

invoice; date of shipment; method of shipment (parcel post, truck line, UPS, etc.); invoice number; customer's purchase order number; terms of payment (net 30 days, etc.); quantity and description of items shipped, their unit price and total amount; plus shipping charges.

Statement

A statement shows an account's balance at month's end. If an account does not pay your invoice, send another invoice, not a statement. Unless you are making several shipments to major accounts each month, statements should not be necessary.

Business Loans and Other Money Sources

Bank Loans

If you ever expect to get a bank loan, you have to know how to speak the language of bankers and write a proper loan proposal. Few individuals are able to get a bank loan at the start of their home business, either because they lack start-up investment capital or the kind of collateral the bank requires, or because they're simply reluctant to pledge to the bank what collateral they do have, usually savings accounts, equity in a home, or cash surrender value of an insurance policy. In the end, many people decide it's easier to borrow from their own savings account or perhaps a relative. Others simply figure out how to raise their own venture capital through a variety of entrepreneurial activities. This is as true in Canada as it in the United States. The blunt truth is that banks simply consider most homebased entrepreneurs a poor business risk.

"Collateral" is an asset that can back up a loan. Generally it means property, stocks, bonds, savings accounts, life insurance and current business assets—any or all of which may be held or assumed to ensure repayment of a loan. In addition to collateral, banks also consider the overall health of your home business— how much money it's generating or can be expected to generate—and your ability to repay the loan. An individual's character, credit history and net worth are also of great importance.

A banker once told me that it's important for a borrower to know the kinds of loans a bank normally offers. For instance, some banks specialize in making loans to people who are into art or oil, as opposed to people who might invest in a chicken farm or a racehorse; still others give "conventional" loans only. In short, each bank has to feel comfortable in its ability to sell the kinds of things it accepts as collateral on a loan. If a bank is not into art, oil, chickens or horses as investments, it wouldn't know what to do with this kind of collateral. But every banker knows what to do with stocks, bonds and other securities, thus their preference for them as collateral. Bankers also like to deal with people who have accounts in their bank, not to mention excellent financial reports. (See Financial Reports.)

Line of Credit

Once your business is well established and showing a profit, talk to your banker about the possibility of obtaining a line of credit instead of a loan. It seems laughable, but the best time to apply for a line of credit is when you don't need the money. But take it anyhow, because the day may come when you will be grateful to have something to fall back on. The best time to apply is when your personal finances are in tip-top shape, all your business bills are paid up, and you're showing a nice monthly profit from your business.

There are both secured and unsecured lines of credit. If your total net worth is, say, between $50,000 and $100,000, you can generally get a $5,000 to $10,000 line of credit against which you can borrow whenever you need it. A line of credit normally has an expiration date of a year, and it may be renewed, providing you have had a profitable year. Although payable on demand, few banks would call in this kind of loan unless they were unduly concerned about a borrower's ability to repay it.

By establishing a line of credit before you actually need the money, you'll have added peace of mind that you'll be able to handle unexpected business expenses in low cash-flow months, take advantage of special sales on supplies or equipment, or make other, major business purchases earlier than you might otherwise have been able to do.

Bank Charge Card Loans

In unskilled hands, charge cards are a dangerous thing. Used properly, however, they can be an effective business tool. In addition to helping you build a good credit rating, charge card receipts provide an excellent tax record of business transactions. A special feature of a bank charge card is it gives you access to emergency cash at anytime, especially useful when traveling. Simply present your card to any bank and receive an immediate cash advance (determined by your account's balance and credit limit).

Many small business owners also use charge cards to obtain short-term loans to cover business expenses. Although interest rates are high, it seems a small price to pay if one has a great and immediate need for a certain sum of cash. If each spouse were to have two bank charge cards with high credit limits, there

Tip:

If you have a friend or relative who has money in savings but is not keen on just lending it to you outright, he or she could move these savings to your financial institution and let you use the savings passbook as collateral for a loan. Although your friend or relative could not spend the money in this account so long as your loan was outstanding, no interest would be lost. As you paid back the loan, you would "free up" that amount of funds in the savings account. Stocks, bonds and notes receivable may also qualify as collateral for this type of loan. As you repay the loan, you would be establishing a valuable credit history that could make future business loans easier to get.

might be access to as much as $20,000 overnight—a comforting thought, indeed.

Life Insurance Loans

Don't overlook this possibility for business capital. If you have an insurance policy with cash value, you may be able to borrow on it at rates as low as 5 percent. (Some smart investors borrow on life insurance policies even when they don't need the money simply to reinvest the loan money in higher interest-bearing investments, such as government securities or money-market funds.)

SBA Loans

In 1993, the U.S. Small Business Administration introduced a new Microloan Program to offer loans of from $200 to $25,000 to budding entrepreneurs through selected private nonprofit lenders. More information can be obtained from an SBA or SCORE office near you (see chapter sixteen). *Guaranty Loans* are also available to certain new/young businesses when a local bank will not provide a loan without additional backing. Before the SBA can process this type of loan, however, it needs the signature of the local zoning officer to verify the business is operating legally—a fact that would automatically eliminate many homebased business owners from consideration. Some *Direct Loans* are also available to handicapped persons and disabled Vietnam-era vets.

Although state and federal governments have an assortment of programs to assist economic development through financing new business, the processing of applications for government loans or loan guarantees is a lengthy procedure. It may be better to consider government assistance as an additional or secondary source of financing once the business is under way, rather than a source for start-up funding.

Other Sources of Money

Your membership in certain organizations (particularly those that focus on women, minorities and other underrepresented sectors of the population) may give you access to small business loans or venture capital. Regular reading of business magazines and newsletters will reveal many such organizations. One example is the National Association of Female Executives (NAFE), which has a venture-capital program for cash-strapped, female-owned businesses. A list of alternative financing organizations is available from the SBA's Office of Women's Business Ownership in Washington, DC.

Check bookstores and libraries for the newest titles on private, state, federal and corporate money sources and grants opportunities. One example is Matthew Lesko's regularly updated book, *Government Giveaways for Entrepreneurs*, listed in chapter sixteen. It describes thousands of sources of money and free expertise available to entrepreneurs who want to start or expand a business—loan sources, grants, venture capital and much more.

Some states now have business enterprise programs whereby would-be entrepreneurs can collect unemployment insurance benefits while they're trying to get a new business off the ground, with income from the business not counting against benefits. If you've recently lost your job, be sure to inquire if such a program is available in your state. If you are on welfare, note that thirty-eight states now have self-employment programs permitting one to use welfare benefits to start a business.

Canadian Money Sources

Canada offers three types of programs to help its growing population of homebased entrepreneurs: direct grants, government-backed loans and loan guarantees. Information about such loans should be available from Business Information or Economic Development Centers throughout Canada. Or contact a local office of the Federal Business Development Bank, which offers a free booklet titled *Assistance to Business in Canada*.

Business Records

"Records are at the heart of controlling your business destiny," says a Department of Labor booklet, and all businesses must deal with a variety of them. Records that should be retained permanently include business ledgers, financial statements, check registers, all legal papers (including contracts, patents, trademarks, copyrights, etc.), depreciation schedules and inventory records, executive correspondence, copies of office forms used, systems and procedures records and tax returns.

For at least three years, maybe longer, you should keep all records pertaining to income and expenses, including accounts payable invoices, bank deposits and statements, payroll registers and petty cash records, sales commission reports, general correspondence and manufacturing records.

Tip:

Here's how to use your customers' money to finance a new project. The "prepublication offer," used mostly by self-publishers, has also worked well for other product makers. A few weeks before a new product is scheduled for release, the publisher or manufacturer will offer its best customers a special prepublication price (usually 20 percent off the retail price) in order to bring in a surge of orders to cover up-front production costs. Keep your customers happy (and avoid problems with the Federal Trade Commission) by meeting the shipping date promised in your offer.

Tip:

Since the IRS can bring assessment or collection proceedings for a given taxable year for up to three years after a return is due or filed, you should keep all records relating to income and expenses for at least this long in case of an audit. Some accountants advise that you keep such records for at least six years. Tax attorney Julian Block adds, "There is no time limit on when the IRS can begin an audit if you fail to file a return or you file one that is considered fraudulent. The tax for that year can be assessed at anytime."

Protecting Your Business Records

As important as the records of your business is the way in which you protect them once they're established. I've heard many sad stories about loss of irreplaceable records and other papers— everything from damage caused by pipes that burst in the winter to flooded basements where such items are stored, to total destruction by fires, tornados, hurricanes and earthquakes. Until you imagine the results of such a loss, you cannot begin to take steps to protect against it.

Ask yourself which of your business documents, mailing lists, correspondence, artwork, printed materials, and so on are *absolutely vital* to the continuation of your business, then take steps to protect this material accordingly. Some of it can be duplicated and stored in fireproof drawers or safe deposit boxes. Other things can at least be centrally located in your home or office so you could grab them on a moment's notice as we did one year when a tornado was sighted a couple of miles from our home.

Since printed materials are an important part of any business, it's a good idea to get in the habit of setting aside a couple of master copies of everything you have printed. Even if the original art is lost, at least you'll have an image to work from and all your valuable copywriting won't have been lost. (One great advantage of a computer is that you can protect all computer-generated material simply by making backup disks or tapes and storing them off premise.)

Business or Trade Name
(See also Licenses and Permits; Trademarks)

After you've picked your business name, but *before* you order stationery and cards, check with your city or county clerk to make sure no one else is using the name you've selected.

Fictitious Name Statement

In the United States, if you are using an assumed name, such as Sally's Catering Service, or Country Classics, you must register (file a fictitious name statement) your name with the county clerk and publish a specially worded notice in the legal section of a local newspaper of general circulation. The purpose of such registration and notice is to give the public information about your identity. A fictitious name has to be connected to the name of a person who can be held responsible for the actions of a business. Your assumed business or trade name should be registered with the state, too, to prevent its use by any corporate entity. Of course, your name must be free of conflict from corporate names already registered. (If it isn't, you'll be notified.)

Note: Some states require registration even when one's real name is part of the business name, so you'll need to check this on your own. To protect your name and business logo on a national level, see the Trademarks section.

Many small businesses do not bother to register their names with local officials, but if you're investing time and money into the development of a business, you'll be smart to protect your business name. I once heard about an unscrupulous entrepreneur who went through county records checking on whether certain local businesses had registered their names. He then filed fictitious name statements for all the unregistered businesses he found, approached each business one by one, and told them they either had to stop doing business under that name (because he now owned it), or pay him a stiff fee to buy it back. Since registration of your name is a simple and inexpensive matter, take care of it today, even if you've been in business for some time. The form you have to complete doesn't ask for the date your business was started, so no one will be the wiser about your delay in registering.

Canadians must register their business name according to their province's regulations. According to the government-produced handbook *Starting a Business in Saskatchewan*, a "business name" is: (a) a name other than the proprietor's family name or surname, such as "John Doe" operating as "Sunrise Hardware"; or (b) a name comprising the proprietor's family name or surname with the addition of some other word or phrase indicating a number of members, such as "Doe and Company." Other provinces may or may not operate in exactly the same way.

d/b/a: This is simply an abbreviation for "doing business as." Banks often use this abbreviation in their records to connect a depositor to his or her fictitious name, as in "Jack Robinson, d/b/a Antiques Galore."

Business Use of Home and Personal Property

Although this tax-related information is for U.S. readers only, my research shows that Canadians enjoy similar deductions. (See nearby chart.)

Home Office Deduction

To take a tax deduction for using a part of your home in business, that part must be used *exclusively* and *regularly* as:

1. The principal place of business for any trade or business in which you engage, or
2. A place to meet or deal with your clients or customers in the normal course of your trade or business, or

Tip:

Find out when you have to renew your local business name registration. In the United States, and possibly Canada as well, you won't be notified about this, and you wouldn't want to lose the name over such a technicality.

Checklist of Home-Related Tax-Deductible Expenses for Home-Business Owners in the United States

Note: Stay aware of changes in tax laws, which could affect the following deductions at any time. Canadians enjoy similar deductions but should double-check individual items with an accountant. (For general information on how to calculate the following tax deductions, see the section on Business Use of Home and Personal Property.)

Direct Expenses:

Those that benefit only the business part of your home. You may deduct all costs of direct expenses, which include:

☐ Decorating or remodeling costs/expenses (that do not result in capital improvements); painting or repairs made to the specific area or room used exclusively for business; or repairs done to change an ordinary room into a place of business, such as rewiring, plumbing changes, walls or flooring, etc.

☐ Certain room furnishings. Larger purchases, such as office furniture and equipment, must be depreciated, as a general rule. Inexpensive items, like an office bulletin board, for example, could be deducted under office supplies and materials.

Indirect Expenses:

Those that benefit both the business and personal parts of your home (only the business part is deductible as a business expense):

☐ Rent (on percentage of home used for business)
☐ Mortgage interest (percentage related to use of home for business; balance of interest is deductible on the personal portion of your tax return)
☐ Insurance premiums on home
☐ Depreciation of home (not the land, however; see note below)

☐ Utilities (gas, electric, oil)
☐ Services (trash removal, snow removal, yard maintenance). The latter two may be questionable unless clients or customers normally visit your home.
☐ Home repairs, plus related labor and suppliers (furnace, roof, etc.)

Other Expenses:

☐ *Personal Computer.* If you use one computer both for personal and business usage, you need to document one or the other with a time log so you can calculate a percentage related to business that may be used to figure your business deduction. You may depreciate the business percentage of the computer's cost and also deduct related supplies and materials.

☐ *Telephone.* Fully deductible are all business-related long distance telephone calls and all extra charges for business extensions or services, such as call forwarding, call holding, etc. However,

homebased business owners may not deduct a percentage of the basic monthly charge for the first phone line coming into the home. (See also Telephone in this chapter.)

☐ *Family Automobile.* See "Vehicle" in Business Use of Home and Personal Property in this chapter. All business-related mileage—or actual operating expenses related to business use—is deductible.

☐ *Child Care Expenses.* If you are self-employed, and you pay someone to care for your child, or an invalid parent or spouse, so you can work, a portion of the cost may be deductible.

> **Note:** Ask your accountant to explain the tax problem that can occur if you take a deduction for depreciation of your home and then sell it at a considerable profit. (In Canada, this is known as "Capital Cost Allowance.") Taxes may be due on the same percentage of profit that you used to figure the deduction. However, an IRS ruling states that if you cease to qualify for the home office deduction in the year you sell your home, the entire gain can be treated as a "rollover," if you buy and occupy a new residence within twenty-four months before or after you've sold the old one.

3. A structure that is not attached to your house or residence and that is used in connection with your trade or business (examples: garage, studio, barn).

A lot of home-business owners got cold feet in January of 1993 when a new Supreme Court ruling set stricter standards for home office deductions. This ruling did not change the above information, but only added to it by emphasizing that now, a home-office deduction would hinge on two things: *the relative importance of the activities performed at each business location and the time spent at each place.* In a nutshell, this ruling suddenly eliminated the deductibility of a home office for everyone who spends most of his or her time outside the office, such as caterers, musicians, salespeople, consultants, interior decorators and others. This action put the industry in an uproar, and within days, several factions were working to get this deplorable situation corrected. Four years later, however, we're still waiting for new legislation that will set up a broader definition of a home office that will not exclude any group of individuals who are currently self-employed and working from home base. Watch business periodicals for updates on this topic.

Most homebased entrepreneurs remain so frightened of the IRS and the possibility of an audit that they are not taking home office deductions to which they are legally entitled. But this is ridiculous! If you're not cheating on your taxes, and you can defend all your regular tax deductions, adding legitimate home-office deductions to your Schedule C report could save you thousands of dollars in the years ahead. Don't let a nervous accountant with warnings of possible audits rob you of this deduction, because the IRS insists that you will *not* be audited simply because you take a deduction for your home office.

In the United States, to deduct expenses for your home, you must be able to show the part of your home that you use for business (take photographs). To figure the part of your home used for business, figure the total square footage of your home, then the square footage used in your business. This will give you a percentage figure you can use to apply to all the expenses related to the maintenance of your home. Another acceptable way of figuring the percentage is to count the rooms of your home—provided they are all about the same size—and divide the number of rooms used for business by the number of rooms in the home. *Example:*

2,500 square feet in home, with 500 sq. ft. used for business = 20 percent; 10 rooms in home, with 2 used for business = $\frac{2}{10}$, $\frac{1}{5}$, or 20 percent

To determine applicable home deductions, then, you would add your total costs for gas, electricity, insurance, repairs, etc.

Tip:

(see checklist) and take the percentage figure that applies to your business or, in this case, 20 percent of each amount.

Although this is the basic principle on which home deductions are calculated, there are some exceptions plus a number of special guidelines for each type of expense. Currently, the deduction is limited to the gross income from the business use *minus* the sum of (1) the business percentage of the mortgage interest, real estate taxes and casualty losses; and (2) the business expenses other than those related to the business use of a home. *Translation: Deductions for the business use of a home cannot create a business loss or increase a net loss from a business.* Deductions in excess of the limit, however, may be carried forward to later years, subject to the income limits in those years. A worksheet introduced in 1991 (Form 8829, "Expenses for Business Use of Your Home," which must now accompany the Schedule C form) makes it easier to calculate and take legitimate home expenses without fear.

Personal Property

What happens when you start a business and begin to use personal property that may already be paid for, or in the process of being paid for? You *can* depreciate this equipment on either a cost or market value basis, whichever is less, says Bernard Kamoroff. But how do you determine a fair market value? "Pick a figure and hope you don't have to prove it," he quips adding that, in his experience, IRS seldom questions any reasonable amount.

Vehicle

All business-related travel is tax-deductible. Although it is no longer mandatory to document this information with a diary, it's a smart move because both the IRS and Revenue Canada keep a sharp eye on such deductions. Note the odometer reading at the beginning and end of each year, and log each business-related trip you make, including visits to the bank, post office, printer, office supply store, sales calls, delivery trips, travel to speaking engagements or workshops, trips to the newspaper to place an ad, appointments with clients and so on. Your mileage logbook should include an explanation of where you've gone on each trip plus a notation of the odometer reading before and afterward. If you make a lot of trips to the same place, such as daily trips to the post office or printer, you could get a mileage reading on the first round-trip and simply multiply that figure times the number of trips made each week or month. Just be sure to keep a calendar record of each trip.

One way to deduct business-related car expenses is to use a mileage allowance, plus parking fees and tolls. The tax allowance per mile keeps changing, so check each year to make sure you're taking the maximum deduction allowable.

Depreciating a New Vehicle

This is a complicated area best left to your accountant. Suffice it to say that if you can document the use of your vehicle for business, you can depreciate an appropriate percentage of the cost on your tax return.

Canadian Orders

U.S. businesses who sell to Canadians must decide whether they will ask Canadians to remit in U.S. funds (a move that may diminish response), or calculate the higher prices in terms of Canadian dollars and accept Canadian checks (a move that may create problems when depositing checks). Many U.S. banks are not equipped to handle foreign checks, and such deposits may incur high handling charges.

Canadians, on the other hand, are happy to accept U.S. dollar equivalents because the higher exchange rate helps offset their extra postage charges in shipping goods into the United States. Of course, U.S. postage costs to Canada are also higher, and because all mail, except postcards, must be sent in envelopes, this often adds an extra ounce to the package. Bulk mail is not acceptable at all.

Note that a bounced check from a Canadian buyer can be expensive since the costs of manually handling a returned check through international channels can amount to $20 or more. One reader who reported this problem was told by the Canadian bank in question that this problem could be avoided by requesting a money order or certified check from customers. In all my years of selling books to Canadians, I've yet to get a bad check from one of them, so think twice before you establish a money-order policy for your consumer mail-order buyers. This might cost more in lost orders than one or two bad checks a year.

Whether you're doing business in the United States or Canada, if you're shipping a large order to a company whose credit you have not yet verified, a money order or certified check with the first order seems only prudent. (See "Pro Forma" in Invoicing Terms.)

Chamber of Commerce

In both the United States and Canada, chambers of commerce are supportive of businesses in their area. Some even publish directories of licensed homebased business owners to help others in the community use their products and services.

Tip:

You may find that your deductions for business use of your vehicle will be larger if you calculate on the basis of total operating costs. In this case, you would add up all expenses for the year, including gas, oil, supplies, repairs, maintenance, parking and tolls, towing, washing, tires, garage expenses, license tags, inspection fees, taxes, insurance, depreciation, even Motor Club memberships. Take total miles driven for business and divide by total miles driven for the year to get a percentage of business use. Multiply total car costs by this percentage figure to get your business-related, tax-deductible automobile expenses for the year.

Tip:

If you offer customers a charge card service, this will neatly avoid the problems associated with checks from a customer in a foreign country. The charge card company will automatically calculate the correct amount in U.S. or Canadian dollars, based on that day's rate-of-exchange figures.

Membership in your local chamber of commerce is an indication that you're a stable part of the business community, and it provides special opportunities for networking with other businesspeople in the area, which leads to invaluable word-of-mouth advertising and opportunities to develop local business relationships. New members may tend to ask, "What will the chamber do for me?" when in fact they should be asking, "What can I do to help the chamber help the community?" Depending on the size of your community, dues may vary from $25-$300 a year. Call your chamber of commerce for more information.

Collection Techniques

Can't collect an invoice? Consider a collection agency. You may not get your money, but at least you'll get some satisfaction that a deadbeat is being legally hassled by a bill collector. The better credit agencies in the United States belong to the American Collector's Association, which has some 2,800 members at present. They will try to collect accounts locally, but when you need to collect from someone out of state, they simply pass along your account to a member collection agency in the appropriate state. All member agencies trade accounts this way, and make regular ninety-day reports back to the originating agency. If and when collection is eventually made, the agency would normally take 40 percent of a local account or 50 percent if the collection was made by a member agency. Since half is better than none, a collection agency is at least an alternative bill collection technique you may wish to try at some point in your business.

Small Claims Court

If someone owes you an amount less than $750 (this amount will vary from state to state), you can sue him or her in Small Claims Court for a modest filing fee. I've been told by people who have done this that "it's cheap, quite direct and painless." Although you may win a small claims court judgment, note that you're still the one who has to figure out how to collect, since many debtors simply refuse to pay in spite of a judgment against them. In that case, collection options include garnishment of wages and attachment of certain property, steps that might take more time than they're worth.

Consignment Laws

Theoretically, consigned goods remain the property of the seller until they are sold to the retail customer, and in normal situations, there are no problems. According to the Uniform Commercial Code (which has been adopted by most states), if an establishment goes bankrupt, consigned goods may be subject to the claims of creditors and be seized by such creditors unless certain protective steps have been taken by consignors. (A standard consignment contract is not enough to protect one in this instance.) It's a good rule of thumb never to consign more than a few items to a new or unknown shop until you have developed a satisfactory relationship with the owner or manager (based on prompt payment after the first merchandise has been sold) and see other indications that the shop is being well managed.

Several states now have consignment laws designed to protect artists and craftspeople. Those known to me include California, Colorado, Connecticut, Illinois, Iowa, Kentucky, Massachusetts, New Hampshire, New Mexico, New York, Oregon, Texas, Washington and Wisconsin. Some state laws protect "art" only, excluding from protection items that fall outside the area of painting, sculpture, drawing, graphic arts, pottery, weaving, batik, macrame, quilting, "or other commonly recognized art forms." Since each state's law offers varying degrees of protection—and since other states may now have such a consignment law on the books—all sellers interested in consignment should obtain complete details from their state legislature.

Consumer Safety Laws

(See also Insurance/Product Liability; Trade Practice Rules and Regulations)

All levels of the government are concerned about consumer protection, and as a consumer yourself, you no doubt are pleased by this concern. As a business owner, however, you must look at consumer safety in a different light. Although the following information is for U.S. readers, it serves as a red-light warning to Canadian readers, who may find similar federal acts exist in their country. (A few of the Canadian Federal Acts are listed at the end of this section.) The following entries describe specific consumer safety laws affecting homebased manufacturers in the United States:

Toys and Other Goods for Children

The *Consumer Product Safety Act of 1972* created the Consumer Products Safety Commission, which establishes and enforces mandatory safety standards for consumer products sold in the United States. One of this commission's most active regulatory programs has been in the area of products designed for children. If you make toys of any kind, avoid problems by making sure your toys are (1) too large to be swallowed; (2) not apt to break easily or leave jagged edges; (3) free of sharp edges or points; (4) not put together with easily exposed pins, wires or

Tip:

Never consign merchandise without a consignment agreement that includes the name of the owner and addresses such things as insurance, pricing and commission, payment dates, how merchandise is to be displayed and maintained, and how and when unsold merchandise will be returned.

nails; and (5) nontoxic, nonflammable and nonpoisonous. (The latter requirement explains why many toymakers do not paint or varnish wooden toys.)

Textiles

Manufacturers—including individual craftspeople—involved with textiles (garments, quilts, stuffed toys, knitting, rugs, yarn, piece goods, etc.) and wearing apparel must affix special labels to their products (including Canadians, who must be concerned with the requirements of their *Federal Textile Labeling Act*).

1. The Bureau of Consumer Protection, in connection with its *Textile Fiber Products Identification Act*, requires a label or hang tag that shows: (a) the name of the manufacturer or person marketing the textile fiber product, and (b) the generic names and percentages of all fibers in the product in amounts of 5 percent or more, listed in order by predominance by weight. Examples: "100% combed cotton" and "50% cotton, 50% polyester." If the item contains wool, it falls under the *Wool Products Labeling Act* of 1939 and thus requires additional identification.

2. The Federal Trade Commission requires all wool or textile products bear information on labels clearly indicating when imported ingredients are used, even if the product is made in the United States. (Example: A tie made in the United States from imported silk must indicate that fact with such wording as "Made in the USA from imported products" or your own variation of that information.) Items made in the United States from materials obtained in the United States need only state "Made in the USA," "Handcrafted in the USA," or whatever words you like. Furthermore, similar information must be passed on to the consumer whenever such products are described in mail-order catalogs.

3. In connection with its *Fabric Care Labeling Rule*, The Federal Trade Commission also requires a permanently affixed "care label" on all textile wearing apparel and household furnishings. Such labels must give care and maintenance instructions for the item, such as "Wash in warm water; use cool iron." Manufacturers can design and make their own labels or use standard ones available from a variety of sources.

In addition to labels, the textiles manufacturer must also be concerned with the flammability of fabrics and fibers used in the production of wearing apparel and home furnishings. Hand-woven, hand-dyed items, as well as fabrics of all kinds, must conform to the standard of *The Flammable Fabrics Act*, which is policed by the Consumer Products Safety Commission.

Items With Concealed Stuffing

The *Bedding and Upholstered Furniture Law* is an aggravating, frustrating state law that affects everyone in the United States who manufactures items with concealed stuffings, including dolls, quilts, pillows, soft picture frames and so on. The law not only requires yet another label to be permanently affixed to each item, *but a license ($100 or more) for each state in which goods are sold.*

The frustrating thing about this law is that it makes no distinction between the manufacturer of pillows and mattresses and the craftsperson who sells a few dolls in the local craft shop. Especially annoying to some people is the fact that this law is arbitrarily enforced. In one state, makers of such items and the shops who sell them are "getting away with it," while those in another state are having their merchandise removed from shop shelves and show exhibits. (Some unhappy people in the latter group have been known to seek revenge by turning in other people who haven't yet been caught.)

Note: If you happen to sell decorator pillows, the "raw pillow" should come with the label already affixed. Crafters who need only a few labels might visit a large fabric store to see if they might obtain the extra labels that normally come with the bolts of fabric the shop buys.

For more information on this topic, contact your state's Department of Health and try to connect with "the bedding official." (In some states, you may have to call or write State Tagging Law Enforcement Officials, usually listed under bedding, milk or food, product safety, health, home furnishing, sanitation or Department of Health and Environment.) Ask for samples of the required tag and a source where labels can be bought.

Canadian Federal Consumer Safety Laws:

- **Consumer Packaging and Labelling Act.** Affects firms who package and label prepacked consumer products, as well as manufacturers and importers of prepackaged consumer goods.
- **Food and Drug Act.** Affects manufacturers, processors, importers, packagers, labellers and sellers of food (and other items unlikely to be produced by homebased entrepreneurs).
- **Hazardous Products Act.** Affects manufacturers of products such as cradles, cribs and toys.

Contracts

A written contract is a lot easier to prove in court than a verbal one, but verbal contracts are just as legal and binding—unless it

Tip:

One enterprising garment manufacturer solved her label-making problem by buying a $35 silkscreen set. She prints her own labels on ribbons and has the flexibility of using different colors of ribbon to match differently colored garments and pillows.

is for the sale of goods over a certain amount. (This amount varies from state to state, but in many states it is $500.)

Any written agreement, dated and signed by the parties involved, can serve as a legal document, and legal language is not required. Complicated agreements, however, should at least be approved by a lawyer, and certain contracts and agreements should never be signed without advice of counsel, as mentioned earlier.

Companies often have standard contracts filled with lots of unacceptable clauses, but remember that nothing is written in stone. Through negotiation, clauses may be amended to the satisfaction of both parties. In some cases, such as when you are selling a book to a publisher, an agent with good negotiating skills will give you greater power in making contractual changes while also increasing your profits from the deal.

Copyrights

(See also Patents; Trademarks)

Canadian and U.S. copyright laws are similar, but not the same. Readers in Canada should use the following information only as a general guide, obtaining complete details from their own Copyright Office. You will recall my lengthy discussion of copyright law in chapter one, which explained how to avoid violating the rights of others. Here, the focus is on how to protect your own intellectual property.

Copyright protects the rights of creators of intellectual property in five main categories, and each category requires a special copyright registration form:

1. **Form SE** is used to register a copyright for a SERIAL, which includes periodicals, newspapers, magazines, bulletins, newsletters, annuals, journals and proceedings of societies.
2. **Form TX** is used to register TEXT of any kind—books, directories and other work written in words, such as the how-to instructions for a crafts project.
3. **Form VA** is used to register a work of the VISUAL ARTS, which includes pictorial, graphic or sculptural works, including fine, graphic and applied art, photographs, charts, technical drawings, diagrams and models.
4. **Form PA** is used for works of the PERFORMING ARTS, including musical works and accompanying words, dramatic works, pantomimes, choreographic works, motion pictures and other audiovisual works.
5. **Form SR** is used to register SOUND RECORDINGS, including musical, spoken or other sounds.

You cannot copyright names, titles and short phrases, but brand names, trade names, slogans and phrases may be entitled

Illustration of a copyright form. The clear instructions provided with each type of form make it easy to complete. (Note: It takes the Copyright Office six to eight weeks or more to process an application and return the registered copy. Be patient.)

Filling Out Application Form TX

Detach and read these instructions before completing this form. Make sure all applicable spaces have been filled in before you return this form.

BASIC INFORMATION

When to Use This Form: Use Form TX for registration of published or unpublished non-dramatic literary works, excluding periodicals or serial issues. This class includes a wide variety of works: fiction, non-fiction, poetry, textbooks, reference works, directories, catalogs, advertising copy, compilations of information, and computer programs. For periodicals and serials, use Form SE.

Deposit to Accompany Application: An application for copyright registration must be accompanied by a deposit consisting of copies or phonorecords representing the entire work for which registration is to be made. The following are the general deposit requirements as set forth in the statute:

Unpublished Work: Deposit one complete copy (or phonorecord).

Published Work: Deposit two complete copies (or phonorecords) of the best edition.

Work First Published Outside the United States: Deposit one complete copy (or phonorecord) of the first foreign edition.

Contribution to a Collective Work: Deposit one complete copy (or phonorecord) of the best edition of the collective work.

The Copyright Notice: For published works, the law provides that a copyright notice in a specified form "shall be placed on all publicly distributed copies from which the work can be visually perceived." Use of the copyright notice is the responsibility of the copyright owner and does not require advance permission from the Copyright Office. The required form of the notice for copies generally consists of three elements: (1) the symbol "©", or the word "Copyright," or the abbreviation "Copr."; (2) the year of first publication; and (3) the name of the owner of copyright. For example: "© 1981 Constance Porter." The notice is to be affixed to the copies "in such manner and location as to give reasonable notice of the claim of copyright."

For further information about copyright registration, notice, or special questions relating to copyright problems, write:

Information and Publications Section, LM-455
Copyright Office
Library of Congress
Washington, D.C. 20559

PRIVACY ACT ADVISORY STATEMENT Required by the Privacy Act of 1974 (Public Law 93-579)

AUTHORITY FOR REQUESTING THIS INFORMATION
• Title 17, U.S.C. Secs. 409 and 410

FURNISHING THE REQUESTED INFORMATION IS
• Voluntary

BUT IF THE INFORMATION IS NOT FURNISHED
• It may be necessary to delay or refuse registration
• You may not be entitled to certain relief, remedies, and benefits provided in chapters 4 and 5 of title 17, U.S.C.

PRINCIPAL USES OF REQUESTED INFORMATION
• Establishment and maintenance of a public record
• Examination of the application for compliance with legal requirements

OTHER ROUTINE USES
• Public inspection and copying
• Preparation of public indexes
• Preparation of public catalogs of copyright registrations
• Preparation of search reports upon request

NOTE
• No other advisory statement will be given you in connection with this application
• Please keep this statement and refer to it if we communicate with you regarding this application

LINE-BY-LINE INSTRUCTIONS

1 SPACE 1: Title

That is a "Work Made for Hire"? A "work made for hire" is defined as: (1) "a ... prepared by an employee within the scope of his or her employment"; or ... a work specially ordered or commissioned for use as a contribution to a ...ctive work, as a part of a motion picture or other audiovisual work, as a ...lation, as a supplementary work, as a compilation, as an instructional ...s a test, as answer material for a test, or as an atlas, if the parties expressly ... in a written instrument signed by them that the work shall be considered ... made for hire." If you have checked "Yes" to indicate that the work was ... for hire," you must give the full legal name of the employer (or other ... for whom the work was prepared). You may also include the name of the ...ployee along with the name of the employer (for example: "Elster ...ing Co., employer for hire of John Ferguson").

...nymous" or "Pseudonymous" Work: An author's contribution to a ... "anonymous" if that author is not identified on the copies or ...ecords of the work. An author's contribution to a work is ...nymous" if that author is identified on the copies or phonorecords ...ictitious name. If the work is "anonymous" you may: (1) leave the line ... (2) state "anonymous" on the line; or (3) reveal the author's identity. ...k is "pseudonymous" you may: (1) leave the line blank; or (2) give the ...m and identify it as such (for example: "Huntley Haverstock, ...m"); or (3) reveal the author's name, making clear which is the real ... which is the pseudonym (for example: "Judith Barton, whose ...m is Madeline Elster"). However, the citizenship or domicile of the ...st be given in all cases.

Birth and Death: If the author is dead, the statute requires that ...th be included in the application unless the work is anonymous or ...nous. The author's birth date is optional, but is useful as a form of ...n. Leave this space blank if the author's contribution was a "work ...re."

...Nationality or Domicile: Give the country of which the author is a ...he country in which the author is domiciled. Nationality or ...st be given in all cases.

...Authorship: After the words "Nature of Authorship" give a brief ...ment of the nature of this particular author's contribution to the ...les: "Entire text"; "Coauthor of entire text"; "Chapters 11-14"; ...isions"; "Compilation and English translation"; "New text."

FORM TX
UNITED STATES COPYRIGHT OFFICE

REGISTRATION NUMBER

_____
TX   TXU
EFFECTIVE DATE OF REGISTRATION

_____
Month   Day   Year

DO NOT WRITE ABOVE THIS LINE. IF YOU NEED MORE SPACE, USE A SEPARATE CONTINUATION SHEET.

1 TITLE OF THIS WORK ▼

PREVIOUS OR ALTERNATIVE TITLES ▼

PUBLICATION AS A CONTRIBUTION If this work was published as a contribution to a periodical, serial, or collection, give information about the collective work in which the contribution appeared.   Title of Collective Work ▼

If published in a periodical or serial give: Volume ▼   Number ▼   Issue Date ▼   On Pages ▼

2 NAME OF AUTHOR ▼

a
Was this contribution to the work a "work made for hire"?
☐ Yes
☐ No

AUTHOR'S NATIONALITY OR DOMICILE   Name of Country
OR { Citizen of ▶ _____
Domiciled in ▶ _____

DATES OF BIRTH AND DEATH
Year Born ▼   Year Died ▼

WAS THIS AUTHOR'S CONTRIBUTION TO THE WORK
Anonymous?   ☐ Yes ☐ No
Pseudonymous?   ☐ Yes ☐ No
If the answer to either of these questions is "Yes," see detailed instructions.

NATURE OF AUTHORSHIP   Briefly describe nature of the material created by this author in which copyright is claimed. ▼

NOTE
Under the law, the "author" of a "work made for hire" is generally the employer, not the employee (see instructions). For any part of this work that was "made for hire" check "Yes" in the space provided, give the employer (or other person for whom the work was prepared) as "Author" of that part, and leave the space for dates of birth and death blank.

b NAME OF AUTHOR ▼

Was this contribution to the work a "work made for hire"?
☐ Yes
☐ No

AUTHOR'S NATIONALITY OR DOMICILE   Name of Country
OR { Citizen of ▶ _____
Domiciled in ▶ _____

DATES OF BIRTH AND DEATH
Year Born ▼   Year Died ▼

WAS THIS AUTHOR'S CONTRIBUTION TO THE WORK
Anonymous?   ☐ Yes ☐ No
Pseudonymous?   ☐ Yes ☐ No
If the answer to either of these questions is "Yes," see detailed instructions.

NATURE OF AUTHORSHIP   Briefly describe nature of the material created by this author in which copyright is claimed. ▼

c NAME OF AUTHOR ▼

Was this contribution to the work a "work made for hire"?
☐ Yes
☐ No

AUTHOR'S NATIONALITY OR DOMICILE   Name of Country
OR { Citizen of ▶ _____
Domiciled in ▶ _____

DATES OF BIRTH AND DEATH
Year Born ▼   Year Died ▼

WAS THIS AUTHOR'S CONTRIBUTION TO THE WORK
Anonymous?   ☐ Yes ☐ No
Pseudonymous?   ☐ Yes ☐ No
If the answer to either of these questions is "Yes," see detailed instructions.

NATURE OF AUTHORSHIP   Briefly describe nature of the material created by this author in which copyright is claimed. ▼

3 YEAR IN WHICH CREATION OF THIS WORK WAS COMPLETED This information must be given in all cases.
_____ Year

DATE AND NATION OF FIRST PUBLICATION OF THIS PARTICULAR WORK
Complete this information Month ▶ _____ Day ▶ _____ Year ▶ _____   ◀ Nation
ONLY if this work has been published.

4 COPYRIGHT CLAIMANT(S) Name and address must be given even if the claimant is the same as the author given in space 2.▼

APPLICATION RECEIVED

ONE DEPOSIT RECEIVED

TWO DEPOSITS RECEIVED

REMITTANCE NUMBER AND DATE

DO NOT WRITE HERE   OFFICE USE ONLY

TRANSFER If the claimant(s) named here in space 4 are different from the author(s) named in space 2, give a brief statement of how the claimant(s) obtained ownership of the copyright.▼

See instructions before completing this space.

DO NOT WRITE HERE

Page 1 of _____ pages

MORE ON BACK ▶ • Complete all applicable spaces (numbers 5-11) on the reverse side of this page. • Sign the form at line 10.   • See detailed instructions.

Tip:

If you're a designer interested in protecting your work through registration, you need not copyright each individual design. The Copyright Office will accept collections of designs that are bound together in any fashion.

to protection under the provisions of trademark laws discussed later in this chapter. Inventions cannot be copyrighted but may be patented. (The "drawing" or written description of an invention, however, could be copyrighted.) Ideas are not copyrightable, nor is the procedure for doing, making or building something. However, the expression of such ideas, fixed in tangible form (in a book or product insert, for instance) can be copyrighted. Here is an example to help you remember the difference between copyrights, trademarks and patents: The *artwork* on a can of cola can be copyrighted. The *name—and the way it is expressed on that can—*can be trademarked. The *formula* for the cola itself can be patented.

Note that the Copyright Office is prohibited from giving legal advice or opinions about your rights in connection with cases of alleged copyright infringement "or the sufficiency, extent, or scope of compliance with the copyright law." Thus, if you have a copyright problem, consult a copyright attorney. Application forms may be ordered by mail or by phone from the U.S. Copyright Office. The completed application form must be returned to the Copyright Office with the required fee (currently $20) plus two copies of the "best edition" of the work (and the Copyright Office has a list of criteria that determine exactly what the "best edition" is in each case). In printed matter, for example, it would mean a hard-cover book instead of the paperback edition; for other graphic matter, the best edition would be the one in color, instead of black and white. In the case of three-dimensional works, photographs or accurate drawings may be accepted in lieu of actual copies, etc.

Length of Copyright

Copyright protection for works created after January 1, 1978, lasts for the life of the author or creator plus fifty years after his or her death. If the work is created anonymously, pseudonymously, or done for hire, copyright protection lasts 75 years from year of first publication, or 100 years from creation, whichever occurs first. For works created before 1978, there are different terms, which a copyright lawyer can explain to you.

Copyright Notice

As of March 1, 1989, failure to place a notice of copyright on copies of protected material can no longer result in the loss of copyright. But the lack of a notice only makes it more inviting to others to steal your creativity, and when this happens, people may claim "innocent infringement" by saying they didn't see a notice. *Because the remedies against innocent infringers are limited, the Copyright Office still strongly recommends the use of a copyright notice.* Thus, if you make or manufacture items of any kind, always include a proper copyright notice on each item offered for sale:

1. the word "copyright" or its abbreviation, "copr.," or the copyright symbol, ©
2. the year of first publication of the work (when it was first shown or sold to the public)
3. the name of the copyright owner. Sometimes the words, "All Rights Reserved" will also appear, which means that copyright protection has been extended to include all of the Western Hemisphere. *Example:*

Copyright © 1994 by Barbara Brabec. All Rights Reserved.

Such a notice notifies the public that you own the copyright and warns them against using your work for their own profit. The copyright notice can be affixed in a number of ways, including handwriting, printing, stamping, burning, etching, sewing, etc.

Copyright Infringements

There will always be people who will use copyrighted works, either innocently or deliberately, and if you become aware of an infringement of one of your copyrights (whether officially registered or not), immediately send a cease-and-desist letter. Because infringers have no way of knowing whether you have registered the copyright, they will probably stop using your work to avoid any legal problems. Naturally, it helps if your letter is written with authority on impressive stationery, and it will carry more weight if an attorney writes it for you.

Under present law, if you decide you want to sue, you can file the registration after you discover the infringer—although such late registration will limit the kind of damages you can sue for. As this edition goes to press, however, there is a strong movement in Congress to abolish the requirement that one must register a copyright in order to sue for infringement. If this becomes law, it will become almost impossible for anyone to know whether anything is copyrighted or not, and to be safe, everyone will have to assume *everything* is protected by copyright.

For now, here's the real trick to the whole copyright business. You can place a formal copyright notice on anything you create and thereby announce your claim to copyright ... *but formal registration is optional.* On the other hand, if you do not file this official claim, you cannot sue anyone who copies, or infringes upon, your copyright. In any case, in each copyright situation, you must decide how important your work is to you in terms of dollars and cents, and ask yourself (1) whether you value it enough to formally register it, and (2) whether you would

Tip:

Computer technology has created a new problem area for graphic artists. Given the ease with which images now can be scanned into a computer, copyright violations in this area are growing unchecked. In working with a publisher, ad agency or other buyer of your artwork, it would be wise to include a special clause in your contract that outlines or limits exactly what may, or may not, be done with your illustrations or art. In the case of unauthorized use, whether you've registered a copyright or not, you would at least be able to sue for breach of contract.

be willing to pay court costs to defend your copyright, should someone steal it from you. If you never intend to go to court to protect your work, there is little use in registering it officially. But since it costs you nothing to add the copyright notice to your work, you would be foolish not to do this.

Note: Although it is not necessary to formally register a copyright claim, there is a "Mandatory Deposit Requirement" for all work bearing a copyright notice. There is no charge for this, and no forms to complete. Simply mail two copies of the work to the Library of Congress.

Computer Software

If you create software for sale, you have added protection in the *Software Rental Amendments Act.* Passed by Congress in 1990, this law prohibits the commercial rental, leasing or lending of software without written permission of the creator. In response to the growing concern over software piracy, a 1992 amendment to this act instituted criminal penalties for copyright infringement of software that include imprisonment up to five years and/or fines of up to $250,000. Thus all computer users must be particularly careful about reading the licensing terms on software they have purchased.

Cottage Industries
(See also Independent Contractors)

Some people call any kind of home business a "cottage industry," but in actuality, a cottage industry is one that is based on a central marketing and management operation, with craft production done by individuals working at home. For example, you might start a small manufacturing company, then hire other individuals in your community to do the actual labor involved in the production process, allowing them to perform this work in their own homes for a per-piece price.

For years, acting on the advice of accountants and attorneys, small business owners have hired such labor on an independent contractor basis (instead of an employee basis) because they were told this would avoid all the usual tax and paperwork problems associated with the hiring of employees. This is now a dangerous practice for U.S. business owners. (*Canada appears to have a more lenient policy about independent contractors.*) Many cottage industries that have fallen under the scrutiny of the IRS or Department of Labor have been sued for thousands of dollars in back taxes and related penalties.

This particular can of worms was opened back in the 1980s, when some Vermont home knitters called attention to their industry by protesting the 1943 Fair Labor Standards Act. This act imposed a nationwide ban on home knitting and other home-based production industries. By 1984, despite extreme opposition from labor unions, the federal ban had been lifted from home production of knitted outerwear, jewelry, gloves and mittens, buttons and buckles, handkerchiefs and embroideries. However, thanks to the power of these unions—especially the International Ladies Garment Workers Union—hiring homeworkers to make women's and children's apparel is still illegal. (The bitter irony is that if you were to manufacture *men's* clothing, you would have no problem.) And several states have enacted their own laws prohibiting homeworkers from knitting outerwear or manufacturing common items such as toys, dolls, purses, men's clothing, pipes and jewelry. (You'll find a complete list under the "Industrial Homework Laws" entry in this chapter.)

What this means is that homebased garment designers, for example, cannot expand a business beyond their capability to sew products for sale, since the hiring of homeworkers to produce such garments is prohibited by federal law and possibly state law as well. To do this legally, a designer would have to open a manufacturing plant and hire regular employees.

Important: In seeking legal advice on any matter relating to the formation or operation of a cottage industry that will employ homeworkers of any kind, *you need an attorney who is fully versed in labor law.* You can no longer rely merely on the advice of an accountant or business attorney in this instance. The small business press has published many horrifying articles about small businesspeople who have been caught in this trap, thanks to poor legal advice.

Credit/Credit Cards

(See also Business Loans and Other Money Sources)

If you do not have a personal credit history, this should be an immediate goal. If you're a married woman with a home business, be sure to open your business checking account in your name only. If you add your husband's name, it becomes a joint account with credit history going automatically to his file.

Apply for a bank charge card whether you need it or not, and use this card to charge as many business expenses as possible. This will give you an excellent paper trail of all transactions. Meanwhile, you're building a credit history in your name. The more you use the card, the higher the credit limit can be set, and the more useful the card in obtaining emergency cash.

Never give your credit card number to anyone on the phone unless you are ordering something with that card. Scam artists use all kinds of tricks to get consumers to "verify a number for their records." Even though credit card companies ask you to write your account number on your check when you make

Tip:

Beware of credit card companies that urge you to buy insurance to protect you against illegal use of your card in the event it is lost or stolen. Under federal law, you are automatically protected against loss provided you call the card issuer before unauthorized charges are made. Even if you don't, you are liable for only $50 on each card.

monthly payments, this is not a good idea, because other people will be handling those checks. Finally, merchants may request a credit card to validate a purchase made by check, but this also leaves you open to fraud. Since merchants cannot cover a bounced check by charging the amount to your credit card, you should merely show them your card—don't let them copy your account number. You have rights of privacy, and this is one of them.

Caution: After several years of using credit cards and having your credit limit automatically increased, you may someday find yourself with more credit than is good for you. If you were to apply for a mortgage, for example, and had available credit of $50,000 on several charge cards, the lending institution might count this against you because it suggests you might actually incur that much debt and become a financial risk where the new mortgage was concerned.

Checking Your Credit Rating

There are over nine hundred credit bureaus in the United States, but only three major credit rating firms: Equifax, Trans Union Credit Information Co., and TRW Information Services. Credit bureaus used to serve local areas only, but thanks to computer technology, each now has credit information on everyone across the country. The three major bureaus all have the same information, but each may process it differently, which means errors might slip into your record from time to time. If you were to apply for a loan, your bank might call any one of the three, so prior to applying for a loan, you might ask your bank which bureau it uses, then check your own credit first. Expect to pay a small fee for your report. (See below, "Credit/Trade References," for information on checking your customers' credit ratings. For merchant credit card information, see the "Banking" section in this chapter.)

Credit/Trade References

Always ask for credit references when you're opening an account for one of your customers. Get two trade references (other businesses your customer deals with on credit) plus the name of a bank. Also make sure you have the business owner's name and telephone number on file. Some accounts go uncollected simply because the owner can't be tracked down.

Of course, you will be asked to provide similar references whenever you open supplier accounts, and having good credit with your suppliers can be one of the smartest business moves you'll ever make. For example, if you can get net 30 day terms from your printer, it means you can order printing, get it in the mail, and start bringing in business before you ever have to pay the printing bill. If you are an especially good customer, a supplier might agree to wait up to ninety days for payment if it meant such terms would guarantee a large order from you.

Checking Your Customers' Credit

While businesses can get credit information on individuals, individual business owners cannot get credit information on other businesses from credit bureaus, "unless you have a permissible purpose that includes a financial relationship with the individual or other party," says a contact at Associated Credit Bureaus in Washington, DC. For example, if you're a crafts seller who wants to check the credit of a particular shop in another state, there's not much you can do to find out how credit worthy they are. By working with a credit bureau in your customer's area, however, you might be able to get a credit report on the *owner* of a particular shop (information you should always have in case of bankruptcy), but this won't be worth much if the business is incorporated. Your best bet may be to call the Better Business Bureau to see if there have been any complaints against the party you're thinking about doing business with. For companies large enough to be rated, the information in *Dun & Bradstreet* directories may also be helpful.

Employees

(See also Independent Contractors vs. Employees; Labor Laws)

As a U.S. employer of *nonfamily employees*, you must comply with certain labor laws discussed on page 144. As an employer of your own family members, however, your concern will largely be one of taxes and corresponding paperwork. The following information is for U.S. businesses only. Canadian readers should contact Labour Canada for information about the *Fair Wages and Hours of Labour Act*.

An often-overlooked tax break is that it may be possible for you to employ your children, which can result in sizable tax savings. As Julian Block, a former IRS agent and author of *Julian Block's Year-Round Tax Strategies*, explains: "Putting your youngster on your payroll can be a savvy way to take care of his or her allowance at the expense of the Internal Revenue Service. Significant tax savings can result merely by moving the money from one family pocket to another."

Since the IRS may scrutinize the tax aspects of transactions involving family employees, be sure they are performing "meaningful work," and keep careful records of the hours they are employed and the manner in which you've calculated wages.

Tip:

*The Tax Court has upheld the deduc-
tion of reasonable salaries for children
as young as seven years old, even for
simple jobs such as cleaning your
workshop. Check with an accountant
about the amount you can pay a child
employee without having to pay
taxes. (This amount would be a deduction for your business that would
lower taxes on your business profits.)*

What are the tax advantages of hiring family members? Wages paid to a child under the age of eighteen are exempt from social security (FICA) taxes. When you pay your spouse to work for your business, you may take this as a business deduction, which lowers the amount of social security taxes paid on your Schedule C business profits; however, your spouse must pay social security taxes on his or her earnings (and state and federal income tax must also be withheld from such income), so the main tax advantage here is being able to place social security deposits where they are most advantageous to the family. (For a tip on how to shelter spousal income from taxes, see the discussion of IRAs under the "Retirement Plans" section in this chapter.)

You will want the help of an accountant when you hire an employee, even one in your own family, because there are a number of aggravating tax forms to be completed and filed. Included are (1) an SS-4 form to get your Employer Identification Number; (2) a form 940, which will exempt you from paying unemployment taxes on wages paid to family members; (3) a W-4 tax registration application for withholding tax, similar to the form you must complete when you file for a tax identification number to collect sales tax; (4) an Employer's Quarterly Federal Tax Return (Form 941), which indicates wages paid to family employees, and taxes withheld—your accountant will give you a handy chart for this; and, at year's end, (5) W-2 forms stating income paid to each employee for the year, plus (6) a W-3 Transmittal form to accompany the W-2 forms you must send to the appropriate Social Security Administration office and your state's Department of Revenue.

This sounds a lot worse than it is. Let an accountant help you get set up. After that it's nothing more than repetitive paperwork.

Employer's Identification Number (FEIN)

This federal taxpayer number is required by the government at the point when one becomes an employer. Partnerships, corporations and nonprofit organizations also need a FEIN. Sole proprietors without employees may also obtain and use a FEIN instead of their social security number on all business forms that ask for a "taxpayer identification number." This number is obtained by filing IRS Form SS-4, available wherever tax forms are found. Only one FEIN is needed, even when you own several businesses, and if you should change your business name or relocate to another part of the country, your FEIN goes with you.

Environmental Protection

There are several restrictions on the taking and use of protected wildlife and plants. If your business in any way involves such things—particularly feathers, bones, claws or ivory—obtain additional information from the U.S. Fish and Wildlife Service, Department of the Interior.

Canadians involved in taxidermy should check on their federal Migratory Birds Convention Act.

Federal Trade Commission (FTC)

In addition to the laws pertaining to consumer safety and the labelling of certain products, the FTC is especially concerned with the following:

Truth in Advertising

It is not what you say in actual words that counts, but what people believe after they have read your ad. In evaluating whether an advertisement has the tendency or capacity to deceive, law enforcement officials and the courts apply certain standards involving (1) the message as a whole (the impression left by the total advertisement); (2) the "average person" standard (ads must be viewed from the perspective of the "average" person, not the sophisticated or skeptical person); and (3) deceptive nondisclosure (giving selected information or omitting facts the average person would need to know to make an intelligent purchasing decision).

Use of the word "new" is restricted. As a general rule, a "new" product can only be advertised as new for a period of six months. An older product, although new and unknown to a particular market, may not be advertised as "new" insofar as it gives the impression it has just recently been discovered, developed or invented. It can, however, be advertised as being new to a specific market area.

Use of Endorsements and Testimonials

These must be based on actual use of the product and the endorser's informed knowledge of the field. Statements of opinion should be so identified to avoid the impression they have a scientific or other authoritative basis.

If you publish a periodical, you cannot use testimonials from readers whose subscriptions have expired. Endorsers must actually use the advertised product. Also, do not use people's names without written permission.

Warranties and Guarantees

Warranties inform buyers the products they are buying will perform in a certain way under normal conditions. An *implied* warranty means a product will perform as similar products of its kind under normal conditions, while an *express* warranty states a specific fact about how the product will perform. Claims made in advertisements may constitute an express warranty that imposes legal obligations on the advertiser.

Guarantees must clearly disclose the terms, conditions, and extent of the guarantee, plus the manner in which the company will perform the guarantee. FTC standards require not just a statement, such as "Satisfaction guaranteed, or money back," but a detailed explanation, such as: "If not completely satisfied with the merchandise, return it in good condition within ten days to receive a complete refund of the purchase price."

FTC 30-Day Mail Order Rule

It is extremely important to comply with this rule, because it is strictly enforced with penalties up to $10,000 for each violation. The FTC says it is unfair or deceptive to solicit any order through the mails unless you believe you can fulfill the order within the time you specify. Or, if no time is specified, then you must ship the order within 30 days after receipt of a customer's paid order. You are not affected by the 30-day rule if you invoice orders after shipment, or if you specify a particular length of time for delivery, such as "Allow six weeks for delivery." If you are unable to ship within the specified time, or within 30 days if no time has been specified, then the FTC ruling demands that you notify the buyer of the additional delay, and enclose a postage-paid reply card or envelope. You must give the buyer the option to either cancel the order for a full and prompt refund or extend the time for shipment. If the buyer does not respond, the FTC ruling states that you automatically get the delay, as silence is construed as acceptance.

The Mail Order Rule passed in 1975 has now been amended to apply not only to mail orders, but to orders placed over the phone, by fax and through online services such as CompuServe or Prodigy. In such cases, the 30-day period begins with the actual charging of a customer's account.

900 Numbers

If you plan to use a 900-number in your business, you must be aware of the FTC's Telephone Disclosure and Dispute Resolution Act. Since a series of new rules regulating the advertising and operation of 900-number services has recently been proposed, you should obtain complete information on this topic from the FTC itself.

Financial Reports

If you ever hope to get a bank loan, you will need well-prepared financial reports such as Income Statements, Profit and Loss

Statements, Balance Sheets and Cash Flow projections. Refer to a book on financial accounting to learn how to prepare these various statements. (Many computer software accounting packages will also generate these reports for you once you enter your income and expense figures.)

Even if you don't want a bank loan, you should prepare quarterly and annual reports because this is the best way for you to monitor your business growth. At times, it may seem as though your business is unprofitable because there is so little money left at the end of a month, quarter or calendar year; yet a study of previous year's financial reports may reveal surprising growth or advancement in terms of lower cost-of-goods figures, higher gross or net profit margins, lower administrative costs and so on. In short, financial reports can be highly informative and very comforting at times when you're not sure if you're just treading water or actually making gains.

Independent Contractor

As a self-employed individual, you will have many occasions to work for others as a freelancer or independent contractor. Payment for such work is made with the understanding that you will be responsible for all taxes related to this work, and at year's end, you will receive a 1099 Miscellaneous Income tax form representing total wages paid by your clients.

If you routinely perform work in the homes or offices of customers of clients, you may wish to obtain liability insurance to protect you from such risks as damaging another's property, possessions or equipment. (See "Insurance" in this chapter.) Note, too, that some corporate clients may require evidence of liability insurance before they hire you—and perhaps worker's compensation insurance as well. They will not want to be held liable in the event you injure yourself while in their plant or office. By the same token, any independent contractor you hire—such as a neighborhood worker who climbs a ladder to remove the leaves from your gutters—ought to have liability insurance too. Without insurance, if he fell and injured himself while on your property, his medical bills could be your problem. (Check with your insurance agent to see what liability coverage you have under your homeowner's insurance.)

Independent Contractors vs. Employees
(See also Industrial Homework Laws)

These days, the use of independent contractors in the United States has become particularly risky because the stand taken by the IRS and Labor Department seems increasingly to be that all workers should be considered employees or employers—*period.*

State tax collection agencies are also getting into the act.

In 1991, the IRS began systematically to identify employers who were misclassifying employees as independent contractors. In their first purging, they reclassified 76,000 workers as employees and socked 16,000 employers with $93.8 million in back taxes and penalties. By mid-1993, according to an article in the *Wall Street Journal*, the IRS had assessed more than $500 million in penalties and back taxes and forced businesses to reclassify over 400,000 independent contractors as employees. But this is only the tip of the iceberg. There may be 5 million independent contractors in the United States, and the IRS estimates 3.4 million of them should be reclassified as employees.

What this means to a business who needs outside help is that it doesn't matter how many "agreements" you may have stating you have an employer/independent contractor relationship instead of employer/employee; the bottom line is, if questioned, you'll have to *prove* the legitimacy of the relationship, and if you can't prove independent contractor status, you may find yourself faced with a huge back-taxes/penalties bill that will bankrupt your business.

The only safe independent contractor relationship these days seems to be when one business or self-employed individual buys the products or services of another business or self-employed individual. The problem comes when you, as a business owner, hire an individual to work for you in some capacity when that individual, in truth, is *not* a self-employed businessperson. To quote the IRS: "If an employer-employee relationship exists, it does not matter what it is called." In short, an employee *is* an employee if the IRS (or the Department of Labor) says so. In general, an "employee" is one who "follows the usual path of an employee" and is dependent on the business she or he serves.

The Supreme Court has offered the following guidelines, which are considered "significant" in the determination of whether a person is an employee or independent contractor:

1. The extent to which the services in question are an integral part of the employer's business (The more integral they are to the employer's business, the more it will tend to show an employee-employer relationship.)
2. The permanency of the relationship (The more permanent the relationship, the more it tends to show an employee-employer relationship.)
3. The amount of the alleged contractor's investment in facilities and equipment (The more substantial the investment, the more it will evidence an independent contractor relationship.)
4. The nature and degree of control by the principal (The more

control exercised by the principal over the person, the more it will evidence an employee-employer relationship.)

5. The alleged contractor's opportunities for profit and loss (The more opportunity he has to make a profit or sustain a loss, the more it will evidence an independent contractor relationship.)

6. The amount of initiative, judgment or foresight in open-market competition with others required for the success of the claimed independent enterprise (The more initiative, judgment and foresight required, the more it will show an independent contractor relationship.)

The IRS also has its own list of twenty factors used to determine proper classification of an independent contractor:

1. **Instructions.** An employee must comply with instructions about when, where and how to work. Even if no instructions are given, the control factor is present if the employer has the right to give instructions.

2. **Training.** An employee is trained to perform services in a particular manner. Independent contractors ordinarily use their own methods and receive no training from the purchasers of their services.

3. **Integration.** An employee's services are integrated into the business operations because the services are important to the success or continuation of the business. This shows that the employee is subject to direction and control.

4. **Services rendered personally.** An employee renders services personally. This shows that the employer is interested in the methods as well as the results.

5. **Hiring assistants.** An employee works for an employer who hires, supervises and pays assistants. An independent contractor hires, supervises and pays assistants under a contract that requires him or her to provide materials and labor and to be responsible only for the result.

6. **Continuing relationship.** An employee has a continuing relationship with an employer. A continuing relationship may exist where work is performed at frequently recurring although irregular intervals.

7. **Set hours of work.** An employee has set hours of work established by an employer. An independent contractor is the master of his or her own time.

8. **Full-time work.** An employee normally works full time for an employer. An independent contractor can work when and for whom he or she chooses.

9. **Work done on premises.** An employee works on the premises of an employer, or works on a route or at a location designated by an employer.

10. **Order or sequence set.** An employee must perform services in the order or sequence set by an employer. This shows that the employee is subject to direction and control.

11. **Reports.** An employee submits reports to an employer. This shows the employee must account to the employer for his or her actions.

12. **Payments.** An employee is paid by the hour, week or month. An independent contractor is paid by the job or on a straight commission.

13. **Expenses.** An employee's business and travel expenses are paid by an employer. This shows the employee is subject to regulation and control.

14. **Tools and materials.** An employee is furnished significant tools, materials and other equipment by an employer.

15. **Investment.** An independent contractor has a significant investment in the facilities he or she uses in performing services for someone else.

16. **Profit or loss.** An independent contractor can make a profit or suffer a loss.

17. **Works for more than one person or firm.** An independent contractor gives his or her services to two or more unrelated persons or firms at the same time.

18. **Offers services to the general public.** An independent contractor makes his or her services available to the general public.

19. **Right to fire.** An employee can be fired by an employer. An independent contractor cannot be fired so long as he or she produces a result that meets the specifications of the contract.

20. **Right to quit.** An employee can quit his or her job at any time without incurring liability. An independent contractor usually agrees to complete a specific job and is responsible for its satisfactory completion or is legally obligated to make good for failure to complete it.

The IRS also offers a mouthful-of-a-form that may be helpful (or possibly more confusing): "Information for Use in Determining Whether a Worker is an Employee for Purposes of Federal Employment Taxes and Income Tax Withholding" (Form SS-8, available at local tax offices or by mail from the IRS).

Obviously, the small business owner prefers to use independent contractors whenever possible because it cuts paperwork in half and eliminates tax withholding. If you hire independent contractors, all you have to do at year's end is complete a 1099 form (Statement for Recipients of Non-Employee Compensation) for each individual to whom you have paid $600 or more. One copy goes to the IRS and the other to the contractor. Just make sure the people you hire are truly independent contractors, and not employees.

Industrial Homework Laws

Still more laws? Yes, and if you've read this far, you're probably ready to throw this book at me. It was so much more comfortable not knowing all this stuff, wasn't it? But as a home-business educator, my job is to present facts and information that will enable you to make intelligent *and financially safe* decisions. As a home-business owner, I, too, resent the way government sticks its nose into the home-business arena, and state homework laws may surprise you as much as they did me when I first learned about them. Until I brought them to the attention of the home-business community in the first edition of this book, this topic had never been discussed in home-business guides, except in passing. ("Be sure to check on any state laws that may apply to you," etc.) State homework laws came to my attention only because of their similarity to the Labor Department's "sweatshop law," which attracted wide attention in the national media in early 1983 (see "Cottage Industries" section in this chapter.) Most of these state laws were meant to reinforce federal law, and they have been on the books since 1937 when the legislature became aware of homework abuses and passed a federal Industrial Homework Law.

Perhaps the key lies in whether you are a licensed manufacturer. To be safe you must obtain a legal opinion about the law in your state. If certain state and federal laws seem to violate your constitutional rights, you'll have to fight to correct the situation. One way to do this is to join and support national business organizations who are now fighting on your behalf.

Insurance

Half of us are probably insurance poor (from paying on several necessary insurance policies), and the other half so underinsured we're worried to death about what will happen if "the worst" happens. Some of us have both problems. Insurance is one of the most important considerations for self-employed individuals, because lack of the right coverage can put you out of business overnight. The following information will alert you to financially dangerous situations you might have overlooked and will help you ask the right questions the next time you meet with an insurance agent. Before you purchase a new policy, take care to check the stability of the insurance company in question. With so many insurance companies going belly-up, you can't afford to take out a policy with any company that doesn't have a superior rating. (The A.M. Best Company in Oldwick, New Jersey, is one of the best sources for ratings of U.S. insurance companies.)

Tip:

To avoid problems with the Department of Labor, do not hire home-workers to manufacture goods. In addition to Labor Department regulations against this, the following states have "industrial homework laws" that specifically prohibit the manufacture of certain products at home. Prohibited articles most often include food and drink, wearing apparel, toys and dolls, cosmetics, jewelry and certain accessories. In some cases manufacturing may be allowed in a home atmosphere if the business owner obtains a special homeworker certificate or permit. Contact your state's Department of Labor for more information. Here is a list of states known to have such laws:

California
Connecticut
District of Columbia
Hawaii
Illinois
Indiana
Maryland
Massachusetts
Michigan
Missouri
New Jersey
New York
Ohio
Pennsylvania
Rhode Island
Tennessee
Texas
Virginia
Wisconsin
and Puerto Rico

Tip:

Before you quit your full-time job and lose its accompanying medical insurance, make sure you can get adequate coverage as an individual. One secret to cutting health insurance costs is to join a large professional organization that offers a group plan. Good insurance is also available to chamber of commerce members. One couple reported they were able to cut their insurance premiums in half by joining the chamber and getting into its United Chambers group insurance program.

Insurance Tax Tip: *For the year 1997, self-employed individuals may deduct 40 percent of the cost of health insurance on page one of their annual tax return. This deduction will increase to 45 percent for years 1998-2002, then gradually increase to 80 percent by 2006.*

Hospitalization/Major Medical Insurance

In spite of the high cost of medical insurance, self-employed individuals can't afford to be without good coverage. In shopping for a new medical plan, look for (a) choice of deductibles; (b) a stop-loss feature that limits your financial risk; (c) a plan that doesn't charge for children if you don't have them; (d) sufficient outpatient coverage for things such as cancer treatment; and (e) benefits that cover organ transplants/implants. Most policies do not cover the latter item and may severely limit the dollar amount of outpatient treatment benefits, so check these points carefully as they are the ones that could bankrupt you.

If you already have coverage, take a moment to double-check the cancellation/conversion clauses in your policy. My husband and I learned the hard way that insurance can be canceled at any time, particularly if a small group of insured individuals is entering too many claims. With only thirty days' notice of cancellation of our major medical policy (obtained through a small writer's organization), Harry decided he'd better have that angiogram the doctor had been advising. Good thing, too, for it revealed an immediate need for quadruple bypass surgery. The old policy covered all expenses, but a month's delay here would have wiped us out.

By law, one is always entitled to some kind of conversion policy, but the benefits are never as good for an individual policy as they are for one obtained through a group, and the premiums are higher as well.

Homeowner's or Renter's Insurance Policies

If you operate a business at home, you stand to lose twice as much as the ordinary homeowner in times of tragedy—both home and business. Make sure you're covered for all possible disasters, be it fire, flood, tornado, hurricane or earthquake. An insurance agent once laughed when I said we wanted earthquake insurance, but it costs less than $100 a year and gives me great peace of mind every time I think of the major quake possibilities in Missouri that also may affect my state. Remember regular homeowner's policies do not cover things such as cracks in the foundation due to earth movement (including sink holes); sewer problems; water damage from hurricanes (unless, for example, a tree first knocks a hole in your roof or wall so the water can get in); and so on. (Most people in flood-prone areas do not have flood insurance, but those who are running businesses at home should give careful consideration to this potential problem.)

Also, if you have special collections of any kind (antiques, diamonds, silver, furs, guns, cameras, artwork, etc.), be sure to have them appraised and insured by a separate, all-risk endorsement. (The typical homeowner's policy limits loss on such items to no more than $1,500.)

Business Pursuits Endorsement

It's important to tell your insurance agent that you run a business at home because your regular homeowner's or renter's policy will *not* cover business equipment, supplies or inventory nor, in all probability, any losses due to fires that may be caused by such things. Note that "goods for sale" are considered business property that must be separately insured, either with an individual policy or a special rider.

A Business Pursuits Endorsement is a good answer for small businesses since it offers some liability coverage for people in your home for business purposes as well as materials and products you are storing. If you are storing over $3,000 of inventory, however, you should probably obtain a separate fire, vandalism and theft policy. Note that a business rider on your home insurance carries no personal liability coverage for your business.

Some insurance companies, quick to capitalize on the work-at-home movement, have developed special policies for home-based entrepreneurs. My insurance agent warns, however, that the biggest problem with such policies is the minimum premium for certain types of exposure can be quite high. In some instances, some of these things can be taken care of by an endorsement of a homeowner policy.

Personal computers used for business will not be covered by your regular homeowner's policy, except possibly against loss by fire or theft. But that leaves you with possible risks related to damage caused by water, high humidity or power surges. The latter can cause extensive damage to circuits, although a voltage surge suppressor can prevent this. The insurance problem can be solved simply by insuring your computer system separately with a company that specializes in this kind of coverage. Such coverage would also protect your computer while it's in transit to and from the repair shop or when you travel with it.

If you sell art or handcrafts, normally taking them to fairs or shows, you might want to investigate special "studio insurance" policies designed to protect such property both at home, in your studio, or in transit to and from exhibitions and shows. Such policies are available from some art and craft organizations, a few of which are included in chapter sixteen.

Replacement-Value Insurance

For about 15 percent more a year, you can obtain "replacement-value insurance" on all your personal possessions. If your insurance agent does not bring this to your attention, be sure to ask

Tip:

To protect your home and office from fire, consider spraying drapes, furniture, carpeting and storage cartons with No Burn, *a nontoxic, nonstaining formula that retards smoke and flames. It is colorless, odorless and harmless to pets. It comes in a trigger-spray bottle.*

Tip:

No policy will be worth much if you can't prove what you owned prior to total destruction by fire or other disaster, so be sure to make a comprehensive list or photographic record of your possessions. Keep this information in a safe place outside the home, such as in a safety deposit box. Also, in the event of theft, you should have a handy record of all the model and serial numbers of all your electronic and computer equipment.

about it. With a regular homeowner's/renter's policy, what you get in the event of loss is figured on the current value *after depreciation.* This often brings dollar amounts down to little or nothing. A replacement-value policy, on the other hand, will pay you whatever it costs to replace any item that's been damaged or destroyed, regardless of its age at time of loss, up to the limits of your policy. Note that this coverage is applicable only to personal possessions; loss of furnishings and equipment in your office or studio would be figured on a depreciable basis and be limited to the amounts shown on your special business rider.

Liability Insurance

Each of us can be held liable for a lot of things, and when you have a business at home you need to be doubly careful. *Personal liability insurance* protects you against claims made by people who have suffered bodily injury while on your premises, while *product liability insurance* protects you against lawsuits by consumers who have been injured while using your product. My insurance agent emphasizes that personal and business liability should not be intertwined since claims will be treated differently because of the different pursuits.

You might ask your insurance agent if, as a sole proprietor working at home, you would be covered in these cases: A delivery person (maybe the UPS driver) slips on the ice on your steps while delivering a business package, breaks his or her back and can never work again. Big lawsuit! Or a customer or client suffers bodily injury while in your home on business and sues for hospitalization costs and loss of job income. *Why* these people are on your property will determine the coverage your insurance policy provides. *Read the fine print and talk to your insurance agent.*

To decrease your personal risk, inquire about a "personal umbrella policy" that will take over where your present coverage stops. You might be able to buy a million dollars' worth of liability insurance for as little as $100 per year. The same kind of umbrella policy is available on your automobile policy as well. Here, the difference in premium costs for one million vs. five million dollars' of insurance may be ridiculously small. As my insurance expert confirms: "Personal umbrella programs are excellent vehicles for providing broader coverage, and they are especially important today where judges and juries are awarding some unbelievable numbers in lawsuits. Business umbrellas are also important but they are a little more expensive than the personal umbrella."

As mentioned in the "Independent Contractor" section, if you perform services for clients in their homes, offices or plants, you may wish to obtain general liability coverage to protect you against things such as your causing injury to someone, or accidental damage of another's property or equipment. Such insurance should be substantial enough to cover costs that would be incurred in a lawsuit against you.

Product Liability Insurance

For many businesses, product liability insurance is simply too expensive to buy, yet it can sometimes be critical to the sale of merchandise. For example, a garment maker had to cancel a large order because the store she was doing business with insisted she have product liability insurance on her products—gifts for babies and children, a touchy area. National mail-order catalog houses often insist on product liability insurance, too.

Many small business owners are faced with a hard decision: Should they continue to operate without liability insurance or cease operation? Before you give up on obtaining insurance, investigate help that may be available to you through a trade association. Some groups are able to negotiate policies for members.

Historically, few craft manufacturers have carried product liability insurance because most handcrafted/handmade items are considered relatively safe. But ceramic pots have been known to break and spill hot contents on the owner's lap, doll's eyes have been swallowed by children, and stained glass windows have shattered while being hung. According to the book *Making It Legal* by Lee Wilson, the legal rule of product liability is this: *"Defective product plus injury arising from customary or foreseen use equals maker or seller pays."* Here are four ways to guard against product liability suits:

1. Set high quality control standards to avoid possible injury.
2. "Idiot-proof" your products and try to design away any potential harm. If the latter isn't possible, at least warn the public of possible harm by including detailed instructions on the proper use of your products to avoid that harm.
3. In advertising your products, don't make any claims or promises you cannot meet.
4. Include a questionnaire with your products, asking for customers' input. Their comments might alert you to potential problems.

In seeking insurance coverage, look first for a nearby agency that sells business or commercial insurance, including well-known companies such as American Family, Allstate and State Farm. One insurance agent told me product liability insurance rates vary greatly from state to state, depending on your annual gross sales (or anticipated sales), the number of products you sell, and the possible risks associated with each of them. An insurance company will look closely at what your products are made of and consider possible side effects you'd never imagine.

Tip:

If you have an employee and ask that employee to run an errand using your personal vehicle (which you normally use for business), you're courting disaster. If your employee should have an accident that seriously injures someone, he or she would be sued, and because your employee was "acting in behalf of the employer," you, too, could be held accountable. Ask your insurance agent about "non-ownership contingent liability protection," which can be included as part of your overall liability insurance policy or obtained separately, or consider having your vehicle rated for business.

If your income is low and your product line small, you may be able to buy an affordable policy. In your desire to save insurance premium money, however, don't overlook the fact that you do need high limits of coverage.

An Idea to Consider

The owners of a party-plan business told me product liability was a major consideration and obstacle in the establishment of their business, but insurance was not available in their area at a reasonable premium because they had no storefront. Their solution was to incorporate under Subchapter S (see "Legal Forms of Business" later in this chapter). Although this didn't give them the product liability coverage they sought, it did work to protect their personal and family properties. Their insurance agent advised that, given the relative safety of their inventory, this type of protection should be adequate for them. (See "Corporation" under "Legal Forms of Business.")

Disability Insurance (or Income Replacement Insurance)

If you are the major breadwinner in your family, what would happen if you could not work for an extended period of time . . . or ever again? To keep premium costs as low as possible, consider a waiting period of three to six months before benefits would begin.

Business Interruption Insurance

Another "for instance": Your home is destroyed by a fire or a tornado, and your business stops until you can piece it together again. Business interruption insurance could make a big difference, and it may not be as expensive as you think. Talk to an insurance agent about it. Investigate group plans offered by professional organizations.

Workers Compensation Insurance

If you hire employees, your state probably requires that you carry worker's compensation for them. Such insurance is available through individual agents, and the amount you pay will vary depending on the number of employees you have and the kind of work they do for you.

Partnership Insurance

If you are in partnership with someone, it is necessary to establish a Buy-Sell Agreement, funded by life insurance. By law, at the death of a partner, your business is dissolved and can no longer operate until it is either liquidated or reorganized. The agreement, prepared by an attorney, establishes the price the survivor will pay for his or her share of the business, and that the heirs will sell for, and the insurance provides the money to complete the transfer.

Invoicing Terms

Pro Forma

If you are uncertain about the credit worthiness of a new retail account, do not ship and bill, but sell your first order to them on a *pro forma* basis, which means you want your money in advance. Simply send a Pro Forma Invoice for the merchandise that has been ordered and ship the goods when payment has been received.

Freight Charges

F.O.B. means "Freight (or free) on board." These initials with the name of a city immediately after them indicate the point to which the seller will pay the freight. If the customer is to pay freight, the notation would read "F.O.B. (your city)"; if you are paying the freight, it would read "F.O.B. (buyer's city)." This F.O.B. notation could be important in the event goods are lost or damaged in transit since, legally, title of the goods changes hands at the F.O.B. point.

Terms of Sale

When full payment is desired within ten or thirty days, simply include the appropriate terms on your invoice: Either "Net 10 days" or "Net 30 days." If you wish to offer your customers a discount for prompt payment, you would state the terms of sale as "2%/10/30" or "2% 10 days, net 30." Either term indicates to a buyer that you will give a 2-percent discount if payment is made within ten days, and full payment is expected within thirty days. When an invoice includes sales tax, you should state the exact amount a customer may deduct, and this deduction should be based on cost of merchandise before tax is added. (If you do not state this figure, your customer may calculate the 2 percent on the total invoice. Over time, this could amount to a sizable amount of lost dollars.) Some buyers pay an invoice a month late and still take the discount, in which case they should be invoiced for the difference. Although they may ignore such a small invoice, such action will show them that you mean business.

Tip:

In analyzing your various insurance needs and discussing them with one or more insurance providers, be sure to lay all the details in front of the agent so proper coverage can be provided. Withholding information can only lead to problems in the event of a claim.

Labor Laws

The U.S. Department of Labor administers several laws that affect the operations of American businesses both large and small. *The sole proprietor, however, need not be concerned with any of them (save minimum-wage laws) until non-family members are hired as employees.* At that point, the following laws apply to one's business:

The Fair Labor Standards Act of 1938, as Amended

This law establishes minimum wages, overtime pay, record keeping and child labor standards for employees individually engaged in or producing goods for interstate commerce, and for all employees employed in certain enterprises described in the act, unless a specific exemption applies. Employers are required to meet the standards established under the act, regardless of the number of their employees and whether they work full or part-time. A complete copy of this act and additional information about the hiring of employees can be obtained from your nearest Wage and Hour Division of the Department of Labor (see "U.S. Government" in your telephone book).

Occupational Safety and Health Act (OSHA) of 1970

If you have even one employee, you need to know about OSHA, which is allowed to inspect or investigate any workplace in response to an employee complaint and issue citations and assess penalties for violations. This statute is concerned with safe and healthful conditions in the workplace, and it covers all employers engaged in business affecting interstate commerce. Employers must comply with standards and with applicable recordkeeping and reporting requirements specified in regulations issued by OSHA.

OSHA regulations also extend to employees' use of your vehicle. If one of them were to be hurt in an automobile accident, you could be held responsible, particularly if they were injured because they weren't wearing a seatbelt. Details about OSHA regulations are available from area offices of the U.S. Department of Labor.

Other Laws Administered by the U.S. Department of Labor

You need not be concerned with these laws unless you are involved in situations that concern (1) garnishment of employees' wages; (2) hiring of disadvantaged workers; (3) federal service contracts using laborers and mechanics; (4) federal contracts for work on public buildings or public works; (5) employee pension and welfare benefit plans; (6) government contracts; and other special situations.

Social Security Act of 1935, as Amended

This act is concerned with employment insurance laws, and each state requires employers who come under its employment insurance law to pay taxes based on their payroll. For more information, contact your local Employment Security or Job Service Office, or talk to an accountant.

Legal Forms of Business

On a nearby page, you'll find a chart that compares the advantages and disadvantages of the four basic forms a U.S. business can take: sole proprietorship, partnership, corporation and limited liability company. Canada has similar forms of business, but readers should note the following information has been written with U.S. businesses in mind.

Sole Proprietorship

Most small businesses are sole proprietorships simply because this is the easiest kind of business to start, operate and end. A disadvantage of this form of business is that the owner is fully liable for all business debts and actions, meaning that personal assets are not protected from lawsuits. Something few sole proprietors ever think about when they launch a business is how they will eventually end that business, but given the high failure rate of all new businesses, one ought to give a little consideration to this idea in the beginning. See chapter fourteen for some perspective on this topic, along with some specific tips on how to exit gracefully.

Partnerships

Many small businesses elect to form a partnership so the work load and responsibility for the management of the business can be shared. It's important to have a contract in any kind of business partnership and advice from legal counsel. Be cautious about entering into a partnership with a close friend because many friendships have been destroyed in the name of business. In a chapter she contributed to the book, *Word Processing Plus*, Colleen Perri says the number of failed partnerships rivals that of failed marriages. "Just as in a marriage, innumerable things can happen to confuse, to hurt and to horrify." She has identified eight reasons why partnerships can go wrong: different priorities (the race horse vs. the turtle); different skills and equipment (overequipped vs. underequipped); different personalities (over-achiever vs. underachiever); different attitudes (long-term vs. short-term thinking); different goals; different philosophies; lack of communication; and the failure to "put it in writing."

To alert you to other partnership problems, consider these stories shared by my readers:

• One learned a bitter lesson about partnerships when, two years after she and her husband had dissolved a partnership with another person, the IRS came in and levied their bank account, right at the time they were trying to refinance a loan. Their former partner had not paid his income taxes for the past two years, and the IRS (and any other creditor) can levy *any* partner's account for uncollected funds—even the account of the partner who did pay his or her share. "A person learns real quick how helpless he is with government agencies such as the IRS," my reader concluded.

In dissolving a partnership, see if you can build into the dissolution contract some kind of safeguard against this kind of tax problem. No one needs a surprise like this two or three years after a partnership has been dissolved.

• Another reader, who bought out her partner, told how difficult it was to determine a fair net worth figure based on inventory totals, raw materials, accounts payable and accounts receivable. An accountant helped in that regard. The partners worked out an agreement whereby payments would be made over a three-year period, and the buyer took out declining term insurance to cover the contract in case anything happened to her before the balance was paid in full. "Dissolving a partnership is somewhat like a divorce in that neither person wants to get shafted by the other," she says. "I suggest that anyone looking for a business partner think ahead, asking, 'What would I do if . . . ?' A partner may die or want out of the business, or you may simply want to buy out your partner as I did."

Or, as newsletter editor Shep Robinson once said, "Just because you get on the wrong streetcar, nothing says you have to stay on it to the end of the line."

Corporation

"The decision on whether to incorporate a business is not as simple as it was a few years ago," says Judith H. McQuown, author of *Inc Yourself—How to Profit by Setting Up Your Own Corporation*. "Nearly every year of the past decade has produced major tax legislation that has impacted the small

Legal Forms of Business in the United States[1]

Sole Proprietorship

Pluses	Minuses
1. Controlled by owner	1. Liability unlimited
2. All profits to owner	2. Limited resources
3. Little regulation	3. No continuity at retirement or death
4. Easy to start	
5. Earnings personally taxed	

General Partnership

Pluses	Minuses
1. Joint ownership and responsibility	1. Conflict of authority
2. Access to more money and skills	2. Liability unlimited
3. Earnings personally taxed	3. Profits divided
4. Limited regulation and easy to start	4. No continuity at retirement or death

Limited Partnership

Pluses	Minuses
1. General partner(s) run the business	1. Limited partners have no say in business
2. Limited (silent) partners have no liability beyond invested money	2. General partners have unlimited liability
3. Profits divided as per partnership agreement	3. More regulations to start than general partnership
4. Earnings personally taxed	4. Special tax withholding regulations

Corporation

Pluses	Minuses
1. Limited liability	1. Regulated by states
2. Ownership interest is transferrable	2. Costly to form
3. Legal entity and continuous life	3. Limited to chartered activities
4. Status in raising funds	4. Corporate income tax plus tax on personal salary and/or dividends

Subchapter S Corporations

Pluses	Minuses
1. Receives all advantages of a corporation	1. Highly regulated both by state and IRS
2. Electing corporation taxed as sole proprietorship	2. Restricted to certain kinds of business and limited number of stockholders

Limited Liability Company (LLC)

Pluses	Minuses
1. Combines the best attributes of other business forms	1. High set up and annual filing fees
2. Personal liability protection is similar to that of corporation	2. Different tax and regulatory requirements in each state
3. Better tax advantages than limited partnership	
4. Owners do not assume liability for business's debt	

Footnote

1. Some of the above information has been adapted from a U.S. Department of Labor booklet. Canada's legal forms of business are similar, except that LLCs do not yet exist there (to my knowledge). In addition, there are different types of corporations (private, public or federal).

corporation," she says, "yet there are still many compelling business and tax reasons to incorporate."

A corporation is the most complicated form a business can take. While it offers special advantages, such as protection for one's personal assets in the event of a lawsuit, it involves a lot of paperwork, plus legal and accounting services. Since a corporation is a legal entity unto itself, it does not die with the retirement or death of its officers. Investments may be transferred from one party to another without affecting the operation of the company. Some small business owners incorporate their businesses merely to obtain legal protection for personal assets in the event of a lawsuit. While incorporation does afford a certain degree of protection, it is not the complete answer. As attorney Leonard D. DuBoff explains, "individuals who are actually responsible for wrongful acts will remain liable for those acts. The corporation will protect your personal assets from being exposed only when your employees or agents are responsible for the business's liability."

In some cases, it may be easier and less expensive simply to purchase liability insurance. Other times, however, a homebased business needs to be incorporated because it involves individuals from two or three families, and this is the best way to protect everyone's interests. An interesting reason to incorporate came to my attention when self-publishing guru Jerry Buchanan said in his newsletter that he had incorporated after seventeen years as a sole proprietor because this was the only way he could avoid giving his social security checks back to the government at the end of the year. Something to think about, at least.

Some experts have said incorporation does not justify its additional costs unless one's business profits have reached five figures and exceed personal income needs. However, only you and your lawyer or accountant can determine what's best for your particular business and personal tax situation. It is entirely possible and quite legal (in some, but not all states) to incorporate without the services of a lawyer, but this is not something a business novice should attempt. One lawyer pointed out to me that it will cost more to unincorporate yourself than to incorporate, so you don't want to make the wrong decision. This is just one more reason to seek professional advice.

Note: In Canada, the words "corporation," "incorporated company" and "limited company," all mean the same. Registration can be done either on the provincial or federal level.

Subchapter S Corporation

This is a corporate structure for new or low-income businesses, and even a one-person business can operate in this fashion. Unlike the usual type of corporation, profits or losses of a Subchapter S are reported on a shareholder's Form 1040, as in a partnership, meaning you're taxed at the lower personal rate. Since this legal form of business offers the advantages of a corporation without double taxation, it's often a good choice for entrepreneurs.

Limited Liability Company

The new business form that made its appearance in several states by the end of 1992 should be available in all states after 1997. "This form of business is similar to an S Corporation, with limited liability for the stockholders, and pass-through profits taxable to the owners but not to the business," says Bernard Kamoroff in *Small Time Operator*. "LLCs offer more generous loss deductions than S Corporations, offer more classes of stock, and are not limited to the S Corporation's maximum of 35 individual shareholders. The IRS does not recognize LLCs for federal income tax purposes, and will tax them either as partnerships or corporations, depending on how they are legally structured."

Licenses and Permits

Many home-business owners have never bothered to get a local (municipal or county) license or permit, even when this is required by law. Fortunately, no one goes around checking to see who has a license and who doesn't, which probably accounts for the lack of attention new business owners sometimes pay to this detail. However, authorities may discover such unlicensed businesses by checking state sales tax returns and resale licenses.

Local Registration

Contact local authorities (city or county clerk or local council) to learn if you need any special permits or licenses to legally operate a business in your area (in addition to the registration of your business name—see "Business or Trade Name" in this chapter). In both the United States and Canada, licenses are rarely required for small craft businesses and others who will be operating quietly without customers coming and going, but you must ask to be sure. If you operate without a required license, you run the risk of discovery, at which point you might be fined or ordered to cease business.

It's a good idea to find out how solid the ground is under any unlicensed business you already may be operating. Take a trip to the city or county clerk's office under the guise of "just wondering about starting a business" and get the facts. You may find it a simple and inexpensive matter to legally establish your business, and then you won't have to worry about it anymore. If

Tip:

A mail-order seller in New York who uses her home address for her business had to obtain a "special use permit" to operate. On the other hand, a homebased publisher in California was advised by the license bureau to obtain a post office box number for his address because "the post office is in a commercial zone," and that eliminated the need for any "special use permit." Check this out, because it may work in your area, too.

you're truly concerned by what you learn on your research trip, ask a lawyer for advice on what to do next.

Note: Some communities in the United States, having suddenly realized homebased entrepreneurs represent a terrific source for extra revenue, have begun charging extra fees of from $15 to $200 for what they're calling a "home occupation permit"—sort of a "taxation without representation" situation in that such permits offer no real benefits to the homebased entrepreneur but do add to city coffers. As seminar leader Sylvia Landman reports from Marin, California, "When I questioned what this money was for, I was told it was to 'police and control the nature of new home businesses in our city.' I then asked who comes out to check on this, and was told that no one ever does this. All this seems to be a case of 'just pay and obey.'"

In Joanne Pratt's paper, *Legal Barriers to Home-Based Work*, she points out that "cities want to cash in on the home business boom by levying additional taxes without voting on them first, and that these fees are but one of the systematic methods used nationwide to discourage homebased business. The question is, will this issue slow the tremendous surge in the home business boom, or just irritate it?"

Whether you get a license or permit for your business may depend on zoning regulations in your area. In some towns and cities, all homebased businesses are outlawed by archaic zoning laws written back in the 1800s, but this hasn't stopped thousands of individuals from operating businesses anyway. Such illegal businesses simply never ask city officials if they need a license, because this would only draw attention to themselves. Businesses in both the United States and Canada have similar problems where zoning is concerned. See "Zoning Laws" section for more information.

Other Licensing Agencies

Depending on the type of business you plan to operate, you may need to get a permit from other municipal or county agencies. In general, food-related businesses will be subject to special restrictions and inspections by both local and state health departments, and day care centers will have to conform to local and state regulations as well. The fire department may have to give some kind of permit or official OK if you work with flammable or dangerous materials. If your business causes the release of any materials into the air or water (even a ceramic kiln), you may need approval from the local environmental protection agency. Door-to-door sellers (if they still exist) may need a peddler's license. If you work with animals or agricultural products, check with your local Department of Agriculture; if you work with the handicapped or elderly, contact the social services department of your local, state or provincial government.

Certain business professionals in the United States—such as accountants, auto mechanics, photographers, cosmetologists, TV repairers and others—will need occupational licenses issued by the state agency that administers consumer affairs. Contact your state capitol to connect with this particular agency to see if you need an occupational license of any kind. Canadians should contact their provincial and federal governments for information.

"Commercial Kitchen Laws"

The person who decides to launch a homebased food-related business must be concerned not just with permits and zoning ordinances, but with local health officials and state regulations as well. (Local health authorities reportedly comb newspaper ads to spot unlicensed food/catering services.) In fact, the "commercial kitchen" law in your state may make it almost impossible to set up a food-related business in your home. (Canada has similar laws.)

Thumbs up to the state of Iowa, which has a "home-bakery provision" that draws a line between commercial food businesses and small operations like bake sales and farmer's markets. (It is possible that other states have similar home-bakery provisions in their food laws, so ask about this.) Iowa's law allows home bakers to operate without a license if they earn less than $2,000 per year and agree not to advertise their products. (All business must come from word-of-mouth advertising.)

Licensing

Are you using a famous copyrighted design or character (Snoopy, for example), or do you make sweatshirts and other products that incorporate university emblems or sports team logos? You cannot legally do these things without a licensing agreement from the copyright holder. Some people who have become "personalities" may also license others to use their name or face on some product or service. In particular, the rights of deceased personalities are protected by state law and aggressive agencies working for heirs (as discussed at length in chapter two).

When working with major companies or institutions, licensing arrangements are likely to be expensive and usually involve royalties that may range from 6½ to 7½ percent of gross sales. But small business owners may be able to work with other individuals on a mutually profitable basis. For example, I recall two needlework designers who made a profitable arrangement with an artist whose work they admired. They sold him on the deal

Tip:

One way around commercial kitchen laws in your state is to rent an outside kitchen in a commercial building. A reader in California said it was popular there to rent bakeries in the evening hours, and pizza parlor kitchens in the early morning. One woman met her state's requirements by buying a storage shed and then putting in the required sinks, two Coleman stoves, etc. to make her jams and jellies in her backyard. Another reader reported that she solved her cake-baking problem by using the commercial kitchen in her church.

Tip:

Be particularly careful when establishing royalty arrangements of any kind. There is a big difference between being paid a percentage of the retail price, net receipts or net profit. You can't bank on the last one, and net receipts may be less than half the retail price due to discounts given to wholesalers.

simply by stitching one of his paintings and explaining how they would market an entire line of his designs in cross-stitch and needlepoint. Working with an attorney, they came to an agreement on royalties and term of contract (which included renewal options and a termination clause). Here are three tips they shared with me:

1. You or the licensor may want to branch out into other related fields, so you need a "Right of First Refusal" clause that will give you first chance at the opportunity to expand into a different area of business. If you decline, the opportunity may then be offered to others.
2. Be sure to work out what will happen in the event of death of either licensor or licensee.
3. Specify the territory in which you plan to sell . . . and don't limit yourself to a small area.

Although you may never have any intention of obtaining such a license, you may someday find yourself in a position to license others to reproduce a design you've created. Before entering into a licensing arrangement, be sure to register appropriate patents, copyrights or trademarks, and establish quality-control standards for the manufacturer of your designs. A licensing agent or attorney can represent your interests.

Occupational and Health Hazards

"100 million Americans may be using dangerous materials without knowing it," says the Center for Safety in the Arts, a national clearinghouse for information on this topic. If you have an undiagnosed illness, it could be related to your improper use of certain materials related to your work. Particularly harmful when not properly used are paints, paint thinners, plastics, photo chemicals, dyes, lead, asbestos and dozens of other materials or substances.

In addition to occupational hazards related to your health, there may be hazards relating to your safety as well, particularly if strangers ordinarily come to your door in the normal course of business. Take these sensible steps to ensure your personal safety:

1. If you don't know your customer, don't advertise the fact that you are alone in the house. There is much you can do to create the impression someone else is at home.
2. Never tell anyone except trusted neighbors and your mail carrier that you're going to be out of town. Casually dropped information like this can easily be overheard by the wrong person, making you a prime burglary candidate.

3. Don't tell people on the phone that you'll "be gone until 4:30" for the same reason; and when recording a message for your answering machine, don't say, "I'm not at home now," instead, word your message to suggest that you are merely away from your desk or on another line.
4. A course in self-defense might make you feel safer. So would a guard dog.

Tip:

Two or three live plants in your office will improve the oxygen supply and help combat the pollutants you're adding to the air with your laser printer and other office machines.

Patents

(See also Copyrights; Trademarks)

In the United States, a patent is defined as "a grant issued by the United States Government giving an inventor the right to exclude all others from making, using or selling his invention within the United States, its territories and possessions." It lasts for 20 years from its issue date, but high maintenance fees ($225-$670) must now be paid at 3½, 6½ and 11½ year intervals, or the patent will lapse.

In Canada, a patent is described in B.C.'s *Home-Based Business Manual* as "A right given for 20 years after filing by the Government of Canada to an inventor to stop others from using his or her invention in Canada." Like copyright laws, patent laws in the United States and Canada are similar, but not the same, so Canadians should read the following information for perspective only, and obtain their patent information from their own Patent Office.

In the United States, patents may be granted to anyone who invents a new and useful product, process or any new and useful improvement of either. This sounds simple enough, but in truth, patents are a very complicated and expensive way of protecting "intellectual property." Actually, all a patent really does is give the inventor the right to exclude anyone else from making, using or selling the invention. It is possible you could get a patent on something, yet not be able to use it if someone has a more encompassing, earlier patent. You cannot patent anything in the public domain or anything that would be obvious to anyone skilled in the process or field. Essentially, to be patentable an invention must add to the pool of knowledge, not take from it. In other words, you can't reinvent the wheel.

You can do a U.S. patent (or trademark) search in one of three ways: (1) by visiting the public search room of the Patent and Trademark Office in Arlington, Virginia; (2) by providing the Patent office with specific information to enable them to do a search for you; or (3) through a search of one of the patent databases now available in some libraries. One of them, PATLEX, has full-text copies of all U.S. patents after a certain date (which apparently changes from time to time).

If you get a patent, and it's contested by a company with

Tip:

If you decide to manufacture a product yourself, get it on the market fast to beat the crowd, says an experienced marketer, because a good idea will be stolen the moment you display it at a trade show. "And," adds Ms. Sears, "if you decide to manufacture, that is the time the patent usually is worth the investment and effort involved—in part because it deters others from suing you on their patents, and in part because it does deter some copiers as well."

Note: The patent system changed dramatically on June 8, 1995 when the General Agreement on Tariffs and Trade (GATT) took effect. Now, instead of the term of a patent running seventeen years from date of issuance, it will run twenty years from the date of filing. Since it can take up to ten years to get a patent, a lot of inventors are going to lose money as a result. Legislation to correct this problem is pending.

clout, it will be child's play for them to prove it resembles some item already patented by them, which in turn will automatically void any patent you may hold. Since a patent gotten with the help of a patent attorney can cost from $3,000-$20,000 (depending on attorney's fees), some inventors might be better off selling their ideas to manufacturers for a flat fee up-front or on a royalty basis when possible. But attorney Mary Helen Sears stresses, "It is dangerous to submit a patentable item to a manufacturer before filing a patent application unless the manufacturer, *in advance* of hearing the invention, commits itself that *you* are the owner. Don't do this without competent legal help or you will lose all."

In an article about patents in *The Dream Merchant*, a periodical for inventors, marketing consultant Mike Rounds emphasizes that patentability has nothing to do with marketability. "Less than one percent of the over seven million products that have been patented in the United States have ever been marketed, and less than one percent of the products on the market have a patent," he says.

If someone infringes on one of your patents, you do have the right to sue. But the smaller you are, the less you can afford the high cost of litigation. "If you're a small person suing a large company, they can outspend you in court and impose so many tasks on you that it becomes difficult to stay the course," says Ms. Sears. She adds, however, that many patents litigated today are being held valid, and because judgments are often quite large, a few lawyers now take patent cases on contingency.

Prepatent Considerations

In his thirty-five years of experience in getting new products and ideas into the marketplace, inventor Jeremy Gorman in Wilmington, Vermont, has learned a lot about the patent process and the value of its protection. Sales of products of his inventions exceed $500 million annually, and he now counsels inventors individually and through seminars. He says that 97 percent of the U.S. patents issued never earn enough money to pay the patenting fee. "They just go on a plaque on the wall or in a desk drawer to impress the grandchildren fifty years later," he says. "Except for your ego, nothing is helped by having a patent on an unsalable idea, no matter how creative it is." Jeremy offers these tips for beginning inventors:

1. Before considering patenting an idea, first determine if there is a market for the product. If so, consider whether you will make the product yourself or have it made under license.

2. Don't spend money to get a patent unless a market study tells you how much money you can expect to make on the product. Be sure a patent is worth the cost, and *be sure it will protect*

you. For example, if you have a simple invention like the paper clip, all a patent would do for you is give you a about a two-year head start. There are ripoff companies whose business is to copy simple things, and they don't give a hoot for patents. They will make a hundred million of your paper clips in three months and flood the market with them. By the time you even know they exist, they will have scrapped the mold, moved to a new address, and be making thumbtacks under another name.

3. If you decide a patent is worth the expense, don't apply by yourself. Get a patent attorney. This will cost between $1,500 and $5,000, but if the attorney is good, you'll have a good patent that legitimate outfits will have difficulty getting around.

4. You can write much of the patent yourself. Go to a store and find a similar product that is patented. You'll find a patent number on the package. For a dollar, you can get a copy of the patent from the U.S. Patent Office in Washington, DC. Use that as a format and write a similar patent for your invention. Take that to your attorney and tell him or her to make it legal and as broad as possible. That gives you the biggest bang for the buck.

Design Patents

Design patents are primarily for manufacturers who want to protect new and ornamental designs on two- and three-dimensional objects. This might include anything from the design of a garment to the motif on a belt buckle to the shape of a coffee mug. Fabric designers are often protected this way, too. Like copyrights, design patents are hard to police and just as expensive to defend in court. Unless you're a commercial manufacturer, they're probably not for you. To qualify, a design must be new or novel, original, ornamental and inventive in character. These patents can be obtained for different terms of years, depending on the fee paid.

Postal Service
(See also United Parcel Service)

As a businessperson, you must acquaint yourself with the way the postal service operates. The following information for U.S. readers will serve as a reminder list of points Canadian readers should investigate on their own. In mid-1996, the U.S. Postal Service improved mail standards by reclassifying mail. There are now only four classes of mail: Expedited, First-Class, Periodicals (formerly called second-class), and Standard Mail (formerly third- and fourth-class). Special discounts are now available to mailers who prepare mail for automated processing. Changes have also been made in the way third-class bulk mail must now be labeled and bundled prior to mailing.

Tip:

Prior to printing a new brochure, catalog or newsletter, always check with your local post office on the regulations for size and weight. Odd sizes and where you've placed the address area on a mailer can cause problems and may incur extra postage. The best strategy is to take a mock-up of your mail piece to the post office to confirm that its size and design meet their regulations and qualifies for the lowest rate possible.

Mail Order Laws

The Postal Service is the watchdog of the mail order industry, and anyone who uses the mail to sell products and services must always be careful to accurately represent themselves and their products to their mail order customers. In chapter two, you learned postal authorities actively pursue promoters of chain letters and pyramid schemes, as well as anyone else who runs a scam that involves the mail. Earlier in this chapter, you learned about FTC rules concerning shipment within 30 days and truth in advertising. Many companies have been put out of business because they have engaged in a scheme or device for obtaining money or property through the mail by means of false representation, a phrase that packs a powerful punch.

For instance, consider the case of a man whom the Postal Service put out of business because he was selling herbs and herbal formulas through a catalog. In itself, this activity would have been OK, but this seller maintained that the advertised products had certain curative powers that dissolved malignant tumors, among other things. To say that certain herbs are believed by some to have curative powers is one thing; to claim they will cure anything is selling by means of false representation. Remember this story whenever you make claims of any kind about your products or services.

Using a Post Office Box

Some people wonder whether they should use a post office box number as their business address since prospective customers might be suspicious of it. All I know for sure is, in over twenty-five years of selling by mail from a box address, I've never seen any indication of concern from buyers, nor has this had any apparent effect on the volume of mail I routinely receive from publicity mentions. Given some people's reluctance to deal with homebased businesses, the use of an easily recognized residential street address might actually deter more buyers than a post office box number.

Although the U.S. Postal Service will deliver business mail to a home address, a post office box number is the best way I know to keep a low profile in the community and discourage drop-in customers. As mentioned in the "Licenses and Permits" section, it can also be a helpful way to get around local zoning laws that prohibit businesses at home.

Moving presents a problem for many mail-order businesses because mail is normally forwarded for one year only (in the United States), after which time it is stamped "Moved, not forwardable" and returned to sender (free, if mailed first class; postage due, if bulk mailed with an "Address Correction Requested" line under your address). Since ads and publicity in books and magazines often pull for several years, this is a great way to lose orders and prospective customers. The answer I've found is *not* to enter a change-of-address card when you move. Instead, retain the post office box as long as sufficient mail is received to warrant its cost, and hire someone locally to pick up and forward the mail. This person can rubber-stamp all first-class mail with your new address (*i.e.,* *"Please forward to . . . "*) and drop it into the nearest mailbox. The post office will forward this kind of mail indefinitely at no extra cost. Other classes of mail, however, must be repackaged and forwarded at regular postage costs.

When you wish to discontinue the use of the box and hiring of an individual to forward your mail, *then* enter a change-of-address card, at which point the post office will continue to forward your mail for another year. Remember to guarantee forwarding postage on second-class mail (periodicals), and keep in mind that third-class bulk mail will not be forwarded even if you guarantee postage.

Retirement Plans

Individual Retirement Account (IRA)

An IRA is a good way for self-employed individuals to shelter some of their income from taxes while building a retirement nest egg. Wage earners are currently entitled to put up to $2,000 of earnings into an IRA. Self-employed individuals may also contribute to a Keogh Plan, discussed below. This money will eventually be taxed, of course, but you will presumably be in a lower tax bracket when you retire. Withdrawals from an IRA may begin at age 59½ or be delayed up to age 70½. There is a 10 percent penalty for a withdrawal before age 59½, and taxes would be due on such funds at that time. (You may draw on an IRA without penalty if you become disabled before age 59½, and in the event of death, IRA funds are paid to one's beneficiary.) Under current law (always subject to change), *deductions* for IRAs are primarily limited to those who do not participate in the pension plan of their employer.

You have until the due date (not including filing extensions) of your tax return each year to establish or contribute to an IRA. Once you open an account, you can contribute varying amounts each year, or make no contribution at all. And if your first IRA ends up paying lower interest rates than new ones that come to your attention later, you can stop paying into the first one and open one or more additional accounts as desired. All will continue to earn interest for you until you decide to withdraw funds. At retirement, you can elect to withdraw all the funds at once (and

Tip:

In addition to contributing to one's own IRA, a current entrepreneurial tax strategy is to hire one's spouse to perform work for the business, pay that spouse at least $2,000 per year, and take this amount as a business deduction. Meanwhile, the spouse places this $2,000 into an IRA, legally avoiding taxes on it until retirement age.

pay taxes accordingly), or withdraw money in installments as needed.

Simplified Employee Pension (SEP)

SEP plans, originally established for self-employed individuals, partnerships and corporations, were repealed in 1996 and replaced with a new plan similar to a 401(k). SEPs adopted before the end of 1996 were not affected by this ruling, however. For more information on the new retirement plan, talk to your accountant, banker or financial planner.

Keogh Plan

Self-employed individuals may establish Keogh plans for purposes of sheltering larger amounts of their earnings each year than is possible with an IRA. There are many similarities between IRAs and Keogh plans, such as withdrawal requirements and penalties, but each has advantages and disadvantages. The main difference with a Keogh is that a self-employed individual may shelter the lesser of $30,000 or 25 percent of compensation per eligible employee on a pretax basis. The amount contributed is deductible from federal and, in most cases, state income taxes, and all earnings grow on a tax-deferred basis. New plans must be established by December 31 and contributions must be made by the company's tax filing deadline. If you have employees, you may have to include them in your plan, too.

Taxes

As a business owner, you need to be concerned about several kinds of taxes, more if you're an employer than if you're not. Canadian readers are on their own here—tax laws are far too complicated for me to try to outline what's applicable in another country. For U.S. readers, however, your taxes include the following:

Local Taxes

In addition to certain local taxes, your state or local governments may impose an inventory tax—a property tax, actually—on business equipment and inventory, such as the for-sale goods you're holding, or the large supply of books you've just self-published. You'll have to investigate this point on your own.

State and Sales Taxes

These include Income Tax, Unemployment Tax (if you have employees) and Sales Tax. Most states have an income tax. Like the federal income tax, it's calculated on your net income or profit and is generally due at the same time you file your annual federal tax return. In addition to state sales tax, there may be local sales tax as well. All are calculated together and paid to the state on a regular basis. In recent years, many states have tried to force businesses to collect use taxes on sales made to buyers in states other than their own. Mail order businesses everywhere heaved a sigh of relief in the fall of 1992 when the U.S. Supreme Court ruled states could not legally do this, but this decision only opened the door to the possibility of a national sales tax. Meanwhile, many states are fighting back by requiring taxpayers to file use-tax returns on out-of-state purchases. Stay aware of what's happening here.

Resale Tax Number. Resale tax numbers are required by sellers in most states. Anyone who sells a product (goods) in a state that collects tax must obtain a tax number from the state even if they do not sell directly to the ultimate user. This resale number may be called different things in different states, but the idea is the same everywhere. You collect sales tax on sales *to the final user* in your state, then send this money to the state with the appropriate form. Small businesses may be able to file annual reports; others will have to file quarterly or monthly, depending on total sales and amount of taxes normally collected. When you apply for a tax number, your state will send you information and instructions on how much tax to collect, when to file and so on.

Some people think their tax number entitles them to avoid sales tax on business-related purchases; not so. *This number applies only to merchandise purchased for resale.* The suppliers you deal with will want your number for their files, and whenever you sell to dealers, be sure to get their number for yours. This documents to the state why you haven't collected tax on a sale. (If you sell wholesale to dealers who do not have a tax number, you have to charge them sales tax on their purchases.)

Another misconception about a sales tax number is it automatically entitles one to buy goods at wholesale prices. This is not true. Each manufacturer and wholesaler has its own terms and conditions of sale. In addition to establishing certain minimum quantities, these suppliers may also have strict policies against selling to anyone who is not a retailer (owner of a shop or store).

Federal Taxes

Included are Owner-Manager's Income Tax or Corporation Income Tax, and Employee Income Tax and Unemployment Tax (if you have employees). Estimated Tax Payments, which are due from self-employed individuals, must be made quarterly, on

Tip:

If you are a self-employed married woman who files taxes jointly with your husband, but uses a different name from your husband's, *it is possible your social security payments are not being properly credited to your account. One woman learned of this problem after she had been married and filing jointly for twelve years. Social Security says it can't correct a problem after three years because their records aren't saved longer than this, but the fact that this woman had kept tax records for all those years made it possible for her to prove she'd actually made the payments. This appears to be a common problem. What apparently happens is that IRS employees assume all women share their husbands' names. By not looking closely enough at the joint return, they send incorrect information to Social Security, causing a mismatch of the woman's name and number, allowing her payments to go uncredited.*

the fifteenth of April, June, September and January. Naturally, there's a penalty for not paying taxes when due, as well as for underestimating them. An accountant will help you figure out the amount you need to pay each quarter.

Hobby Income. The IRS says you are in business if you (1) are sincerely trying to make a profit, (2) are making regular business transactions and (3) have made a profit at least three years out of five. (There have been exceptions to the last rule. In the end, the most important factors are the amount of time you devote to your activity, plus the way you present yourself to the public as being engaged in the sale of products or services; also the way you keep records of your business.) If you do not meet IRS criteria, your business will be ruled a "hobby" and any loss you deducted will be disallowed. (You can show a loss on a business, but not on a hobby.)

If you decide you want to work at home only as a hobby, you are still required to report your hobby income on Schedule C of Form 1040, and list all the expenses you incurred to earn this income. If you end up with a profit, you'll have to pay taxes on it. If you end up with a loss, however, you are not entitled to a deduction, but you *can* deduct expenses up to the amount of your hobby income.

Social Security Taxes

When the profit on your Schedule C tax report reaches $400 or more, you must file a Self-Employment Form along with your regular income tax form and pay into your personal social security account at a rate and wage base that is continually being increased. However, with the last increase, self-employed individuals received some relief in the form of an income deduction (or credit) equal to half the amount of self-employment tax (which could be taken from us at anytime). Check with the IRS or an accountant each year to learn the new rate and periodically request a statement of the earnings posted to your social security record. To get it, send a request for "Summary Statement of Earnings" to Department of Health & Human Services, Social Security Administration, Baltimore, MD 21235. Include your social security number and date of birth.

If you are collecting social security and want to start a business, be aware that until you are seventy, you are limited in the amount you can earn without losing any of your benefits. This dollar amount (available from your local social security office) has been rising slowing through the years, and someday it is hoped Congress will allow senior citizens to work and earn unlimited income without losing benefits. After the age of seventy, there is no earnings limit, but by then we may be too tired to work that hard.

SCHEDULE C
(Form 1040)

Department of the Treasury
Internal Revenue Service   (T)

Profit or Loss From Business
(Sole Proprietorship)

▶ Partnerships, joint ventures, etc., must file Form 1065.

▶ Attach to Form 1040 or Form 1041.   ▶ See Instructions for Schedule C (Form 1040).

OMB No. 1545-0074

1995

Attachment
Sequence No. **09**

Name of proprietor

Social security number (SSN)

A Principal business or profession, including product or service (see page C-1)

B Enter principal business code
(see page C-6) ▶

C Business name. If no separate business name, leave blank.

D Employer ID number (EIN), if any

E Business address (including suite or room no.) ▶
City, town or post office, state, and ZIP code

F Accounting method: **(1)** ☐ Cash **(2)** ☐ Accrual **(3)** ☐ Other (specify) ▶

G Method(s) used to
value closing inventory: **(1)** ☐ Cost **(2)** ☐ Lower of cost or market **(3)** ☐ Other (attach explanation) **(4)** ☐ Does not apply (if checked, skip line H) | Yes | No |

H Was there any change in determining quantities, costs, or valuations between opening and closing inventory? If "Yes," attach explanation

I Did you "materially participate" in the operation of this business during 1995? If "No," see page C-2 for limit on losses.

J If you started or acquired this business during 1995, check here . . . . ▶ ☐

Part I   Income

1 Gross receipts or sales. Caution: *If this income was reported to you on Form W-2 and the "Statutory employee" box on that form was checked, see page C-2 and check here* . . . . ▶ ☐	**1**	
2 Returns and allowances	**2**	
3 Subtract line 2 from line 1	**3**	
4 Cost of goods sold (from line 40 on page 2)	**4**	
5 Gross profit. Subtract line 4 from line 3	**5**	
6 Other income, including Federal and state gasoline or fuel tax credit or refund (see page C-2)	**6**	
7 Gross income. Add lines 5 and 6 . . . . ▶	**7**	

Part II   Expenses. Enter expenses for business use of your home **only** on line 30.

8 Advertising	**8**		**19** Pension and profit-sharing plans	**19**	
9 Bad debts from sales or services (see page C-3)	**9**		**20** Rent or lease (see page C-4):		
			a Vehicles, machinery, and equipment	**20a**	
10 Car and truck expenses (see page C-3)	**10**		**b** Other business property	**20b**	
11 Commissions and fees.	**11**		**21** Repairs and maintenance	**21**	
12 Depletion.	**12**		**22** Supplies (not included in Part III)	**22**	
13 Depreciation and section 179 expense deduction (not included in Part III) (see page C-3)	**13**		**23** Taxes and licenses	**23**	
			24 Travel, meals, and entertainment:		
14 Employee benefit programs (other than on line 19)	**14**		**a** Travel	**24a**	
15 Insurance (other than health)	**15**		**b** Meals and entertainment .		
16 Interest:			**c** Enter 50% of line 24b subject to limitations (see page C-4) .		
a Mortgage (paid to banks, etc.)	**16a**		**d** Subtract line 24c from line 24b	**24d**	
b Other.	**16b**		**25** Utilities	**25**	
17 Legal and professional services	**17**		**26** Wages (less employment credits) .	**26**	
18 Office expense	**18**		**27** Other expenses (from line 46 on page 2)	**27**	

28 Total expenses before expenses for business use of home. Add lines 8 through 27 in columns. ▶	**28**	
29 Tentative profit (loss). Subtract line 28 from line 7	**29**	
30 Expenses for business use of your home. Attach **Form 8829**	**30**	
31 Net profit or (loss). Subtract line 30 from line 29.		
• If a profit, enter on **Form 1040, line 12,** and ALSO on **Schedule SE, line 2** (statutory employees, see page C-5). Estates and trusts, enter on Form 1041, line 3.	**31**	
• If a loss, you MUST go on to line 32.		
32 If you have a loss, check the box that describes your investment in this activity (see page C-5).		
• If you checked 32a, enter the loss on **Form 1040, line 12,** and ALSO on **Schedule SE, line 2** (statutory employees, see page C-5). Estates and trusts, enter on Form 1041, line 3.	**32a** ☐ All investment is at risk. **32b** ☐ Some investment is not at risk.	
• If you checked 32b, you MUST attach **Form 6198.**		

For Paperwork Reduction Act Notice, see Form 1040 Instructions. **105**   Cat. No. 11334P   **Schedule C (Form 1040) 1995**

Self-employed individuals also have the option of using Schedule C-EZ (stands for "easy"). It has just three lines: gross receipts, total expenses and net profit. To qualify, one must use the cash method of accounting, have no inventory, own only one business, have no employees, and not have a net loss. Gross receipts must be $25,000 or less, expenses $2,000 or less, and you can't take deductions for the business use of your home.

Telephone

Telephone companies in both the United States and Canada have taken notice of the growing work-at-home industry, and some now publish promotional newsletters designed to educate home-office workers to the wonders of telephone technology now available to them. Be sure to contact your local telephone company to see what special literature they may be able to send you about extra lines or numbers for business, special phone equipment, voice mail, electronic mail, availability of toll-free numbers and so on.

Many home-business owners use their personal telephone for business, then list this number on their business cards and stationery, not realizing this may be a violation of local telephone company regulations. In the United States, each state has a separate commission that determines the usage of a residential phone, so you need to check on this, too. In some instances, a fine may be imposed for improper use; in others, you may only be asked to stop doing this. Still others may simply start charging you business rates.

Getting an extra line for business may be easier and less expensive than you think. Some phone companies offer special "Remote Relay Services" or "phantom phones." Here, you keep your personal line and the phone company sets up a separate business number for you. Calls to the business number are relayed through your personal phone line and charged separately. Such approved business numbers can then be legally advertised.

Although you cannot legally advertise a personal phone number in connection with a homebased business in the United States, you can receive business phone calls on it and make outgoing calls, deducting expenses for long-distance business calls. (The IRS now limits deductions of other portions of a personal phone bill, and since they may question your long distance business charges, it would be a good idea to keep a telephone log to substantiate your business deductions.)

Until you have a separate business line or other approved arrangement, do not answer your residential phone with your business name. Instead, answer with your name. For example, "This is Barbara Brabec. May I help you?"

Canada's telephone policy seems liberal. In B.C., for example, B.C. Tel is an active supporter of the work-at-home movement and has made it easy for people to switch over from a residential to a business line by removing some inequities in their rate structure to make the move more desirable. They also emphasize that a business phone includes a free listing in the yellow pages.

Save on Long-Distance Calls

As you know, there are many long-distance providers such as AT&T, MCI and Sprint. But are you aware that a growing number of U.S. entrepreneurs are now buying time from AT&T and reselling it to small business owners at rates lower than those offered through regular long-distance companies? These companies are known as AT&T Software Defined Network (SDN) Resellers, and by signing up with one of them, you may be able to save up to 20 percent on long-distance calls, enjoying the same low rates enjoyed by major corporations. Such companies advertise in business periodicals.

Toll-Free Numbers

They've been in use since 1967, and now that they have become so affordable, more and more small businesses are using them to draw prospect inquiries and orders resulting from advertising or publicity. For example, AT&T advises that a homebased business can add a toll-free number that will come in on its regular line with no on-site hookups required. There is a one-time installation charge and a small, fixed monthly fee, plus the cost of calls, of course. Check your local phone company for more information.

See chapter twelve for information on 900 numbers, which are good extra-income or diversification tools.

Answering Machines and Voice Mail

You can leave one message on your answering machine and take one call at a time. This may be all many businesses need. But voice mail is an option some businesses have chosen because it allows them to leave a variety of messages for callers while taking several calls at once. Many phone companies and outside service bureaus offer voice mail services at affordable fees. Those who receive many calls or those who spend a lot of time providing the same information to many callers should find it most advantageous. Be aware, however, that many consumers dislike voice mail because they find it cold and impersonal.

If you're using an answering machine, be sure to keep your message short and to the point. "Move the caller from 'Hi' to 'Bye' as quickly as possible," says executive business specialist Laura M. Rubin. "If you're tempted to record an announcement in your best Donald Duck or Bela Lugosi voice, think again. Since one person's 'Ha Ha' is another person's 'Oh, No!', the safest thing to do is leave the cutesy greeting for contests and special occasions."

Fax Machines

Facsimile (fax) machines have become standard equipment for many home offices, their primary advantage being that they

Tip:

In selecting a business phone for your office, you might look for special features such as two lines (one for home and business), a hold button, speaker button, conference call button, pre-programmed memory buttons and auto redial. PureWater dealer Victoria Turner suggests you get a mute button, too, because it allows you to "hiss at the children while listening."

speed communications and make waiting for the mail a thing of the past. Many business owners have installed a fax machine not because they need to communicate by fax, but because they wish to accommodate customers and clients who now prefer this method of communication. Read home-office magazines for information on how to select a machine that's right for your needs.

Note: If you are planning to market your business by sending fax advertising, don't. The FCC's Telephone Consumer Protection Act, which became law in December, 1992, strictly prohibits the sending of unsolicited fax advertising or prerecorded telemarketing calls unless a prior business relationship exists or the sender has granted permission for such messages. (Five companies filed a lawsuit in mid-1993 to void the ban, which they claim violates free speech. Read business periodicals to stay current on this topic.)

Trademarks

A U.S. trademark "includes any word, name, symbol or device, or any combination thereof adopted and used by a manufacturer or merchant to identify his goods and distinguish them from those manufactured or sold by others," according to the Trademark Act of 1946. The primary function of a trademark in both the United States and Canada is to indicate origin, but in some cases it also serves as a guarantee of quality.

Generic and descriptive names in the public domain cannot be trademarked, nor can you adopt any trademark that is so similar to another that it is likely to confuse buyers. Trademarks thus prevent one company from trading on the good name and reputation of another.

Trademark searches can be done by an attorney, of course, but in the United States you can also do a search using the annual *Trademark Register of the U.S.*, which includes over 800,000 registered trademarks in use. Large city libraries may have a copy for your reference. Many libraries also subscribe to an online computer service such as Trademark Scan or Thomsen and Thomsen. Ask your library for more information since they may be able to help you make an economical trademark search. (There is a per-minute charge for this service.)

To establish a trademark in the United States, you first decide which mark you want to use, then do preliminary research to be reasonably sure no one else is using that mark. Then you take steps to prevent others from also using it on the same or related goods by filing an application for trademark with the Patent and Trademark Office in Washington, DC. Once the trademark registration has been confirmed, you place the notice of trademark, an *R* with a circle around it, after every use of the trademark word or symbol. (You may also use the words "Registered in U.S. Patent and Trademark Office" or "Reg. U.S. Pat. and Tm. Off.")

On the surface, it sounds simple enough to get a trademark, but the process could take as long as two years in the United States. If you do it yourself, the basic filing fee is only $200 (at present). Be sure to avail yourself of some of the self-help legal guides available in any library to lessen the chances of your application being rejected. In this event, you would be wise to hire an attorney to help you resolve any problems. Since the use of an attorney (whose rates may be as high as $300 an hour) could bring your total costs for filing up to $2,000 or more, you have to do some soul searching to decide whether the benefits are worth the cost.

Note: A 1989 change in trademark law made it easier for companies to register and protect a trademark. Under the old law, a trademark could not be registered until it was used in commerce, a requirement that has heretofore given a competitive edge to foreign companies who could obtain a U.S. registration without first using a mark in commerce. Under current law, a business is able to apply for a trademark and protect it for up to three years before actually using it in commerce. Renewals now take place every ten years, instead of every twenty, and there is a fee for renewal and a penalty for late renewal applications.

Common Law Trademark

Your constant use of an unregistered mark can gain trademark status through the years. Take this book's title, for example. As attorney Mary Helen Sears emphasizes, "Because it is strongly associated with Barbara Brabec in the minds of persons engaged in, or interested in engaging in, home-based business enterprises, the term 'Homemade Money' has acquired a secondary meaning, not only as the identification of a book that has the reputation of being *the* handbook and primer in how to start, maintain and conduct a home-based business, but as the trademark and service mark for educational materials relating to home-based business, and for educational and informational activity of all types in regard to such business." Thus, anyone using this phrase for their own profit would be in direct violation of trademark law 15 U.S.C. 1125(a), and I could take appropriate legal action against them.

Trade Secret

A "trade secret" is something a business owns that gives it a competitive advantage over others who do not know it. The

Tip:

U.S. companies generally use a "TM" symbol (or "SM" for a service mark) to indicate they are claiming a particular mark and may also be in the process of filing a trademark application. Although this symbol offers no statutory legal benefits, it does tend to deter others from using the mark. Since use of the TM symbol does not obligate you to actually file for trademark, you have nothing to lose by tacking it on to anything you're trying to protect.

Department of Labor provides this legal definition of trade secret: "Any confidential formula, pattern, process, device, information or compilation of information that is used in an employer's business, and that gives the employer an advantage over competitors who do not know or use it." More specifically, a trade secret might be the secret recipe that makes your catering service special; a VIP contacts list you've spent years developing; a foreign source of supply for a product much in demand, etc.

"If you invent a small device for cutting fingernails that can be easily copied, get a patent," says inventor Jeremy W. Gorman. "If you have a complex formula which will be essentially impossible to copy, keep it as a trade secret. Colors, flavors, perfumes and shampoos are commonly trade secrets."

Common law trade secret protection exists, and if anyone were to steal your trade secret, you might have grounds for a lawsuit.

Trade Practice Rules and Regulations
(See also Federal Trade Commission)

In addition to the laws pertaining to consumer safety and the labelling of certain products (as discussed earlier in the "Consumer Safety Laws" section), the FTC is especially concerned with truth in advertising, use of customer testimonials, guarantees and warranties, and the mail-order industry. When requesting information from the FTC, mention your type of business and specifically ask for information about rules relating to it. For instance, there are certain rules for industries such as jewelry making, leather, ladies' handbags, feathers and down, the catalog jewelry and giftware industry, millinery, photography, furniture making and mail order. When an FTC rule has been violated, it is customary for the Federal Trade Commission to order the violator to cease the illegal practice. No penalty is attached to most cease-and-desist orders, but violation of such an order may result in a fine.

United Parcel Service

You don't need an introduction to UPS, the most economical and dependable shipping service in the country, so this is just a reminder that UPS packages are rarely lost or damaged, and delivery halfway across the country takes only a few days. ("Blue Label" service is available at extra cost for packages that need even faster delivery.) UPS will pick up packages anywhere with just one day's notice—and that includes your residence. There is a modest weekly pickup charge that applies to the first pickup of the week and covers all other packages and pickups in that same week. Packages must be weighed beforehand by the mailer, who then calls the nearest UPS office (toll-free numbers provided) for postage applicable to each package. A simple form plus a check for total postage completes the process. Packages are automatically insured for up to $100 and additional insurance may be purchased if desired. Call your nearest UPS office and ask for information about their "Ready Customer Pickup Service."

Note for U.S. Shippers: Do not use UPS when shipping items into Canada that could just as easily be mailed. All UPS packages must go through customs, causing delays and extra charges to customers who must pick up packages themselves. Fourth-class mail, however, is free from customs inspection and is delivered right to the customer's door.

Zoning Laws

Many homebased businesses in the United States are walking a thin line between being legal in the eyes of the IRS and illegal in the eyes of their local zoning boards. The problem is most zoning laws were written in horse-and-buggy days when no one could have imagined the millions of people who would someday be working in homebased occupations or businesses. However, due to the national media attention to this topic—the impact of flexible worksites, the electronic cottage, and the growing work-at-home movement—it is believed that more and more communities will soon be updating their laws to accommodate homebased entrepreneurs.

If you haven't done it already, learn where you stand by reading a copy of your community's zoning regulations (either at city hall or the library). Find out what zone you're in, and read the section that pertains to home occupations. Remember it's your right to see this information without explaining your interest in it.

If you rent, or live in a condominium or town house, be sure to check your lease, apartment regulations or condominium covenants for any clause that may prohibit a homebased business. A business in one unit of a co-op apartment, for example, can affect the tax-deductibility aspects of others in the building. So even if local zoning ordinances aren't a problem, this sort of thing could stop you dead in your tracks.

If you decide your business is violating local zoning laws but isn't going to create any problems for your neighbors or the community at large, you can either keep working as quietly as possible—and hope no one ever notices what you're doing—or you could ask for a variance or, more likely, some kind of "conditional use," "special use" or "special exemption" permit. This is generally issued following a public hearing about which your neighbors must be informed. If you can get support from

Tip:

If a customer asks you to send a UPS shipment C.O.D., and there is more than one carton or box per shipment, be sure to put a C.O.D. tag on each carton. One reader reported that a customer who ordered five cases of products returned the one case bearing her C.O.D. tag marked "delivery refused," but kept the other four cases and never paid for them.

Tip:

City officials do not go around checking to see who's violating zoning ordinances, but generally act only when a neighbor complains. Thus, many home-business owners have found it best to keep a low profile. They avoid loud noises, strong odors and obvious customer traffic. They don't tie up neighborhood parking places, use business signs, or do anything else not in keeping with the character of their residential neighborhood. In fact, they do their best to keep their business a complete secret—especially from busybody neighbors.

neighbors, the special permit may be easy to obtain.

Generally, there are no financial penalties for violating U.S. zoning laws provided one immediately ceases the activity when caught. In some Canadian cities, however, zoning convictions may result in a stiff fine.

If you enjoy a good fight, you might want to organize a group of homebased business owners in your community and try to get outdated zoning laws changed. Start now to build a list of all known homebased business owners who can give support or testimony when the time is right. (See chapter seven for encouraging examples of how others have fought and won their particular zoning battles.)

Endnote

The in-depth information in this chapter—*material that will not be found in any other home-business guide*—is possible only because hundreds of caring readers have shared their experiences with me through the years in hopes of helping others avoid problems they've encountered. Remember, too, that all material relating to accounting, banking, insurance, taxes, patents, copyrights, trademarks and labor law has been verified by attorneys and other business experts—an extra step taken to give readers added assurance of the accuracy of my research on each topic. In spite of this extra attention to detail, however, readers are once again reminded that it is neither my business nor the publisher's to render legal or accounting services, and both disclaim any personal liability, either directly or indirectly, for advice or information presented herein. *It would be prudent to consult a qualified professional before making an important business decision based on information in this chapter.*

If you would like to contribute a tip based on an expensive business or legal lesson you've learned, or share additional insight on any other topic discussed in this book, I'd be happy to incorporate this information into the next edition. Address such mail to: Barbara Brabec, HMM Feedback, P.O. Box 2137, Naperville IL 60567-2137.

PLANNING YOUR MOVES

BUSINESS PLANNING NEVER STOPS. It is something we must do at the beginning, in the middle, and even at the end of a business. In every business, there is a need for a variety of plans, including time plans (short-, medium- and long-range planning); creative, routine and problem-solving plans; marketing plans; and comprehensive business plans. In addition, the business novice needs to develop a start-up plan that takes into consideration all things discussed to this point in the book.

7

The first management job is planning, a combination of realistic calculations and crystal ball gazing. It is an exercise in arithmetic and imagination, in separating the possible from the impossible.
— from a booklet published by the U.S. Department of Labor

Writing a Business Plan

Few people would try to build a house without a blueprint and some skill as a builder. However, year after year, thousands of people with little or no real business sense try to build a business without any kind of plan. Often, new business owners—particularly home-business owners—begin as dreamers, believing their good ideas and willingness to work hard will get them through. But that is not enough. Statistics from Dun & Bradstreet and the U.S. Small Business Administration tell us that between 55 to 60 percent of all businesses fail within the first five years, and about 95 percent of these failures are attributable to poor management. Don't let these statistics frighten you away from your own business, but do let them serve as a constant reminder that certain business and management skills are essential to success in any money-making endeavor.

Business experts generally stress the importance of a business plan in connection with getting a loan. Experience has shown, however, that small, homebased businesses seldom qualify for bank loans, at least in the first few years of existence. Generally they are financed with money from personal savings or family loans. So if you're not planning to apply for a loan, and you are the only person who will ever see your business plan, why should you prepare one?

Peace of mind is one answer. "The benefit of a business plan is security in knowing what you need to do, how much it's all going to cost, and where you can go wrong," says one entrepreneur. Adds Laura M. Rubin, Executive Business Specialists, "Creating a business plan forced me to think specifically about my goals and the path I would take to reach them. I feel it is important to review your business plan on a regular basis. Not only will this keep you on track, it may also spark new ideas. I have found that change is the name of the game for my business plan; I have updated it on numerous occasions and will continue to do so."

No plan is etched in stone, and all plans have to be changed regularly, based on the records of past experience. Planning thus becomes more realistic and easier the longer you are in business.

A business plan need not follow any set pattern, nor be any set length, but it is important to get as much information on paper as possible. For instance, a business plan might cover thirty pages and contain several elements, including these (not necessarily in this order):

- **Business history.** How, why and when it came into being.
- **Business summary.** A definition of your business, a description of your business goals, products and services, including unique features or customer benefits.
- **Management information.** Who's behind the business, his/her experience, background, qualifications; the legal form business will take.
- **Manufacturing plan.** (if you are a manufacturer or creator of goods). Description of required equipment and facilities; how and where raw materials will be obtained, their estimated cost; how/where you will store/inventory them; labor and overhead costs involved in the manufacturing process.
- **Production plan.** How the work will get done; by whom, and at what cost.

- **Financial plan.** Your expected sales and expense figures for one year, cash flow figures for a year, and a balance sheet showing what the business has, what it owes and the investment of the owner.
- **Market research findings.** Your market, your customers, your competition.
- **Marketing plan.** How you are going to reach and sell to your market (distribution), and the anticipated cost of your marketing effort.

If you do not plan to apply for a loan, why should you bother with a written description of the first three elements in the above business plan outline? You'll know the answer to this the first time you have an opportunity for publicity. These are the points of most interest to many interviewers, reporters and editors who may give your business publicity in a feature article. Thinking them through in the beginning not only will make you feel good about yourself, but actually will give you ideas on how and where to get publicity once your business is rolling. Press releases are often "hooked" on news pegs like these, as you will learn in chapter eleven.

If you're a manufacturer, you will need to incorporate a manufacturing plan into your overall business plan. (Anyone who makes anything—by hand or by machinery—is a manufacturer, so when this word is used in later places in the book, remember it applies to you even if you make only one-of-a-kind, handcrafted wares.)

An important consideration in a small, one-person manufacturing company is who eventually will make the goods when demand for a product increases beyond the owner's ability to produce it. At this point, many business owners turn to independent contractors for assistance, forming small cottage industries that involve a number of homeworkers in one's community. Before you decide on the direction your growing company will take, however, be sure you are well versed in all the legal and tax aspects of using independent contractors vs. employees, a tricky gray area for today's entrepreneurs. (See "Independent Contractors vs. Employees," in chapter six.)

Your "Am I Legal?" Plan

In chapter two, I alerted you to business ideas that were unprofitable or illegal. In chapter five, I spoke about the importance of being legal in the eyes of tax authorities, and why it's a trap to generate money "under the table." In chapter six, you got a crash course in many other things legal and financial, including laws you wish you'd never heard of.

Some people violate a law out of ignorance (an excuse you

Zoning Laws Can be Changed

Before giving up on outdated zoning laws in your area, consider what you might do to get them changed. An organized group, especially one with some support from a notable person, has power. For example, one woman, concerned about the legality of her homebased sewing business, approached her state representative with the problem. Given assurance that her business would not be brought to the attention of local authorities, she gave her representative copies of a model zoning ordinance she had obtained from an organization to which she belonged. The representative met with city officials and in time brought about acceptable changes in the law. My reader concluded her letter with this note: "Please encourage your readers to write their legislators on all levels and to join and support home business organizations. I have . . . and I know it works."

Homebased entrepreneurs are now legal in Tigard, Oregon. The law change began with complaints from neighbors about a piano teacher who was holding evening recitals at home and tying up too many parking places on the street. After due consideration, the city council loosened its grip on the old zoning law. The new law allows for two kinds of permits: Type I allows no customers, employees or signs and requires no annual review, but the resident pays an annual business tax. Type II permits up to six customers daily, one employee and one small sign. The permit is given only after review by city staff and notice to nearby property owners. There is a one-time fee and business tax.

can't use with this book in hand), but others do it deliberately, perhaps because they feel a law is unfair. It well may be unfair—even unconstitutional in the eyes of many—but the fact remains that ignorance of the law is no excuse, and anyone who deliberately or unknowingly breaks the law must be prepared to pay the consequences. This might mean the complete stoppage of a business, a stiff fine, back taxes (plus interest), even a jail sentence. In some cases it could mean an expensive lawsuit instigated by your state or federal government, or another business whose rights you may have violated. By following the guidelines in chapter six, however, you'll be able to avoid many legal and financial pitfalls that will catch other business owners unaware. As you can see, it pays to "do your homework" in the beginning.

A primary goal of this book is to help you understand what you can and cannot do legally as a home-business owner, as well as make you aware of the personal and tax advantages of operating your business in an up-front manner. At one of my workshops, after I had talked for three hours about all the technicalities and legalities of home-business start-up, a small voice in the back asked, "Is it really worth all this effort?" I said I didn't know if it was worth it to her, but it was worth it to me. Only you can answer this question. Just remember every big job seems intimidating at first, even to a professional. The secret is to make a plan of the big job, then break it into a lot of little jobs. The task then becomes not only less frightening, but easier to do. As someone has said, "The only way to eat an elephant is one bite at a time." By putting your plans and ideas on paper, and addressing each sticky question or problem as it arises, you will enable yourself to take small business bites that are easy to mentally chew and digest.

Zoning Problems and Solutions

Zoning is just one of the those "sticky wicket" legal problems homebased entrepreneurs need to address. As you now realize, you could have the world's greatest idea for a profitable home business only to discover it is restricted by your local zoning ordinance. This has not stopped people from starting or operating homebased businesses, however. While you, too, may choose to operate illegally until things change, you do need to plan on the possibility that you might someday be caught and forced to cease business operations. (People are rarely fined for zoning violations unless they persist in the operation of a business after they've been warned to stop.)

Canadians seem to be faring better on the zoning front than their U.S. counterparts. A Canadian magazine, *Home Business Report*, indicates hiding business activities or ignoring licensing requirements could soon become unnecessary, thanks to the support Canadian homebased entrepreneurs are receiving from all sectors. "The education of both municipal leaders and home business people regarding their mutual needs will soon make the unlicensed home business cowering behind the furnace in the basement a thing of the past," said Carol Cram in a zoning update article for the magazine.

For perspective on the zoning problem in the United States, take a look at some of the reports my readers have sent me through the years:

- **Springdale, Arkansas.** A reader sent a newspaper article about a man who operated a wood framing business from his home. He had been reported by a neighbor who objected to the noise from customers and the parking of customer vehicles near the residence. When the city council decided not to renew permits for cottage industry in a residential area, the woodworker replied, "Whether you grant this license or not, the noise will continue because woodworking is also my hobby." The mayor then asked that the home occupation ordinance be reviewed, but as one alderman put it, "There are three different ways to cut this thing, and none of them will please all parties concerned."

- **Herndon, Virginia.** A quilting teacher who decided to be aboveboard obtained the required personal service license and zoning permit, which prohibits the following: signs, accessory buildings, displays, sales, consultation visits from clients for commissions, employees, and more than four students at a time, or more than eight in a day (which certainly limits this teacher's financial prospects). "What's especially irritating," she says, "is that I know at least ten people who flagrantly violate the ordinance, either with students or sales." It's this kind of situation that often prompts people to enter complaints against neighbors and friends. And if your neighbors don't get you, the competition might. (As soon as you give your illegal homebased business visibility with a shot of publicity or an ad in the paper, people can find you and turn you in.)

- **Andover, Massachusetts.** "When our town tried to outlaw homebased businesses on a technicality in the law," a reader reported, "several local homebased people, including myself, met with the building inspector and the Board of Selectmen. We reached this unofficial agreement: So long as the business did not disrupt the *general* residential area (one neighbor's complaint might be ignored), the business would be allowed to continue. Current law is vague in some areas and quite specific in others, so it was agreed that if a specific area of the law was violated, then the business would be asked to 'cease and desist' the activity that violated that particular part of the law."

- **Wichita, Kansas.** Some home businesses are allowed, others aren't. A reader reports you can make arts and crafts, but you can't "manufacture or process anything" (though, in truth,

One Woman's Zoning Battle

It took her five years, but Janet Hansen finally won the small zoning war she started in the Chicago suburb of Mount Prospect. While actively involved in a homebased business, Janet's efforts to change zoning laws were discussed in a feature newspaper article that clearly broadcast the illegality of her homebased business to everyone in the community. Curiously, nothing adverse happened as a result of this visibility and Janet's many meetings with city officials.

Her situation may have been helped by the fact that she was on the board of directors of the local chamber of commerce, and was president of its entrepreneur council. In short, everyone knew what she was doing, but no one wanted to do anything about it.

After trying to win the support of the chamber of commerce, Janet met with the mayor, who merely said that, since she had had no complaints against homebased businesses, she would not instruct the village to go after those running a business.

Janet later reported the village manager said they definitely did not want to change the zoning laws because of the opposition they expected from people with offices and stores. Five years later, however, Janet reported that her years of persistence had finally paid off. "Mount Prospect trustees have approved an ordinance that allows residents to operate businesses from their homes," she said. "Businesses will be allowed as long as they do not disturb the neighborhood or violate certain restrictions, which include no signs, no separate entrances, no customer visits and no outside employees."

Postal Outlets

If you don't want to use a post office box for your business mail but can't use your street address because of zoning problems, check into the services of Mail Boxes Etc. (a franchise operation found in both the United States and Canada) or similar postal outlets, which provide a business street address and suite number, telephone answering and mailing services, acceptance of packages from carriers (in case too-frequent deliveries to your home are a problem), and fax sending/receiving services.

if you make crafts, you are manufacturing them). You can't sell anything you don't make yourself, display a sign, conduct any business in the garage, or have an employee who doesn't live in your home.

Wayne R. Glass, director of Washburn University's Small Business Development Center in Topeka, says both the City of Topeka and Shawnee County have had an ordinance on the books for some time requiring a permit for operation of a business out of the home. "This was in addition to zoning laws that prohibited certain types of businesses, particularly retail, in residential areas," he adds. "Now Topeka has changed its ordinance to include a fee, supposedly to pay for inspections required by the law. It is unclear what purpose these inspections serve, although they are conducted. In order to stay consistent with Topeka, the county also changed its ordinance a few months later to include a fee.

"It's safe to say," he concludes, "that most homebased businesses are either ignoring the law or ignorant of it, although we now make a point of telling folks. The funny part is *the law is almost unenforceable and apparently carries no penalty for noncompliance.* In passing a law with no enforcement, and no obvious purpose, the politicians create a class of unwitting criminals."

What's curious is the fact that, in many communities, zoning officials who are well aware of the growing number of home businesses in their area simply continue to "look the other way." Apparently this is easier to do than changing the law.

In some areas, groups of home-business owners have formed networking groups or official organizations, done all the work involved in writing proposed zoning amendments, and then presented this information to city officials for consideration. After further discussion, sometimes in a town meeting, such efforts have resulted in changes in the law.

Many people operate in violation of zoning laws simply by keeping a low profile. But this means you can't advertise or seek publicity, and it's tough to make gains that way. Someone once asked me why so many homebased businesses are located in small towns and communities, or out in the country. Maybe it's because zoning ordinances are less of a problem there. If a home business is important to you, and it's currently prohibited by zoning ordinances, perhaps a relocation to another area is your best solution.

Business Incubators

Although most homebased entrepreneurs prefer to work in their homes, supplementary use of outside facilities known as business centers or "incubators" is one way to avoid zoning problems because a business would have a legal presence at the center itself.

A "business incubator" is a physical facility used to "hatch" small businesses by providing under one roof all the resources and facilities needed for their survival. Some entrepreneurs house their entire operation in such centers, while others simply use their "business identity package" service, which may include a business address, telephone answering service, secretarial, word processing and copying services, and the use of fax machines. Often, such business centers are started in small business development centers or by individual entrepreneurs in a position to acquire a building for such purposes.

Some business owners rent office space on an occasional basis. For example, a woman in one of my workshops said this had been the perfect solution for her business, not because of zoning problems, but because it was impossible for her to meet with clients with a baby underfoot. So each time she needed to confer with a client, she would grab her "office box" and set up temporary shop in the business center, just for an hour. In the box was an assortment of things one might normally expect to see in an office: a desk pad, pen set, calendar, pictures, etc. When she was finished, she packed up and went home with the client thinking this was her regular office. All her business calls were forwarded to her home phone through the business center, with only one small problem: There was an automatic cutoff after fifteen minutes, so every time the phone rang, she had to set a timer; if the call ran long, she sometimes had to get creative in making excuses for why she had to hang up and call back.

The Many Hats of Business

If you are like most home-business owners, you'll end up doing all the work for a while, so you may chuckle a bit when you get to the production plan. Still, it's important for you to figure out, in advance, exactly how you are going to get everything done in the time available to you. Stop and think about all the business hats you may have to wear, and be realistic about your ability to do all the work that may be involved. Following is a list of the many different people you may have to be at one time or another:

• **General Manager.** You get the worrisome jobs simply because you're the decision maker and risk taker. You also get to write all the business plans and read a wide variety of business publications to stay informed.

• **Marketing Manager.** You get the job of figuring out who customers might be, where they are and how you can sell to them. You, too, must read a variety of business and marketing publications to stay abreast of what's happening in your industry and which marketing strategies are likely to work for you.

- **Advertising Manager.** You work closely with the marketing manager to decide when and where to place ads, and what type (classified or display) to place. It's your job to send for rate cards and sample magazines (ad media kits).
- **Copywriter.** You get to write the copy that goes into the company's sales brochures, flyers and catalogs, not to mention press releases and advertisements. You will need to constantly hone your writing skills by studying the finer points of copywriting shared by experts in books and magazines.
- **Graphic Artist and Printer Liaison.** Naturally, you must work very closely with the copywriter to achieve the right blend of copy and art on all printed materials, and you get the job of pasting everything together for the printer, as well as following through to the completion of each job.
- **Production Manager.** You get to make the work schedules and determine the quality control standards of your product line.
- **Production Worker** (maybe the whole line). You must complete the work on schedule while meeting the above-mentioned quality control standards.
- **Mail List Supervisor.** You're the one who sets up and maintains the company's 3×5-card decks or other list addressing systems, adding and deleting names, making address corrections, etc. (The sooner you get a computer for this job, the better.)
- **Bulk Mail Expert.** And you get the irritating jobs of figuring out the post office requirements for third-class bulk mailings and of redoing the entire mailing when the post office tells you your rubber bands are all wrong.
- **Order Fulfillment Clerk.** You get to process orders and type the necessary order forms and shipping labels.
- **Shipping Clerk.** In addition to receiving shipments of raw materials for the manufacturing of products, you get to pack for shipment all outgoing orders, plus take a physical inventory at the end of the year for tax purposes. You will be greatly relieved when you can afford to hire an outside fulfillment center to handle all orders.
- **Secretary and Customer Relations Service.** You get to order office supplies, sign for packages, compose and type business letters, handle customer complaints and send away for everything needed by management (such as the resource materials listed in chapter sixteen).
- **File Clerk.** And you get the job of figuring out what to do with the mountain of paperwork everyone else in the company is generating every day.
- **Bookkeeper.** You will keep inventory records and post all income and expense figures to the company's journals and ledgers—after you have set them up, of course. You (or the accoun-

tant) will also approve and pay bills, balance the checkbook and organize and file all receipts for tax purposes.

- **Accountant.** You will analyze the books and handle whatever the bookkeeper can't do, such as fill out government forms for tax deposits or payments, do paperwork related to employees, and prepare quarterly and annual financial reports and tax returns. You will also take time to stay abreast of changes in tax laws that might affect your business.

- **Computer Expert.** One of you guys is also going to have to become the computer expert if you hope to long survive in business. (Let's give this job to the general manager, who started this whole thing.)

Some list, isn't it? Speaker, columnist and consultant Patricia Katz in Canada has taken a humorous approach to this topic by creating special cards for her entire family (see illustration). As you can see, she came up with some categories I hadn't thought of, such as manager of the humor department, cheerleader and captain of the "Knock 'Em Dead" Squad. The awesome list above still isn't complete because we've yet to add family and home responsibilities. Since there is a limit to what one person can do alone, it's wise to acknowledge your limits and plan early to find outside help, particularly within your own family. Include all possibilities for assistance, and think of creative ways you might pay for it, including bartering of services or products with business acquaintances, sales commission plans for people who might help you market your product or service and family bribes, if necessary. (Don't forget you can pay your kids a salary for meaningful work, and take an appropriate deduction on your taxes, as explained under "Employees" in chapter six.)

You may be thinking it's impossible for any one person to do all the individual jobs listed above; yet, that's exactly what you'll have to do if you are a sole proprietor with no money to hire outside help. Now do you understand why so many new businesses fail? Too many people start with no idea of all the work that must be done, let alone the special skills or experience some jobs require. As you can see, there are many individual and important jobs to be done, even in the smallest business, and your main job now is to decide which ones you are capable of doing—or learning—and which ones you'll have to get help with.

Except for the final preparation of tax forms (which I hate and never intend to do), I have learned to do every job on this list. But I've become familiar with every facet of the tax forms and monitor them like a hawk to make sure my accountant hasn't made a mistake. Although I do not have a college education, I've been working and studying all my life, always believing I could do exactly what I wanted to do. So far I've been able to learn everything I've needed to know and have attained every goal

Sheltered Workshops

Consider the use of sheltered workshops when you need outside help. Through the years, readers have often reported their satisfaction with the work done by such organizations, which hire mentally or physically handicapped individuals. Routine work of any kind, from handpainting to packaging, stuffing, cutting, etc. is offered at reasonable prices. In addition, you avoid problems with the Labor Department or IRS, which might consider other workers you hire as employees instead of independent contractors.

I've set for myself. I believe you can do the same with time and perseverance.

Remember there are how-to books for everything you can imagine, and your self-education can be reinforced with free information and assistance from your government as well as with seminars and workshops or outside consultants. True, it may take the next five years for you to learn what you need to know, but if self-sufficiency is your ultimate goal, what's five years in the scheme of things? Keep reminding yourself of what I emphasized in the beginning of this book: *Each new thing learned broadens your economic base, and each new skill increases your income potential.* Go for it!

Your Financial Plan

You may hate the idea of having to prepare a written financial plan, but it can be critical to the success of your endeavor, whether financing is being sought or not. You simply must know, in advance, how much everything is going to cost, and where you are going to get the money you need. So many businesses start in a whirlwind of activity only to falter a few months down the line because there is not enough money to keep going.

If you're already in business, it's not difficult to estimate the next year's sales and expenses. But how do you do this if you are just starting? It takes a lot of assumptions, to be sure. You are the only one who can project sales for the first year, and this projection can be based only on what you believe to be the salability of your product or service and your ability to market it. Much also depends on the time you're going to give your business. If you are a manufacturer, you probably can determine an estimated number of units that might be produced in a year, based on how long it takes to make one, and the number of hours you plan to devote to production each week. By setting a suggested retail price for each unit, you can estimate the revenue that would be generated if certain quantities were sold to certain markets at certain discounts.

If you offer a service, figure out the price you're going to receive for it and estimate the number of customers or clients you could reasonably expect to get as a result of your planned marketing efforts.

If you have difficulty thinking of all the expenses you might incur in the first year, refer to the checklist of tax deductions and other business expenses in chapter six, and use it to prepare an estimated expenses worksheet.

"Wise planners will take a somewhat conservative view of what is realistic when estimating what can be accomplished with any given level of staff and other resources," notes the Department of Labor in one of its booklets. "It is a disastrous mistake to assume that everything will go according to an ideal utilization of these resources, with no allowance for breakdowns of machinery, delayed deliveries, sickness and other disturbances of the perfect plan. You must build in a generous contingency factor in any plan—slippage is part of the human condition."

Slippage? You bet. The most important thing I have learned in over three decades of working at home is nothing is as simple as it seems, everything takes longer than expected and unexpected happenings will always force us to change our well-laid plans. There is so much more to running a business at home than just taking care of the business details involved in it. In addition to business, *there is life*, with its infinite variety of large and small crises—family problems, accidents, illness, death, divorce, fires, flooded basements and what have you. Experience has taught me to build a disaster element into all my plans. Given the unpredictability of life in general, and home businesses in particular, it's wise to anticipate the worst possible thing that could happen to your plans. (Remember Murphy's Law?) Once the worst has been imagined, you can plan around it—or "build in a generous contingency factor," as the Department of Labor suggests. Quick decisions, on the other hand, can be disastrous.

I recall a newspaper publisher who set her subscriber rates according to her print costs. She was working with the least-expensive printer in town and when he went bankrupt, she found that she could not afford the higher rates of other printers. After publishing only a few issues, she was forced out of business. *No matter what your business, always have an option in reserve. Never leave yourself without an escape route.*

A Few Words About Business Loans

You'll recall the general advice in chapter six about getting a business loan. Just remember banks love to loan money to "consumers" for worthwhile things like home improvement. (I got my first bank loan at age eighteen—for a vacation on a dude ranch.) Home equity loans are now common, but you may not know that home equity *lines of credit* are now available from many lenders, and this money could be used to start or advance a homebased business.

When you apply for a regular line-of-credit loan, your banker will tell you that collateral is needed. I learned from experience that such credit is also available on one's signature only, particularly if the business is profitable and you have a good credit rating and an account in good standing with the bank. When I started shopping for a line of credit after four years in business, I visited two local banks, explaining my needs and presenting each of them with what I felt was an impressive package of business and financial information. I was surprised when both banks indicated

Barbara's Beliefs

Nothing is as simple as it seems, everything takes longer than expected and unexpected happenings will always force us to change our well-laid plans.

Hope for the best, but prepare for the worst . . . and always leave yourself an escape route. Figure out the worst that could happen, then plan how to get out of trouble if it does. That knowledge alone will give you tremendous courage to try new ideas.

Tips on Time: How to Find It, Save It, Use It More Efficiently

- Try keeping a time sheet for a while so you can see exactly what percentage of your time is being spent on personal and business endeavors; then seek ways to cluster your various jobs to save time.

- Organize your home and your work space. You waste time every time you look for something that isn't where it ought to be. In getting organized, don't ask where to put something; ask how you plan to use it. This will suggest where to put it. If you don't need it, throw it away.

- Learn to do two things at a time, and develop production techniques in all your routine jobs.

- Time represents money to any businessperson, so don't give it away by selling your products or services too cheaply. And be selective in giving time and advice to others who would "pick your brain" once you have become successful in a given area of endeavor.

(continues on page 181)

an interest in loaning money. I selected the bank I wanted to do business with and went in for a visit. When the banker asked what collateral I was offering, I said with a smile, "You're looking at it: me." He pointed out (with a smile) that the bank's depositors aren't too thrilled with this kind of collateral and said that if I were truly serious about building my business, I ought to be willing to risk a second mortgage on the house or give up access to the family savings account.

I said no—it was a matter of principle at this point—that I was tired of having to use personal funds to advance my business, adding, "I've proven myself, shown what I could do with an initial investment of just $1,000—and besides, I have it on good authority that business loans do not have to be secured in this way, particularly when one's credit is excellent."

Grinning, he took another look at my papers. In the end, my ploy worked. I walked out of the bank with an unsecured line of credit (signature only) for $10,000—more than enough to meet my needs at any given time. All it took to get it was the right paperwork and a little moxie.

Time Management Strategies

Although one does not submit a time management plan to the banker along with the regular business and marketing plan, it's a good idea to think about this topic in the beginning. Full-time entrepreneurs should establish regular starting/stopping hours and try to adhere to them, although experience has shown that most new business owners will flog themselves relentlessly, working as many as 80 to 100 hours a week in the beginning. In chapter fourteen, "Maintaining Control," you'll find a discussion of where this may lead, and what to do when you burn out from overwork. If your business will be part-time, I suggest you try to identify at least 20 hours a week to devote to business. (This seems to be the average most part-time business owners work.)

Time management, like money management, requires an awareness of how much one has to spend. Although it takes time to plan how to spend time, such planning generally saves more time than it takes. That's because disorganization wastes time. Organization saves it.

The first principle of time management is to do one thing at a time, and finish it before starting another. That's fine if you happen to be talking about task consolidation, but all the successful businesspeople I know say their time-management secret is to do two things at once. Certainly that's my secret. Take this book, for instance. The original edition and all subsequent revisions have been done on a start-and-stop basis. Write a while; stop and do mail for a day. Write a while; go out of town for a speaking engagement. Write a while; stop to get out my newsletter, write a column, handle important correspondence, do a new PR mailing, or create my next direct mail piece. At any given moment in the daily life of my diversified home business, I am apt to be juggling a dozen different jobs at once.

Ideally, it would be terrific to have to think about only one of them at a time, but so often one thing is dependent upon another, and what you do in one area automatically requires some kind of counteraction in another area of the business. (Anyone who has a business knows exactly what I'm talking about. The rest of you will learn soon enough.)

Doing two things at once may sound difficult, but we do it all the time. For instance, I always work on the next day's meals as I am fixing the evening meal, and I always have pen and paper at hand to jot down ideas that come to me while I'm cooking. If a business phone call is a chatty one, I'm apt to be reorganizing or dusting my desk while I talk. I never fold laundry during the day, but during the evening, while watching the news; and when I do watch TV, I have reading material nearby for commercials. I pay bills in the morning while waiting for my husband to come to the table, put last night's dishes away while the cereal is cooking, throw in laundry on my coffee break, and on and on.

As homebased workers, we often will find ourselves in the position of rushing to complete a job or meet a deadline while also preparing to entertain guests for the weekend. In airports or in a doctor's office, we may wait, but we may also be doing business reading or planning. The more time we need for our business, the more creative we become in our attempts to save it by doing two things at once. Here are other ideas on how to accomplish more in the time available to you:

- Don't let family and friends steal your time, either. Be firm about having some private time for yourself, and set specific times for family activities or visits with friends.
- Establish a regular working schedule. Start work at the same time each day. Learn to leave business behind at the end of your working day, so you can enjoy a personal life, too.
- Change your attitude about time. Plan. Make lists. Study to improve skills and speed work processes. Move faster, sleep less. In short, use the time you do have in the most productive way possible . . . and quit wasting time talking about your lack of time.

Speed Production

"We all have 24 hours a day," says Dottie Walters, a popular author, speaker and owner of several businesses. "Most people waste much time. Do all the things in one direction together," she advises. Dottie is one of the busiest and most productive people I know, and she practices the advice given by Kipling, who said, "Fill every unforgiving minute with 60 seconds worth of distance run."

To do this, you have to look at everything you do—production, paperwork, mail handling, etc.—with an eye to grouping certain jobs that require similar physical movements, tools, supplies or a particular mindset. You lose time each time you have to change mental gears or physical position, so any time you can do a large block of work that takes a certain kind of mental concentration or physical movement, you will save time.

If you make a product, you will find you'll greatly increase output if you do the same step on at least two dozen items (one

No Jam This Year

"I began narrowing down my life in my mid-thirties," says Miriam Irwin, owner of Mosaic Press, a publisher of miniature books. "I gave up bridge, needlework and reading current novels to concentrate on writing and researching.

"In my mid-forties, I planned my publishing company. I gave up even more things I love to do. I have zeroed in on the one thing that has become by now almost a passion: I absolutely *love* publishing miniature books. It uses all my skills; all my talents, all my maturity, all my *patience*!

"This past year, I have given up one more thing in order to buy time to pursue publishing. I have a raspberry patch, and last summer it occurred to me that if I didn't pick and preserve raspberries, I would gain three or four days a year. This is the second year I haven't given in to the raspberry urge; and would you believe I still have jam left over from three years ago? This just shows that whatever I did, I did with great gusto—but it diverted precious time and I have the discipline now to *not do everything*.

"Of course, by next year I may be out of raspberry jam and feel entirely different about all this."

craftswoman says she does 100) at a time, then move on to the second step and do that on those same items, etc. For example, imagine you're making a sawed-out, handpainted toy. First you would transfer the pattern to the wood for 24 items, then cut out (saw) 24 items, then sand them and so on. If your painted design involved six colors of paint, you would add the first color to 24 items, then the second color, etc. *Every unnecessary movement you can eliminate will save time and speed production.*

Production techniques like this can be applied to every part of your daily and business life, resulting in the saving of many precious minutes each day that can be put to better use. Start thinking now about things you can do to give yourself the extra hours you are going to need for your business.

Speed Mail Handling

Many people waste time in handling daily mail, doing a little bit every day just to get it out of the way. This can be a real time-waster, especially if your mail-handling job involves numerous operations, as ours does. For instance, each day we have a considerable volume of information inquiries, orders for a variety of books and reports, and correspondence that requires special handling or phone calls. Each step of our mail-handling operation requires a different type of handling, and we have found we can save several hours a week merely by doing mail only two or three days a week, instead of piecemeal, five days a week. All book orders are handled at once, then all other orders and information requested. The idea behind this is simple: Whenever you can do twenty or thirty things at a time, versus five or six, you'll save time because you are incorporating production-line techniques into your work schedule. (Your customers will never notice this short delay in handling orders; in fact, ours frequently compliment us on our speedy service.)

For example, if you are putting out a batch of mail that involves say, a letter, a two-page, stapled report and possibly other insertions as well, you'll waste a lot of time if you do each package as one unit. Instead, collate all the two-page reports laying them crossways in a pile to separate each unit. Then go back and staple all the reports; then go back and fold all the reports. Next, fold all the letters. Then, lay all folded materials and other insertions in stacks in the order in which they are to go in the envelopes, and collate the individual packets, either laying them crossways in stacks to keep units separate from one another, or placing several items inside a common carrier, such as the cover letter. Finally, insert those packets into envelopes. And if you have dozens or hundreds of such pieces to mail, try my technique for speeding the stuffing and sealing process.

Barbara's Secret Envelope Stuffing/Sealing Trick. Here is one of the greatest time-savers you'll ever discover in the handling of mail in quantity. I developed it out of sheer desperation many years ago when we were doing cooperative mailings of 5,000 pieces and doing all the work ourselves because we had no money to hire help.

Take about ten business-size envelopes in your left hand and ruffle them out to the right so you can see about ⅛″ of the bottom of each envelope, a movement you might make if you were going to count them easily. While you continue to hold these envelopes in your left hand (reverse everything if you're left-handed), use your right hand to pick up a packet of material to be inserted into the first envelope. Now, with the little finger of your right hand, flick the flap of the envelope open and, as the hand starts the downward swing, insert the packet of material into the envelope (all the while holding the other envelopes in position beneath). Drop the stuffed envelope off to the right with envelope flap still in the up position—still holding the rest of the envelopes in your left hand in their original position—and repeat the process until you have all envelopes stuffed. Then stack the stuffed envelopes in their original envelope box or similar container, flaps up.

Sealing the envelopes can be done in quantity, as follows: Fan about ten stuffed envelopes, flaps up, one on top of the other, until only the glue area of each envelope's edge is showing. Now hold the flaps down flat with the fingers of one hand while taking a wet pastry brush or sponge in the other, and lightly coat the entire glue surface of all envelopes in a couple of quick movements. Now—quickly, before the glue starts to dry—turn down the flap of the first envelope on the pile and with the left hand flick it away from the rest of the stack, then press down the flap of the next envelope, flick it away, and so on until all envelopes are sealed. Then pick up all packets and give them an extra press to ensure a good seal. You can work with as many as 20 stuffed envelopes at a time once you get the hang of it. (To really save time, challenge your kids to master the technique and let them have races to see who can stuff and seal 50 envelopes fastest.)

Speed Paper Handling

I laugh every time I hear an organizational expert say that, to be efficient, we must handle mail or paper only once. "Respond to it, file it or throw it away," sounds good in theory but works in practice only if one has tons of time or a secretary or file clerk. In working alone, I must give all my paper triage, assigning it to piles of (1) telephone; (2) respond immediately; (3) answer A.S.A.P.; (4) follow up; (5) send for; (6) read it later; (7) file for (some special later use); and (8) send to. (I got a good chuckle

Handling Information Overload

To successfully manage information, you must have a clear picture of how you are using it. As you handle your print material and electronic files, always ask yourself how you plan to use the information at hand. Forget about filing things alphabetically or by subject category. Instead, consider the thing you thought of when you first encountered the information, which will automatically tell you how you plan to use it in the future. My proven system is to sort information as it relates to:

- letters to write
- networking calls to make
- things to send for
- things to send to other people
- new projects in progress, or idea files for books, newsletters, workshops, reports, etc.
- information that updates my various books and reports
- resource material on a variety of special topics
- mail list update information (I keep folders for each database that regularly requires address changes or other notations)

(continues on page 185)

the day I read that the real definition of "FYI" [For Your Information] is "I got this in the mail and don't know what to do with it.")

While I take the time to thumb through my first-class mail every day, I simply can't "process it" daily because to write well, I need two- or three-day blocks of time when I don't have to think about any of the questions or problems in my daily mail. Thus double or triple handling is the name of the paper game for me.

Keep Track of Time

People who have learned to control time, instead of letting time control them, are generally organized, self-disciplined workers. You can't begin to save time if you don't know how you're spending (wasting) it, so, for a while at least, keep a written record of how you spend your time. (It's the same principle as noting everything you eat when you are on a diet, to see where all those extra calories and pounds are coming from.)

This exercise proved beneficial to me back in 1985 when I began to wonder whether I was wasting my time by performing certain routine tasks or doing other jobs that ought to be farmed out. I didn't have a computer at that time, so I also needed to know exactly how much time I was spending on the development and maintenance of my mailing list. It took a great deal of discipline, but I kept a faithful log for an entire year, logging a total of 2,235 hours on the business, not counting 5 full workshop days out of town. At year's end, I felt as though I had worked around the clock all year long. In truth, I found that time not devoted to the business totaled the equivalent of 93 days—including normal days off plus lost time of all kinds.

The average employed person who works a 40-hour week puts in 2,000 work hours a year (allowing a 2-week vacation). When one works at home, however, work hours may run from early A.M. to late P.M., yet with normal home and family interruptions, one is lucky to end up with eight hours a day in which to conduct a full-time business. Unlike employed workers, home-business owners must work irregular hours, and because we have to squeeze in work time whenever we can, we get the feeling that we're working *all the time*. Therefore, you may feel better about your business if you keep a true record of the time devoted to it. You may find that, for the hours you're expending, you're earning a better hourly wage than you thought. Or, you may find you're wasting time on one facet of your business that isn't profitable. You can then take whatever steps are necessary to correct the situation.

In studying how I'd used my time that first year, I began to see what I had to do to become more efficient. This was when I knew I could not long delay the purchase of a computer, for I found that management of my mail list was eating up 12 percent of my time, and handling my mail (including processing of subscriptions, renewals and routine address changes) was occupying another 20 percent. Two months after getting my computer (while continuing my time log), I saw a dramatic saving of time and an overall increase in productivity in both my writing time and management of my ever-growing mail list.

Make Lists

Time management experts always advise, "make lists," and busy, organized people do tend to be list-makers. As a list-maker myself, I know this saves not only time, but mental anguish. Often, without a list, you may feel there is so much to do you can't possibly handle it all. Yet, once a list is made, it seems less impossible. In addition to being time-efficient, lists of things to be done are great spirit-lifters. The very act of scratching off each task as it is completed gives one the sense of accomplishing yet another small goal. It's little things like this that keep us going when the pressures of business tend to pull us down.

In setting priorities on the things to be done, note that the 80/20 rule will apply. In mail order, this rule relates to the fact that 20 percent of your customers generally account for 80 percent of your business. In an office, it means that 20 percent of the people do 80 percent of the work, and, in matters of time, it means that 20 percent of what you do will probably yield 80 percent of the results. So be sure you identify—and place uppermost on your list—the 20 percent of the work that's the most important to your business or personal life.

Rarely will you get to the bottom of any list, but don't fret about it. Just keep putting the most important things at the top, and as time goes on, the jobs at the bottom that you never have time for will seem less important, or will automatically take care of themselves. (It's like leftovers in the refrigerator; we keep them because we'd feel guilty if we threw them out, but after a respectable "holding period," it's easy to justify dumping them.)

Get Organized

A record of how you spend your time will automatically help you get organized, but if disorganization is a problem for you, I suggest you read a book or two on this topic, any lengthy discussion of which is beyond the scope of this book. I do wish to emphasize, however, that being organized is not the same as being neat. Years ago, one of my favorite bosses, then co-owner of a direct mail advertising firm in Chicago, had a desk I couldn't believe. It was always loaded with foot-high stacks of one kind of paper or another, and I longed to organize it. But on my first day in the

- marketing activities (promotional and copywriting ideas, sample mail pieces, etc.)
- marketing leads (people to call, promotional mailings to make)
- publicity contacts (send news release or press kit)
- office management (tax info, insurance, suppliers, computer reference)
- material requiring library research
- new business or money-making ideas

At year's end, set aside a day to browse through your information files to see what can be dumped. While some information will always retain its value, other information gradually ages until it can no longer be used.

"Everyone has the ability to be orga-nized," says Stephanie Winston, au-thor of Getting Organized *(Warner Books) and owner of a time manage-ment consulting firm. "If you can man-age to cross Columbus Circle in New York, an intersection of eight streets, you have the potential to be orga-nized. It's simply a matter of negotiation."*

office, Bob warned me sharply, "Don't ever touch a thing on my desk. It may look a mess, but I know where everything is." And he did. Often when I would ask him for a certain file, he'd run his fingers down a stack of material and, to my astonishment, pull out exactly what I needed.

Now that my office looks just like Bob's, I know why he worked this way. Out of sight, out of mind. I worry about things I can't see, and if I file something that requires any kind of later action, I forget about it because I have too many things on my mind all the time. So the best way for me to remember what has to be done is to actually see the work stacked somewhere, beg-ging my attention. Thus, my desk is loaded with racks of manila file folders, mail-holding trays, spindles of notes and other piles of "to do" work. It doesn't look beautiful, but I know where every-thing is. If you work like this, and are criticized for it, tell your critics this is one of your time-saving devices. (If you can manage to keep the entire surface of your desk covered with paper, you'll never have to dust it.)

It's not that I'm disorganized, it's merely that I cannot seem to do my kind of work in any other manner. Or, as Harold S. Geneen says in his book, *Managing*, "If you are on the firing line with the leadership of several projects, you are going to have 89 things on your desk, ten others on the floor beside you, and eight others on the credenza behind you."

In *Organizing Your Home Office For Success* (the first book dedicated to teaching home-office professionals how to or-ganize their offices), author Lisa Kanarek says, "It's easy to con-fuse perfectionism with organization. Perfectionists stuff papers, supplies and anything else that would otherwise clutter a desk into drawers to be dealt with later. They want to give the appear-ance of being organized, yet when it's time to work, they spend extra time taking everything out again. Being organized means setting up your office to be functional, so that you don't have to rearrange your desk when you are ready to work."

Designer Judy Mahlstedt used to feel guilty about the way she worked—until she read that people who are dominated by the right half of the brain (as the majority of creative people are) often function better in controlled chaos than they do in an organized environment. "Right brain people are stimulated by working on several projects at once," she wrote. "We need to be surrounded by the tools of our trade. We think better when we are facing a deadline and will often put our action off until the last moment, although our minds are constantly hashing over the problem for days or weeks in advance. We can actually sabotage our creativity by attempting to follow the suggestions of well-meaning left-brain people who can't resist trying to physically organize us." Judy closed her letter by saying she naturally could not find the magazine in which the article appeared because she was trying to get organized by discarding her reading material as soon as she finished it.

After writing about this topic in my quarterly report, several subscribers wrote to say they were greatly relieved to know there was a term ("organized chaos") for their style of working, and that they weren't disorganized slobs after all. One reader found the perfect sign for this situation, but said there wasn't room to put it on her desk: *Neat desk—empty mind. Cluttered desk— genius at work!*

DEVELOPING A MARKETING STRATEGY

8

. . . [O]f all the hats the small entrepreneur must wear, none is more deserving of time and attention than that labeled "Marketing/Sales Manager."
—Herman R. Holtz, in
The Secrets of Practical Marketing for Small Business

DON'T FEEL EMBARRASSED IF YOU don't understand what marketing is all about at this point. Even people with a college education in business and marketing don't understand some of the basic marketing principles you're about to learn. As a marketing major once told me: "The nuts-and-bolts rules of business are not mentioned in business school. It's assumed 100 percent of graduates will go to work for someone else who's already figured it out. A marketing major is trained to be a salesperson. I was taught to sell but learned nothing about the channels of distribution, advertising or sources of supply for businesses outside of the Fortune 500. It is expected you will learn these things on your way up the corporate ladder in your chosen industry."

Don't let the word "marketing" intimidate you. It is just a cumulative word that describes a company's total promotion, advertising and sales activities. There is a difference between sales and marketing, and you should know it since you may have to do both jobs for a while. A *salesperson* is concerned with what products he or she has to offer, and which of their features can be emphasized to make the sale. The *person in marketing*, on the other hand, needs to be concerned with what customers want, how many different kinds of customers there are (called the "universe"), how they can be located, and how they then can be convinced of the benefits of the company's products.

"The marketer must know what he wants the customer to perceive," says author and marketing consultant Herman R. Holtz. "All marketing must then be directed toward creating that image and making it a credible one. Your perception of your business is not worth two cents unless it agrees with the customer's perception. Or perhaps we ought to turn that around and point out that you must somehow create a customer perception that fits the perception you have."

So what you need to concentrate on is not your product or service per se, but its benefits to users. More important to customers than the quality of your product or the swiftness of your service is how well it's going to satisfy their needs or desires. Or, as one writer said in a marketing article, "People buy drills because they want holes."

In an article in *Publishers Weekly*, Leonard Felder explained how marketing concepts have changed in recent years. In the old days, he pointed out, all you had to do was build a better mousetrap, then go out and sell it. Now, he says, "Any old mousetrap can catch mice. But consumers want a silent unseen trap that leaves no mess and won't hurt domestic animals; they want, in other words, not only relief from mice, but also safety, cleanliness, convenience and peace of mind." In short, Felder explains, "the goal of selling mousetraps has now been replaced by the goal of marketing a service to customers who need safe, clean and convenient protection from mice." If you are going to bring in the dollars from a business today, you need to apply this kind of thinking to every product or service you sell.

Most entrepreneurs learn about marketing the hard way, by making expensive mistakes that teach them what not to do the next time around—like placing display ads in the wrong publications, exhibiting in trade shows without a knowledge of industry pricing structures or channels of distribution, or offering the right product or service to the wrong audience and vice versa.

Like Alice in Wonderland, many business beginners lack a sense of direction:

Alice asks the cat: *"Can you tell me, please, which way I should walk from here?"*

Market Research

Although sophisticated marketers use demographics available from government sources (such as the Census Bureau) and statistical information compiled by trade associations, publications and private research firms, small businesses rarely need to go to such lengths to learn about their market. Many simply talk to potential buyers to see if there's any interest, network with other business professionals at conferences or trade shows, or browse shops, stores and mailorder catalogs to see what's selling at what price.

Here are five reasons why people don't buy:

- No trust
- No need
- No money
- No hurry and
- No desire

The cat replies, *"That depends on which way you want to go."*

So it is in marketing. Once you have determined your most likely market, you need a plan—some kind of roadmap—to get your products from here to there. It begins with market research.

Market Research

Before you can successfully launch a business, you need to do *market research* to identify, describe and categorize the current and future market for a particular product or service. This research is concerned with the customer, the product or service, the competition, and outside forces (like the economy) that might affect one's business. It is interesting detective work and a critical part of your marketing plan.

To take the mystery out of marketing, look for clues to who your customers or clients might be, where they are located, and how you might reach them with publicity, advertising or sales calls. It's not enough to know that a market exists for what you offer. *What is important is that you know—in advance—exactly how you're going to connect with it, promote to it and sell to it.* Too many sellers make the mistake of offering a product or service that pleases them, rather than one people may want to buy. This is backward thinking. You will find it is a lot easier to fill an existing need than it is to create your own market. The following questions will help you define the market for any new product or service:

- What exactly am I trying to sell? (If you can't define your product or service in 50 words or less, you will have a hard time trying to publicize or advertise it.)
- Why do I think my product or service will sell?
- Is my product or service something people want or need? What are its benefits to buyers?
- If it's something people do not need, why might they want to buy it anyway? (As a gift? For leisure-time enjoyment? Business convenience? To save time, money, aggravation? To beautify their home, enrich their life, or satisfy a nostalgic desire?)
- Who is my ideal customer or client? (Male? Female? Young, middle-aged, older? A white-collar worker? Blue-collar worker? Corporate executive? Homebased businessperson? Professional or technical worker, homemaker, consumer . . . who, exactly?)
- Where do my clients or customers live or work? (In the community, my county, my state, a specific geographic region or nationwide? Worldwide, maybe?)
- How can I connect with these people? What trade or consumer periodicals, organizations, trade shows, directories or

mailing lists are available? What established networks exist for my clients or customers?

- Is my product or service available elsewhere, in stores or by mail? At retail or wholesale prices? Can I compete pricewise?
- Is there currently a strong demand for my product or service? Why? Is it related to the economy? Is demand likely to increase or decrease with a change in the economy? Is the current demand a fad or should it endure for a long time? If a fad, can I move quickly to capitalize on it before it dies?
- Is the market for my product or service likely to expand slowly, quickly or not at all? Is my product or service closely tied to some other, similar product or service for which the market could expand—or collapse—very quickly?
- Is my entry into the marketplace more dependent on price than on quality? If so, can I successfully compete in this type of market, given my access to raw materials or supplies, and my ability to purchase them?
- What kind of competition will I/do I have . . . locally, regionally, nationally?
- Is my product or service newer, better, different from that of my competition? Does it offer higher quality? Longer life? More speed or efficiency? (The very fact that competition exists proves a demand, or at least a need, for what you offer. In the end, your competition may become your marketing strength, provided you work with it and not against it. More about this later.)
- How does my competition publicize and sell? Will the same techniques work for me? What can I offer, say and do that they can't?
- Is the competition overlooking a segment of the market I can reach? (Larger companies often ignore smaller markets because they are not worth the time and trouble, but such markets may be perfect niche markets for homebased entrepreneurs—particularly those who sell by mail.)
- If there is no competition, why? (Maybe the need for your product or service is being satisfied in some other way; maybe it simply is not a profitable idea to begin with; or maybe your idea is so new and unique, no one has thought of it yet.)

Positioning Your Business

"Positioning" is a common marketing strategy even the smallest business can employ. It is not something you do to your business so much as what you do to the minds of your prospects to make them perceive you in a particular way.

People's Needs Vs. Wants

What's the difference between selling something people need, as opposed to what they may only want? Here's how a family income development report, issued by Michigan State University, answered this question:

Most items produced by home industries . . . represent wants (discretionary purchases) on the part of the final consumer, not needs or necessities. The closer an item is to a necessity, and the farther the market extends beyond the local community, the greater the potential for success of the business.

Now Here's a Positioning Statement for You!

The owner of a homebased beauty shop doesn't just "do women's hair." No, she says, "I satisfy the need for physical enhancement among working women in my town who don't have much time."

Ask yourself what special needs your business satisfies, then create a strong positioning statement of your own.

In creating a "positioning statement," you need to consider what business you're in, your primary goal, what you feel your strengths and weaknesses are compared to those of your competition, and how you see the need for your product or service in today's marketplace. In short, you need to be able to state *why your product or service has value, and why it should be purchased.* (See example in sidebar.) No product or service can be all things to all people and if you do not deliberately position your products, services and your business itself, you may find they have been positioned by circumstances you do not control, and not always to your advantage.

Once you've written a positioning statement, try to create a "core concept" statement—a tight seven-word summarization of your positioning statement. Remember what you do isn't exactly what you *do.* For example, I write and publish books, produce a newsletter, speak and consult—but what I *really* do is *help people succeed in a homebased business.*

If you've already launched your business but got started on the wrong foot or just aren't doing well in the marketing department, maybe it's time for a change. "Change requires awareness," says Herman Holtz. "You must keep up, know your industry, know what's happening in the marketplace." Change is inevitable, but it requires courage, he stresses. "Timid, fearful business people tend to cling to the old way stubbornly, irrationally and *fatefully.*"

Perhaps you've heard the old adage about how stupid it is to keep doing the same thing in the same way while expecting different results. Yet this is just what many unsuccessful business owners are doing. They keep placing the same kind of ineffective ad or sending the same kind of direct mailer, or attending the same kind of shows, hoping each time for a different response than they received the last time around, when what they really need to do is *try a different marketing strategy.*

These examples will help you understand the importance of properly positioning your business in the marketplace:

- When the JCPenney Company decided to quit selling appliances, automotive parts, lawn and garden supplies, paint, fabric and certain hardware items, they reportedly spent more than a billion dollars to reposition 450 of their largest stores as "apparel and home furnishing stores."
- When the traditional cedar chest (often called the "Hope" chest) fell out of favor with young brides, the Lane Company began to call its products "love chests," thus positioning itself as "the company that makes furniture for lovers."
- A candymaker who began with a mailing to 75 friends on his Christmas card list went on to generate candy sales of more than a million dollars a year. Positioning in the marketplace was

his key to success. Instead of selling candy in food and gourmet shops, where it was expensive in relation to other items being sold, he sold it in fine gift shops, where it was inexpensive when compared to other items being sold. (In addition, it was often the only edible in the shop.)

• When management of a local hospital started getting flack from its patients about the $16 charge being made for an ice pack, they neatly repositioned that ordinary item in the minds of patients by giving it a more expensive-sounding name: a "Thermal Therapy Kit."

Puppeteer Tim Selberg is an example of a businessperson who repositioned his business not because it wasn't doing well, but because he was ready to expand. For years, he sold his hand-made puppets exclusively to professional ventriloquists. In 1993, he repositioned his business by changing his logo to appeal to a younger, more contemporary audience. (See before and after illustrations.) He still sells to ventriloquists, but because he has gained a reputation as an artist in his field, he has launched a new line that appeals primarily to collectors.

As you will learn in the next chapter, one way to position products is to give them a special name or identity, as Tim Selberg has done. The title you use for yourself is also a powerful positioning tool and has much to do with the kind of customers and clients you will attract. For example, are you a "legal typist"

Top: Old image.
Bottom: New, younger, happier image.

Positioning

Positioning is an exercise in shaping customers' and prospects' perceptions of you and what you are selling. For positioning to be of maximum value to you, the image you build must be one that inspires the prospect to do business with you, and include within it the promised benefit—what I prefer to call "the promise."

As a consultant, I must sell my credentials as an expert to close sales, but that is not the primary positioning objective. In my case, positioning is creating the promise that I can help clients win government contracts. My clients see me as an avenue to winning the proposal competition and thus the contract. It is only when and if they gain this perception that they have even a slight interest in my credentials as an expert.

So for me, positioning means an image of someone who helps clients win contracts because he writes winning proposals. The expert credentials are secondary. Positioning works far better if you help the prospect think things out and work the promise into the image you are creating.

—Herman Holtz, business consultant and author of numerous business books

Customer Testimonials

In my continuing informal review of hundreds of marketing documents, I find only one in ten offers even the most cursory testimonial, even though testimonials, properly used, constitute a superb means of expediting sales.

Moreover, those who do use testimonials are not attempting to get and use endorsements that do them much good. A good testimonial must confirm the precise benefits a satisfied customer has gotten from the product or service you are now offering while also identifying the person giving the testimonial as someone your prospects can relate to.

Ever notice how many testimonials end with "Mrs. J.D., Sioux City"? My cynical mind immediately assumes there is no Mrs. J.D., that in fact she has been invented by the seller who actually doesn't have anyone who will stand up publicly and endorse his product or service.

Once you have obtained good testimonials, use them in every marketing document you produce. Every
(continues on page 195)

or a professional whose motto is "The Lawyer's Best Friend"? Are you the fellow down the street who fixes old furniture, or are you an "Old World Artisan" who offers expert refinishing of antiques? When I began my business, I called myself a "crafts marketing authority" because I began as a crafts seller, then went on to write a book and publish a crafts marketing newsletter. Initially, I attracted creative people only. With the publication of the first edition of this book, however, I had a product with a market much broader than the crafts industry. To tap it, I had to reposition myself and my business in the eyes of book buyers. I did this by (1) changing the name of my business from "Artisan Crafts" to "Barbara Brabec Productions"; (2) changing the name of my periodical from *Sharing Barbara's Mail* to *National Home Business Report*; and (3) changing what I called myself. I was the first one in the United States to use the title of "Home Business Development Specialist"—now there are quite a few of us. In total, this repositioning move greatly broadened my market, increased my sales, enhanced my reputation as an expert, and enabled me to command higher speaking fees—not bad for just changing a few words here and there.

A motto (a short expression of a guiding principle) is a good positioning tool, particularly when it points to an unfilled niche in the market or emphasizes something that is lacking in a competitor's product, as in "the only soap that floats." Many businesses use slogans as well. A slogan is *a word or phrase used to express a characteristic position, stand or goal of endeavor* and, like a motto, it is generally included in advertising to make a point. Slogans often "play on words" or add a touch of humor customers appreciate and long remember. For example, I spotted a window cleaning service that's using "Your Pane Is Our Pleasure" and a lawn service that claims "We're Easy To Get a Lawn With." My favorite is Art's Electric in Pullman, Washington, which coaxes, "Let Us Remove Your Shorts."

Reconsidering Your Pricing Strategies

The most expensive marketing mistakes are often those made as a result of hasty decisions based on inadequate market research or knowledge about one's industry. Such business ignorance, coupled with a lack of self-confidence or a fear of losing sales (or not getting customers at all) may also cause novice business owners to charge much less than the market will actually bear, making business survival almost impossible.

I can't begin to tell you how many business beginners have told me they've deliberately set their prices low so they can undercut the competition. One fellow who bragged about his low prices and the fact that he was taking business away from others said he could afford to do this because he didn't have to make a living at it like the others. What can I say, except that I deplore such an attitude, and I don't know a single professional who operates this way. Yet I understand how timid most of you are when you begin to set prices on the value of your time and the worth of your special products and services. Do you recall my earlier comments about the psychology of pricing and how the mere change of a name can make a product seem worth more in buyers' minds? Now consider your pricing strategies on a broader scale, and think how they might affect the way buyers will position you or your business in their minds.

If you enter the marketplace with prices that are too low to begin with, buyers may think you less worthy than your competition, being naturally suspicious of anyone who would offer good products or services at too-low prices. On the other hand, prices that are too high can just as easily position you in prospect's minds as being totally out of their financial reach when these may be the very people you're counting on to build your business. Thus pricing becomes an important part of your overall marketing strategy, and you can't set the right prices without a thorough understanding of your costs, your industry, the economy and a dozen other factors, not the least of which is your reputation as a business owner, entrepreneur, expert or whatever.

There comes a time, I've learned from experience, when it's necessary to raise prices not merely because they are justified by increased inflation or the cost of doing business, but simply as a matter of principle. For example, through the years I've gradually raised the fee I charge for seminars and keynote addresses, not out of greed but because the audience I'm now marketing to expects an internationally known author and industry leader to charge accordingly. I would soon lose credibility as a business authority if I didn't demand prices similar to other professionals in my field.

Now relate this logic to your own business. If you do something better than someone else, don't be afraid to say so, and *charge accordingly.* Be prepared to lose a few customers and prospects when you raise your prices, but don't fret about it because you will automatically attract a whole new audience of buyers who can finally relate to you *because your pricing fits their preconceived notion of what a business like yours ought to be charging.*

I firmly believe that, as water always seeks its own level, so too will a business find its own level (market) by the way it prices its products and services.

time you make a major claim for what you're selling, provide a satisfied-buyer testimonial for that claim. For example, when I tell prospects that my book, Money Making Marketing, *"tells you precisely what you need to know to write direct mail letters that your prospects will read and respond to faster," I follow this major claim with this kind of testimonial: "Using Jeffrey Lant's* Money Making Marketing, *my direct mail letters are not only better, they are getting a greater response. My last mailing got an 8 percent return!" (Then use the person's full name and city/state location.)*

Don't be sheepish about prompting your customers for testimonials. Ask them about particular aspects of your product or service, write down what they say, and then ask for their permission (which you must always have) to use it. The meek do not do well at marketing.

—Jeffrey Lant, author and publisher of *Money Making Marketing* and other marketing books for entrepreneurs

The Age of Skepticism

A new reader once wrote: "You may be a hoax and you're really a grumpy gremlin raking in money in a cave—but your publication

Don't Discuss Prices!

It's great to network with the competition . . . but are you aware you can't legally meet with your competition to discuss the prices you're charging?

You can keep tabs on what your competitors are charging, then adjust your prices accordingly, but it's a violation of the Sherman Antitrust Act to *discuss* this action with the competition. Each year, many small businesses who mistakenly believe this law applies only to "big business" find themselves facing lawsuits, so be careful.

comes across as being written by a warm and caring person, so I shall picture you that way."

While this letter gave me a chuckle, it also reminded me that we are living in what *Direct Marketing Magazine* once called "The Age of Skepticism," which is "the age in which nobody believes anybody, in which claims of superiority are challenged just because they're claims, in which consumers express surprise when something they buy actually performs the way it was advertised to perform."

So how do you sell to skeptics? First, be sincere when promoting yourself, your products, your services. Offer testimonials from real people who endorse and embrace what you're offering and always include a money-back guarantee of satisfaction. Also remember to play to the three great buying motivators, which are *GREED*, *GUILT* and *FEAR*.

In your ad or promotional copy, approach *GREED* as "what you can get here with less effort"; *GUILT* as "what you'll miss if you don't respond"; and *FEAR* as "what may happen to you if you don't order *NOW*." I admit it's a challenge to be sincere while also being clever enough to play on people's emotions like this, but this is a knack we must all develop if we are to become successful sellers.

Studying and Working With the Competition

One of the smartest marketing moves you can make is to work with your competitors, not against them. Donald Moore, a publisher in England, says it best: "Your competitor as an enemy will give you nothing but competition; as a friend, he will give you information you can obtain in no other way. Everyone running a business should be keen to meet as many men and women in the same field of endeavour as can possibly be managed." I agree. As a leader in the home business industry, I have worked very closely with my competitors for years and, in fact, credit much of my success to their support of my work.

There is a feeling of family among home-business owners that enables many of them to work cooperatively, even when one might imagine the businesses would be natural competitors. One example that comes to mind is two word processing businesses in the same small community who work together passing job referrals back and forth. Because each specializes in a particular area and doesn't want the kind of work the other does, they are happy to trade business. They also use one another as independent contractors when the press of business becomes too heavy for them to handle alone.

"Some entrepreneurs believe that all competition is harmful to them," says business consultant and author Herman Holtz. "But there are others who believe that competition is the best thing that can happen to them because the combined effect of everyone's advertising and sales promotion creates a much larger market than anyone can create through his or her own efforts alone."

Networking

Business-to-business networking has become one of the most successful marketing strategies of homebased entrepreneurs. A *network* is a system of supportive people who are interested in one another and willing to help each other succeed. Your involvement in even one established home-business network could make the difference between success or failure in your particular endeavor. An involvement in several could double, triple or quadruple your chances for success.

While the obvious benefits of networking include industry contacts, a source of "inside information" and client referrals, many see networking as the ultimate advertising tool: Through networking you "get the word out" about your business without an outlay of cash.

Networking offers other benefits as well, says Joyce Zimmerman, an artists' representative and consultant. "It not only generates business leads but is a source of support and sharing of ideas and expertise between business owners. It also alleviates the loneliness and isolation of a homebased business."

"It works!" exclaims crafts business owner Donna Heidler. "I was once told that you are always only three people away from the person you want to talk to. A retail needlework shop owner (#1) introduced me to a published crochet designer (#2), who exposed me to the Society of Craft Designers where, after joining, I met a publisher (#3) who bought my first design for a magazine. One of the most important things I've learned is the importance of talking to everyone about my business."

Enthusiastic home-business owners are the first ones to recognize the need for organized networks that will enable them to trade information and ideas on a regular basis while also gaining encouragement and motivation. If a network doesn't already exist in your area, consider starting one. Two or three people can meet for lunch, or announce a meeting in the local library or chamber of commerce with a press release to the local paper. Although it's fairly easy to bring a local group together for the first few meetings, it's often difficult to hold it together. The demands of business tend to prevent attendance at meetings, and the one or two individuals who start a network may eventually pull back when they can't get any help from others. While such networks exist, however, they can be invaluable to beginners and pros alike, and they are always worth joining or starting.

Membership in a professional or trade organization is a

Networking

To build her market base, word processing specialist Jackie Herter began by networking statewide with court reporting firms and hospitals for transcription work. Now she also corresponds with federal and state agencies looking for contracts or subcontracts, is active in her local chamber of commerce and elementary school PTA. Through CompuServe's online services, she also networks with others in the legal and medical transcription field.

Equally important to many who now network online to advance their business are the many personal online support groups that now exist. People who are dealing with grief, medical problems and other personal situations may find hope and encouragement from others who share their problems and concerns.

wonderful way to make networking contacts. My younger sister Mollie Wakeman, who runs a busy music teaching studio in her home in California, has never found it necessary to advertise for students. In fact, she has always had a lengthy waiting list. After joining a music teachers association, she quickly learned the benefits of networking with the competition. Once she acquainted them with her special skills and background, teachers with too-busy schedules or a lack of expertise in a certain area began to refer students to her. For Mollie, a skilled teacher and performer, word-of-mouth advertising did the rest.

It was my other sister, Mary Kaufmann, who taught me the importance of networking with chamber of commerce members. When she was actively engaged in her own insurance business, her regular attendance at chamber meetings enabled her to get to know virtually everyone who was anyone in the Denver area—including many attorneys, bankers, doctors and other professionals who sent her a steady stream of referrals while also serving as an information pipeline to business happenings in the area.

And me? I haven't spent a dime on traditional advertising since 1983. Through networking, use of the media, promotional articles and newsletters, and regular direct-mail promotions to my prospect and customer lists, I have all the business I can handle.

Networking is not something that must be done in person. Many businesses network by mail or by phone after connecting at a conference or trade show or after reading about someone in a newsletter or magazine article. My readers have often reported on business gains they have made as a result of networking through one publication or another. Eileen Anderson of Word Enterprises in Minnesota told me she once thought networking was a waste of time. But that was before she wrote to me, had her letter published, and began to receive phone calls and letters from other readers. And because she made her business known to me, I later found an opportunity to refer her to a writer who gave her publicity in a national business magazine.

"Due to all this exposure," she wrote, "I have received numerous letters and phone calls from men and women across the country wanting help on starting their own homebased word processing business. That led me to write a book that contains all I have learned through years of research and personal experience. It's titled *Help! There's an Entrepreneur Inside Me!* I never would have had any of the exposure, nor would I have received the motivation to write my book, without the networking that resulted from the publication of my letter in your newsletter."

Niche Marketing

Any time is a good time to look for market niches—little "pockets of riches" your competition may be overlooking. Many businesses that have failed during hard economic times might have succeeded if they had simply concentrated on selling not to the masses, but to niche markets. Others might have survived if they had taken steps earlier to diversify their business. (Niche marketing and diversification are closely connected since the discovery of a niche market often requires one to create, or at least vary, an existing product or service. You'll find a wealth of diversification ideas in chapter twelve.)

What can you do to stand out in the crowd? Is there a niche your competition has failed to fill? Can you, perhaps, become a specialist in an area where there are many generalists? Specialization is an important marketing key today. In looking for niche markets, you've got to narrow your thinking and remember different segments of the marketplace will require different copywriting and advertising approaches. For example, if you have a product or service for mothers, are you really trying to reach every mother in the country, or only young working executives with preschool children and discretionary income? If you offer something for gardeners, are you trying to reach every gardener in the country, or only those who are interested in growing herbs or roses? If you're a business specialist, are you planning to help everyone in business, or will you target specific groups, such as retailers, small manufacturers, homebased entrepreneurs, or other business professionals such as doctors, lawyers and accountants?

The most successful niche marketers will always be those with special expertise in a particular area. Their knowledge and experience will enable them to speak to the market as a friend who knows and understands what they're going through. (I'm a perfect example of this kind of marketer.)

To find new niches for your products and services, begin by dividing your market into logical segments. Then take a closer look at each of the products and services you currently offer and relate them to the market segments you've just identified. Which of your products or services can be modified to serve a different segment of your market? Have the needs of one or more segments changed because of the economy, technology or other factors? If so, start brainstorming for new products and services you can add to your business mix, because each group of people or businesses with similar needs or demands adds up to another market niche just waiting to be filled.

Star Quality

In an interview, comedian Tim Conway once said he didn't think of himself as a "star," but that he had learned early on the importance of surrounding himself with people who were stars. He said the very fact that he was always in their company made others think of him as a star, too.

Interesting, isn't it? It works that way in business, too. To become a professional in any endeavor, it's a good idea to surround yourself with professionals. That old saying, "You're known by the company you keep," makes a lot of sense in this light, and Conway's remarks also add weight to the illusion-of-success comments nearby.

The Illusion of Success

While you're waiting for success to happen to you, remember the importance of maintaining the *illusion of success,* especially in those darkest hours when even you begin to have serious doubts about what you're doing. Make your business look financially successful even when it isn't by having classy stationery, cards, brochures, catalogs or other appropriate promotional materials. And when dealing with business contacts, always speak confidently.

People in the business world like to deal with confident, successful people because it makes them feel more important. Half of all big business is one big bluff, and you might as well play the game. Since nothing sells like success itself, even the illusion of success may be enough to convince a prospective buyer your products or services ought to be seriously considered for purchase. Nowhere is it written that you have to be honest to the point of saying, "You're my first client" or "I have only a few accounts right now." Instead, you could say, "My new service is generating considerable interest" or "You wouldn't believe the response I've received." You won't be lying, but you'll certainly be giving the impression that business is good.

It's rather like the story of the egotistical violinist who was looking for compliments after a bad performance. "How did I play tonight?" he asked a friend. Not wanting to hurt the violinist's feelings, the friend said, "I've never heard anything like it."

After publishing my "illusion of success" remarks in my newsletter, a reader responded: "You cleared up a point I had accepted in theory—maintain the illusion of success—but which I had not really been practicing. Sometimes we have an idea firmly in mind, but only in mind, and need a comment from a different angle to see how it can be put into practice for us."

Another reader saw it quite differently, however, saying that what I was suggesting was borderline dishonesty. "My business acquaintances are friends," she said, "and therefore my business relationships have to be built on trust and honor, just like my personal relationships." I agree, but my early years of experience in the "hard, cold business world" taught me it's not good business sense to tell all you know when you're negotiating a business deal or trying to close a sale. You can be honest and loyal while still "playing your hand close to your vest."

It's natural for different people to have different opinions on a topic like this and, in the end, we must all do what we believe to be right for us.

A crafts producer agrees: "I try to base my life on the Golden Rule," she says, "and I don't see any conflict with that if I tell a shop owner, 'This is my most popular item.' It doesn't matter whether you've sold three dozen or three hundred; if you've sold more of them than anything else, it's your most popular item. It also sounds more positive to say, 'This is a new design,' instead of, 'I haven't sold any of these yet,' though both statements are true. We've all found ourselves in a strange town at meal time, and nearly all of us will choose to eat at the restaurant with the larger crowd. That's reacting to the 'illusion of success,' so if we really want to be successful, looking as if we already are is a good way to start."

I'm reminded of a job my husband got shortly after we were married. He was a freelance drummer in Chicago at the time, and there was a great deal of competition for each job in town. When a contractor called and asked Harry if he had four kettle drums, he said yes. "But you don't have *one* drum, let alone *four*," I said worriedly. "Yeah," he replied with a grin, "but I know where to *get* them. If I'd been totally honest, I'd have lost the job."

Outline for a Simple Marketing Plan

I hope this chapter has given you a better understanding of what marketing is all about. Once you have answered the market research questions posed at the beginning of the chapter, it should be easy for you to write a marketing plan, even if the only marketing you've ever done before was shopping for groceries. Here's an outline to help you tighten your focus and draft a plan that will enable you to develop successful strategies for your business:

• **What do I do?** (Write a description of your business in 25 words or less.)

• **How does my product or service benefit buyers?** (Remember, buyers do not buy products or services per se, but rather the benefits offered by those products or services.)

• **How do I want to be perceived by my buyers or clients?** (Your positioning and core concept statements.)

• **What are the characteristics of my target audience?** (Indicate age, income, lifestyle, geographic location, etc., along with whatever your market research information to date tells you about the total number of potential customers in your target area, the share of the market you expect to capture, and why.)

• **Who is my competition?** (Write a description of your competitors, what you think their share of the market is, what you think their strengths and weaknesses are, what they might do to take business away from you and how you'd fight back.)

• **How will I market my product or service?** (Will you sell to the private sector or to the business community, and will you deal with buyers or clients directly or indirectly; retail or wholesale; market by mail; through reps, trade shows and so on. Also, could you diversify by licensing products or franchising a service?)

Marketing without a specific goal is futile. What are you really trying to accomplish with your advertising and promotion? Do you want to strengthen your professional image locally or nationally? Do you want orders with cash up-front . . . sales leads . . . or a mailing list you can use for direct mail promotions?

- **How will I advertise, and where?** (Display ads or classifieds in national magazines, ads in local papers, distribution of flyers, direct marketing methods, trade ads or shows and conventions? And don't forget your publicity opportunities!)
- **What are my selling policies?** (You'll need to establish standard credit terms, guaranties, customer discounts, returns policy, shipping or delivery charges, etc.)
- **Is my pricing OK?** (Is it in line with industry standards? Does the present economy in your market area justify higher or lower prices for certain products or services in your line? How do your prices compare to those of your competitors? If lower, are you sure you can make a profit after all costs are considered, and do you really want to accept anything less than what your competition gets? If your prices are higher, can you justify them by offering something special your competition does not? Why might your prospects gladly pay a higher price for what you offer? Again, think of the *benefits* you offer.)

You've got the idea now. After creating your first rough-draft marketing plan, you'll have something to build on. And, as you gain additional marketing information and expertise, you will begin to fully understand how better marketing automatically leads to greater income.

"A sound marketing plan," says one marketing expert, "is a prophecy of coming events. It contains the specific steps designed to make the prophecy come true." Like a business plan, a marketing plan will always be changing, based on sales results and the results of any special tests you may run. Marketing is something you must do throughout the entire life of your business, so don't think you can rest on your laurels once you have come up with a good marketing plan. It may work beautifully for a while. But you cannot expect to stay ahead of your competition unless you constantly test new markets, new marketing methods, and new advertising and promotional ideas. Nothing stays the same, least of all business, so be aware of changes taking place that may affect your business. The best way to do this, as I've emphasized before, is to subscribe to a variety of periodicals related to your field and join professional organizations so you can meet and network with your competition and customers.

In time, you may find it necessary to change your prices, your product or business name, your packaging, designs or colors, your marketing outlets, the function of your product or service, even the entire image or personality of your business. You will know when its time to make changes, too, because your sales will level off or begin to drop for no apparent reason. By doing a little planning before the worst happens, you'll be prepared to take off quickly in a new and more profitable direction.

PRICING FOR PROFIT

9

PRICING CAN MAKE OR BREAK YOUR business. That's why it must be your first marketing consideration. "If your price is wrong, it hardly matters whether you do everything else right," one expert has said.

Unless you are involved in a product business where the retail price of the merchandise you sell already has been set or suggested by someone else, you are going to have pricing problems of one kind or another throughout the life of your business. Product and service sellers alike need to be concerned with the same basic pricing factors: The value of one's time, profit, overhead, labor costs and so on. In addition, there are a number of intangible factors to consider, such as the way price affects one's image (and thus the growth of a business), the preconceived notions buyers have

Never charge a client what you think you're worth; charge what you think he's worth.
—Author unknown

about the worth of certain things, and market trends, among others. Product makers (manufacturers) have yet another major factor to consider: the cost of raw materials and their availability at wholesale prices.

As a consumer with a lifetime of shopping experience behind you, it's only natural to ask yourself how much you would be willing to pay for your product or service if you were the buyer instead of the seller. This kind of commonsense logic in evaluating the prices you set is fine if you happen to be selling to a market of buyers much like yourself. But unless you're rich, or at least a "free spender," you may find it hard to believe some people might actually pay the price you need to make a profit on whatever it is you are selling. People in this category tend to keep their prices low because they are afraid no one will buy at a higher price.

This is just one of the little traps sellers sometimes fall into. Time and again I have heard people say, "But no one will pay more than this for what I offer." Sometimes that's true, but often this statement is based on belief, not fact, and such belief is directly tied to one's own spending habits. While fearful sellers sit around complaining no one will pay more, smart entrepreneurs come along and offer the same kind of products and services at two or three times the price—and get it. Why? Because they know some things fearful sellers do not. They know their marketplace, they have marketing savvy, and they know exactly what it takes to get people to part with their money.

The Value of Your Time

Few people seem willing to set a price on the worth of their own time, yet everyone in business must do this, and soon. Most people who work at home don't have enough time to begin with. As their home-business workload increases, each hour seems more precious and fleeting.

The decision as to what one's time is worth is quite personal. It is influenced by many factors, including one's education or degree of skill, age, professional reputation (if any), amount of salaried job experience, level of confidence, and degree of boldness or nerve. Where a person lives also has much to do with the pricing of a product or service, as does a person's need for money or lack of need for it.

Homemakers-turned-business-owners often feel as though their time has no real value, particularly if they lack salaried job experience. But it is not job experience that determines the worth of one's time in a business, it is what one does with the time that counts. It's what you know, and what you know you are capable of doing. Don't sell yourself short. Your time is worth as much as anyone else's.

People with full-time jobs naturally equate the value of their time to their present salary, while others may decide on an hourly rate by asking themselves what they could earn if they went out and got a job. This is a good place to start, but Kate Kelly, author of *How to Set Your Fees and Get Them*, reminds us that self-employed people should multiply the hourly rate they receive in a salaried job by at least 2.5. In her book, she explains:

"Let's suppose that you're making $16,000 per year on staff. That means you earn approximately $308 per week; $62 per day, and $8 per hour.

To arrive at a starting figure for your hourly rate once you are self-employed, multiply $8 by 2.5 (some even say by 2.8 or 3). This means that you would use $20 an hour for your initial estimate as to what you might charge. . . . the true reason for the multiple figure is overhead."

I can just hear some of you product makers hollering, "But I can't charge $20/hour for my time. That would put the price of my products totally out of reason." If you're making all the products you sell, you may be right. But this only emphasizes the fact that it is difficult, if not impossible, to make a large amount of money when you—the business owner—are also the entire labor force. In that case, maybe what you ought to do is set several different hourly rates for the various jobs you do—perhaps $20/hour for design time or marketing and a lower rate for labor (based on whatever you would have to pay to hire a production worker).

Remember that while owners of product businesses can make a profit from the individual items they sell, owners of service businesses must include in their hourly price whatever profit they hope to realize at year's end. In truth, the only product they have to sell is their time and expertise, and it must be valued accordingly.

In this light, then, $20/hour isn't much money at all, especially when one considers what professionals in many fields currently receive. I think one problem here is many of us are still living in the past (particularly if we have been out of the job market for some time), before inflation took its toll and dramatically increased the price of everything. Many professionals who work at home command and get $50-$100 an hour and more for their services. But hourly rates like these are generally based on special skills, knowledge or years of experience in a particular field. You may have a long way to go before you reach this point, or you may be there now and just don't know it. One thing is sure: No matter how much an hour we are finally able to get, there will always be someone else who can get more, and all we can do is shake our heads in wonder. I felt terrific when I was finally able to get $1,000 a day as a speaker . . . until I met a fellow

Finding Supply Sources

One of the easiest ways to find the special suppliers you need—from raw materials to service providers—is to obtain copies of the Yellow Pages from large cities such as Chicago, New York or Los Angeles. Call your telephone office for information on how to obtain the directories you need.

Other suppliers can be found through library directories such as the *Thomas Register of American Manufacturers* and annual directories published by trade magazines such as *Gifts & Decorative Accessories* and *Profitable Crafts Merchandising*.

Another way to find the special suppliers you need is to network with others in your industry, through membership in professional or business organizations, as well as through subscriptions to newsletters and trade periodicals. Sometimes members of an organization band together to buy supplies on a cooperative basis—something you might want to explore.

who said he charged $1,000 an hour for his business advice. But as my husband has so often said, "Charging that much—and getting it—are two different things entirely."

Buying Materials Wholesale

Next to labor, cost of materials is the most important consideration in setting the price on any product. Small manufacturers and other individuals who create a limited number of products for sale each year often run into trouble when it comes to obtaining wholesale prices. Manufacturers and distributors in certain industries (the crafts industry, in particular) often will not sell to anyone lacking a storefront. (It doesn't matter whether a buyer can meet their minimum quantity order requirements or not.)

In other industries, suppliers don't care where one works; mostly they want evidence that you are a legitimate business and not a hobby buyer, have a resale tax number, and can meet their minimum order requirements. (Small budgets, however, sometimes make this impossible. And whenever any material used in the production of goods for sale has to be bought at retail prices, a lot of the maker's profit goes down the drain.)

Some manufacturers sell to dealers, bypassing wholesalers and distributors entirely, while others sell only through wholesalers and distributors. When you find a manufacturer who will sell to you at dealer prices, but whose minimum quantity requirements are too high, ask for the name of the distributor nearest you. If you cannot meet the distributor's minimum quantity requirement, the next thing to try is to approach a dealer who carries the materials you want. Ask for a 20 percent "professional discount," but if this is a retail store, don't do it in earshot of customers or you'll get a fast turn-down. Instead, telephone for an appointment to discuss your situation and explain the benefits to the retailer. (Your orders might enable the store to buy in greater quantity and thus get a greater discount on the material or item in question. This strategy has often worked for fabric buyers.)

With supplier catalogs in hand, your next job will be to convince them you are entitled to wholesale prices—a legitimate business. Do this by having a professional letterhead, and send well-typed letters requesting catalogs. Don't give explanations. Just say, "Will you please send me a copy of your current catalog? Thank you." The businesslike appearance of your letter should do the rest. (If you don't know the proper format for typing a business letter, obtain a secretarial how-to book from the library. If you don't have a typewriter or computer, plan to buy one and learn how to use it; or find someone to type your letters for you. Few businesses can function without a typewriter or other word processor, and even if they can, they won't be taken seriously by other businesspeople.)

When you receive a catalog and decide to order, be prepared to meet the company's minimum quantity requirements without question. If you are concerned that you might not qualify in their eyes as a legitimate dealer, send your first order on a purchase order (get them at any office supply store), include your resale tax number and enclose a check for the total amount of the order. (Few companies will turn away an order with a check attached.) You might also send a cover letter saying you are enclosing payment because you need the materials quickly. If you plan to continue ordering from this company, ask for a credit application at this time so you can be invoiced the next time around.

Finding reliable and affordable suppliers is a major challenge for all business owners regardless of size or type. It's a job you must do for yourself, and it may take a couple of years before you finally solve your particular supplier problems. Warning: Never build a business around a product that's available from only one source because you'll be out of business if that source ever dries up. Keep looking for alternative sources of supply you can tap in an emergency.

The Profit Factor

Many product makers think they are making a profit when in fact they are only *making money*. They may spend hundreds of hours building their inventory for a show. Then, when they come home with a sizable chunk of money in hand they think, "Gee look at all this money I made." They simply subtract the cost of their materials and show expenses from the total amount of money they have made and consider the difference their profit.

"Profit" and "wages" are not the same thing, though many who work at home tend to forget this fact. After all expenses (including owner's salary) have been deducted, the idea is that there still should be something left over as profit for the owner or company. But there won't be if you forget to include profit in your pricing formula.

It can be an expensive mistake to set the retail and wholesale price of a product based only on the cost of materials, labor and overhead. The following example illustrates what happens when you add a 10 percent or 20 percent profit factor to your pricing formula:

10 percent profit: $18 wholesale price $\times$ 10 percent = $1.80 + $18.00 = $19.80 adjusted wholesale
20 percent profit: $18 wholesale price $\times$ 20 percent = $3.60 + $18.00 = $21.60 adjusted wholesale

A Checklist of "Overhead" Items

In trying to determine your business's overhead costs, remember to include all of the following:

- Rent
- Utilities
- Telephone
- Postage
- Office supplies and equipment
- Insurance premiums
- Car expense
- Other transportation costs
- Employee expenses
- Maintenance
- Cleaning and repairs
- Business
- Interest expense
- Packing materials
- Freight charges
- All other costs related to the overall operation of a business

While this small hike in the wholesale price may mean little or nothing to the buyer, it can mean a lot to you. For example, if you sell 500 units of this item in a year, look what happens:

10 percent profit: $1.80 × 500 units = $900 profit for you
20 percent profit: $3.60 × 500 units = $1,800 profit for you.

And while you are thinking about that, here's another thought to ponder: If you work on a 10 percent profit margin, you will have to sell $1,000 worth of goods to offset a $100 loss; but at a 20 percent profit margin, you must sell only $500 worth of goods to offset the same $100 loss.

Bringing Overhead Into the Picture

Overhead includes all the operating costs of a business that are not directly related to the production of a specific product or service. Such costs are generally fixed, monthly expenses. Even when a business is generating zero income, overhead costs will be adding up. (See sidebar for list of typical overhead costs.)

If you have been in business for at least a year, it will be fairly easy for you to pull all these overhead figures together to arrive at an average monthly cost. If you are just starting, you can do some fancy guessing and estimating. (You might start with a figure that is 8 to 10 percent of anticipated gross sales.) To illustrate how overhead figures fit into the pricing picture, let's assume your annual business overhead costs are $3,000, and you're working 1,000 hours per year on your business. That means your hourly overhead rate is $3 per hour. You can either add this hourly figure to the one you arrived at earlier for your time, or, if you make goods for sale, you can apply it proportionally to each product on a percentage basis.

Assume for example a $3 per hour overhead cost. If you can make three of something per hour, you would add $1 to the labor and materials cost for each of those three products. Or, if it takes two hours to make a product, you would add $6 in overhead costs to each product.

Some production workers use a different method based on the total cost of labor plus materials. For example, if you spend $15,500 to produce your goods in a year, and you have $3,000 in overhead costs, you would divide $3,000 by $15,500 to get a 19.4 percent overhead to production. That translates to $.19, the amount that should be added to every dollar of production costs on an item.

Example: An item costs $10.39 in labor and materials. Add 19 percent of this figure ($1.97), increasing total cost to $12.36.

Start now to document all the overhead costs that will affect the profitability of your business in the months and years to come. At the beginning of each new business year, refer to these figures to see how much your overhead costs have increased because of inflation and other expense factors, then increase your prices if necessary.

Raise Profits by Cutting Costs

One of the smartest things I ever did was to become "unit price conscious." See the card below? At the end of my third year of business, I took the time to set up a three-year cost history of previous printing jobs, office supplies and other materials used in the business. I continue to use these cards today. Now, each time I order supplies or printing, I have a handy record of where I last got them, and at what price. By checking invoices against these cards, I can quickly spot any billing errors that might occur, and what I see on the card may also prompt me to look for a new source of supply, or perhaps increase the size of certain orders to get a better discount. (I don't include shipping costs in my per-unit figures because I want to compare apples to apples when

Analyze, Analyze!

The only way to assure continued profits for any business is through constant analysis of what's happening in that business. Whether you are selling products or services, it's important to periodically study sales and cost figures relating to your business. In them you will discover clues to what you must do to increase profits each year. Sometimes it means cutting expenses or increasing the price of certain products or services; sometimes it means adding something else to your line (which, incidentally, may have little effect on your overhead costs); and sometimes it means dropping a product or activity that clearly is proving to be unprofitable.

ARTICLE				
71629				
Date	Quantity	Price	Per	Purchased From

comparing suppliers. Freight costs mount up, and you may get not only lower unit prices from new suppliers, but cut shipping costs if they're nearer to you.)

Becoming unit-conscious in your business can result in increased profits at the end of the year. Whenever you see your suppliers increasing their prices, consider whether it's necessary for you to increase prices as well. Small business owners cannot afford to waste any of their profits, and attention to small details like this can often make a big difference.

Since profit is so closely tied to both sales and costs, you must consider both of them whenever you are looking for ways to increase your business profits. Selling more goods won't mean much if your costs also increase to any degree. On the other hand, if you can lower your costs, your profits will increase even when you don't make additional sales.

An accountant once told me it was a lot easier to increase profits by decreasing costs than by increasing sales, because of the high cost of marketing and obtaining each new customer. I can see the wisdom of that remark from a study of my own business records. I worked at my present business for almost two years before I found the time to get serious about my record books and the information in them. What I finally learned came as a real surprise.

A thorough analysis of your books after a year or so will no doubt surprise you, too, particularly if you make and sell a variety of products, or if you are involved in a diversified business involving both products and services. For example, I write articles and books, publish books, reports and a periodical, speak, and do some consulting. Each of these activities takes a certain amount of my time, a factor that is fairly easy to estimate on an annual basis. Although I always have kept track of the income each of my business activities has generated each month and year, it was not until my third year in business that I decided to break down all the business expenses and overhead costs relating to each of these income categories. Suddenly I could see what really was happening with the business. Then I knew the direction I had to take to realize greater profits in the years ahead.

At the same time, I began to analyze the income and expenses related to each item in my product line. Now I saw that some products that seemed to be making money (based on gross sales) really were not profitable at all in terms of their material and handling costs. As a result, I dropped some of them.

Perhaps a fictionalized account of a business that involves the sale of both products and services will give you a better idea of what I'm talking about. Let's assume a business grosses $120,000 one year, $100,000 of which is from the sale of products, the balance from some service—let's say teaching. Here's how the figures might look on the Schedule C tax report:

Gross receipts or sales	$100,000	
Cost of goods (labor + materials)	- 25,000	(25% of gross sales)
Gross profit	$ 75,000	(75% of gross sales)
Other income (services)	+ 20,000	
Gross income	$ 95,000	
Less business deductions	- 40,000	(42.1% of gross income)
Net profit before taxes	$ 55,000	(57.9% of gross sales)

There are many costs related to a product business, but the costs related to the service portion of this fictional business are nominal (a few materials and overhead expenses) because all direct expenses are paid in addition to the teacher's fee. That means the profit margin is going to be very high on the service side of this business, as the following illustration shows:

Product Portion of Business

$100,000		gross receipts
- 24,500	(24.5%)	labor + materials
$ 75,500	(75.5%)	gross profit
- 38,400	(38.4%)	deductions
$ 37,100	(37.1%)	net profit before taxes

Service Portion of Business

$ 20,000	
- 500	(2.50%)
$ 19,500	(97.50%)
- 1,600	(.08%)
$ 17,900	(89.50%)

In total, this fictional business has $65,000 in expenses. Although the bottom line is still the same—$55,000—the service portion of the business is clearly the most profitable in terms of labor, materials and other expenses. But, to really understand what's happening here, one would need to continue the analysis by separating all the income and cost figures for *each individual product or service*. Although there might be ten or twelve products in a line, such an exercise might show one of them was generating 50 percent of the income, and one or more were, in truth, costing more to inventory and ship than they were worth.

Whether this business owner decides to expand the service area or the product area would have much to do with the particular business and the market for the products or services it offers.

Setting a Cost-Competitive Price

"No matter which method is used to monitor costs," says the U.S. Department of Labor in one of its booklets, "costs alone are insufficient to fix a price. Expenses must tell the entrepreneur one important fact: the price below which he is losing money. Costs only set a floor. Consumer demand will set the ceiling. In between, the business person must fix a cost-competitive price. In the last analysis, your price must lie somewhere between a product's cost and the ability of the buyer to get it somewhere else."

Industry Pricing Guidelines

When trying to set the best selling price, keep industry guidelines in mind. For example, if you are in catering, you may learn from a book, as I did, that caterers all over the country just sigh when asked how they figure prices. Many say the question is too hard to answer concretely, but they do use a couple of "rule-of-thumb" formulas. In large cities like New York, caterers simply multiply the cost of ingredients by four or five, which amount is said to allow for all overhead, profit and labor costs. Other caterers, in smaller cities, multiply the cost of ingredients by three, then divide that figure by the total number of guests the client plans to invite to come up with a per-guest cost figure for the client.

Similar guidelines for other professions and industries will be found in books, some of which are listed in chapter sixteen; others can be found in a library. In one book or another, you are likely to find special pricing guidelines for people who offer typing, business and computer services, as well as those whose businesses include cooking, consulting, teaching, herbs and gardening, animals, music, child care, fine art, crafts, design, graphic arts, photography, repair services and so on. In short, you don't have to work in the dark; you just have to do a little research.

If it is a one-person manufacturing company, and no plans are being made to hire employees to increase productivity, then perhaps it would pay to drop part or all of the product line and concentrate on providing additional services. Choosing the right direction for this business may not be a simple matter, but with figures to work with, at least the owner will not be making plans in the dark.

At least annually, try this kind of income-versus-cost analysis for each product and service you offer. The answers you get will help you evaluate the correctness of all your prices and give you the comfortable feeling that you know where you're going and why, even when the profit picture is not as rosy as you would like it to be.

How to Quote a Job

You'll recall Kate Kelly's pricing advice at the beginning of this chapter. In quoting a job, Kate stresses you should give yourself plenty of time to figure the price you need. "No matter when the subject of money comes up," she says, "make it a practice of getting back later with a figure. Unless you're simply quoting an hourly or daily rate which you've set in advance, or if it's a fee on a proposal you've written (when you've had ample time to consider how much work is involved), then it's too early to talk money."

Different jobs will require different rate structures. You will need to consider quoting by the hour, versus by the day, per head or per project. Some jobs lend themselves to a flat rate charge, while others need to be charged on a retainer or contingency fee basis.

Some professionals charge by the hour when their services are required for only an hour or two, and offer a more economical hourly rate for a full day's work. In setting a daily rate, much has to do with the amount of preparation time required, not to mention time lost to travel. When I first began as a speaker, I thought I was doing well to get $250, then $500 a day and expenses. But reality soon set in when I considered this "daily fee" actually had to cover at least four days of my time: a full day of preparation (planning the program, gathering handout materials, packing, etc.); a day of traveling (often to rural areas with poor plane connections and possibly a long car ride once I landed); the day of the workshop, and another long trip home the next day. Not to mention that such trips wore me out physically and emotionally (fifty workshop students picking your brain is mentally exhausting), so I didn't accomplish a lot the next day back at my desk. That's why I no longer do day-long workshops unless they're in my backyard, and why I now charge higher fees for speaking engagements.

Some jobs are better quoted by the project, particularly if the job is one you know you can do easily and quickly but may seem difficult to the client. As Kate points out, people often react poorly to knowing how much she earns an hour. "When they compute and compare their hourly staff pay with mine, they tend to forget that I must pay for my own insurance, set aside my own pension benefits, and budget for any vacation time I take. What's more, I couldn't possibly bill out forty hours a week, so my overall income is almost surely less than they expect."

In setting fees of any kind, consider your overall experience and expertise. Just because you may be able to do a job in a day doesn't mean someone else could do it that quickly, or as well as you. The client, after all, is buying *your* experience and expertise. You are not obligated to tell him how quickly you have done the job. There are definite advantages in not delivering a job too quickly, lest the client thinks he has, indeed, been overcharged. As Kate confirms, "I once billed $1,200 for a project due in seven days' time, and the client never knew whether I polished it off in a day or burned the midnight oil for a week, though I feel quite certain that he preferred to think the latter."

Setting fees and quoting on specific jobs is both an art and a skill most business professionals acquire gradually with time and experience. But sometimes you just luck into higher prices when you least expect it, as I did the time I was asked to speak in Canada. Remembering the awful experience I'd had going through customs on my first speaking trip to Canada, and recalling how tired the trip made me, I figured the easiest way to say no was to double my prices. "That will be fine," I was told, and the job was mine whether I wanted it or not. Stunned by the simplicity of this experience, I quoted that same price to the next three prospects and was astonished when each one said yes. So the next time you want to test your wings, and you're presented with a job proposal you really don't want, you have little to lose and perhaps a lot to gain by simply asking twice your normal fee. In the process, you may accidentally discover, as I did, a whole new market that's prepared to pay you what you think you're worth.

Or, as Hugh Rome, publisher of *Home Office Computing*, said in one of his editorials: "you may even use high prices to make it worth your while to deal with overly demanding SOBs."

Think Twice Before Lowering Price

When business is sluggish, and particularly in recessionary times, many sellers lower their prices in hopes of selling more products or services. Before you do this, stop and consider that a lowering of prices by 20 percent will mean you have to bring in more than a 20 percent increase in sales just to offset your loss of revenue.

Pricing Psychology

If you can't sell something at a certain price, try reverse psychology. Don't lower the price—raise it! Yes, you may lose some customers, but your higher price will automatically attract a totally new audience of buyers.

Once there was a woman who started a teddy bear repair service. When she eventually decided to do something else, she thought she had an excellent strategy for killing her bear business: She would simply double her prices to discourage customers. To her amazement, business increased. As one customer explained, "I was reluctant to bring my antique teddy to you before because your prices seemed suspiciously low. Now I'm confident you can be trusted to do the job."

After reading this story in one of Barbara's magazine articles, artist Grady Harper reported on his experience:

"One of my full-sheet paintings just never would sell even though it seemed to be the main attraction in my exhibit at all of the shows. After reading your pricing article, I decided to follow your suggestion about doubling prices instead of lowering them. I increased the price of my painting from $325 to $750 and it was purchased after being on display only a few hours."

A Connecticut student had some terrific advice for people who have consulting or service businesses. "If
someone objects to your fee," she
said, "tell them, 'My fee includes this,
this and this. What would you like me
to leave out?' "

—from Barbara Winter's
Winning Ways newsletter

It's tough to increase sales by 20 percent in a good year; in recessionary times, it's likely to be impossible. Perhaps a better strategy is to keep your prices the same, but introduce new and less
expensive variations of your stand-by products and services. For
example, I learned during one recession that, while fewer people
purchased my books, more of them purchased my inexpensive
line of special reports. And they often spent more on several
reports than they would have spent on a book, indicating that
lack of dollars was not the issue here; in recessionary times, people simply become more careful about how they spend the dollars
they have. Perhaps buyers perceive my reports to be worth more
to them when money is tight because they zero in on specific
topics of interest to them at the moment.

An even better solution to lowering prices is to increase
them—even double them. I've been giving this advice to product
sellers for years, and many have told me it works. (See sidebar,
"Pricing Psychology.") In one of my monthly magazine columns,
I offered one of my books at $11.45 (postage-paid), but due to a
typographical error the price appeared as $22.45. Nevertheless,
I received almost as many orders for the book as I'd received
when it had been offered earlier at the correct price (and had to
send a lot of refund checks as a result). Clearly a certain percentage of my column's readers felt this book was worth twice what
I charge for it, proving once again you can double your present
prices and still find a market willing to pay for what you offer.
Think about it.

Some Pricing Formulas to Try

Before any pricing formula will work, you have to come up with
some kind of hourly rate for your time or labor. Here is one of
the most sensible formulas I have ever found.[1] It can be applied
to any kind of business.

Hourly Rate Formula

Desired annual net income ÷ number of working hours per year
+ annual expenses ÷ number of working hours per year =
hourly rate needed to realize desired annual net income.

Here, the hourly rate is determined through a calculation
based on time and expenses. Decide how much you would like
to net for the year, then estimate the number of working hours
per week and multiply this figure by 50 weeks (giving yourself
two weeks vacation). Then add your fixed, variable and selling
expenses for the year and divide by the number of working hours

[1]Libby Platus's Pricing Principle, as noted in *The Crafts
Report*.

per year. Add this hourly figure to the first hourly figure to get the final hourly rate you will need to charge to realize your desired net income at year's end.

Example: Let's say you desire $30,000 net income, and you work full time 40 hours per week × 50 weeks, or 2,000 work hours per year. Divide net income by 2,000 work hours to get a $15 hourly rate for your time. Now add up expenses for the year. Let's assume they are $38,249. Divide this expense figure by 2,000 hours to get an hourly expense rate of $19.13. Add this to the $15 figure to get a total of $34.13, or the amount you must charge per hour to realize $30,000 net income at year's end.

Classic Formula for Manufacturers

Cost of labor + materials for one unit × number of units to be produced in a year + estimated annual overhead costs + desired annual profit ÷ number of units to be produced in a year = wholesale cost per unit × 2 = retail price.

   Here, the idea is to get into the price of each item not only all the costs and expenses, but the profit as well. Whether you are planning to produce several thousand units per year, or a limited edition of 250 handmade items, this formula clearly shows any pricing problems you are going to have.

Example: Let's assume you're going to make laminated walnut-and-pine breadboards. Based on the time it takes you to make one, you figure you can make 800 a year. Let's then assume you will have to invest a total of two hours' time in each breadboard, and you want at least $10/hour for your labor. Materials cost will be $2.85 per board (you have a good source for scrap lumber). That gives us a total labor + materials cost of $22.85/unit.

   Let's also assume you will have $3,000 overhead costs for the year, and you would like at least $2,500 annual profit from your money-making enterprise. Here's how the figures would work out:

$22.85 × 800 units = $18,280 + $3,000 + $2,500 = $23,780 ÷ 800 units = $29.73 (wholesale price) × 2 = $59.45 (retail price).

   Logic tells us $59.45 is too high a price for a breadboard, even one that is to be offered as an exclusive handmade item in a gourmet catalog. What this exercise has done, then, is point out that you either will have to be satisfied with a lower hourly labor rate or less profit. It's clear you would not be able to reduce your materials cost much, if at all. On the other hand, if you could produce this item in half the time, the figures would change considerably, as follows:

The Last Two Digits

"Some researchers believe that there exists some magic in ending a price in six, seven, or nine" says marketing professor Donald W. Caudill. "Seven, as you know, is a lucky number; six and nine double and triple the powerful and mystical three. Others suggest pricing on the even dollar because buyers automatically round up to the nearest round figure."

Before deciding on the last two digits of your price, check to see how others in your industry are pricing. For example, If you're selling quality handcrafted products or art, avoid the $5.98, $10.99 type of prices found in discount stores; if you're selling a book, set figures that end in $.95 like most other publishers; if offering a service, use round figures like $35 an hour and so on. The use of weird prices in an industry that traditionally uses a certain type of pricing will mark you as an amateur.

$12.85 (labor + materials) × 800 units/year = $10,280 + $3,000 + $2,500 = $15,780 ÷ 800 units = $19.73 (wholesale price) × 2 = $39.45 (retail price)—a more reasonable price, but still high.

When your recalculated price is still too high, you must consider your options: to sacrifice profit, trim your overhead costs, do something to the product itself to give it a higher worth in the customer's mind . . . or make something else that will be more profitable.

If you want to work with this formula, but have no idea what overhead costs and profit might be, simply begin with what you know a product will cost you in labor and materials, then estimate how many you can produce and sell. The difference will be what's left to cover overhead and profit.

Example: Let's suppose you want to write and publish a simple book, and you plan to do the writing and the page layout on computer, eliminating the need for typesetting costs. You find from a printer's estimate it will cost you $988.55 to print 1,000 copies of a 64-page, perfect-bound book, or $.99 each. To this per-book print cost, you should add production costs (art and cover design, $250), and something for the hours you will spend actually doing page layout or paste-up for the printer—let's say 40 hours at $15/hour or $600. Production costs thus add up to $850, or $.85 cents per book. Add this to the per-book print cost to get a total book cost of $1.84.

Now let's assume you can sell 1,000 copies of this book on the retail level for $6.95. Multiply that figure times 1,000 books for a gross income of $6,950. Deduct your costs of $1.84 per book, or $1,840 and you have $5,110 left. Now ask yourself if this is enough to cover your time in writing the book, plus the overhead costs connected with your endeavor. Don't forget your marketing costs and time that will be required to advertise and sell the book by mail. The arithmetic looks like this:

(a) $988.55 ÷ 1,000 books = $ .99 per book (print cost)
(b) $250.00—art and design
      $600.00—labor

      $850.00 ÷ 1,000 books = $.85 per book (production cost)
(c) $.99 print cost + $.85 production cost = $1.84 total book cost
(d) $6.95 (sug. retail price) × 1,000 books = $6,950.00 gross income
(e)   –$1,840.00 ($1.84 × 1,000 books)
(f) $5,110.00 left.

Is it enough? I would say so, because a book, once written and printed, can produce income for years and may require only minor updating from time to time. But now assume you want to write a larger book of 200-300 pages. Your investment of time to write it will be considerably larger, as will production costs. The higher these costs, the higher the retail price. (Trade book publishers generally figure the retail price of a book needs to be from 6-8 times the total production cost to make it a profitable title, but self-publishers rarely are able to set prices more than 3-4 times their production costs because their print quantities tend to be so low. This leaves too little room in the pricing formula to allow for wholesale prices, which limits marketing options.)

Pricing Formulas for Handcraft Sellers

Craftsellers and makers of other products often use simple pricing formulas like the ones that follow, but only as a general guideline. In the end, they know an item is worth only what it can be sold for, and a pricing formula is worthless whenever it yields an unrealistic retail price. But just for fun, let's apply the same basic figures to each of the three formulas below, to see how they work.

Without identifying the object we are making, let's assume that our materials cost is going to be $1.50, we can make three units an hour, and we want $10/hour for our labor. (Labor cost per unit, then, will be $3.33.) In the last formula, we also will add $.20 for overhead and a 20 percent profit based on the wholesale price.

A. Materials × 3 + Labor = Wholesale price × 2 = Retail price
   $1.50 × 3 = $4.50 + $3.33 = $7.83 × 2 = $15.66

B. Materials + Labor × 3 = Wholesale price × 2 = Retail price
   $1.50 + $3.33 × 3 = $14.49 × 2 = $28.98

C. Materials + Labor + Overhead + Profit = Wholesale price × 2 = Retail price
   $1.50 + $3.33 + $ .20 + 1.01 = $6.04 × 2 = $12.08
   ($1.50 + $3.33 + $.20 = $5.03 × 20% = $1.01)

Interesting, isn't it? Now if the item we were making happened to be a piece of jewelry, all three items would be realistic, since jewelry runs the gamut in both price and style. However, if the item happened to be a Christmas ornament or a ceramic coffee mug, all prices would be high, although certain mugs and ornaments might sell for $12-$16 in exclusive shops. The point I'm trying to make is that formulas are fun, but they often are impractical, and the retail price still has to be adjusted to whatever consumer market one is trying to reach.

Here, for comic relief, is my favorite pricing formula, from Raymond Martell, a jeweler in New Jersey:

Cost of materials + labor (at the rate it would cost to pay someone to replace owner at the bench) + 40% of the labor-plus-materials figure + 10% of the labor-plus-materials figure for overhead × 2 = retail price. "Then," quips Ray, "I throw the whole thing out and figure what I can *get*."

In the end, common sense must take over, and the retail price must be set by the maker based on what the market will bear. If the maker cannot realize a profit in addition to his or her wages, perhaps the product should be dropped from the line.

The Break-Even Point

Sometimes the price decision on a product or service can be made as a result of a break-even analysis. The "break-even point" is the point at which your annual income from sales covers your costs. The income received after this point is profit. Let's suppose you've created a new product you think will sell for $25 at retail. You estimate you can sell 1,000 of these items in one year. You know your direct costs per item (materials, labor) will be $10, and you estimate your annual fixed expenses for the business (overhead) to be about $6,000. Here's how to find out how many items you would have to sell to break even:

1. The difference between the selling price of $25, and the direct costs of the item ($10) is $15, which is your "contribution to fixed costs per item." Until you reach your break-even point, every penny of this amount has to go toward covering your fixed expenses.
2. Now apply the following formula to find out how many items you have to sell to break even:

$$\frac{\$6{,}000 \text{ total fixed costs}}{\$15 \text{ contribution to fixed costs per item}} = \text{400 items, or number of sales needed to break even}$$

3. To prove the calculation:

400 items × $10 direct costs   = $ 4,000 direct costs
+ $ 6,000 overhead
$10,000 total costs
or 400 items × $25 = $10,000 total sales

Thus, if you have built in all your direct costs and other expenses related to this particular item, you would break even for the year when you had produced and sold 400 items.

By keeping careful records, you can determine the break-even point on a service-oriented project, too. My literary agent, Barbara Doyen, shares this tip on how her husband, Bob, helps her track the break-even point on the seminars they run together:

"Bob maintains a project spreadsheet in his computer so we

know when we've recouped our expenses on each seminar series. By keeping the bookkeeping current, we know whether we can afford more advertising, and whether we can fly instead of driving, etc. I do the same thing, only I tally our 'time expenses,' and by comparing our figures, we can determine if the results of our project were worth the investment in terms of both time and money."

Markups and Discounts

If you are a small manufacturer, you may think you cannot sell at the wholesale level because of pricing or problems of limited production. Often, this is true. Other times, however, a product can be changed or redesigned in some way to permit increased production at a retail price that's high enough to allow for wholesaling, at least to some markets.

Whether you're an importer, distributor or manufacturer, once you decide to enter the wholesale marketplace your thoughts probably will turn to retail shops and stores, mail-order catalogs, trade shows and a variety of special markets. One point I need to stress is this: *You will find it impossible to crack certain wholesale distribution channels unless both your product and its pricing structure are right for those markets.* This requires industry research that can be obtained through books, consultation with industry experts, membership in trade organizations and subscriptions to trade periodicals.

The pricing formulas I gave you earlier were all based on the idea of doubling the wholesale price to get a suggested retail price. While a 100 percent markup is standard for many retail outlets, other markets, such as chain stores or mail-order catalog houses, need larger markups than this, anywhere from 150 to 400 percent. Thus, the product you make and the wholesale price you set may or may not permit selling to certain markets. If a buyer tells you he needs a three-times markup in order to accept your product, you can figure out easily enough if your wholesale price is low enough to still yield a retail price that consumers will accept. For example, let's say you offer a hobby kit with a $2 cost in materials and labor. A general rule of thumb is you must mark up this price five times to realize a profit, which means your wholesale price must be $10. You may be able to sell the kit in a store that marks up your price 100 percent, but will your kit sell for $30 or $40? The answer you get to this question will suggest your wholesale outlet possibilities.

Sometimes a buyer will tell you a discount of 50 percent is needed. That's easy enough to understand—just divide the retail price by two. (Actually, this is the same as a 100 percent markup of your wholesale price.) But you may become confused when buyers start talking about discounts of 50 + 10 percent, or worse,

Understanding Markups and Discounts

Markup: The percentage a retail outlet *adds* to the wholesale price it pays for any item. For example, if you wholesale an item for $20, in most cases it will be marked up 100 percent to arrive at a retail price of $40. (Some stores use a higher markup, depending on what the traffic will bear.)

Discount: The percentage a retail outlet *subtracts* from the retail price to get the wholesale price they'll pay for merchandise. For example, if stores want a 50 percent discount off your retail price, it means they will expect to pay $20 for an item you retail for $40. Thus, in dollars and cents, a 50 percent discount is the same as a 100 percent markup.

Don't Undercut Your Dealers

If you sell products directly to con-sumers, as well as to wholesale buy-ers (shops and stores), *do not* sell these products at a lower retail price than your retail outlets sell them for. If you do, you not only will jeopardize the retailer's business, you will hurt your own as well because the retailer will stop buying from you.

In other words, if you make something that wholesales for $10 and retails for $20, don't sell this item to a shop for $10, then go to a crafts fair and also sell it to the consumer for $10. This is extremely unprofessional.

$50 + 10 + 10 + 5$ percent. A $50 + 10$ percent discount is standard for many distributors, but in certain industries, distributors try to get additional discounts. I have heard of some that are $50 + 10 + 10 + 10 + 5$ percent, in fact. What all these figures mean is that an additional discount is taken off each adjusted amount. Here is the way to figure such discounts, so you will know what these buyers are talking about:

Example: Suggested retail price of item is $20. Buyer wants a $50 + 10 + 10 + 5$ percent discount:

1. First turn the percentage figures into decimals:
   $50\% = .50$; $10\% = .10$; $5\% = .05$
2. Multiply $20 \times .50 = \$10$
   (equivalent to a 50% discount)
3. Multiply $10 \times .10 = \$1$
   Subtract $1 from $10 to get $9
   (equivalent to a $50 + 10\%$ discount)
4. Multiply $9 \times .10 = \$.90$
   Subtract $.90 from $9 to get $8.10
   (equivalent to a $50 + 10 + 10\%$ discount)
5. Multiply $8.10 \times .05 = \$.405$ (round off to $.41)
   Subtract $.41 from $8.10 to get $7.69
   (equivalent to a $50 + 10 + 10 + 5\%$ discount)

Note: If you sell wholesale to a shop or store figuring your price will be marked up 100 percent, as is the normal custom in such outlets, but you later find the shop has marked up the price by 200 percent, do not get angry. It is none of your concern at what price the shop sells your wares. The only thing that should concern you is the fact that you are receiving a fair wholesale price for the merchandise. Some shops price items for what the traffic will bear, and they have every right to do this. However, if you notice that shops and stores in different parts of the country consistently mark up your products more than 100 percent, it probably is a sign you are wholesaling them at too low a price. Maybe you don't know the value of what you are selling and should raise your wholesale prices.

The Game of the Name

You will recall that I talked about positioning in the last chapter, explaining how this affects the marketability of certain products and services. (Remember the candymaker who sells in gift shops instead of food shops?) What you call a product has a lot to do with how well it's going to sell; in fact, there is quite a game to this business of a name, and it can greatly affect your ability to command a good retail price or successfully wholesale a product.

A common complaint from many product makers—particularly those who make handcrafts—is they can't find the right market, or worse, they have the right market in mind, but their pricing structure will not allow for wholesaling to it. If this is your problem, one solution might be to change the name of whatever you're selling (i.e., reposition the product), double or triple its price, add a fancy designer label and hang tag, and offer it to a more affluent market.

For example, if you offer an originally designed vest and call it a "handmade patchwork vest," you're likely to appeal to the type of buyer who might pay from $25-$45 for the item at a crafts fair or in a small shop. On the other hand, if you were to take this same item, create half a dozen other unique vest designs and call the line "InVESTments," you might be able to sell the garments for up to $500 or more in the right outlets. (The "InVESTments" word just came to me out of the blue—I don't know if it's original or merely remembered. I would not suggest "lifting it" without a thorough trademark search.)

Merely by changing the name of a product or giving it a unique identification, while adding other professional touches— the fabric labels required by law, a "designer label" (in this case, an InVESTments logo), and a fancy hang tag that proclaims each vest to be "One-of-a-Kind Wearable Art"—you would be in a position to sell to exclusive shops in major cities, reaching a whole new audience of women who are used to spending hundreds or thousands of dollars on designer clothing because they know they're not going to meet themselves coming down the street. In a word, they are paying for the benefit called *prestige*.

Every time we turn around today, we find something that used to be called one thing is now called another, and these changes are generally made for marketing purposes or because someone has decided the public's preconceived image of a particular product or certain group of people needs to be changed. For example, "garbage collectors" gained new respect when they were dubbed "sanitation engineers," and the secondhand-car dealer down the street makes more money when he promotes his "used Cadillacs" as being "previously owned luxury cars."

To further illustrate, consider the following list of common handcrafted items now being made for sale in countless homes across North America. Merely by changing the names of such items—and thus suggesting greater consumer benefits—higher retail prices can often be commanded:

- *Candles* can be sold at higher prices when their image is not merely functional, but decorative, as in *Wax Sculptures*.
- *Folk paintings* may seem more valuable to buyers if they are called *Early American Folk Art*.

Look What a Name Change Can Do!

A catalog seller found a charming brass doll bed he wanted to offer, but he was concerned its high price would discourage sales. After all, one will pay only so much for a *doll bed*.

Solution: He added a colorful mattress and a doggie bone and offered the item as a *Deluxe Dog Bed*, which, not surprisingly, became a hot seller.

Hang Tags: Cheap Advertising

A music box seller reported that, shortly after she began attaching hang tags to her seashell music boxes, she received over $2,000 worth of business from shop owners who had spotted her boxes in other shops. Although her tag did not include her full address, they were able to track her down by phone.

Note: Shops will remove any tag that bears a manufacturer's complete name, address and phone number because they don't want their customers to know how to contact their suppliers. Therefore, list only your business name and logo, city and state on merchandise tagged for resale in shops.

- *Crude wood carvings* attract a more affluent buyer when they are called *Primitives* and sold in art galleries instead of craft or souvenir shops.
- Large *cloth dolls* can command higher prices when they become *life-size sculptures* or *mannequins* for use in fine shops and stores.
- *Found-art jewelry* made from pieces of wood, bone, shell, etc. might bring higher prices if given a fancy name, such as *Nature's Treasures*.
- *Sewing machine embroidery* takes on a new image when it is called *Machine Artistry*.
- *Quilts* will sell for more when they are offered as *fine art collectibles*.
- *Replicas of antiques* may be worth more in buyers' minds if they are called *Authentic Period Reproductions*.
- *Knick-knacks* of all kinds will be worth more to buyers if they are identified as *collectibles*.

Back in the 1960s when I was selling handpainted boxes and other crafts, I had an interesting shop experience that taught me a valuable lesson. I took several of my boxes to an exclusive shop on the north shore of Chicago and was amazed when the manager opened them and said, "But there's nothing in them." Of course not, I said; people buy empty boxes because they have things they want to put in them. But she just wasn't interested.

I thought about her strange attitude and came up with an idea. When I went back a few weeks later, I presented the same line of boxes, with one difference: This time, each one had a musical movement in it. "Ah!" she exclaimed. "What lovely *music boxes* these are." Voila! The same boxes I could not sell empty were now attractive to her at three times the price. Yet my only extra cost was an inexpensive movement and fifteen minutes of labor to insert it.

You don't have to make boxes to apply this kind of thinking to your product line. Just look at everything you make and ask yourself what changes or additions you could make that might enable you to call things by a different and more expensive-sounding name.

There's quite a game to this business of the name, and don't you forget it.

The Importance of Tags and Labels

One of the best ways to get higher prices for handcrafted merchandise and gift packages is the inclusion of a "hang tag," a decorative and informative printed selling aid that makes all products sell better at the retail level. While hang tags cost only pennies, they send an automatic signal to consumers that a

THE ART WAX WERKE
CINCINNATI

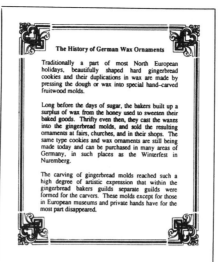

The History of German Wax Ornaments

Traditionally a part of most North European holidays, beautifully shaped hard gingerbread cookies and their duplications in wax are made by pressing the dough or wax into special hand–carved fruitwood molds.

Long before the days of sugar, the bakers built up a surplus of wax from the honey used to sweeten their baked goods. Thrifty even then, they cast the waxes into the gingerbread molds, and sold the resulting ornaments at fairs, churches, and in their shops. The same type cookies and wax ornaments are still being made today and can be purchased in many areas of Germany, in such places as the Winterfest in Nuremberg.

The carving of gingerbread molds reached such a high degree of artistic expression that within the gingerbread bakers guilds separate guilds were formed for the carvers. These molds except for those in European museums and private hands have for the most part disappeared.

Left: This is a three-fold product tag that, unfolded, measures 4½″ × 11″ (six panels of copy). It's printed black ink on tan, as is the hang tag shown below.

Below: Folded, this hang tag measures 2⅛″ × 2¾″. It's punched in the top left-hand corner for a string tie.

Three hang tags for crafters from Carol Carlson's Kimmeric Studios catalog.

Gourd art is an ancient form of expression. The gourd was used by early civilizations for its versatility, durability, practicality, tactile and visual beauty. The gourd was manipulated into both functional and decorative works of art, a gracious combination of nature and man's ingenuity.

As far as I have been able to determine, the oldest known American gourd doll is dated circa 1850. It was created by a slave woman, fashioned from a dipper gourd, twigs and cloth. It is on display in the Atlanta Antique Toy Museum.

Personally, art has always been a passion, a joy and a source of great fulfillment. As a professional artist, specializing in graphic design, I realized the gourd held enormous creative potential. The idea surfaced to revive this primitive folk art form establishing my own style and characters, each with a distinctly different personality. Perhaps they will remind you of someone dear, or stir within you a favorite childhood fantasy.

Each gourd doll is lovingly hand-crafted every step of the way and as no two are identical, you

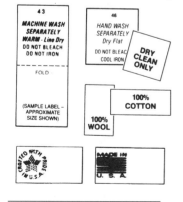

43	46
MACHINE WASH SEPARATELY WARM - *Line Dry* DO NOT BLEACH DO NOT IRON	HAND WASH SEPARATELY *Dry Flat* DO NOT BLEACH COOL IRON

DRY CLEAN ONLY

FOLD

(SAMPLE LABEL – APPROXIMATE SIZE SHOWN)

100% COTTON

100% WOOL

CRAFTED WITH LOVE IN U.S.A.

MADE IN U.S.A.

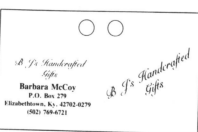

B J's Handcrafted Gifts
Barbara McCoy
P.O. Box 279
Elizabethtown, Ky. 42702-0279
(502) 769-6721

B J's Handcrafted Gifts

Roger B. Sandstrom
Rt. 4 — Box 95
Seymour, Mo. 65746

Kind of Wood

Early American TREENWARE

A GIFT FROM THE HEART by Jeanne

Banners of His Word

Handcrafted with love
© 1985 Dayle DeBry
Bear Hug Bouquets

Sample care labels, some required by law, furnished by Charm Woven Labels, Portland, Oregon.

These hang tags (show in reduced size) illustrate the variety of sizes and shapes one can use. Note some tags provide information about one's business while others tell how products are made, type of materials used, care and cleaning instructions, or technical information about the manufacturing process. Some tags simply convey a whimsical note designed to tug at a buyer's heartstrings. Some hang tags are folded while others are simply printed on one side, with the other side left blank for the price.

product is special and thus worth more.

A tag not only adds a professional touch to products, but it is a sales tool each time it carries your message home with buyers who may later reorder. Nearby you'll find a page of fabric labels and hang tags used by a variety of product makers. Fabric labels are generally sewn to garments, toys and other "soft items." Some are required by law (as explained in chapter six), while others are optional image tools, such as a designer's name or logo. Standard labels of all kinds are available in quantities as small as fifty, and your own custom-designed label can be reproduced for a nominal setup charge. (To find suppliers, read craft and gift industry magazines.)

Hang tags are easy to design and simple to produce. They can be laser-printed on lightweight card stock or "quick-printed" locally. (You could cut costs by printing hang tags and business cards at the same time.) Children or sheltered workshop employees could punch holes, add ties and attach to products.

The size of a hang tag and the message you put on it are up to you; options are unlimited. For starters, anything that makes you or your products unique is information that can be put on a tag, such as any of the following:

- Type and source of materials used to make the product (Georgia clay, seashells from around the world, hand-dyed yarns)
- A statement about the quality of the product ("Our treenware is designed to give you fitness for purpose, beauty of form and a love of old-time craftsmanship.")
- Colorful information about a business ("It was our grandmother's idea to start this business . . .")
- How products are made (interesting technical information about the manufacturing process)
- Care and cleaning instructions
- Consumer safety warnings ("This is not a toy—keep out of children's hands!")
- History of an old or little-known art or craft
- A whimsical note designed to tug at a buyer's heartstrings (often the most effective way to get higher prices)

The designer who shears her sheep to make handmade felt that is then turned into toys . . . the ornament maker whose wax creations are made from museum fictile ivories . . . the rosemaler whose designs are completely authentic—all should use such information to their advantage on a hang tag because such stories give a product personality, and personality *sells*.

I'm reminded of a little handpainted picture on wood my husband and I once bought. It was just a sailor standing by a rowboat, and we never would have bought it except for the fact that beneath the picture was a "personality message" that made it the perfect gift for Harry's old school chum, a sailboat enthusiast: "Old sailors never die; they just get a little dinghy."

Packaging With Flair

I'm not talking about wrapping here, but packaging as it relates to the marketing of products and services. I encourage you to offer a little pizzazz and *charge* for it. Let's take products.

Instead of trying to market all your handcrafted products on an individual basis, take a look at what you have to sell and see if you can't combine several items (some handmade, some commercial) and market them as a:

- "Holiday Gift Pak"
- "Gourmet Selection"
- "Beauty Care Kit"
- "Designer Bathroom Ensemble"
- "Mother's Sanity Kit"
- "A Bundle for the Baby"
- "Gift Basket" (gift basket ideas are endless)

Not only would you sell more product this way, but you would surely increase profits as well. People are always willing to pay more for a complete package if they perceive it as something that will save them time, stress or merely aggravation (i.e., shopping for a gift when there's no time).

The same concept also works for service sellers. Business people often speak in terms of the "business package" they offer, and maybe you should be offering a business package, too. It can be presented either in a plain brown wrapper for a plain brown price—or you can add some glitter and command whatever the traffic will bear.

To sell the glitter, you must identify and promote your true customer benefits. Why should people use your service instead of that of your competitors? Do you have more experience, a better business reputation, do you offer special guarantees of satisfaction, faster service, more attention to detail, glamour . . . what? Remember, buyers often will pay extra for intangible benefits like these. (How many times have you heard yourself saying things like "Well, you only get what you pay for" or "This is important to me, so I want the best I can find—price is no object"?)

A savvy party planner, for example, would not limit her service to merely planning a party, but would offer a wide variety of separate services that included every little detail: from sending invitations to planning the menu and decorations, to finding just the right entertainment. And perhaps she will also diversify into the sale of products related to parties, from nut cups and decorations to gift wrap, hand-printed announcement cards, even a photography service that provides framed mementos or novelty items (cups or plates with photos on them, for example).

If you offer a wide variety of services and products, you need to give yourself a special title, your business a special name and professional image and your complete "package" a title that will make prospects beat a path to your door. When you successfully play "the game of the name" and professionally package your products and services, you may advance to "GO," collect the money, and wave bye-bye to the competition.

SCOUTING FOR BUSINESS

I WOULD NEED THE SPACE OF A whole book to detail the hundreds of low-cost marketing strategies home-business owners can use to bring in business. It is beyond the scope of this book to be that specific, but if this is something you need right now, I suggest you subscribe to some small business newsletters and read a few books devoted to the topic of marketing. (A list of such publications will be found in chapter sixteen.) Also check out your networking opportunities online.

In my limited space, I will concentrate on the special marketing needs of two groups of readers: beginners who may not yet have their first customer or client; and established—but young—businesses who may not be properly building on what they've got.

10

"We're marketing on a shoestring," says a beginning business owner, "but the ends keep coming untied."

Let's take a moment to recap the marketing information you've received so far in this "workshop in book form." In earlier chapters, my emphasis has been on what I feel are the most important marketing *concepts* you must have to survive in business. You've learned why you need to develop business and marketing plans and know what you must do to present yourself and your business in a professional manner. You've gained perspective on such intangible marketing concepts as the psychology of pricing and the importance of positioning. You've been reminded that, to succeed as a self-employed individual, you must pay attention to all things legal and financial and work hard to develop pricing policies that are fair both to you and your buyers.

My reader mail suggests that, at this point in the book, your brain is ready to explode and your good ideas are keeping you awake at night. You're fired up now! In spite of all the hard work involved in building a business at home, you think you can do it. You know what you want to do and you think your business idea has great potential, either as a part-time endeavor or a full-time venture. You believe in your product or service, and you're sure there is a need for what you offer because you've done your market research (or will soon confirm your gut instincts about the market through such research). You are committed to the idea of excellence, and although you lack money for advertising and promotion, you're rarin' to go!

You may have customers or clients already, since so many homebased businesses start with the cart before the horse. (They do something for themselves, someone asks if they will do it for them, and they've got their first customer automatically.) Once satisfied, buyers begin to tell others; the thing that may have begun as a hobby or just a part-time money-maker suddenly begins to look a lot like a *business*.

Maybe you're a crafts hobbyist who entered a local show and were astonished when you sold half of everything you took with you, and came home with some custom orders besides.

Or as an individual with confidence aplenty, maybe you simply looked around, saw a need for your service, approached a few likely prospects with your spiel on how you could solve their problem, and were in business overnight.

Or perhaps you lost your job suddenly and immediately went to work for your former employer as an independent contractor. Wow! That was easy . . . your first client, just like that.

There will always be a demand for worthy products and services, and getting the first few customers or clients is not what's hard. What's *hard* is coming up with a steady stream of interested prospects month after month. What's *harder* is getting enough of them to buy to turn your little money machine into a year-round income producer. And once you have a good customer list going for you, what's *even harder* is keeping them interested by always coming up with something new and different, and getting them to buy again and again.

If you are selling products, and in need of ideas on where to sell them, see charts in this chapter titled, "Retail Markets to Consider," "Wholesale Markets to Explore," and "Retail Outlets That Buy Products or Services." Many of the retail shops named on the latter chart are also markets for a variety of services, as are the market categories presented on the "Checklist of Mailing Lists You Can Rent." For a reminder list of your various direct-mail marketing options, see "Direct-Mail Options to Consider." Product and service sellers alike should be able to use all of these charts as idea stimulators for markets that might be tapped through direct selling methods, advertising, publicity, direct-mail promotions or telemarketing efforts.

Remember: Every individual, every business, and every organization, institution and government agency represents a market for someone's special products and services. To find *your* most likely prospects and customers, first decide which problems or needs your product or service addresses or solves, then aggressively seek those who need what you offer.

Advertising Perspective

Now take a look at the chart titled "Advertising/ Promotion/Marketing Options at a Glance," page 244. As you will see, there are several no-cost ways to start the flow of business, but to get all this free advertising, you must first:

1. Get over your shyness about telling people what you do;
2. Get a couple of customers or clients who will get word-of-mouth advertising started;
3. Hone your networking skills as explained in chapter eight;
4. Learn how to get publicity (see chapter eleven);
5. Get serious about library research to turn up media contacts and find directories that offer free listings (see chapter sixteen);
6. Keep your eyes open for places where you can tack up a business card or small poster; and,
7. Actively look for opportunities to have your flyers or brochures circulated by others.

A few words about directory listings: There are more than 14,000 directories published worldwide, and they are described in a two-volume reference called *Directories in Print*. It's published by Gale Research and is available in many libraries. I doubt, however, that this directory includes the many small, self-published directories now being issued by homebased entrepreneurs in various fields. Such directories are often publicized in

How to Shift Gears From Retailing to Wholesaling

With few exceptions, the same marketing methods are used to sell on both the retail and wholesale levels. The primary difference is that, in wholesaling, the marketer has to shift mental gears because dealers and retailers do not think about merchandise in the same way as consumers.

Whereas you must sell a consumer on his or her need for your product, you have to sell dealers and retailers on this point plus one other: *why consumers will want to buy your products from them.* That's one reason why wholesalers and manufacturers work so hard to make it easy for their dealers to sell, and why they offer them free or inexpensive counter display racks, finished samples (to sell kits), promotional literature they can give to consumers, camera-ready advertising copy and so on.

In trying to find new wholesale markets for your products, shift your thinking by looking for the wholesale counterpart of each retail market you now sell to. With few exceptions, you will find both consumer and trade shows, magazines and organizations for each industry and each specific interest. This kind of "detective work" is what good marketing is all about. The sharpest marketers are those who not only dig around to find just the right distribution channels for their products, but also the most efficient and cost-effective way to use them.

Retail Markets to Consider

RETAILING is *direct selling to consumers*. This is *personal* selling, involving face-to-face meetings with buyers or the public at large through:

Shows/Fairs/Festivals (art, crafts and related products)[1]
Flea Markets (both new and used goods)[1]
Home Sales and Holiday Boutiques (generally products created by sellers)[2]
Open Houses or Party-Plan Sales (both craft and commercial product lines)[3]
Person-to-Person Selling (sales calls to prospects who have indicated interest)[4]
In-Home Demonstrations (generally by appointment to show commercial product lines)
State and County Fair Exhibits (generally commercial product lines or service businesses)
Other Consumer Shows and Product Fairs (all types of products and services)
Business Opportunity Fairs (for general public)
Business Trade Shows (for business owners)[5]
Shopping Malls (products and services—temporary leased space)[6]
Craft malls and Rent-a-Space Shops (retail space rented by the month)[7]

Footnotes

1. See chapter sixteen to tap into sources of information for local, regional and national art and craft fairs, shows, festivals and flea markets.

2. Often set up to run on a weekend, home shops and holiday boutiques provide an interesting and profitable alternative to selling at fairs or through local shops. Twenty or thirty exhibitors may be able to ring up sales of as much as $10,000 in a couple of days, particularly if the sale has become an annual event noted for high-quality merchandise. Such events generally cause few, if any, problems with local zoning officials since they seem to be viewed in the same light as ordinary garage sales. It's always a good idea to check with authorities, however, before planning such an event.

3. Although some handcraft manufacturers successfully market through open houses and party plans, such events are commonly associated with multi-level marketing (also known as "network marketing") and the sale of commercial products such as cosmetics, housewares, jewelry, lingerie, etc. While open house visitors generally take products with them when they leave, party-plan selling usually involves later delivery of products. In some instances, however, zoning regulations prohibit one from using the home to transfer the sale of merchandise, so rather than let customers walk out of the door with the product, sellers may have to deliver goods later to be in strict compliance with the law.

4. This used to be called "door-to-door" selling, but the phrase has become outdated as most sales today are generated by appointments arranged by telephone, instead of door-knocking. Besides, say companies involved in this field, the new phrase has more sales appeal.

5. The growing number of trade shows for "home-office professionals" is providing many homebased entrepreneurs with excellent opportunities to sell products and services to others in their industry. Read trade magazines in the industry to learn of such events.

6. Many shopping malls in the United States and Canada now offer space that can be leased on a temporary, seasonal basis—from kiosks and carts to vacant storefronts. Call malls in your area for details about plans they may offer. Artists and craftspeople might find this an excellent way to sell during the Christmas season.

7. Craft malls and rent-a-space shops are a unique way to market artwork and handcrafted merchandise at the retail level without any face-to-face selling. Sellers simply rent whatever size space they desire or can afford, fill the space with an attractive display of merchandise, maintain the sales display over a period of time, and leave the selling to those who own the individual craft mall or retail shop. Detailed information on this and other innovative retail marketing concepts will be found in the author's book, *Handmade for Profit*.

Wholesale Markets to Explore

WHOLESALING is *indirect selling to consumers*. This is *impersonal* selling, involving sales through retailers, dealers and other distribution methods. All types of products are purchased for resale by buyers such as:

Retail Shops and Stores (See related chart, "Retail Outlets
   That Buy Products or Services")
Mail-Order Catalog Houses[1]
Trade Shows/Sales Reps/Merchandise Marts[2]
Institutional Buyers[3]
Premium Sales[4]
Bookstores and Libraries[5]
Foreign Markets[6]

Footnotes

1. In the United States alone, there are currently more than 55 billion catalogs mailed annually. To successfully sell to this market, you will need a product that allows for a four-time markup; i.e., you'd have to wholesale a $30 item for $7.50. Best way to sell here is to telephone the catalog company of your choice, ask for the "Director of Merchandise" or the "Catalog Merchandise Buyer." Try to determine level of interest, then follow up with a good information package that includes a glossy photo of the product. (Don't send samples unless requested; they won't be returned.)

2. Although trade show exhibiting is neither simple nor inexpensive, it can often be the most important marketing move a small business can make. Find trade shows by reading *trade periodicals* (see chapter sixteen). Because of the high cost of trade show exhibiting, many small businesses find it better to use sales representatives who not only call on certain retail outlets but regularly exhibit in certain trade shows as well. Many also have permanent exhibits in merchandise marts. Reps generally expect a commission of at least 15 percent, but on low-ticket items with limited sales potential the rate could be as high as 30 percent. Conversely, commissions may be as low as 5 percent on items with huge sales potential. You can find reps at trade shows or through reading trade magazines.

3. Institutional buyers often purchase self-published books and periodicals. They like (but don't insist on) a 20 percent discount and prefer that you ship and bill.

4. "Premiums" are marketing tools used by companies to entice buyers into purchasing some product or service. A difficult market to crack, but any product or publication that can be produced in quantity may have premium appeal to buyers. You can connect with interested premium buyers by working with a marketing firm that specializes in premium offers or by placing ads in trade publications that reach catalog buyers, premium users and fund raisers.

5. If you are a self-publisher, you may prefer not to sell directly to bookstores, since their trade's purchasing and payment practices irritate even the largest publishers. Independent bookstores generally order only one or two copies of a book at a time, then take sixty to ninety days to pay, retaining the right to return books up to a year after date of invoice if the books don't sell. Even more frustrating, the books are not always returned in resalable condition. Your best wholesaling option here is to connect with Baker & Taylor, the world's largest book wholesaler, and let them order from you and ship to the independent bookstores. (Their current practice is to send payment with order.)

Libraries generally prefer to order from library distributors but occasionally purchase directly from publishers, desiring the same 20 percent discount they get from their distributors. ("Over the transom" purchase orders from libraries and bookstores are common if you receive a lot of national publicity for your books.)

6. Exporting to other countries is not something the average small business plans to do, but it is a possibility for aggressive marketers. To avoid the paperwork hassles involved in exporting, it is best to work with agent-buyers or bona fide distributors. The Department of Commerce is the place to start when you want more information on this topic.

Display Advertising Tips

The advertising director of a trade magazine offered these tips at a seminar:

1. In planning an ad campaign, make sure your strategy is consistent with your objectives. Always follow up on the leads and inquiries generated by your advertising, and have a plan to evaluate the results of each ad.

2. Few readers are motivated by one ad only, so one ad in one issue of a magazine is probably a waste of money. When running an ad more than once in the same publication, figure that the response will peak somewhere between the second and third insertion of the ad, and be "worn out" by the fourth exposure.

3. Ads placed on the right-hand side of a page will get 5 to 10 percent more attention from readers, and those placed on the top corner of the right-hand page may attract as much as 25 percent greater viewing attention. (You may not get preferred positioning when you place an ad, but always ask for it.)

4. There is no right or wrong way to write an ad, but there are five basic elements of a good display ad: (1) Heading, (2) Sub-head, (3) Body copy (details of offer), (4) "Call to action" (coupon, toll-free number, or anything else that motivates response) and (5) Company's signature (name and address).

5. You'll increase the pull of an ad if you add a second or "spot" color to it. This will cost about half again as much as a regular black-and-white ad but much less than a four-color ad.

6. If you use a toll-free number in a display ad, you can figure that you probably will be able to make a sale to at least half the people who call.

the small business press and are worth investigating. Directory listings work for me, and they work for designer Pamela Spinazzola, who reported that when her commemorative gifts and fine art note cards were listed in the annual *Gifts and Decorative Accessories* directory, she received hundreds of inquiries from 46 states.

About signs: While advertising signs on your vehicle or business signs in your yard will generally be prohibited by zoning ordinances, temporary signs may be OK in your community if you want to advertise a Holiday Boutique or Open House. And remember signs may be as small as a business card and posted anywhere there is a bulletin board. If you have a computer and modem and use online services, you may also find opportunities to promote your business on electronic bulletin boards. Some craft sellers wear their signs in the form of wearable art they sell at fairs, or jewelry they've made (which attracts compliments and opens the discussion on how to buy it).

While taking advantage of free advertising opportunities and exploring your possibilities for publicity, your thoughts will naturally turn to paid advertising as well. Unfortunately, the lament of beginning advertisers everywhere seems to be, "but I expected a much greater response than I got. I don't know what went wrong." A *lot* of things can go wrong in advertising, and experienced marketers are as likely to encounter problems as beginners. The only difference is the former can more easily afford mistakes than the latter.

Display Advertising

Large corporations live by the old rhyme, "You always buy familiar names/the ones you recognize; that's why the adman always claims/it pays to advertise." Each year, they spend millions of advertising dollars just to remind us they are in business. (Food and drug product companies, insurance companies, car manufacturers, and oil and utility companies come readily to mind.) Because of exposure to intense media advertising, we consumers often are subconsciously persuaded to make certain buying decisions. Even on the smallest scale, homebased business owners cannot afford this kind of image advertising—unless it comes in the form of publicity.

Few small businesses can afford the high advertising rates of most national magazines. Those who decide to risk such an ad often lose their investment because an ad can fail even when the product being advertised is salable and correctly priced. Most ads fail either because they are placed in the wrong publications or are poorly written or designed. There is so much more to preparing an ad than just making it look good. If the advertising copy doesn't motivate people to buy, they simply will not respond. My best advice is this: *Do not spend money on display advertising until you know something about graphic design and ad copywriting.* If you insist on advertising this way at the beginning and don't know how to do the job right, hire a professional because this will save you money in the long run.

Meanwhile, you can "test the water" with less expensive display ads in some of the smaller, special-interest periodicals (which may actually pull better than some of the national magazines). The addresses of such publications will be found in the resource chapters of various books, magazines and library directories; a few of the better-known ones are listed here in chapter sixteen.

As you will learn in the next section, it's important to calculate the per-inquiry cost of all your advertising efforts. In addition to comparing the costs of display advertising versus classifieds, you should also compare the pull of various sizes of display ads. For example, a one-column inch ad might draw 150 responses for a per-inquiry cost of $.75 each, while a three-inch ad might draw twice as many responses but have a per-inquiry cost of $1.10. And a full-page ad could be the least cost efficient of all, even though it might draw thousands of quick responses. That's why it's best to start with small display ads and classifieds to minimize your financial risk while you test several publications. As you increase the size of your ads, keep analyzing response and measuring actual results against the cost of each ad.

If you have a mail-order business, always indicate you want the mail-order ad rates of any consumer magazine you are contacting. These rates are lower than regular ad space; for many advertisers they actually pull better because they're placed in a special mail-order section of the magazine where interested mail-order buyers are most likely to look.

If you should become a serious display advertiser, ask about the availability of "remnant space," which usually is offered at highly discounted rates and available only for a short time. Sometimes a magazine will sell a particular page of an issue to an advertiser who wants distribution only to certain sections of the country. This means this particular page for the remaining sections of the country must be filled. Major consumer magazines would be a logical place to find such space.

Newspaper Advertising

If you plan to advertise in your local newspaper, pay particular attention to the day your ad runs, remembering that each day's paper may include special sections targeted to specific readers. One service seller told me that her newspaper ads had failed until she began to place them on a Friday when more men were reading the paper to get a certain feature in that day's edition.

Marketing on the Internet or World Wide Web

Do explore your online opportunities, but don't believe the hype about how easy it is to make direct sales on the Internet or World Wide Web. Remember that the people who are making the most money now are entrepreneurs who are selling ad space or charging exorbitant fees to design fancy homepages for people who don't know they can learn how to do this themselves.

If you are hoping to sell your products worldwide via the Internet or your own website, consider that personal Internet access is still very expensive in other countries. Since most individuals here can't afford Internet access in their homes, it means your international audience is likely to be mostly businesspeople for some time.

Several different surveys have revealed that most of today's online users are just looking for information. Few of them are buying products direct from advertisers. (If you have a success story to share, I'd love to hear it.) Advertisers who use their online presence to increase sales of their products in retail outlets may be faring better, however. After more than a year of promoting my books on three different websites, I had received only a handful of orders by phone, fax or mail, and only one order from a foreign country. My books continue to sell well in bookstores, however, so I believe the retail sales of my books have been enhanced by my online presence.

Classified ads may be used effectively to attract prospects interested in buying a service (such as lawn services, typing, housecleaning, child care, etc.), and by business service providers who offer "complete details on request." Never try to sell craft products in a newspaper ad, however, because this is not a good direct response medium. Like radio (see below), newspapers often serve local retailers best.

Many small businesses have commented to me that their ads in "penny-pincher" newspapers have yielded surprisingly good results—perhaps because the people who like such publications tend to read them cover to cover, so as not to miss anything of possible interest. If your community has such a newspaper, you might want to give this type of advertising a try.

Radio and Cable Television

While advertising on radio is a great way for retailers to get business, it doesn't work well for homebased businesses. People expect a radio ad to lead them to a retail shop or store, not to someone's home (and zoning laws would probably prohibit this anyway). Certainly one cannot sell products effectively on radio without a toll-free number and charge card services, and if this is what you want to do, you don't have to pay for the privilege. There are many opportunities for radio publicity, as you will learn in the next chapter.

Cable TV presents some interesting advertising possibilities, as Sylvia and Philip Landman discovered. These California-based consultants help others start up small businesses or solve small business problems. After running a 30-second commercial (which cost $600 to produce), they received a surprising number of clients interested not only in their consulting services, but the small business books and tapes they sell by mail. "Right there sandwiched between pizza parlors and manicure salons, viewers watched and followed our suggestions," says Sylvia. "They called. They wrote. They bought. They made consulting appointments, and the fee from our first client paid our production costs."

The hardest part about doing the commercial was writing the 30-second script, Sylvia adds. "We were advised to keep it to no more than 78 words since that is all most people can say in thirty seconds. I wrote 325 words, then went to work editing, revising and condensing. I continued to extract words until only the most concentrated remained—92 strong, effective words survived, and I divided them into a professional script for Philip and me to share. There was no friendly 'hi' or hand waving, no dogs or kids. Just the facts, including our phone and fax numbers."

Don't be discouraged if you lack money for advertising because this may turn out to be a blessing in disguise. Without money, you'll find yourself using creativity instead of dollars, or as one marketer puts it, "substituting brains for bucks." The less money you have, the more creative you're likely to become in your marketing efforts; the less money you have to invest in paid advertising, the less you'll stand to lose if your ads fail to pull results. So let's proceed on the premise that you have only "pennies for promotion" and don't know how to bring in the business you need. One by one, I will discuss what I believe to be *the six most important, low-cost marketing steps you can take, not only at the beginning of a business, but throughout its life*:

1. Establish a word-of-mouth advertising base to limit your need for paid advertisements
2. Develop a variety of mailing lists for marketing and publicity purposes
3. Use inexpensive "two-step" advertising techniques to build a large prospect list
4. Consistently mine both your prospect and customer lists with follow-up direct-mail promotions
5. Become an expert at getting publicity
6. Keep looking for new ways to diversify and expand

The last two items on this list are deemed so important that they have been given separate chapters of their own immediately following this one.

Building Word-of-Mouth Advertising

The first way to assure word-of-mouth advertising is to offer products and services that give people real value for their money. Satisfied customers will always be quick to tell others about good books they've read, handy products they've discovered and helpful services that save them time, money or aggravation.

Once you begin hearing from satisfied customers, don't hesitate to ask them for testimonial copy you can use in your promotional material. If written testimonials don't come automatically, jot down verbal comments you receive from customers (wording remarks to your advantage), then send them a copy asking permission to quote them by name in your brochure. (Many will be flattered by this request.) Once you have developed a small list of satisfied customers, make it easy for them to help you by asking if they would like a few of your cards or flyers for their friends or business associates. (Be careful not to load them down with printed materials that will only be thrown away.) Some people just naturally like to help others and will want nothing in return for their kind words on your behalf. Others will talk about you even more if you offer them a small incentive for spreading the word—a discount, perhaps, on purchases of your product or service each time one of their friends contacts you and mentions their name.

Fax Marketing

Facsimile (fax) machines have become a hot direct marketing tool as more customers are being urged to place their orders through fax numbers. Direct-mail experts thus see the fax machine as the wave of the future and the kind of technology that will ultimately change the catalog industry.

In an article in *DM News*, catalog marketer Jay Walker spoke of how the combination of fax, telephone and computer technology will help the consumer become the ultimate decision maker in what he wishes to receive. "This self-selection process is called 'demand fax.' With demand-fax interactive systems, all the rules of the direct marketing game will change," he says.

Several sellers in my network have reported an increase in business since they began to use a fax number in connection with charge card services. One reason may be that fax numbers are tapping an audience of businesspeople who don't have time to order if they have to write a check and send it by mail. Thus "fax" translates to "customer benefit."

A benefit to the seller is that chargebacks from customers who claim never to have ordered merchandise are practically nil, because when a customer uses a fax line to place an order, the seller has documentation of the fax being sent from a traceable phone number.

Sheila Young, who sells hand-loomed, personalized hats by mail and through "Hat Parties," gets her customers to send prospect names by affixing a special label to her order form and rubber-stamping its message on all outgoing sales literature. It reads:

Send me 10 addresses of friends who might appreciate my catalog, and eliminate the postage and handling charge from your order.

If you decide to try this idea, determine its value to you by keeping track of how many referred names actually order. My experience shows that your response will increase greatly if you include a little note with your brochure or catalog that explains why you are sending people something they haven't asked for. (Example: "Your friend Helen Smith thought you would enjoy receiving my catalog.") A rubber-stamped or laser-printed label with a blank allowing you to write in a person's name would also work here.

When new business comes in "over the transom," always ask people how they heard of you. By keeping track of where most of your prospects are coming from, you'll know where to place advertising or promotional emphasis in the future. To keep the word-of-mouth advertising flowing, always thank those who are helping you.

Judy Schramm, owner of Judy's Maternity Rental, says when her customers name a specific person or company, she pops off a thank-you note folded over a lottery ticket. "I've been looking for a long time for a way to say thank you to all the people who refer customers to us," says Judy. "From comments I've heard, very few of them play the lottery, so this is unusual and fun for them."

With this idea, Judy not only found a way to capitalize on the goodwill she had created during her several years in business, but she also got a terrific wave of publicity in the small business press when she sent out press releases titled "Maternity Rental Shop Rewards Referrals With Lottery Tickets." (Just one of the hundreds of innovative marketing strategies I mentioned earlier.)

Without question, the easiest way to promote any businesses is to "talk it up" by telling everyone what you're doing: family, friends, business acquaintances and anyone else who looks like a prospect. And never go anywhere without your cards or brochures because prospects are everywhere, says Sylvia Cronin, who sells personalized Cradle Gram(R) birth and religious announcements. "Whenever we go to the supermarket or a restaurant, I always carry a supply of our brochures. If I see a woman who is obviously expecting, I just hand her our brochure and walk away. This is a wonderful way of getting new sales. We have made many sales in supermarkets, waiting in line at the movies, etc. A creative brochure that 'tells it all' is a marvelous sales tool for any homebased business."

Because she lives in Florida where there are many Spanish speaking people, Sylvia has created her brochure in both English and Spanish, a simple marketing idea many businesses would do well to consider.

I've already emphasized the importance of networking as a business and marketing tool, but if talking to strangers doesn't come easily to you, read a book on the topic to gain confidence and learn how the game is played. Remember that networking should not be abused by always asking people to give something to you; true networking requires that you give back to others, not necessarily at the time the original networking is going on, but somewhere along the line. I'm always impressed when businesspeople I don't know take the networking initiative by asking me if I could use an article for my newsletter, or suggest that they might hand out my flyers at an upcoming seminar, or ask if some of their special business contacts might be useful to me. This immediately makes me eager to trade information and referrals I think could be valuable to them and sets the stage for a long-term networking relationship.

Once you've built a good customer base, you can spur your word-of-mouth advertising with regular mailings—follow-up letters, reminder postcards, self-mailers, brochures—or try a promotional newsletter, which many home-business owners now use to promote a variety of products and services. Even when your customers don't buy, your follow-up mailings will often be passed along to others with a word-of-mouth recommendation to "check this out."

"Everyone you meet knows 250 other people," says Stephan Schiffman, president of a sales training and consulting company in New York, and author of several books. "Thus, every time you meet someone, you are, in essence, meeting many more—some of whom may be interested in your product or service. The best way to capitalize on word of mouth is to proudly tell everyone you meet (relatives included) what you do for a living."

"Not all word-of-mouth commentary is spread orally; some of the most important comments may be written," adds Godfrey Harris, coauthor of *Talk Is Cheap: Promoting Your Business Through Word of Mouth Advertising*. This book offers nearly 200 practical ideas on how to systematically stimulate customers into talking about your products or services.

Developing Your Mail Lists

A good mailing list is like a gold mine that just won't quit. All you have to do is grab your pick and start digging. If it's a prospect list you have developed through advertising or publicity (as opposed to a list you have rented or traded), you can send a new

---

Run a Perception Check

We want different things from different people. Prospects are the same. They may want price, quality, a problem-solver, a friendly ear, an intelligent discussion. Your job is to discover needs which you are able to fulfill. Then convince the prospect you can.

Run a perception check. Ask your present clients why they decided to buy from you. You may be surprised by their answers.

—Tom Stoyan, author of *Sell More—101 Ideas to Increase Sales . . . Now*

follow-up mailing as often as every six weeks and count on getting business from a new segment of the list that just didn't get around to responding before. If it's a customer list, your chances of a response are even greater.

My mail lists are so valuable to me that I think of them almost as a trade secret. In total, the thousands of names on my lists not only generate day-to-day business, but they also form the basis of my tremendous word-of-mouth advertising army, which in turn gives me an edge on my competition and unceasing national publicity. It has taken me years of concerted effort to develop my various mail lists, and it requires constant effort to keep all of them up-to-date with regular promotional mailings. Since these lists are one of my most important business assets, I see their maintenance as one of my most important marketing jobs, one I would never trust to an outsider. My whole business revolves around these lists, and if I were suddenly to lose them, I'd be out of business overnight. That won't happen, of course, because I go to great lengths to regularly back up all my computerized database files and then store my backup disks in a safety deposit box. To give you an idea of the kind of mailing lists you ought to be developing, here's a list of mine:

- Names of former newsletter subscribers
- Prospect and book-buyer lists (always growing, always changing)
- Magazines, newsletters and newspapers that publish small-business information and regularly use my press releases
- Special media contacts (syndicated columnists, freelance business writers and authors who often quote me in their articles or books)
- Educators (small business development center directors, cooperative extension specialists and home economists who regularly "talk it up" for me, plus teachers and seminar leaders who distribute my flyers at conferences and promote or sell my books in their classes or workshops)
- Government contacts (SBA offices, SCORE specialists and people in economic development who pass my name on to others with regularity)
- Radio and TV shows on which I've appeared, plus others known to do telephone interviews with authors
- Libraries that have purchased my books
- Schools that offer small business or entrepreneurial courses (several of which use my books as classroom texts)
- Business resources (all the information suppliers in my industry)

From time to time, I mail something to everyone on my various mailing lists, just to stay in touch and keep addresses up to date. It might be a sample issue of my periodical, a copy of

Retail Outlets That Buy Products or Services

Many of the following retailers represent good markets for services of one kind or another, and if you are marketing a service by mail, note that you can rent mailing lists of all these market categories from one list house or another. (See also the chart in this chapter titled "Checklist of Mailing Lists You Can Rent.")

If you are retailing products, generally expect these retailers to ask for a discount of 50 percent off the retail price (although some may be accustomed to buying at 40 percent). You will have to do some market research to learn what is standard in each industry. Exceptions known to the author are indicated by a footnote.

- ☐ Appliance stores
- ☐ Art and craft galleries[1]
- ☐ Baby shops
- ☐ Barber shops
- ☐ Beauty shops
- ☐ Bookstores[2]
- ☐ Bridal shops
- ☐ Camera shops
- ☐ Candy shops
- ☐ Card shops
- ☐ Christmas shops
- ☐ Clothing shops
- ☐ Coffee and tea stores
- ☐ Coffee shops
- ☐ Computer stores
- ☐ Craft supply shops[3]
- ☐ Department stores

- ☐ Fabric stores
- ☐ Fancy cookware stores
- ☐ Florists
- ☐ Garden centers
- ☐ Gas stations with food/gifts
- ☐ Gift shops, general
- ☐ Gourmet food stores
- ☐ Grocery stores
- ☐ Gun shops
- ☐ Handcraft shops
- ☐ Hardware stores
- ☐ Health food stores
- ☐ Hobby shops
- ☐ Home shopping centers
- ☐ Hospital gift shops
- ☐ Hotel gift shops
- ☐ Ice cream parlors

- ☐ Lawn and garden centers
- ☐ Magic and novelty shops
- ☐ Military exchanges
- ☐ Museum shops
- ☐ Needlework shops[3]
- ☐ Office supply stores
- ☐ Pet shops
- ☐ Print shops
- ☐ Record/CD stores
- ☐ Religious bookstores[2]
- ☐ Religious gift shops[2]
- ☐ Restaurants
- ☐ Shoe stores
- ☐ Sports shops
- ☐ Toy stores

Footnotes

1. Like many handcraft shops, art galleries rarely buy outright, preferring work that can be placed on consignment. They may sell for you, keeping from 25 to 40 percent of the retail price, and there may also be extra space rental fees involved here. Consignment selling means increased bookkeeping and paperwork for both shop and seller, and for the latter, merchandise is tied up, but not sold, which presents cash-flow problems. Common consignment hazards are shop owners' lack of concern for goods they do not own, thus losses due to shoplifting, breakage or mishandling are the consignor's problem. *(See also "Consignment Laws" in chapter six.)*

2. If you are selling books to bookstores, they will expect a discount of from 20 to 40 percent, depending on number of books ordered. (See also note 5 on "Wholesale Markets to Explore," page 231.) If a bookstore also has a greeting card or gift division, they will no doubt expect to buy this merchandise at the 50 percent discount that is standard in the gift industry.

3. Craft retailers rarely buy directly from a manufacturer, preferring instead to purchase through craft wholesalers (whose 50 + 10 percent discounts were explained in chapter nine). Needlework retailers, however, often buy patterns and kits from individual manufacturers, expecting only a 40 percent dealer discount.

Criss-Cross Directories

If time allows, you can use "criss-cross directories" or "cross-reference directories" to build a mailing list of potential customers in a specific market area. Call the Chamber of Commerce or the reference librarian at your city library to find out which publisher serves the market area you want to reach. These directories can be leased or used free of charge in a library. With a local criss-cross directory in hand, you can establish a mailing list of apartments and homes within specific areas. You cannot get individual family names, but you can address your mailing to "Occupant" at each address on your list.

my *Home Business Success Catalog* (which describes all my books and reports), a self-mailer that focuses on selected information products, a postcard mailing of one kind or another, or a promotional newsletter that adds to my image as an expert. I do not look for a direct response when I send promotional mailings since these are primarily designed to spur word-of-mouth advertising or generate new publicity, but every other mailing I send to prospects, book buyers or subscribers has one primary purpose: *to generate orders for my various small business information products*.

In the next chapter, you'll find tips on how to build a media (publicity) list. Following are suggestions on how to build a good *prospect* list:

- Begin with the names of friends and business associates with a possible interest in using your products and services.
- Collect business cards at any meeting you attend.
- Ask everyone you know to give you names of their friends.
- Add any names you get from regular publicity, ads and other promotional efforts.
- Donate something that requires people to write their full name and address on a card for a drawing.
- Obtain exhibitor lists from trade shows or attendee lists from conferences and meetings.
- Compile targeted neighborhood lists using criss-cross directories available in your library (see sidebar).
- Order membership directories from organizations serving your targeted market (often—but not always—available).
- Glean from small business publications the addresses of individuals and other business owners for networking or business-to-business marketing purposes.

Your own prospect lists will always outpull any you can rent, but you *must* keep them up to date with periodic mailings. Always include an "Address Correction Requested" notation beneath your return address on any mail piece you send to alert the post office that you want the piece returned to you with the new address. Although first-class mail will be forwarded automatically, it won't do you any good if you don't capture that new address at the time. After only a year, at least 15 percent of your names will be out of date (and in hard times, the percentage could soar to 30 percent), so if you're sitting now with a list that hasn't been mailed in a couple of years, it may be more expensive to clean it than to start all over again.

The cheapest way I know to salvage a badly outdated list is to create an exciting first-class postcard that announces some new product or service. When mailed first class with an "Address Correction Requested" notice, you will get back not only undeliverable cards but those with new addresses. Then you can update your list and remail once again. *Note: If you elect to mail an old list without asking for address corrections and just ask people to let you know if they want to stay on your mailing list, fewer than 5 percent (of addresses that are good) are likely to respond.*

Renting Prospect Lists

Be cautious here. There are countless commercial list compilers who offer mailing lists priced between $45-$110 per thousand. The minimum quantity you can buy is generally 5,000 names, and while the cost of names themselves may seem affordable, mailing 5,000 pieces at current bulk-rate prices will cost you a bundle. (Figure about $.50 per contact—list rental, addressing charge, printed materials, preparation of mailing and postage—for even the most ordinary direct-mail package.) If the list is bad for you, or your mail piece is wrong for the names you've selected, you could easily lose your entire investment. For what you might spend on such a mailing, you could buy quite a few ads likely to bring a much better response. In short, traditional direct mail is great for the pros, but beginning marketers will be better off if they concentrate first on direct mailings to their own "hot lists" of fresh prospect and customer names and hold the idea of rental lists (called "cold mailing lists") as an option to explore later on. (See other notes on this topic on "Checklist of Mailing Lists You Can Rent," page 242.)

The time may come when you are approached by another home-business owner who offers a list for rent or trade. In some instances this can be profitable, particularly when it's a business associate you know and trust. But always ask when the list was last mailed and whether address corrections were requested from the post office. (Remember what I said about how quickly lists go out of date.) *Never* clean someone else's list, and if it is suggested that you will get twice the number of fresh names for every address correction you send, pass on this "opportunity," because this is a clear signal the list is one of those worthless mail-order opportunity lists—names of individuals who have responded to get-rich-quick programs, work-at-home ads and so on. These individuals are not likely to buy your high-quality products and services.

I regret there isn't sufficient space here to include all I've learned about building, using, managing, renting and cleaning mail lists through the years, but if you need more information on this topic, see chapter sixteen to order my publications list, which includes a 5,000 word report on this topic.

Direct Response Guidelines

In making direct mailings of any size, you need to monitor results closely to gain response guidelines for future mailings. Mailings should be considered profitable any time you can get back at least 100 percent of the direct costs of your promotion. After you have made a mailing, how soon can you tell if it's going to produce a good response? Various marketing experts tell us that

- The heaviest day's response to a mailing will come the second Monday after the first response arrives;
- Half the total response to a direct mailing will come within the first thirteen days of returns;
- By the fifth or sixth day after the first response has been received, you will have about 30 to 35 percent of the total response you are going to receive. By the end of two weeks you will have about 75 to 80 percent of the total response you're going to receive.

These helpful guidelines may also be used to project response from publicity and magazine advertisements.

Checklist of Mailing Lists You Can Rent

Following are just a few categories of lists that will be of interest to small businesses. Whether or not you plan to rent such lists, you will find these market categories helpful in determining the most likely groups of buyers for your particular products and services. In fact, a study of several list catalogs will reveal hundreds of market categories you've probably never thought of before. To find companies who sell lists, check the *Standard Rate & Data Service* publications in libraries, or check the ads in any direct marketing trade magazine.

In addition to renting mail lists of market categories I've listed on charts in this chapter, you can also reach many of these same market categories through press releases to organizations that publish member periodicals, privately published newsletters serving these niche markets, and through classified ads and publicity in trade or consumer publications aimed at these groups.

- ☐ Boat owners
- ☐ Business executives
- ☐ Business opportunity seekers
- ☐ Clubs, organizations, societies
- ☐ Collectors (categories are endless)
- ☐ Colleges and universities
- ☐ Corporate gift buyers
- ☐ Crafts enthusiasts
- ☐ Day care facilities
- ☐ Doctors
- ☐ Editors
- ☐ Ethnic groups (various)

- ☐ Farmers
- ☐ Garden clubs
- ☐ Gift shops
- ☐ Gourmet cooks
- ☐ Hobbyists
- ☐ Homemaker groups
- ☐ Knitting and yarn shops
- ☐ Libraries
- ☐ Meeting planners
- ☐ Millionaires
- ☐ Mothers-to-be
- ☐ Music teachers
- ☐ New Mothers

- ☐ Nursery schools
- ☐ Photography buffs
- ☐ Professionals (all fields)
- ☐ Religious and ethnic groups
- ☐ Self-improvement buyers
- ☐ Senior citizens
- ☐ Small businesses owners
- ☐ Sports lovers (all categories)
- ☐ Subscribers (of many publications)
- ☐ Teachers
- ☐ Ultra-affluent women

Note

The fact that you may have to purchase 5,000 names from a list house does not mean you have to *mail* to all of them. In fact, you can test the list with a mailing of as small as 1,000 and get a good indication about whether this is a profitable way for you to find new sales outlets.

The most important thing to remember about direct mailing to cold lists like those above is that a 1 to 2 percent response is considered good by major mailers (who would be ecstatic with 3 to 4 percent). One percent, of course,

translates to only 50 orders on a 5,000-piece mailing, and you need not be a mathematician to see how easy it would be for inexperienced direct mailers to lose their shirts the first time out. Now you know why only the more expensive products are offered by major direct-mail marketers. In fact, a product with a retail value of less than $50 probably would not be profitable to them, given the high costs of direct mail and the average response to a "cold mailing list," which is all rented lists are.

Using Two-Step Advertising

One thing homebased entrepreneurs can afford—and can count on to yield a fair response even when the copywriting isn't great—are classified ads designed to pull in interested prospects who can then be sold with a good follow-up mailing or telephone call. It's called "two-step advertising," and it's a lot like going fishing. First you get the nibble . . . then you sink the hook.

This is the preferred method of advertising for all businesses with limited budgets, but it works so well major marketers also use it to build mailing lists of qualified customer prospects. While major companies may place expensive display ads to attract buyer prospects (manufacturers trying to interest dealers, for instance), smaller businesses are more likely to think in terms of placing classified ads in a number of magazines. And for as little as $500, one can run quite an effective campaign.

Average Response From Classified Ads

The response to any classified will bring you a number of "hot prospects" (people who are obviously interested in learning the details of your offer), as opposed to the "cold prospects" you normally would reach in a direct mailing to a rental list. (The latter prospects, never having asked to receive your literature, may simply throw it in the wastebasket when it arrives.)

Since all ads attract a certain number of curiosity seekers, don't expect to sell more than 5 percent of your hot prospects with your first mailing, and be satisfied if you get an order response of 2 to 3 percent, which most mailers consider good. (Again, much depends on what you are selling, and to whom. I have received order conversion rates everywhere from 3 percent to 18 percent, but the catalog I now send to interested people generally brings a 10 percent order response. I did notice, through the years, that my order response gradually increased the more professional my printed materials became.)

About six to eight weeks after your first mailing to a list of prospects gained from a classified ad, send a follow-up mailing, and *keep on mailing to these prospects as long as you get back enough orders or client business to cover all your costs.* In my experience, repeated mailings to a good prospect list will generate new business every time it's mailed, and this seems to hold true even if you mail the same people the same offer over and over again.

Figuring Per-Inquiry/Per-Order Costs

If you wonder whether a display ad or the two-step method would be best for you, try a test and evaluate the results on a

What You Should Know About E-Mail Addresses

A 1996 survey revealed that 75 percent of users go online just to be able to send e-mail. If this is your main reason for going online, here are a couple of things you might like to know.

Once you have an e-mail address, you may begin to receive "junk e-mail." That's because e-mail addresses are now being captured and rented to electronic advertisers in the same way that names and addresses are compiled and rented to mail order marketers. (One list seller I read about rents five million addresses at a time for less than a hundred dollars.) As this is being written, various steps are being taken to protect the privacy of e-mail users and enable them to get their names off existing lists.

Legal Problems. If you use e-mail, be careful what you say, especially if you are sending e-mail messages while on the job. As one business adviser warns, "People are being sued for what they've said in e-mail messages they believed to be private. If your e-mail is deleted, it can still come back to haunt you. Computer sleuths can exhume deleted e-mail long after you've buried it."

Advertising/Promotion/Marketing Options at a Glance

Free:

Word-of-mouth advertising (from satisfied customers and business peers)

Referrals (from business associates)

Publicity from press releases (print and electronic media)

Publicity from articles you contribute to other publications

Publicity from your being interviewed on radio or television

Directory listings (many free listings available)

Signs and bulletin board announcements

Flyer distribution at meetings, workshops, conferences (from contacts gained through networking or study of business periodicals)

All sales made in connection with activities you initiate, such as holiday boutiques, open houses, instructional classes or speaking engagements.

Per-order (PO) advertising *(See "Direct-Mail Options to Consider," page 245.)*

Inexpensive:

Press release mailings to media contacts

Telemarketing (cold calls to get prospects or follow-up calls to existing prospect lists)

Direct-mail promotions (to your own prospects and customers)

Selling to dealers or distributors who will makes sales for you (you need only supply sales aids such as camera-ready artwork for ads or flyers)

Marketing on a drop-ship basis (dealers send you orders with payment enclosed for product and shipping costs;you need only package and ship for them using their labels)

Classified and display ads in self-published periodicals of all kinds (generally small circulation but often reaching important niche markets)

Two-step classified ads in small circulation magazines

Free product samples (to prospective buyers or reviewers)

Free sampling of your service (to individual prospects and particularly to prominent individuals in a position to influence other buyers)

Donation of product or service to a community event, conference or meeting (where your name will be mentioned as a contributor)

Moderate Cost:

Presentation packages or press kits to selected clients or media contacts

Two-step classified ads in large circulation magazines

Display ads in small-circulation magazines or trade publications

Yellow pages listing or small ad

Per-inquiry (PI) advertisements *(See "Direct-Mail Options to Consider," page 245.)*

Selling through an authorized agent (products such as books, designs, licensing and other sales rights—your cost is sales commission to agent)

Selling through sales reps (who take a commission and require color flyers and samples)

Advertising specialties (calendars, emery boards, magnets and other devices with your name and address on them)

Expensive:

Display ads in large circulation magazines

Advertising through special point-of-purchase displays for retailers

Package inserts *(See "Direct-Mail Options to Consider," page 245.)*

Direct-mail promotions to a rented mailing list

Trade show exhibits (high booth fees and related expenses)

Exhibiting in merchandise marts (high space rental fees)

Direct-Mail Options to Consider

1. Cooperative mailings
2. Per-order (PO) advertising
3. Per-inquiry (PI) advertising
4. Package inserts (commercial insert programs)
5. Commercial card deck (or card pack) programs
6. Your catalog or direct-mail package sent to a rented list

Notes:

1. Many small businesses work cooperatively with other noncompetitive businesses, adding their flyers or brochures to their outgoing mail, subscriber mailings or special promotional mailings to their entire prospect base. In addition to a special per-piece insert charge, you would have to pay for all printed materials. (*Note*: Offering a cooperative mailing to other businesses in your industry is an excellent way to expand your own profit base.)

2. PO advertising is free, no-risk advertising offered by some special interest magazines and some radio and television stations. These opportunities are rarely publicized; to find them, contact the advertising department to see if PO (or PI—see below) advertising opportunities are available. If your product is deemed likely to sell to their audience, they will run your ad without charge to you, directing orders to their address and keeping half the product's retail price as their commission. You would then ship orders as they are forwarded to you, a practice known as "drop shipping."

3. PI advertising is similar to PO advertising, except in this case you would be expected to pay so much per inquiry, depending on whether you were offering free literature or some kind of for-sale booklet. One problem here is that volume of response might overwhelm a small business.

4. Most package insert programs have to be purchased in minimum quantities of 100,000, but a diligent search may yield interesting markets with minimum test quantities of between 10,000 and 25,000. These programs include everything from "take-one" posters distributed on college campuses, to new-mother packages distributed in hospitals, to package inserts in merchandise shipments made by major catalog houses. Although cost is similar to display advertising, response tends to be higher because information is going directly into hands of likely prospects. For more information about special distribution programs of this nature, check the *Standard Rate & Data Service (SRDS)* publications available in libraries, or look for ads in direct marketing magazines.

5. A "card deck" is a collection of from 25 to 65 postcards from a wide variety of sellers, each trying to get interested prospects to order directly from their card or at least return it for more information. There are hundreds of commercial card deck programs, each directed to a specific, targeted market (most often business professionals in one field or another), but most are too expensive for use by home-based businesses because of 100,000 minimum quantity requirements, which may cost $3,000 or more for participation, depending on the targeted market. The least expensive, and perhaps most responsive business card deck now in existence is the one offered by homebased entrepreneur and author Dr. Jeffrey Lant, whose address is found in chapter sixteen as a primary provider of reliable small business information.

6. See "Renting Prospect Lists" under "Developing Your Mail Lists," and note on "Checklist of Mailing Lists You Can Rent."

Classified Ad Writing Tips

- Eliminate unnecessary words.
- Write in telegraphic style. Use as many one-syllable words as possible.
- Don't try to sell two things in the same ad, because the average reader can only retain one basic idea at a time.
- Don't try to sell products or services directly in a classified ad—it doesn't work. Just fish for prospects and let your mail piece do the selling job.
- Use the *A-I-D-A* formula in writing ads:

  A = ATTRACT your reader

  I = INTEREST the reader by appealing to his or her wants or needs

  D = Stimulate *DESIRE* for your product by listing benefits to be derived from it

  A = Demand *ACTION* by closing with a phrase that gives readers something to write for or do. Examples: (1) For information write; (2) Send for free details; (3) Catalog, $1.00; (4) Order *Now!*

per-inquiry/per-order cost basis. This is far more important than the cost of an ad or mail promotion. For example, if a classified ad costs $60 and generates 110 inquiries, your per-inquiry cost would be $.55 ($60 divided by 110).

If you were to place a small display ad—one that cost $250—in the same publication, and it brought in 197 inquiries, your per-inquiry cost would be $1.27 ($250 divided by 197). In this instance, then, classified ads would certainly be the most cost-effective way to generate inquiries *in this particular magazine.* (You might get an entirely different response from a different magazine.)

Your per-customer (or per-order) costs are even more important to you. Let's say that you send a catalog or other direct-mail package to customer prospects, and it costs you $.73 to print and mail first class. Using one of the examples above, let's assume that you send this mail piece to the 110 prospects who have responded to the classified ad, for a cost of $80.30. Add to this the cost of the ad itself, which was $60, for a total of $140.30. If you were to get a 4.5 percent order response (conversion of prospects to customers)—only 5 new customers—your per-customer cost would be $28.06, as illustrated below.

Depending on the cost of your product, or the size of your average order, you can easily see whether you're going to make or lose money in this kind of situation, and determine whether you should be charging some kind of fee when you "fish for prospects." As you know, many advertisers charge from $.50 to $3 for brochures or catalogs, depending on how elaborate or expensive they are to print and mail. If you were to place the same $60 classified ad and ask $.50 for your catalog, you might get only 65 prospects instead of 110, but they would probably be better buyer prospects, and your order response might increase from 4.5 to 8 percent. On this basis, your actual ad investment would be $60, less the $32.50 your customer prospects send you for postage and handling, or just $27.50. To this, add $47.45 in costs to send them a catalog, and you've lowered your costs to $74.95. On the basis of an 8 percent order response (5 customers), your cost per customer now drops to $14.99 instead of $28.06. Quite a difference, isn't it, from an ad that reads "free catalog" to one that reads "Send 50 cents for catalog." Certainly you'll be money ahead whenever you can lower your advertising costs by charging for your promotional literature.

These days, few sellers can afford to put anything into the mail without at least a dollar charge for postage and handling. Such a small charge will rarely deter serious prospects and only further "qualifies" them as likely buyers once they get your literature in hand. A popular strategy is to charge $1 or $2 for the information package and mention in the ad that the charge is "refundable with first order." This means you would include a $1 credit memo or money-off coupon with your outgoing literature so prospects can get their dollar back if they decide to order.

To illustrate the above figures:

Step One of Two-Step Advertising Method

Ad reading "free catalog"		**Ad reading "50 cents for catalog"**	
Cost of ad:	$60.00	Cost of ad:	$60.00
		Less $.50 sent by each of 65 prospects:	−$32.50
		Adjusted ad cost:	$27.50
Per-Inquiry cost: $60 ÷ 110 = $.55		Per-inquiry cost: $27.50 ÷ 65 = $.42	

Step Two of Two-Step Advertising Method

Cost to send catalogs to 110 prospects: 110 × $.73 =	$80.30	Cost to send catalogs to 65 prospects: 65 × $.73 =	$47.45
Plus ad cost (above):	$60.00	Plus ad cost (above):	$27.50
Total invested in this ad promotion:	$140.30	Total invested in this ad promotion:	$74.95
If 4.5 percent order response (5 customers) per-inquiry cost would be: $140.30 ÷ 5 = $28.06		If 8 percent order response (5 customers), per-inquiry cost would be: $74.95 ÷ 5 = $14.99	

Instead of asking for money, some advertisers ask interested prospects to send an SASE (Self-Addressed, Stamped Envelope). In doing this, remember the importance of making it easy for people to respond to your offer. Sometimes the extra effort involved in getting an envelope and finding a stamp kills the impulse to order at all. In fact, experts say a request for an SASE will automatically decrease by 25 to 35 percent the total number of responses you may receive. "You're cutting your own throat to save a first-class stamp and an envelope," says one mail-order seller.

And now I'm going to tell you what works best for me and many other mail-order marketers. Instead of offering free information, asking for an SASE, or charging $.50-$1 for your catalog or brochure, think about creating a special information package you could sell—a tip sheet, reference chart, resource list, sample or special report that your prospects will perceive as being

Brochure Copywriting Tips

In creating your brochure, ask what you want the brochure to accomplish:

1. Are you trying to get orders from individuals by return mail with check enclosed?
2. Are you trying to sell wholesale to shops, who may request shipment with invoicing?
3. Are your trying to get the recipient to return an enclosed postage-paid reply card or other vehicle that says, "Yes, send me detailed information by mail"?
4. Or are you mostly interested in getting an expression of interest so you can follow up with a personal sales call?

The primary goal of a brochure should be to show recipients how your product or service can solve some particular problem or need they may have at the moment. Stress the benefits of what you're selling in terms your particular market can relate to. The inclusion of testimonial copy will show that others value your products or services and help persuade many people to buy. Finally, make it easy for the recipient to respond by providing a convenient order form or reply vehicle of some kind. (It need not be prepaid to be effective.)

valuable to them. In my experience, people will gladly pay up to six bucks to get unusual or hard-to-find information targeted to their special needs. When such orders are received, you simply tuck your promotional material in with the special information ordered. To increase bounce-back orders or client business, you may wish to include a money-off coupon on one of your high-profit products or services. Surprisingly, a $2 information package may pull two or three times the response of an ad that requests $.50 for a catalog or brochure *because now you're appealing to a niche market with specific interests.*

For comparison's sake, let's say that your $60 ad will generate 200 requests for "valuable information" you have decided to offer for just $2. The figures look like this:

200 inquiries with $2 checks	$400.00
Less your cost to mail package:	
200 × $.83 ($.73 plus $.10 for the 'info package" offered):	–$166.00
Less cost of ad:	–$ 60.00
Up-Front *net profit:*	$174.00

Voila! Now you've got 200 hot prospects *at no cost to you.* If NONE of them buy, you'll still be ahead, but chances are good that your response will increase because the value of the information you've included in your package has added to your professional image and given prospects more confidence in whatever product or service you're selling. (In the next chapter, you'll find specific examples of information packages and samples that can be offered not only in ads, but in press releases.)

Getting a Response to Your Second Step

Obviously, the material you send to prospects who respond to your ad has a lot to do with the number of orders or volume of business you'll get. The easier you make it for people to order, the more likely they are to respond to your offer. That's why flyers or brochures without any kind of order form do not pull as well as a brochure or catalog with an order blank; better yet, a standard direct-mail package with a cover letter, brochure, separate order form and postage-paid reply envelope. In the beginning, your goal should be to get started with the best package you can afford. Test the response to each mailing you send out, and test a number of direct mail pieces. Then decide which kind of mail piece works best for you.

Note that handcrafts and gifts, in particular, will *not* sell well to consumers through inexpensively printed, black-and-white brochures or catalogs with line drawings or poor photographs. One reason is because buyers may be able to buy such items locally, where they can see every little detail. When ordering by mail, they have no visual assurance of the color, texture and quality of such products. Conversely, the same products that will not sell this way may sell beautifully if they are featured in a full-color catalog produced by a nationally known company, such as Horchow or Lillian Vernon. The difference here, of course, *is buyer confidence in the company making the offer*. This is just one more key to success in selling by mail. Guarantees also go a long way in mail order, as do testimonials from satisfied customers. (It is said that a money-back guarantee may increase order response by as much as 40 percent.)

Follow-Up Mailings

The greatest mistake made by inexperienced marketers is to concentrate only on selling their products and services to new (first-time) buyers. They run ads or get publicity that brings in hundreds, even thousands of prospect names, mail to them once, and let the original letters or envelopes rot in a box. The buyers acquired from the initial prospect mailing are apt to suffer a similar fate: once orders are processed, or a service delivered, they may never be contacted again because the names and addresses were not preserved on computer.

As one who considers a good name and address worth its weight in silver—if not gold—I am always astonished that anyone would waste such a valuable business resource in this way. Yet business novices tell me all the time this is exactly what they are doing, mostly because they either lack a computer to organize the names or have nothing else to sell. It's difficult to succeed in business with only one product or service (at the very least, you need "variations on a theme")—which is why this book includes a special chapter on diversification strategies. And although I once managed 20,000 names on $3'' \times 5''$ cards and paper label masters, I practically went crazy in the process and wouldn't be in business today if I had continued to operate this way past 1986. That's why this book also includes a special computer chapter. In the event you are not yet "computer literate," I want you to realize how easy it is to learn to use computer technology not only to manage your business and mailing lists, but to develop multiple profit centers built around the computer.

As important as it is to regularly contact your list of prospects, it's *doubly* important to stay in touch with your existing customer base. The two most expensive things a business can do is *get a customer* and *lose a customer*. "We often put so much time, effort and money into finding new customers that we forget and neglect our past and present ones," says Doug Kipp, editor of *The Entrepreneurial Spirit* in Calgary, Alberta. "It is far more expensive to make a customer buy from you the first time than it is to get a satisfied customer to return for additional sales. Therefore, we must keep the ties with our customers as tight as possible."

If you lack ideas on how to promote to your existing prospect and customer lists, here are three approaches you might use in a direct mailing:

1. **Offer a Discount.** In hard economic times, it might boost your sales to offer $3-$5 off on the first order for an advertised product or publication. In selling a service, try a 10 percent discount for using the service before a specified date (usually 15-30 days).

2. **Offer Old Products in a New Way.** If you have no new products, publications or services, try offering old favorites in new, money-saving combinations, or try packaging one product with another product or service. Think about offering a "Sizzling Summer Selection," "Buy Three—Get One *Free*," "Trial Sampler," or "Special Introductory Offer." Such offers could be presented in a letter, postcard or inexpensive four-page self-mailer (folded to size 5½″ × 8½″).

3. **Offer Something *Free*.** The key here is to be selective, offering freebies only when their cost will be offset by an order; but remember free product samples tend to generate valuable word-of-mouth advertising even when direct sales do not result. Two things that have worked well for me are (1) "Free $10 cassette tape with $40 catalog order"; and (2) "Subscribe Now—Get Bonus $6 Report."

If your product is too big or too expensive to give away free, consider the following alternatives:

1. Creating a miniature version of the item
2. Publishing a booklet with helpful information and tips
3. Offering a free trial (like magazine publishers do: Return invoice if not delighted)
4. Offering a free service that would attract the product buyers you want to reach (e.g., free makeup analysis for people who might then purchase cosmetics)

The offer is just part of what must be considered when planning a direct-mail promotion of any kind. Copywriting also comes into play here, and for that reason you'll find some helpful copywriting tips in sidebar material and at the end of this chapter that can be used in the development of both brochures and advertisements.

Telemarketing

The telephone is one of our best and most affordable marketing tools, yet many business owners fail to utilize this simple technology to their advantage. In just one minute on the telephone, you can accomplish what it might take two pages of a letter to do. In the process, you not only save some of your precious time but also make a greater impression on a prospective customer, client or business associate than may be possible using a letter.

Let's say you're trying to sell a special product to a major mail-order catalog house or offering a particular service to a corporation or organization. Instead of agonizing over what to send them (how to phrase an "are you interested in this?" question) and worrying about whether your letter will even reach the proper decision maker, simply *pick up the phone*, ask for the name of the specific individual you need, and forthrightly present yourself as a seller of (whatever). Say, "I just wanted to check first to see if you had any interest in this. May I send you a complete presentation package?" When you hang up, you'll know *exactly* what must be said in a letter, and the worst part of your selling job will be over.

Consider Carol Starr's approach to telemarketing. Although she says she dislikes making phone calls to solicit orders for her Starr Gift Baskets, she was forced to do this when she couldn't find anyone else to do the job. Beginning with a list of names she had acquired from membership in such groups as the Convention and Visitors Bureau and Chamber of Commerce, she had an easy opening for her call: "Hi, I'm a member of the (group), and I just wanted to say hello, tell you what I do, and get some information about your business."

"Everyone loves to talk about their business," says Carol, "so this sets the tone for a comfortable conversation. I then ask them if it is OK to send a brochure about my business, and if I may follow up with a phone call. They always says yes."

By making only ten calls a day, Carol says she does not feel rejected and frustrated because she has not tried to "sell." Yet in her first attempt at telemarketing, she got two basket orders. Now the telephone has become one of her best networking and sales tools.

Other Follow-Up Strategies

After you've given prospects your best brochure, catalog or direct-mail piece and made the first follow-up contact, it's time to follow up again . . . and again with other direct-mail promotions, telephone calls or personal visits to the client's door.

"Don't stop with just one follow-up contact," says super-salesman Tom Stoyan. "It has been reported that of all new sales, 80 percent are made after the fifth call. Yet a survey of sales-people revealed that 48 percent gave up after one call and 25 percent after the second call."

It's much easier to persuade an already-interested prospect to buy than it is to dig up brand new prospects who have never

Selling Your Services

My number one commandment for selling a service is Listen!

Most people who sell do it absolutely wrong. They go in and tell the prospect what they want to say, reciting a memorized list of product features and benefits. But what prospects care about is what is important to them—*their needs, their problems, their concerns, their fears, their desires, their goals, their dreams. Successful salespeople tailor their presentations to show how the* features *of their products or service can give every client what he or she desires most or needs to solve his or her problem.*

—Bob Bly, marketing consultant and author of several books, including *Selling Your Services—Proven Strategies for Getting Clients to Hire You (or Your Firm)*

heard of you before. If you're financially strapped, don't invest in an expensive advertising campaign until you have made a special effort to once again "touch base" with everyone currently on your in-house mailing list.

Prospects who already are familiar with what you offer may need only a small nudge to buy. Satisfied customers are likely to be interested in whatever is new. These strategies have worked for me and many others. Give them a try:

"Sock-It-To-'Em-Again!"

Ninety percent of those who ask for information about my books and newsletter do not place orders after receiving detailed information in my catalog, my best sales piece. Yet when I send these prospects one of my routine follow-up postcards, self-mailers or promotional newsletters two or three months later, I can be *certain* of receiving a 2 to 4 percent order response (sometimes more). And I can count on a similar response each and every time I remail the list over the next three years or more. (When I reach the point where response drops to a level that I cannot make a profit on a mailing to a particular segment of my prospect list, I dump those names.)

In applying this "sock-it-to-'em-again" strategy to your own business, ask yourself what your prospects need most, then create a follow-up promotion that offers them a *specific benefit* for buying *now*. Once you have a prospect's interest, you need only find the right "response button" to get an order or close the sale. Different people respond to different buttons, but the bottom line is benefits, benefits, BENEFITS.

Consultant Bob Bly says repeated follow-up should convert at least 10 percent of prospects to buyers. He also suggests this follow-up strategy, particularly effective in hard times:

"Help existing clients or customers create new sales for you. Call existing accounts with new ideas that will benefit them while requiring them to buy more of what you're selling. They get your ideas, suggestions and solutions to problems at no charge, while you sell more of your product or service to help them implement the idea you suggested." Bob is the author of several marketing books, including *Advertising Manager's Handbook*, perhaps the best collection of expert advertising advice you'll ever find. (See chapter sixteen.)

Send a Postcard

A great way to bring in cash almost immediately, while also updating your mail list, is to announce new products or services with an illustrated postcard. For the personal touch, use your picture on the front of a card, and have yourself "speaking" (in a cartoon-style bubble) a benefit-oriented message. Include an illustration and description of your new offer on the back, asking people to return the card with payment, call your toll-free number to order, or arrange to receive a free consultation or sales presentation. (See sample postcard illustrations nearby.)

Craftseller Kay Nelson uses postcards to promote to customers who have purchased from her at craft fairs. Beginning with 250 names, she originally hand-addressed cards. Three years later, with the help of a computer, she was sending follow-up announcements to nearly 5,000 customers and racking up extra sales at every show as a direct result. "As many as 75 to 85 percent of show sales have been from customers who have received these mailings," says Kay, who now mails everyone on her list twice a year. She sends a postcard announcing shows in the spring, and a new catalog and show schedule in September.

Copywriter and consultant Bob Westenberg sends monthly copies of a postcard called *IMP—The World's Smallest Newsletter*. Each "issue" features a dozen or so interesting tidbits of information on a variety of topics, with the last tidbit always being a subtle reminder that Bob is available to help. For example, one card reads, "Most of my jobs come from referrals. If you know someone who might want to use my services, give me (or them) a call. Thanks." Another card reads, "IMP is more than a keep-in-touch newsletter. It chips away at customers/prospects and gets business. It's my best-ever business-getter. Ask about your own IMP to get new sales for you, too." Once you start receiving Bob's impish postcard reminders, it's pretty hard to forget him. Even harder when he follows up these cards with personal notes and letters that may include an amusing cartoon, interesting clipping or helpful business resource.

"*IMP* is my best business-getter," says Bob. "Last year its water-on-the-rock contacts netted me $21,000 in freelance work. Not bad for a monthly circulation of 150." Not bad, indeed, for an advertising cost I calculate to be little more than $500/year. As a believer in the idea that "little things mean a lot," Bob Westenberg is an excellent example of how to come across as a real person, not an "organization." "It's the little things that build strong, invisible bonds between you and customers that competitors can't break," he reminds us.

You can also use postcards effectively for prepublication announcements, invitations, customer thank-you notes and other personal customer correspondence. (For the latter, try a full-color photographic card that shows your best product, you sitting at your desk in your office, or an action shot of you at work.)

Send a Promotional Newsletter

Newsletters are an effective marketing tool for product and service businesses alike. I have developed two follow-up newsletters

How to Get Some Business (*Money*) in a Hurry!

- Call some of your best customers to see if they need your products or services at this time.
- Make telephone calls to a selected list of "hot prospects."
- Contact the rest of your prospect and customer bases with postcard mailings promoting specific products or services likely to be of interest. (Turnaround time: two weeks.)
- Check your business competitors to see if they could use your help in handling overflow work.
- Call your former employer to see if you could work for the company on an independent contractor basis.
- If you sell a service, look closely at prospects in your community to identify a few who clearly need your business. Depending on what you do, a quick, observant walk around the neighborhood might do the trick.

REVISED UPDATED
Includes information about using compu... in your work.

SELL & RE-SELL YOUR PHOTO

How to sell your pictures to a world of markets as close as your mailbox.

ROHN ENGH

IS YOUR ADVERTISING HOT ??

If your advertising doesn't provide hot leads, try our attention grabbing professional photography plus superb color printing that will demand immediate interest in your business products or services.

We handle it all — Photography, copy, layout, and printing !! Call Today !

Post Cards / Catalog Sheets / Brochures

Visions Photography
Philonese Simmons
Oak Park, IL 60302

---

imp
The World's Smallest Newsletter
Published on the 17th by:
BOB WESTENBERG
Copywriter / Consultant / Fund Raiser
6020-E Highway 179 • Sedona, AZ 86336 • (602) 284-1111

To make room for 5,000 RV's coming to MI for '88 "Campvention of National Campers/Hikers" 30,000 trees were cut down.

Poor listener traits, per Sales/Mktg. Mgmt.: "Helps others finish sentences; Does all the talking; 'Steps on peoples' sentences'; No eye contact; More feedback than needed using, 'Uh huh's.'"

U.S. has 70% of world's lawyers; one per 335 people. Japan has one per every 9,000 people.

Leonardo da Vinci wrote all his notes backwards so they had to be read in a mirror, to prevent theft of his ideas.

In '91, CEO's averaged $143,600...

"A committee can make a decision dumber than any of its members."

To cut procrastination: Mix unpleasant chores with pleasant ones; Reward yourself after doing unwanted chore; Focus on what you gain from doing the job, don't worry about finishing... just start." *(Bottom Line)*

Smoking is associated with more deaths and illnesses than drugs, alcohol, auto accidents, AIDS combined, Bruce!

Looking for new ideas? Isolating yourself from others can be a mistake. Contact with others is an idea stimulant.

Dottie Walters, "Starmaker"-President of Walters International Speakers Bureau, author of Prentice Hall book, **Speak & Grow Rich**, Publisher of Sharing Ideas magazine, is coming to <u>Nashville</u>!

Full day Famous Seminar: "Speak & Grow Rich"

STONE MILL... PARK
BOX 219
ROCKLAND, DE 19732
ADDRESS CORRECTION REQUESTED

HOLIDAY FONT SPECIAL

BUY ONE GET ONE FREE!

It's time to renew your subscription to KEYBOARD CONNECTION!

It's as easy as returning this post card with your check or money order made payable to **Keyboard Connection**. Go ahead: fold, spindle, or mutilate this card to fit it in an ... to the label below.

... year ...). Canadian

... **Connection** (a savings of

Hi _____. You're invited to attend an informal art & craft exhibit. Come & see thousands of unique items from across the country. The selection includes:

- Personalized water color cartoons
- Calligraphy (some personalized)
- Original water color prints
- Custom aw...

- Frames & prints
- Miniatures
- Framed quotes & quips
- Pencil drawings
- and more...

...he local shops. Many are available

FIRST CLASS
U.S. Postage
PAID

National Home Business Report
P. O. Box 2137
Naperville, IL 60567

Address Correction Requested

SEE OVER. . .to receive my *"Niche Marketing Ideas"* report FREE! It could have a dramatic impact on your business!

Barbara Brabec, Author of
Homemade Money & Creative Cash

SUBSCRIBE WITHIN 15 DAYS...
☞ Get BONUS "Niche Marketing Ideas" Report!

"NHBR is chock-full of good information. . . one of the best publications in the field." - **HOME OFFICE COMPUTING**

Serious about a homebased business? Increase your chances for success with a subscription to *National Home Business Report*. Subscribe now--AT NO RISK—and we'll send a complete <u>Home Business Information Package and $6 BONUS Report</u> (see left) by return mail and start your subscription with the next issue (Report #53). Focus of this issue is on **Sharpening Communication Skills: How to Get Your Message Across to Prospects and Customers.** (Also available as a SAMPLE for $7 ppd.)

Each 28-page issue of *NHBR* (now 13 years old) features INSIDER INFO for home-business owners and other self-employed individuals--with industry news, articles, special departments, DOZENS of low-cost marketing ideas, and <u>up to 70 business/networking connections</u>. A subscription (4 issues) also includes a unique FREE publicity service.

JOIN THE WINNERS! To subscribe...
Return this card with payment of $24. (Check accuracy of address on other side.) **Satisfaction GUARANTEED or money back!**

BONUS Report:

- ☐ 60 Business Contacts!
- ☐ 34 Niche Markets Identified
- ☐ 12 Diversification Success Stories
- ☐ Checking Credit Ratings
- ☐ Postcard Marketing Tips
- ☐ Independent Contractor Warning (IRS)
- ☐ How to Sell to the Federal Government
- ☐ Niche Publishing

that are "soft-sell" self-mailers I bulk mail in quantity whenever I have some new information products to offer my list (or I want to remind my word-of-mouth army to keep talking). Each newsletter includes a personal message, a list of my newest reports (with an emphasis on topics under discussion in the current issue of my subscription quarterly), a collection of valuable small business tips and resources, an excerpt from one of my books, reader testimonials, and an order form for whatever information products are mentioned in that particular mailer. This has been a far more effective sales tool than the old "hard-sell" self-mailers I used to do (and hated to write). Doing a friendly newsletter for my following of readers is not only more fun, but more profitable. A lot of other marketers apparently agree with me since dozens of promotional newsletters cross my desk every month. (I only wish space allowed for a longer discussion of this topic here.)

Pick Up the Phone

Earlier, you learned the value of using the phone to get initial orders. It's an effective reorder tool as well, as Jane Wentz, owner of From Wentz It Came, illustrates:

"When a saleswoman at a clothing store called to give me her name and thank me for my business, the call gave me such a positive feeling that I decided my own customers might like to receive a similar call. So I phoned my best customer to chat for a while, and ended up with an order. That encouraged me to call several other accounts. I got three orders from the next eight calls, and it felt good! Since then I've begun to personally deliver selected orders just so I can meet the interesting people behind the signatures I've come to know. I have little to lose and so much to gain."

Marketing studies have revealed it costs the average company six times as much to get an order from a new customer as it does to get the same order from an existing customer. And, since your existing customers will always be your most profitable source of new orders, it pays to go out of your way to keep them happy—with special money-saving offers, special attention to order inquiries and personal service. In short, when you need cash in a hurry, dig in your own backyard first. Your mailing list of interested prospects and customers is a virtual gold mine just waiting to be worked!

General Copywriting Techniques

Because good copywriting is so important to the overall success of your business, you should make it a point to acquire some skill in this area. You do not have to be "a writer" to do this, but you

The sample postcards on page 254—including two used by the author—have been successful in getting book, software and subscription orders and renewals; seminar registrants; clients for photography and copywriting services; and in drawing customers to an informal art and craft exhibit (card sent by Fax Marketing).

The reverse side of each postcard offers additional information. For example, the seminar card includes a picture of seminar leader Dottie Walters with some benefit-oriented copy; the other side of the Visions Photography card is a full-color photograph that shows the quality of work clients may expect to receive; the "Sell & Re-Sell" postcard includes a description of what's in the revised edition of the book being promoted; the art/craft exhibit card and renewal card show the business logos used by each business owner; and the software postcard describes the individual font packages being promoted. Bob Westenberg's "IMP" postcard is blank so he can add a personal, handwritten message and address. Sometimes he just stuffs these postcards in with his outgoing mail. (See text for more information on this unusual marketing tool.)

Note: *The author ceased publication of her newsletter in 1996 after fifteen years of publication.*

Powerful Words and Persuasive Phrases

The following words and phrases are used regularly by successful advertisers. Incorporate them into your advertising copy whenever possible.

Bargain	Love
Bonus	Money-back
Check	guarantee
Compare	New
Complete	Now
Confidential	Offer
Discover	Personalize
Earn	Popular
Easy	Profit
End	Profitable
Exciting	Proven
Facts	Quick
Free	Refundable
Fun	Reliable
Gain	Safe
Gift	Sale
Guaranteed	Save
Helpful	Secrets
Here	Stop
How to	Success
Important	Tested
Improved	Try
Informative	Wanted
Interesting	Winner
Last chance	Your
Learn	*You*

Act *Now*

A Special Invitation

Buy three—Get one free

Do not delay

Free details

Get started today

Here's news

It's easy

Judge for yourself

Never before

Proven results

Save time and money

Send no money

There's no risk or obligation

Three good reasons

Trial offer

You can trust

do need to acquire some of the writer's skills. Probably the best way to learn ad copywriting is to study the advertisements of other advertisers and businesses in your field. Look carefully at what you have been calling "junk mail" and pull out good examples of cover letters, flyers and brochures you can study for style and technique. Remember that major advertisers pay a small fortune to professional copywriters, and you can get their expertise *free* simply by reading your daily mail! For continuing help, subscribe to at least one marketing magazine that includes articles on how to write better advertising or sales copy. Like every other skill the homebased business owner must acquire, this one just takes a little time and effort. Meanwhile, here are a few tips to get you started on the road to better copywriting:

• Use everyday language. Short sentences. Short paragraphs. Don't ever try to be funny. Just be sincere and conversational.

• People like to deal with people, so establish a personality, flavor and atmosphere by your name, concept and what you are trying to do.

• Speak to your audience as if you were speaking to one person. Use the words "you" and "your" often. Avoid "we-centered" remarks.

• Make your offer believable by avoiding exaggerated claims and words like "astounding," "unbelievable" or "sensational." Be prepared to prove any claim you make.

• Don't use opinionated phrases such as, "You'll love it" or "It's really beautiful." Instead, stress the product's or service's benefits, such as "comfortable," "practical," "lasting." Remember that people have basic wants and needs. Among other things, they want to save time and money, worry or discomfort, and they want to be successful, healthy, informed and attractive. They also want more money, security, confidence and a feeling of importance. (*Note*: In a *Reader's Digest* ad test of two different headlines, the "save time" ad outpulled the "save money" ad.)

• Speak always in positive terms. Do not say, "You will not be disappointed," because this is a negative thought. Instead, say, "Satisfaction guaranteed."

• People often are motivated to buy out of greed or fear. Whenever you can inject these elements into your advertising message, you will increase response. For greed, stress what people will gain from your product (money, getting ahead in business, envy of neighbors, etc.), and for fear, tell people what they will lose by not ordering. (Loss of time, money, convenience? Will price soon increase? Is this the last chance to order?)

• Make a special offer. Examples: Buy three, get one free. Free (product) if you order within ten days. Buy one at full price, get the second at half price. Free freight on all orders over $100. Free lesson to first ten people to respond. Save 20 percent by ordering our "Early Bird Selection." And so forth.

Headline Ideas for Ads or Flyers

The headline is all-important, because this often is the only thing people read. According to ad experts, five times as many people read headlines as read body copy.

Try to incorporate some of the twelve most powerful words in your headline copy (see sidebar) and use action verbs for more power, such as : How to . . . *GET, BE, DO, SAVE, MAKE, STOP, WIN, HAVE, START*, etc.

If you study full-page display ads, you'll note many headlines (proven to be successful) begin with the words, How I . . . *BECAME . . . MADE . . . STARTED . . . SUCCEEDED . . . IMPROVED* and so on. A variation on this theme is to speak directly to the prospective customer by saying, How *you* can . . . *BECOME . . . MAKE . . . START . . . SUCCEED . . . IMPROVE* and so on.

Other successful headlines for ads and flyers often involve numbers, such as "10 ways to . . . ," "25 tips for . . . ," or "100 ideas on how to. . . . "

Use good typography in setting your headline. Help people read your ad more easily. Avoid use of all capitals as this retards reading speed. Never use the kind of flowery typeface that forces readers to look at it twice to make out the letters.

Increase response to any ad or offer by giving customers the option of charging an order to a bank credit card. The average mail order by credit card is said to be 20 to 40 percent higher than a cash/check order.

Perhaps I've tried to cram too much into this chapter, but for many of you, I suspect it alone will be worth the price of the book. Don't try to absorb all of this in one sitting, but come back to this chapter from time to time for ideas on how to get more prospects while also getting repeat business from satisfied customers and clients. None of us was born with marketing skills, but with time and experience, most of us can become creative marketers. As your business grows, I'd love to hear about shoestring marketing strategies that are working for you and perhaps feature you in one of my columns or my next book. Do let me hear from you.

The twelve most persuasive words in the English language, according to ad copywriters, are these:

You . . . Save . . . Money . . . New . . . Love . . . Easy . . . Health . . . Safety . . . Results . . . Discovery . . . Proven . . . Guarantee

The ten words that spell direct-mail success are said to be these:

Free . . . You . . . Now . . . New . . . Win . . . Easy . . . Introducing . . . Save . . . Today . . . Guarantee

THE PUBLICITY GAME

11

"HOLLER" IS ONE OF THOSE QUAINT old words few people use anymore, but the technique of hollering is well known to publicity experts. Whether you are calling the hogs or people in the media, the idea is the same: *to get attention.*

What does it take to capture the attention of magazine and newspaper editors? What do you have to know to get an interview on radio, be a guest on a TV talk show, get your story on local or network television? What are the keys to getting publicity? This chapter answers those questions and many more. As a "publicity hound" who has built her business through effective use of the media, I've shared some of my experiences plus those of many home-business owners in my network. And to make sure you're getting the broadest perspective possible, I've included expert tips and advice from leading PR (public relations) consultants and authors whose books, reports and directories you'll find listed in chapter sixteen.

"We live in a world that is literally media-driven," says Alan Caruba, veteran PR counselor, owner of The Caruba Organization and editor of *Power Media Selects*. "Knowing who to reach and how best to influence media coverage is an essential aspect of any business or nonprofit activity."

"Anyone can purchase the opportunity to have access to the public," says Doug Swanson, former reporter, news director and TV news assignments manager, owner of The Swanson Group and author of *Business Building . . . in the '90s*. "All you need is money. But obtaining free access to the public—access which is much more valuable than anything you could have purchased—often takes work. You need to acquire the knowledge necessary to understand the process and manage the tools."

Unlike advertising, which is the expensive way to get attention, publicity is virtually free. (Your only costs, in addition to the time you spend on your publicity campaign, will be for printing and mailing press releases or media kits, plus some follow-up telephone calls.) Publicity can be generated in many ways, using techniques that run the gamut from a simple letter, telephone call or standard news release mailing to expensive campaigns involving publicists and high-priced media kits. Since home-business owners traditionally have little or no money for advertising, this chapter's emphasis is on inexpensive and practical PR methods any creative-thinking individual can use to increase the visibility and income of a business. As with advertising, the primary goal of small businesses should be to get the kind of publicity that will generate a direct response from customers or prospects.

Regardless of the publicity method you use, remember that editors and program directors are not interested in giving you free advertising. What they want is news or information that will inform, benefit or at least entertain their readers and listeners. Actually, all publicity pivots on the answer to one question: *Is your information or news "newsworthy" or at least interesting to a large number of people?* If the answer is yes, you'll get your publicity. If it's no, the wastebasket will get your release.

In her book, *Writing Effective News Releases,* Catherine McIntyre points to a survey by the Associated Press that reveals that newsrooms receive on average 122 news releases each day. Some editors reported receiving up to 600 releases a day. "The participating editors in the survey reported that 80 percent of all the news releases they received were unusable and rejected," says Catherine. "Why? In many cases the releases contained material that may have been newsworthy, Catherine explains, but it was presented in a manner unsuitable for use by the media. Releases may also be tossed when a contact person is not listed or can't be reached by telephone; when the news is received too late; when copy is lacking in reader appeal; or is simply too wordy, boring or filled with "puff." (Self-serving press releases that blatantly advertise a product or service are never used.)

"When you approach the media with a news release, don't write about yourself or the great new widget you've created," says Mitchell Davis, owner of Broadcast Interview Source and publisher of the annual *Yearbook of Experts, Authorities & Spokespersons*, a major newsroom and talk show reference. "The most important element for success is to identify what is most newsworthy about one's product, service or field of expertise," Davis emphasizes. "Push the story. Susie opening a cookie factory isn't news. But if Susie's release explains why her particular kind of cookies are a HOT NEW TREND, she's going to get some nice publicity for her business."

What Exactly Is "Newsworthy"?

A press release (or "news release," if you prefer) does not have to be filled with actual news to be newsworthy, but it must be worth publishing as news because it cannot be published as advertising. What editors want, more than anything else, is a "news peg" on which your story can be hung. Actually, the key word here is "new," not "news." Anything that's new may be newsworthy, as in a new business just starting, a new product that offers some special benefit to consumers or business owners, a new achievement of some individual in a community, locality or industry, a new twist to an old idea and so forth. The news peg or "hook" for a story can be almost anything. Sometimes it is the very thing that makes you, your business or product stand out from the rest; often, it's the benefit offered to consumers in your press release.

All businesses have characteristics or qualities that lend themselves to a press release, but not all press releases are appropriate for all media. In fact, it may take several different releases to get all the publicity that's available to you. If you shoot a shotgun loaded with buckshot, you will get an interesting scatter effect; aim a rifle, however, and you hit one target dead center. In thinking about publicity, you need to consider both approaches.

An example of the rifle technique would be to target a specific magazine or TV talk show and send a sensational press kit that might include a letter, press release, biographical release (see related sidebar and sample release), fact sheet, photo and product sample, if appropriate. Another option is to send a release headed "*Exclusive to* (name of publication)." This is the technique I once used to get publicity in *Family Circle*.

Contact: Dorothy Glenn
            Moss, Finley and Tupper
            510 Court Street
            Cleveland, Ohio 44114

            (216) 555-3267

                          RON FINLEY

   By day, Ron Finley sits in a wood-paneled office meeting with clients,
discussing financial planning and poring over figures. By night, Finley dons
make-up and costume and assumes any number of roles.

   When meeting Ron Finley, a partner in the accounting firm of Moss, Finley
and Tupper, one would hardly suspect he is the same Ron Finley who performs
professionally in many productions at the Hayden Playhouse in Cleveland. At 6'2",
Finley traditionally wears pin-stripe suits and sports a distinguished salt-and-
pepper beard. He looks far more the businessman than the actor.

   To Finley this split life is the most natural thing in the world. "I love
my work at the office. I enjoy meeting with people and solving the complexities
involved in managing money," he says. "But at night I become a very different
person--taking on new roles is a challenge I enjoy immensely."

   Finley's schedule is a challenge as well. Hayden Playhouse performances
are held Friday and Saturday nights and Sunday afternoons. Each play usually
runs four weeks. Prior to the run, Finley's evenings are filled with rehearsals.
"Tax time is the only time when I can't work at the Playhouse. We're just too
busy here," he explains. "Otherwise I love the schedule. I can't think of
a better place than the theatre to spend the rest of my time."

   Finley was bitten by the acting bug six years ago while helping the
Playhouse with its initial fundraising drive. It was the classic cliché when
director Alfred Bush asked, "Ron, have you ever considered acting?" Finley has
been at it ever since. His most recent role was as the doctor in A Doll's House.

   Ron Finley helped form Moss, Finley and Tupper twelve years ago. A
1946 graduate of Ohio University, he is single and resides on Northridge Drive.

                              -0-

A sample of a "feature bio," a special release which often accompanies a news release. Its purpose is to encourage a feature article instead of just a news announcement. From The Publicity Manual. *© by Kate Kelly. Used by permission.*

"Bio" Releases

Many businesses could take a tip from the press releases used by book publishers. They are often printed on legal-size paper and contain copy suitable for a feature article. Some even contain illustrations. Such releases are actually a combination news release and biography press release, or a "bio," as it is called in the trade. If a separate biographical press release and a photograph accompany a news release, you will greatly increase your chances of getting a feature article in newspapers and magazines. Basically, the bio tells who you are and why your business is interesting. It generally reads exactly like an article, the idea being that a busy editor can simply run it as is, or a lazy reporter can submit it under his or her byline. (See sample bio release.) Many writers, of course, use bios to form the basis of their own, lengthy feature articles. If you can't write this kind of story about yourself, hire a freelance writer to do it.

Different products and businesses require different approaches, and you should be prepared to adjust your thinking and strategy at any time. For example, a press release that is designed to attract attention from local media—newspapers, radio or television—probably will not work for a national publication or station because the news impact is not the same. It can work just the opposite, too. I am reminded of a story I heard on National Public Radio. A Chicago woman was stopped in a parking lot outside a bowling alley by a would-be robber who demanded all her money . . . or else. Obviously a quick thinker, she put a stop to his plan by dropping her bowling ball on his foot, so disarming him that she was able to get away. Curiously, this story was not noticed by Chicago newscasters, but National Public Radio heard about it and presented it as an amusing anecdote, just as I have done.

Thus, information that is not news to one editor may be news—or at least human interest material—to another. For this reason, small businesses that may be taken for granted in their own community may find it easier to get publicity in national media. Surprisingly, national publicity often leads to a feature story in one's hometown paper along the line of "local business recognized nationally." That, you see, is newsworthy.

I recall the time I wrote about Sweeter Measures, a small garment business in rural Nebraska then owned by Susan Winchester. A reporter for the *Wall Street Journal* picked up on my story and gave Susan a nice mention in his column. That publicity so impressed the editor of *The Omaha World Herald* that he put Susan's business on the front page of the Sunday edition with a color picture. (This publicity did aid the growth of Susan's farm-based business, which she later sold.)

Freelance writers doing articles for major business magazines often come to me for referrals to home-business owners in my subscriber network who might like to be interviewed, and I've thus been instrumental in placing many of my readers in the national media. Although such publicity rarely results in direct sales, it is invaluable "image advertising" few small businesses could afford to buy.

Consider Nancy and George Hammes, who live in a small town in Illinois where news travels faster than butter melts on toast. After receiving a two-page color spread in a major entrepreneurial magazine, the Hammes wrote to tell me the bank had hung a copy of their article in the lobby. "Now the banker calls us by our first names," Nancy said, which prompted me to wonder how this article might affect the bank's decision should the Hammes ask for a business loan in the future.

"I keep getting noticed more and more by national publications," says Mary Ann Chasen, owner of Accurate Typing Service and a specialist in getting government contracts. "It seems that the more state-wide and national publicity I acquire, the more local businesses want to do business with me." Carla Culp knows just what Mary means. After sharing the TV spotlight with me on the *Home* show one year (more about that later), Carla said this national publicity was a turning point in her Memos to Manuscripts word processing service. Because she had a how-to book and newsletter to offer, she benefitted from the many telephone calls this publicity generated. In addition, her local newspaper gave her terrific coverage while the TV show was still running, so everyone in town tuned in.

"Local customers perceived me differently after my television appearance," she said, "and my business boomed as a direct result." Carla later expanded by moving her business outside the home.

Creating a Newsworthy Press Release

Before you can make publicity work for you, you have to ask yourself what you expect to gain from it. First, are you seeking local, regional, national or international publicity? Do you want the names of interested prospects so you can send them your brochure or catalog, as in two-step advertising? Or, better yet, are you hoping for orders with payment enclosed? Maybe your primary goal is to get people to look for your product in retail shops and stores, either locally or nationally. Or perhaps you are seeking publicity that would generate telephone calls from prospective clients locally or nationally—calls that might lead to freelance assignments, consulting jobs, speaking or teaching engagements. Or maybe you just would like to get your name in the paper so your mother will be proud of you.

Before I explain the seven basic elements of a press release, let me offer a few tips on how the release should look and why it may work better if photographs are included.

"The appearance of your press release is important because it must compete with many other pieces of mail for a journalist's attention," says Tana Fletcher, editor, writer, lecturer and co-author of *Getting Publicity*. She stresses the importance of the quality of the paper, the legibility of the type and the layout on the page.

Above all, a press release must look "crisp" and be easy to read with ample margins all around. Releases can be printed on plain white paper, on your business letterhead, or on a special news release letterhead you may wish to design. Publicity experts used to advise against using anything other than plain white paper because editors are concerned with the newsworthiness of a release, not how "pretty" it is. Now that so many small businesses have laser printers and access to colorful papers, however, I'm seeing more releases printed on light-colored, textured stock

To make your news release stand out on an editor's desk, design a colorful *news head* using these sample releases as a guide. ArtNetwork's release is plain—black ink on white paper. Universal Software's release is printed on grey paper with a red design block and accent lines across top and down left side. Different shades of blue are used on the releases for HIA, SBA and Bradley Communications, and the HIA release also has a touch of red in the star logo. The "Late Breaking News" head is printed in green with text in black ink. Silver Streak's news head is the most eye-catching, with color "blocks" in four colors: red, blue, gold and green.

Press Release

FOR IMMEDIATE RELEASE
CONTACT: Sue Viders 800-999-7013
Constance Franklin-Smith 916-692-1355

Marketing Solutions
Premiere Consultation Program for Fine Artists

Constance Franklin-Smith, director of ArtNetwork, and Sue Viders, marketing consultant for Color Q Education Division, have expanded their consulting services to provide fine artists at all levels of their career an in-depth analysis of their marketing needs.

"Our service has grown since its inception in May 1991, and we both find we are spending much more time on each artist than anticipated. Both of us spend approximately six hours on each review—reading, researching and responding via audio cassette tape and writing—finding ways to help, suggesting practical strategies and motivating the artist to create for themselves a more marketable position," says Sue Viders.

Marketing Solutions offers two options:

The first is the complete review for $385 in which, based on an extensive 24-page questionnaire that the artist answers, Franklin-Smith provides a written analysis and marketing plan, as well as specific comments and contacts, while Viders presents an hour-lon...

marketability, along...

The second option is...

books and manuals.

Artists rave about th...

Franklin-Smith:

"I will continue
of its value."

"I've now been s
the expanding

"The consultatic
and need to de

For a free brochure ...

13264 Rices Crossing Road
PO Box 369
Renaissance, CA 95962
916 692 1355
916 692 1370 Fax

Universal Software Solutions

PRESS RELEASE

P.O. Box 87968 • Canton, MI 48187 • (313) 455-7510

Marketing Consultation

*

Graphic Design & Illustration

*

Personalized Directed Mailings

*

Custom Computer Services

For Your Information...

Silver Streak Publications
1823 Sussex Ct., Bettendorf, IA 52722

For immediate release...   Contact: Les R. Schmeltz (319) 355-3341

...Garage Sale?

...pt to make a few extra dollars by
...Garage Sale. Surprisingly few of
...th a little more advance planning

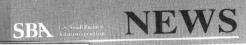

SBA U.S. Small Business Administration **NEWS**

...1993

For more information.
contactJuanita Weaver
(202) 205-6742

...TKINS NAMED ACTING ADMINISTRATOR
...SMALL BUSINESS ADMINISTRATION

...financial manager with 17
...and the Government of the
...named as the Acting
...Administration (SBA).

...ects a comprehensive array
...note and expand U.S. small
...ership in the development
...delivery of financial,
...rams by the agency's 4,000
...e.

...ve experience in municipal
...al, investment and cash
...nancing and management and
...Most recently, he served
...bia, at the Department of
...e acting deputy director of
...for management of housing
...in excess of $50 million.
...tment include: the general
...utive assistant to
...i Revenue he held
...Division (1982 -
...urer/cash manager

...lping Build America's Future

For Immediate Release

hia Hobby Industries of America
319 East 54th Street
PO Box 348
Elmwood Park, N.J. 07407
(201) 794-1133

ELEVEN CPDS ADDED

Late Breaking News:
INFORMATION UPDATE ON LISTS AND DATABASES

...E RELEASE

...& TELEMARKETERS:
...ROM ZELLER & LETICA!

...t is consumers at home or
...Zeller & Letica can help you
...iently ... and economically.

...ased their new 1993 Consumer
...full of every imaginable
...ffer a wealth of ideas for

...Ad Agencies. Magazine
...nies. Car Dealers. Real
...Distributors. Importers.
...ls. And on and on. Since
...ping people build their
...rect marketing and
...of mailing lists and sales
...arketing tools available today.
...als offer sound advice at a

...or FREE BUSINESS AND CONSUMER
...& Letica, Inc., 15 East 26th

...#

NEWS FROM Bradley
Communications Corp.

CONTACT: Bill Harrison
(215) 259-1070

Tips for Promoting Your Business as a Guest on Radio/TV Talk Shows

A sixty-second commercial on the *Oprah Winfrey Show* would cost you about $50,000.00. However, if Oprah interviewed you as a guest on her show, it wouldn't cost you a penny to promote your product or service to her 20 million viewers.

Appearing as a guest on radio/TV programs -- whether they're national like Oprah or simply a local radio show -- can be one of the best ways to promote your company, IF you know the secrets of obtaining and capitalizing on this type of FREE publicity.

Dozens of tips for using broadcast exposure are contained in TALK SHOW PUBLICITY SECRETS, a 70-minute audio cassette with written outline, available for $25 from Bradley Communications, Box 28926, Philadelphia, PA 19151. Here are some highlights:

Four Ways to Profit from Radio/TV Publicity

Increase Sales -- Most radio shows will let you give an address or phone number out over the air so the audience can can order your product or request more info. TV shows will often put your ordering info on the screen. Be sure to ask

or on brightly colored NEWS heads.

I receive dozens of press releases every month from businesses of all sizes. Many are single-spaced and totally devoid of style, suggesting either that the sender is a publicity novice, or someone who has chosen to ignore professional advice on this topic. Alan Caruba says the old rule of "always double-space a release" is no longer applicable, but I think many editors still prefer it. While I was publishing a newsletter, I rarely used a release exactly as it was written because my needs, like those of other editors, were special. Now, as an author and columnist, I still have to hunt through press releases to find material that qualifies as "news" for my particular purposes. A single-spaced release only makes copy more difficult to edit.

Although many PR experts, including Alan Caruba and Tana Fletcher, say releases should be printed on business stationery, I believe business stationery should be reserved for correspondence and feel press releases command more attention when they are printed on specially designed NEWS letterheads. Just my opinion, of course; use your own judgment here.

Press releases should be printed, never photocopied. Thanks to computers and affordable laser printers, press releases are now a snap to produce in a home office. You can create a variety of releases, printing as few or as many as needed, modifying copy as may be necessary for different audiences. I have designed two press release NEWS heads. One I have printed in red ink, usually 500 at a time, by my local offset printer. Then, as releases are needed, I simply use these preprinted pages in my laser printer, fitting copy to the form's margins. Other releases sent in smaller quantities are entirely computer-generated and often individualized for certain applications.

Photographs

"Although every press release does not require a photograph, high-quality pictures definitely improve your chances of being mentioned in print," says Tana Fletcher. You may also elect to send sketches or diagrams if they add to the impact of your story. Since inclusion of photos in a press release adds greatly to promotional costs, make sure the publications you are promoting to actually use photos. (You wouldn't believe how many photographs I trash every week from companies who have no idea what my periodical looks like. I use line art illustrations only.)

"Newspapers and magazines need 5″ × 7″ or 8″ × 10″ black-and-white prints for reproduction," says Steve Meltzer in one of his photography columns for *The Crafts Report*. "Bigger prints have more impact and are likely to be printed larger. Newspapers love visually striking, human-interest photos."

While major business magazines (and most newspapers) will

Positioning Your Copy

You may have the right product but be promoting it with the wrong hook, as Mary Hansen's experience illustrates. When this Canadian self-publisher released *Joyful Learning— Learning Games for Children Ages 4 to 12*, she began to promote the book as "a fun way to learn," which did not work at all in getting publicity, she reported. "But when I decided to be totally direct and say that my book was a method of helping kids who were underachieving, who had not succeeded before, the media leaped upon my story!

"Before, I was afraid that parents would shy away from this idea because they don't want to admit that their kids are underachievers. But I was wrong. They like my fun, humor-filled approach to teaching such children."

Emulate, But Don't Copy

"You must always steal, but only from the best people," says actor Michael Caine.

Everyone in business studies the work of others for ideas and inspiration (particularly the competition), and to some extent we all borrow ideas and techniques from others. But we must be careful not to directly copy anyone else's material since this has dangerous legal implications. This book contains hundreds of ideas and techniques being used by others. While you may borrow their concepts, you must never take their words. Use a similar format, but add a new twist. Lift an idea, but improve it with your own creative touch.

send a photographer to your home or office if a picture is needed, entrepreneurial magazines on tighter budgets will probably ask you to provide pictures for consideration—either black-and-white glossies or color slides. Once, when I offered to refer a writer to specific businesses in my network she might interview, she said she wanted only successful businesses *in cities where it would be easy to dispatch a photographer to get a picture for the article.* This is one reason why some businesses get publicity and others don't. It also suggests that the inclusion of a professional photo with a press release might sometimes make the difference in whether you get a PR mention or not.

Another time, when *Entrepreneur* magazine asked me to provide the names of five unusual homebased business owners they might profile in an upcoming issue, I later heard from some of them about how their pictures got into the magazine. One woman quickly "hired" her husband to take a picture of her in her office. One couple rushed to have pictures taken, and when they weren't acceptable to the magazine, a photographer was sent to their workshop where he spent hours doing the "shoot."

When I was interviewed for a home-office article in *Time* magazine, they asked if they might send a photographer to my office and I said yes, providing I could have a day to "organize my chaos." A top professional in the Chicago area came in with four cameras and over a period of four hours shot four rolls of film, taking snaps of me from every possible angle and even rearranging my office. I could not have afforded this professional's shooting fee, but he did agree to sell me four color slides (of his choice) for $200, and I've gotten a lot of mileage from them. By having a color slide to send when magazines have asked for a picture, I've gotten several nice color spots in articles. From one slide, I pulled a black-and-white print for use as a standard press photo, and I also use this picture on or in my various printed materials.

Press Release Copywriting Tips

Before you begin to write a release, answer the question all editors and readers will ask: *What's in it for me?* List the benefits of your product or service and work them into the copy.

Always use simple English and short sentences, and watch your grammar, spelling and punctuation. To avoid embarrassing errors, ask a knowledgeable friend to read your copy or, if you have a computer, use one of the inexpensive software grammar checkers. Since spell-check software won't catch words that are correctly spelled but misused, double-check for such words as "to" for "too" and "you" for "yours," etc.

You can talk about yourself in a press release, but always write copy in the third person, as though someone else had written it about you. This makes it easy to quote yourself, which is important. Since publicity legitimizes information, you can make strong statements about your business or yourself through quotes in a news release, and people will believe them simply because they have appeared in print. However, if you said the same thing in a sales brochure, it would be suspect, simply because *you* said it. Example:

- Brochure copy: *I believe my service is the only one of its kind. Give it a try. I'm sure you'll benefit from it because I get thank-you letters from satisfied customers every week.*
- Press release copy: *To his knowledge, the service offered by Bob Jones is the only one of its kind. "I know it helps people, too," says Jones as he shuffles through the week's stack of thank-you letters. "I get mail like this every week."*

Avoid first-person voice and "me-centered" releases. Unless you're a notable personality, don't begin a press release with your name, which will only generate a yawn from editors. Releases written by PR novices often contain good information but sound like brochure copy unsuitable for media use. To illustrate, here is copy from one release I received (the owner's name has been changed):

Tom Rowe, owner of Rowe Landscaping, offers a full service, fully insured landscaping business. We are professional and businesslike but our friendly touches make us different. Four years in the business has given us a name we are proud of.

And then the release continued on its boring way to talk about the personal touches this business owner offers, how he gets new business by hand-delivering flyers, through word of mouth, the importance of communication and the free newsletter he now offers his customers. Throughout the release, the writer kept changing voice, from "we" to "I" to "our." By itself, the headline, "A Full Service Landscaping Business With a Personal Touch," was enough to cause most editors to toss the release.

And yet . . . the basic information in this example is sound, and with a few simple changes it can suddenly become powerful PR copy. First, we must change the voice to third person. (Just pretend you are a reporter interviewing yourself.) Second, we must change the slant. The purpose of this release—of most releases, in fact—is to generate new business or more sales (in addition to image advertising). But this can often be done more effectively by giving the illusion that you don't need new business at all—*that you're already quite successful, thank you.* (Remember what I told you in an earlier chapter about the "illusion of success.")

With so many businesses in trouble these days, editors like to include good news about local businesses, *particularly if their advice might help other businesses in the community.* (There's your answer to "What's in it for me?") More than ever, small businesses today need marketing help not only in finding new customers or clients but in learning how to keep old ones. The following revised copy suggests how *all* small service businesses everywhere could use a press release to help other business owners in their community while also positioning themselves as successful entrepreneurs:

COMMUNICATION: THE KEY
TO GOOD BUSINESS IN THE '90S

Having a hard time drumming up new business or keeping old customers in these hard times? *(Notice the news peg lead?)* Take a tip from a local landscaper who says service with a personal touch can make a big difference in year-end profits.

"Communication is the key to good business," says Tom Rowe, who has operated Rowe Landscaping in Durham since 1987. *(Note use of direct quotes and the way Tom's location is included without making it sound like an advertisement.)* "I start off each year by hand-delivering flyers, which enables me to target areas and build growth. Word-of-mouth advertising and referrals from existing customers take it from there."

Tom says little extras can make a big difference in any business that is service-oriented. *(Notice how the "reporter" takes over here, quoting Tom indirectly. Strive for balance in the use of direct and indirect quotes.)* For example, he sends out welcome letters to new customers, thank-you notes to customers who have referred new business, and Holiday Greetings at year's end to thank old customers for their continued patronage. This year, Tom is offering a free newsletter filled with how-to landscaping tips and other news of interest to homeowners. For a free copy, call Rowe Landscaping at (phone).

This release could also be used for national publicity—one businessperson helping another. Although Tom won't get any new landscape customers from such visibility, it would certainly enhance his local business image. People who never get their names in print tend to be impressed by those who do.

Or as my music teacher/sister Mollie Wakeman put it after I'd gotten her a spot of publicity in *Entrepreneur* magazine, "I know I won't get any new students from this mention, but if I put a copy of this article where my students' parents can see it, they'll be so impressed I can raise my rates!"

Try to keep your release to one page if possible unless it is written in a style that lends itself to use as an article. In this case, you can make the copy as long as necessary. Write "MORE . . ." at the bottom of each continued page. The old rule said "never print on the back side of a release," but no one pays much attention to it anymore. In the interest of conserving trees, I vote for printing on the back side, which also saves stapling time. Paper size can be standard ($8\frac{1}{2}'' \times 11''$) or legal-sized, depending on your copy needs.

Mastering the Seven Elements of a Release

The seven elements are (1) source information, (2) release date, (3) headline, (4) basic facts, (5) important details, (6) supplementary information and (7) the "for more info" line. Use them as an outline for all releases you write:

1. Source Information

This information, which should be placed near the top of the release either to the left or right side of the page, gives the media the name and telephone number of the person to call should more information be desired. Generally, the line reads, "For more information, contact (person's name and phone number)." (Including a number here doesn't mean it will be published, but its omission will make it impossible for editors to double-check points of interest or verify that a release is still timely.)

2. Release Date

Most news releases carry the line, FOR IMMEDIATE RELEASE (typed in capital letters and underlined) on the right-hand side of the page, positioned just above the headline. But I also have seen this line centered or positioned to the left, and sometimes it's not there at all. The release dateline tells the media that the release can be used immediately upon receipt, or at their earliest convenience. If news is of a particularly timely nature, a specific date may be given for release. Press releases bearing the line USE AT WILL may have a longer life, held in reference files until space is available or the copy fits into an issue with a special theme.

3. Headline

The headline, also typed in capital letters, should be neatly centered on the page. It should summarize the content of your press release. Although most editors will write their own headline, the one you put on your release may have a lot to do with whether it's read or not. Following are some headlines from press releases I've received from my readers:

Publicizing a Handcrafts Business

A common error made by crafters seeking publicity is to include flowery phrases and descriptive words such as "lovely" or "unique" (one of the most overworked and abused words in use today). Such words merely express the product maker's opinion, suggesting no buyer benefits. Stick to facts. Also avoid: (1) the inclusion of copy pertaining to all the colors, styles, sizes or patterns a product comes in; (2) information about all the methods of payment or charge cards you will accept; and (3) reminders about adding sales tax. The more of this information you include, the more the editor will perceive your release as an advertisement.

Be grateful if you can get the simple line, "To order, send $21.95 ppd. to. . . . " Or, if you accept charge cards, you might say, "to order on VISA or MasterCard, call toll-free (number)."

Although we've gotten lots of national exposure, a little more never hurts (just like chicken soup).

—Claudia Burns, Breadwinners

- HEALTHY EXCHANGES COOKBOOK SATISFIES "REAL PEOPLE"
- REEDSPORT BEEKEEPER TAKES NATIONAL HONORS
- THIS HAIRDRESSER COMES TO YOUR HOME, OFFICE OR JAIL!
- HOMEMAKER'S INVENTION HELPS RECIPE COLLECTORS
- FIBER ARTIST'S QUILT TOURS STATE OF MARYLAND FOR TWO YEARS

4. Basic Facts

The first paragraph of your press release should include the most important facts the media should know—the who/what/when/where/why and how of your story. If you can't get all of them into the first paragraph, get them into the second one. Here are the opening paragraphs of three press releases I received while I was working on this chapter, along with a discussion of how each release incorporates the seven basic elements. Use these samples as a guide to how to write your own attention-commanding release.

Sample A: NATIONAL CONTEST FOR THE DISORGANIZED

February 5, 1993, Dallas, TX. *Home Office Computing* magazine and Everything's Organized, a Dallas-based consulting firm, are conducting the "Search for the Most Disorganized Home Office."

During March and April, disorganized home-office professionals will be asked to submit a 200 word or less description of why theirs is the most disorganized home office along with a black-and-white or color photo of their home office. The prizes for the contest are as follows. . . .

Sample B: AREA RESIDENT CURRENTLY APPEARING ON TV SERIES

Aurora resident, Mary Mulari, is appearing as a guest on the PBS television series, "Sewing With Nancy." The programs will air on Channel 8 on Saturday, June 20 and 27, at noon.

Currently celebrating ten years on television, "Sewing With Nancy" is hosted by nationally recognized sewing expert, Nancy Zieman. The program features a variety of sewing projects and instructions. Frequently, guests are included in the programs, and for the current series titled "Designer Wearables," Mary Mulari appears to share ideas and garments from her book.

Sample C: BRIDAL FASHIONS FOR MOTHERS-TO-BE

Every bride deserves to look her best on her wedding day, and that includes wearing the wedding gown of her dreams. But when the bride is also a mother-to-be, finding that special dress can be nearly impossible.

The marketplace is only beginning to meet the needs of expectant brides, says Judy Schramm of Judy's Maternity Rental in Arlington, Virginia, the exclusive location for maternity wedding fashions. Judy designs her own gowns and knows of no other source for maternity wedding dresses. . . .

Now go back and read the copy in each of the three examples, and look for the *news* in each release. In Sample A, the news is a major business magazine is conducting an interesting contest. (This release is pegged on the suggestion that all home-based workers may be disorganized.) In Sample B, the news is a local resident of Aurora, Minnesota, is to be the guest of a prominent sewing expert. (An example of how to "hook" a release on a celebrity connection.) In Sample C, the news is many pregnant brides have wardrobe problems that can be solved. (My, how times have changed—the hook is obvious.)

In each example, the additional news in paragraph two is also newsworthy, giving editors a double reason to publish it: In Sample A, home-office professionals have a chance to win exciting prizes; in Sample B, the PBS television series is now ten years old; and in Sample C, there is a new need in the marketplace.

5. Important Details

In addition to the basic facts of your press release—the news peg and vital news—a good press release will include other details as well, the kind of material that might prompt a feature story instead of just a short announcement. Although I have not included the entire copy of each sample release, I will describe it for you as I move along.

In Sample A, the important details are a listing of prizes, including a $4,000 custom-designed home office, $500 in products, a $500 gift certificate, and copies of a book by the magazine's senior editor. In Sample B, the details are that this is Mary's second appearance on the show and that, for nine years, she has been sharing sewing ideas through a series of books and seminars in the United States. In Sample C, the details are the U.S. Bureau of the Census statistics stating that 12 percent of all mothers ages 15-29 were married for the first time while pregnant with their first child.

6. Supplementary Information

When the press release reaches this point, we're talking about the kind of background information that adds color to a feature story. Sample A included no supplementary information—a mistake, since not everyone reading this story will be familiar with this particular magazine. This release could have benefitted from copy that mentioned how long the magazine has been in publication, the specific types of articles it carries or an indication of its broad range of readers. (The sender of this release, cosponsor Lisa Kanarek, also could have tooted her own horn a bit louder.) In Sample B, the supplementary information is Mary is the author of seven creative sewing books, with a new one about to be published. In Sample C, Judy Schramm provided detailed information about the different styles and colors of gowns available from her. She also emphasized another benefit: that rental fees were a money-saving alternative compared to purchasing a new gown, and the rental fee included any necessary alterations and cleaning.

7. "For More Information" Line

Not all press releases include this line, but small businesses should always include a last, short paragraph that serves a particular marketing purpose. If you seek a direct response, make some kind of promotional offer that includes your address, telephone or fax number (depending on how you want to be contacted). If your primary goal of publicity is to promote sales on the local level, or a combination of both direct response and sales support, include an appropriate closing line. For example, my releases always state that my books are "available in bookstores or by mail from the author at . . ."

Sample A stated that official entry forms would be available in the current issue of the magazine—a great way to stimulate newsstand sales of this particular issue. In Sample B, Mary Mulari announced the title and publication date of her next book, concluding with the sentence, "Her books are sold through fabric and sewing stores, sewing notions catalogs, and through mail order." Sample C, which was designed to draw local inquiries only, closed with a comment, "Judy's Maternity Rental works by appointment only," then gave a number to call. (Note that Judy's release has a national peg because she has identified a national problem and supported it with statistics. She could get a lot of image advertising in national media if she wants it.)

Although the "for more information" line definitely is advertising, editors often will include this information, *particularly if it will benefit readers to have it*. The most effective product releases concentrate on one product at a time. Here are other examples of closing paragraphs you might use:

• Free information is available from (name and address) or (your business number or special toll-free number).

or

- (Name of product) is available in (kind of retail outlets), or directly from the (manufacturer, publisher, etc.) for (postpaid price) from: (name and address).

or

- To receive a (special offer: tip sheet, sample, newsletter, promotional tape, etc.) send (SASE, or postage-paid price) to: (Use a coded address so you can monitor results from this promotion).

Make an Offer They Can't Resist

You will increase your chances for publicity if your press release includes a free or inexpensive special offer for readers. This might include a sample newsletter or magazine, a tip sheet or minireport, informational pamphlet or brochure, small booklet or resource list.

When *Homemade Money* was first published, I made it a goal to get mentioned in *Family Circle* magazine. My first releases and letters were ignored . . . until I thought of offering an exclusive "home-business information package" to this magazine's readers. I created a special list of the top 20 books and periodicals in this field and offered it with a copy of my catalog for just a dollar. (I wouldn't do this today for less than $3.)

I was given terrific coverage, with a special mention on the editor's page, and was both astonished and delighted when the mailbox started filling up, every envelope containing either a check or a dollar bill. It was the most fun (and work) Harry and I had had in ages, and we got a kick out of the bank clerks, who couldn't figure out where we were getting all those dollar bills every day. In all, that publicity brought in 10,000 responses. Going out, it was close to a break-even proposition, but nearly 30 percent of these prospects placed book or subscription orders, which ultimately put thousands of dollars into my pocket. Many other small business owners before and since have enjoyed this kind of publicity bonanza in one magazine or another.

What kind of special offer could you make in a press release to promote yourself or your business and fill your mailbox with dollars? Here are examples of what some of my readers are offering in their press releases:

- To promote his *Yearbook of Experts, Authorities, and Spokespersons*, Mitchell Davis offers free media guides and an invitation kit that explains how to participate in the next edition.
- A publisher of books on the art of silhouette cutting promoted one of her new titles by sending press releases to craft media offering, for an SASE, a free holiday design, ready to cut and mount.
- The publisher of *Roman Reports*, which helps individuals

Authors: Offer Something Free!

One of the most effective ways to get continual media notice is to offer their audience something free. It is very difficult, almost impossible, to get media to feature a book more than once. But they will feature new free offers as often as you come up with them. Plan to start a new promotional campaign at least four times a year for each book you publish.

How do you find something to give away free? Easy. Your book should be full of valuable information you can excerpt in short two-page or four-page brochures that you can offer free to anyone who sends you an SASE or $1 for postage.

For example, a travel publisher could offer a list of the ten most exciting places in Iowa (if their book was about Iowa). Three months later, the same publisher could offer a report on holiday happenings in Iowa. Three months later, a report on how to plan your next vacation in Iowa. And three months later, a list of 10 major historical sites in Iowa. And three months later . . .

—John Kremer, author, editor and publisher of *Book Marketing Update*

determine the value of opportunity ads, has promoted his news-letter by offering a special $4 report on the kind of businesses the Postal Inspection Services puts out of business each year.

• The owner of a graphic arts business showed off her design abilities and knowledge by creating a specially designed information product she offered in a release for $3.75.

• A seminar leader in Minnesota promoted her self-employment workshops by offering an inexpensive directory of information to help small businesses in Minnesota.

• Marketing consultant Howard L. Shenson promotes his services in a $4 booklet on how to get quoted and talked about by the press.

• Bruce David promotes his *Starting Smart* newsletter by offering a sample for a dollar and sometimes tosses in a special report relative to the times (such as how to increase sales in tight economic times).

You have the idea by now. These days, readers seem to be responsive to any offer up to $7, but you may double your response by keeping the offered item under $5. I would suggest not using an uneven dollar amount, such as $3.75, and always include your postage and handling figures into the total.

Be very careful about making *free* offers because this can cost you a young fortune and yield nothing but names of curiosity seekers who won't buy anything. One of my readers once told me her sorry tale, about the time she was trying to promote her machine-knitted line of wearable and decorative art in *FREEBIES* magazine. This consumer publication regularly runs offers from all kinds of companies and has been known to generate thousands of responses for its "advertisers." It costs nothing to have an offer published, and advertisers have the option of making the offer totally free, or charging up to $3 for postage and handling.

To show the quality of her work, the knitter sent *FREEBIES* her offer of a free knitted lace bookmark—a terrible mistake. Her publicity mention brought her over 900 requests, and she said she nearly lost her mind trying to produce this many bookmarks. Worse, orders from the advertising material she enclosed with the bookmark were practically nil.

Consumer magazines sometimes feature free pattern offers for readers, and many advertisers take this opportunity to get publicity, hoping that once a pattern is in the consumer's hand, reorders will result. But this doesn't always happen. Consider this report from one of my readers:

"We participated in such an offer where the consumer sent a self-addressed stamped envelope for the pattern. It cost me $2,500 just to have the patterns printed and to hire a schoolgirl to stuff the envelopes. We've concluded that too many people order something free even when they're not really interested in using the item. We gained only a few customers from our pattern caper—very expensive lesson. In another pattern offer we participated in, customers had to send $2 to help cover costs. Again, we gained only a few customers, but this time we got enough to cover our costs."

Another pattern designer in my network reported that she, too, once offered a free pattern for an SASE as a means of building a mailing list. She got 7,000 requests for the pattern and "a discouraging response on pattern orders." Like the first pattern seller, she did better when a pattern was offered for a $1 postage and handling charge.

People seem to love $1 items. It's a kind of magic number these days, and many who respond to such an offer will send cash instead of a one-dollar check. Silvana Clark asks a dollar for her "PANIC button" (see sidebar), and that's the price Lynn Hallett and Georgia Feazle put on one of their promotional booklets, designed to sell their newsletter and line of fabric-painting pattern books. Titled *Wearable Art* (16 pages, 3½″ × 8½″), it explains what wearable art is, how to create it, care for it and, of course, how to order their patterns by mail. They told me it got a lot of publicity, and generated a lot of orders for them.

Tie Your Publicity to an Event or Anniversary

Press releases are often hung on national holidays or other proclaimed events. When September was proclaimed by the sewing industry as National Homesewing Month, it provided people in sewing businesses across the country a wonderful reason to send press releases to their local papers every September announcing this fact, and also mentioning the availability of their workshops, classes, custom-sewing services, new products, supplies and so forth.

"Anniversaries of major events and days or weeks established to commemorate certain causes are a publicity seeker's dream," says Kate Kelly, author of *The Publicity Manual*. "If you can tie your business in with one of these occasions, then you will likely have a good chance for additional press coverage."

Publishers, writers, speakers, publicists, businesses, organizations, consultants and others can easily tie their promotion plans into special days, weeks, months and anniversaries. For example, Bruce Fife, author and publisher of *How to Be a Goofy Juggler,* timed the publication of this book to coincide with National Juggling Day, then wrote a press release promoting his book and commemorating the day. (See also sidebar copy, next page.)

Although Congress no longer recognizes special events sponsored by associations and corporations, they are still being used to promote various products and services. Examples

PANIC Buttons

After receiving a PR mention in *Meetings and Conventions* magazine, Silvana Clark was astonished when the first response was an order for 3,000 of her red PANIC buttons, a novelty item she created as a promotional tool. (It fits on any typewriter or computer keyboard, and the media ate it up.)

A simple press release got Silvana a half-page color spread in the above-mentioned magazine. "I'm almost embarrassed to have such a big ad for free," said Silvana as she gleefully counted the profits of her aggressive publicity campaign.

Finding a News Peg

Using a media guide such as *Chase's Annual Events*, look for special days, weeks and anniversaries you can relate to your business. For example:

• Handmade items could be promoted during "National Home Improvement Month." (What better way to improve one's home than to beautify it with handcrafts?)

• If you have a business related in any way to pets, you can profit during "Pets Are Wonderful Month."

• Child-related businesses can tie into "Week of the Young Child" in April while photographers can "snap to it" during "National Photo Week" in May.

• There's also "Michigan Week" in May, and what better time to teach Michigan citizens more about the state, such as the many talented artists and craftspeople it has.

Other interesting events include "National Anti-Boredom Day," "Swap Ideas Day," "Be Late for Something Day," and a host of anniversaries, national and ethnic days, festivals, fairs, presidential proclamations and commercially sponsored events.

include National Bookkeeper's Day, National Business Women's Week, Fun Mail Week, National Goof-Off Day and "I Am In Control Day." (Note: Canada doesn't have special days and weeks like this—only a few "awareness months.") Information on American events will be found in Contemporary Books' *Chase's Calendar of Annual Events* and in *Celebrate Today* by John Kremer, who maintains a national special events registry. (Anyone can create and register their own special event. For John's address, see his *Book Marketing Update* newsletter in chapter sixteen.) In addition to being useful promotional tools, annual event books are fun to read because they include so many humorous entries. Three that amused me were "No Socks Day," "Lumpy Rug Day" and "Stay Away From Seattle Day."

There is one week in particular all U.S. business owners can capitalize on. For the past thirty years, the President has designated a week in May as "National Small Business Week," and each year the U.S. Small Business Administration sponsors special events recognizing the achievements of America's outstanding small business entrepreneurs. This would be a perfect time to issue a press release that hooks your homebased business on this important news peg.

Local Publicity Opportunities

A lot of small businesses have found that publicity in the local paper is as easy as picking up the telephone or stopping by the newspaper office to talk to a reporter. You have nothing to lose and everything to gain, so make a little effort here by deliberately seeking such publicity. "People are so impressed by the fact that we have been featured in the local paper," Susan Winchester told me. "I cannot believe how easy it was to get the publicity . . . all I had to do was ask." Many other *Homemade Money* readers have told me the same thing.

To get started, analyze local papers to see which businesses have been mentioned, and why. What consumer benefits are indicated in each story? If none, then what else about the story interested you? Note the human interest features that appear every day. Editors like them, and people in general like to know what others are doing. If you are doing something you find interesting, you can bet there are people in your community who would like to know about it. If you can tie your release to a local event or national holiday, your chances for publicity will increase. Crafters, for example, often get publicity at Christmastime because handcrafts are a wonderful gift idea.

"I followed your suggestion and sent a press release to each of the two San Antonio newspapers," writes Doreen Barrett of that city, who makes *Karrot Top Tots*. "I mailed the releases on a Thursday. One paper called on Monday, came to my house with a photographer on Tuesday, and the article appeared in the following Monday's paper. I was surprised by the quick response, but I'm sure my timing had a lot to do with it since Christmas was then just around the corner. The article resulted in a number of calls and orders, not only from strangers, but also friends I had not heard from in a while. The other newspaper featured my dolls in a 'Count down to Christmas' shopping column, and it also generated many calls and orders."

As you study a paper, notice its special sections and try to relate your business to one of them. For instance, in the home section, small businesses often get publicity by offering tips related to the care or maintenance of one's home (such as how to clean a chimney or carpet, be a better landscaper or gardener, or make general home repairs). Any business that offers a related product or service that can be promoted in a free brochure should explore the possibilities of either writing a short how-to article for the paper, or asking that the brochure be mentioned as a reader service.

Similarly, the business or marketplace section of the paper is the perfect place to promote business-related products and services; the lifestyle section is appropriate for things related to weddings, anniversaries, entertainment and so on. Note especially the regular columns in each section of the paper. These columnists are always looking for interesting people and things to write about.

Local newspapers like to publish articles about generous people in their community, thus an involvement in community activities, or a donation of your time, services or special products will always draw favorable attention to you and your business while providing the same kind of image advertising major corporations routinely pay for. While image advertising doesn't put dollars directly into your jeans, it can be invaluable in terms of the national recognition it gives to your accomplishments. It also adds to your overall business credibility while offering encouragement to others who may be trying to follow in your footsteps.

When Stephanie Heavey became aware of the Quasquicentennial (125) Celebration of her city, Palatine, she designed a special doll named "PalaTINA" and offered it to the centennial committee for promotional purposes. "They were delighted to exhibit her at several events before using her in a raffle," Stephanie reported. "Then the *Daily Herald* picked up on the doll and sent a reporter to do a feature. This generated several calls and letters, which led to sales for both PalaTINA and another doll that was pictured in the article."

Joellen Buzinec explains how donations of goods for worthwhile causes often leads to sales: "One of our local elementary schools has a fund-raising drive each year with a variety of ways

Warning!

Before you seek local newspaper publicity, be sure your business is operating legally as far as zoning ordinances and licenses are concerned. Zoning officials and other local authorities may pick up on such publicity and pay you an unexpected call.

Give to Receive

After following the publicity advice in an earlier edition of this book, Dessie Durham, a seventy-four-year-old crafter in Springfield, Missouri, sent copies of her PR clips, which mentioned her charitable contributions.

Each time she has a special sales event coming up—a crafts fair, exhibit in a new shop, etc.—Dessie draws a crowd by sending press releases to local newspapers and radio stations announcing she plans to donate a certain percentage of her sales to charity. For example, one of Dessie's special products is a sculpted Santa. At Christmastime, she got a lovely feature by sending a release announcing she was going to donate a portion of her sales to The Kitchen, a shelter for the homeless. (Dessie was orphaned when she was three years old.) The headline on her feature story read, "Senior helps fulfill kids' holiday wishes."

To promote an Easter crafts fair, Dessie chose the American Lung Association to be the recipient of fifty cents from each piece of her handcrafted "Bunny Pin" jewelry sold at a particular shop in the Ozarks.

"I always thought when people talked about the things they did it was bragging," says Dessie, "but Barbara calls it 'self-promotion,' and if it's done in the right way, it works!"

to gain extra revenue for special projects. My homebased business, JOBEE, makes children's jogging suits and personalized towels for children, so naturally I donate several of these items. The return on this investment is always many times over.

"For example, a donated towel worth $12.99 landed me a $4,200 sewing contract for a group of barbershop singers. The father of the child who won the towel started reading my brochure, and as a result called and asked me to bid on the job."

When the owners of a little-known shop volunteered to decorate a well-known museum in their city that was open for special tours during the Christmas season, they received considerable publicity for their decorating efforts, and a great deal of attention for the shop as well. You don't have to be a retailer to benefit from this kind of "rub-off publicity" idea.

The donation of a product or service to a charity or fund-raising group can be a good news hook for your release, as Dessie Durham has learned. (See related sidebar.) The donation of a product or service for raffle at a conference will provide image advertising while also leading to sales, if only indirectly. For example, I often donate a copy of *Homemade Money* for raffle at home-business conferences, with the understanding that the book will be announced as "also available in bookstores."

Local publicity opportunities are not limited to newspaper mentions or radio and cable television appearances (see following section). Consider the library, for example. "Our local library system has a public display case that goes begging for interesting displays," a reader comments. "They were very glad to have ours on 'The History of Photography,' " says a couple who sells 3-D cameras.

Wire Services and Syndicates

Newspaper publicity need not be limited to local papers. If you can find a national angle to your local story, it may be picked up by a wire service, such as Associated Press (AP) or United Press International (UPI), or news syndicates such as King Features, New York Times News Service, and the Los Angeles Times Syndicate.

You have to have interesting, well-written material to get their attention, but once you do, it could mean your story would appear in newspapers or on radio stations across the country. In promoting her children's book Mary Hansen reported that Montreal, Calgary and Regina did articles on the book, resulting in many orders. "Best of all," she said, the "CP wire service (which goes across Canada) picked up my story, including my address and how-to-order information. In three weeks alone, I received over 1,400 orders for the book."

You will find a list of news services and feature syndicates in the media directories listed in chapter sixteen. There seems to be no end to the kind of material they will consider. Many syndicates seem to be interested in material related to "living and lifestyle," which includes everything from cooking to car care, from contemporary living to coping with old age, from growing plants to raising a family. Health, nutrition and money topics also are of interest.

Note that many of the regular columns in newspapers are syndicated. If you can connect with a syndicated columnist who will mention your product or service, you may derive huge direct or indirect benefits. (Check your library for a directory of syndicated columnists.) Because I've relentlessly pursued columnists through the years, I've struck paydirt many times, getting valuable publicity in small and large papers alike. Example: Niki Scott, who writes the syndicated *Working Woman* column, received my "Gloom and Doom" release illustrated nearby and then called to interview me at length. She gave me all the space in two of her columns—including my address as a reader service. One article was titled "Home Businesses Well-Placed for Recession"; the other was "Recessionproofing a Small Business."

My first mention in a syndicated column did not include my address, and at the time I was distressed because people could not connect with me to get information about my newsletter. But in the years since I have come to realize all publicity mentions have power, even when there is no chance for a direct response. The idea is to "get your name out there" so the people you're trying to reach will eventually buy simply because they remember reading about you earlier.

Radio and Television Publicity

"There are four ways to profit from radio/TV publicity: increase sales, gain credibility, expand distribution and build a mailing list," says Bill Harrison, owner of Bradley Communications Corp. and publisher of *Radio-TV Interview Report*, a twice-monthly magazine that reaches 3,800 radio/TV producers nationwide. "Most radio shows will let you give an address or phone number out over the air so the audience can order your product or request more info. TV shows will often put your ordering info on the screen. Be sure to ask about these arrangements before agreeing to do the interview. Also, consider having a toll-free number you can give out on the air."

When appropriate, send your press releases to local television stations. If you can give your story any kind of national angle, it may later be broadcast nationally, giving you the proverbial "fifteen minutes of fame." While waiting for your big break on national television, don't overlook your opportunities on local cable stations. Sometimes program directors will come to you as

Radio Results

Canadian self-publisher Mary Hansen reports she was interviewed for fifteen minutes on Toronto's second largest radio station when she was promoting her children's learning book. Although her name and address was given twice, she got just three book orders from the show.

"On the other hand," she said, "I was interviewed for about four minutes by a much smaller station (a more intellectual, classical type of station than the other one), and I received forty-seven orders from that. Obviously, listeners on the smaller show were the ones most interested in kids' educational products. Just shows you the importance of 'target marketing.'"

Home Business

news

From Barbara Brabec
"America's Most Trusted Home-Business Adviser"

To receive a review copy of any report
by fax or mail, call Barbara Brabec,
(630) 717-4188 or fax to (630) 717-5198.

FOR IMMEDIATE RELEASE

New Problem-Solving Reports for Homebased Professionals

New reports from Barbara Brabec, America's most trusted home-business adviser, offer solutions to four major problems faced by homebased business owners and other self-employed individuals. These reports include special resource lists, insider tips and answers to the following troublesome questions:

- What are the benefits of joining a small business organization, and which ones cater to the special needs of homebased professionals and self-employed individuals?
- As a self-employed individual, where can I get affordable hospital/major medical insurance coverage for myself and my family?
- If a bank won't give me a loan, where can I get the money I need to launch or expand a homebased business?
- How can I get merchant status (offer my customers credit card privileges) after my bank has turned me down, and what are the pitfalls of getting a card through an ISO (independent sales organization)?

"With the right information in hand, all small business problems are solvable," says Brabec, author of *Homemade Money*. Now in its 5th edition, this home- print. In April, after fifteen years of publishing a home-busines her periodical to concentrate on writing new books and report consulting. Her newsletter subscribers are being served by the Paltz, NY. Issues of this quarterly now carry Brabec's "Busines

Her newest reports are *State & National Organizations Employed Individuals* (**#R25**); *Small Business Organizations Tha Quick Money Sources for Homebased Businesses & Self-Employe Merchant Status and Increase Sales up to 46% by Offering Your* Each report is $6 ppd. (U.S. funds). Orders should be sent wit Business Reports, P. O. Box 2137, Naperville, IL 60567. To ch

For Immediate Release

For a review copy or FREE article excerpts for your periodical,
call Barbara Brabec (630) 717-4188 or fax request to (630) 717-5198.

BARBARA BRABEC'S NEW BOOK
OFFERS HUNDREDS OF SECRETS TO SUCCESS
IN SELLING ARTS & CRAFTS

— A Selection of Two Book Clubs —

Has anyone ever told you that you ought to sell your beautiful art, craft or needlework creations? If so, your first thought may have been, "Sure. . . but HOW, *exactly*?" Maybe you've been selling your work for years but are bored with marketing through the same old outlets, or maybe you're just discouraged because the profits you once dreamed of making aren't there.

Whether you're a beginning seller or a burned-out professional, you'll find hundreds of creative crafts marketing tips and ideas in Barbara Brabec's new book, *Handmade for Profit—Hundreds of Secrets to Success in Selling Arts & Crafts* (Evans). You may be familiar with two of Barbara's earlier books, *Creative Cash* and *Homemade Money*. Both have achieved classic status with sales of more than 100,000 copies each.

"Many people have a serious leisuretime interest in crafts or needlework," says Barbara, "but few realize the true value of their creativity and fewer still know how to find the right market for their products, let alone price them profitably. Most crafters limit their retail marketing activities to selling at craft fairs, in consignment shops, craft malls or holiday boutiques," she adds, "but only a few have learned how to successfully sell through all of the sixteen retail markets discussed at length in *Handmade for Profit.*"

Unlike Brabec's other books, this is not a home-business manual but rather a "crafts marketing idea book" that focuses on selling at the retail level. It explains, in detail, how to successfully (and more profitably) sell:

- at art and craft fairs, festivals and mall shows
- in your own home shop or studio
- through home parties and open houses
- in bazaars, holiday boutiques and community markets
- in craft malls and rent-a-space gift shops
- in consignment craft shops and art galleries
- through local retailers and service providers
- with a pushcart in shopping malls
- in schools, hospitals, clinics and retirement centers
- through your own craft cooperative
- on a military base

(continued next page)

Samples of computer-generated news heads and releases used by the author.

Above: News head designed by the author with WordPerfect software. Two of the special reports mentioned in this release were publicized in Jane Bryant Quinn's syndicated newspaper column and "Money Watch" column in *Good Housekeeping* magazine. This publicity generated over $3,500 in business in the form of initial orders and bounceback book sales.

Right: A release laser-printed on pre-printed stock available from Paper Direct. (The solid block is blue with NEWS and border design printed in gold.)

a result of seeing your publicity in the local paper.

If the idea of being on television scares you to death, consider how well dollmaker Eileen Heifner, owner of Create An Heirloom, did her first time around. After receiving local newspaper publicity, she got a call from the director of a local cable TV show who asked if she could do an hour-long demonstration on how to make porcelain dolls.

"We had several meetings to discuss how we would format the show," says Eileen. "I rehearsed endlessly, talking to a spot on the wallpaper as a mock camera. The show was presented live, and when the producer said quiet on the set, I almost died of fright. However, once we started talking, it was no problem at all. I forgot all about the camera as I got involved in showing how to make the dolls. The station gave me a tape of the show that I can loan out to customers so they can better understand the dollmaking process."

Being prepared really paid off for Eileen because a producer from another cable show saw her and suggested a whole series of dollmaking programs. "You were right when you said that publicity generates more publicity," Eileen reported. "In addition to all this television exposure, the newspaper article ultimately led to another feature that my library placed on their bulletin board for a month."

Cathy Gilleland, who organized The Crafters, a cooperative in Chelmsford, Massachusetts, explains how an organized group might obtain publicity on cable television. "When our community began to broadcast on its own station, The Crafters did a regularly scheduled series of craft programs," she said. "Various members of the cooperative demonstrated techniques and gave how-to instructions. Tapes of each show went to the local library for additional viewing after each broadcast."

Although commercial aspects were downplayed, this provided wonderful exposure for each craftsperson. "Names and addresses were given at the end of each show, and inexpensive instruction sheets were also offered," says Cathy. "This not only helped viewers, but got the craftperson's material into community mailboxes."

To increase your chances of appearing on cable TV, first do your homework by learning what kind of guests are interviewed, what topics are discussed and what kind of promotional push guests receive. When you think you have an idea of interest, write or call the show's producer or interviewer and explain it.

If you're shooting for the big time—major television talk shows—read some publicity how-to books for inside tips on how to crack this market. It takes the right talk, PR savvy and extra effort to get invited to appear on the big talk shows. More opportunities exist on smaller radio and television shows, and sometimes they come automatically, as a direct result of print

How Authors Reach Millions

Authors can have a field day on major radio and TV talk shows, sometimes raking in thousands of dollars in sales with a hot topic and a toll-free number for their books. You can either send media releases to a list of stations or place an ad in a media guide such as Bill Harrison's *Radio-TV Interview Report*. To increase your chances of being interviewed, Harrison suggests that you be able to provide other guests and offer localized information that relates to your product or service.

"A sixty-second commercial on the 'Oprah Winfrey Show' would cost you about $50,000. However, if Oprah interviewed you as a guest on her show, it wouldn't cost you a penny to promote your product or service to her twenty million viewers."

publicity. Years ago, after being mentioned in an article in *Money* magazine, I got a call from the magazine's publicity director who wanted to know if I would like her to arrange a few live radio interviews for me. "Sure," I said, trying to sound confident while shaking in my boots. (Never having done this before, I naturally was uneasy about it.) As it turned out, each interview was easy and fun, just like talking to an interesting friend on the phone. Some conversations were only minutes long, others ran as long as an hour. Like everything else in business, doing this kind of thing just takes a little getting used to. Experience breeds confidence.

After I had done four or five interviews, I wrote a press release and sent it to several stations, which resulted in still more interviews. The opening paragraphs of my release read:

Millions of Americans have a leisuretime interest in arts or crafts, and a growing number of them are currently wondering if their craft or hobby could be turned into a profitable home business.

Barbara Brabec, author of the best-selling book, *Creative Cash—How to Sell Your Crafts, Needlework, Designs & Know-How*, has the answer to that question, and she welcomes telephone interviews on this topic.

When *Homemade Money* was published, I began to promote it the same way I'd promoted my first book, aggressively seeking printed publicity and using radio when I had blocks of time to give interviews. I still do this today, not with the idea of soliciting orders on the phone, but to generate consumer interest at the bookstore level. Although I always get a little direct response (on average, between five and twenty people may call or write), it is publicity like this that has kept *Homemade Money* in print since 1984. Hogging all the sales to myself could have resulted in too few sales at the bookstore level and lack of interest on the publisher's part to keep it in print. What's really nice is when radio or TV hosts begin to publicize you on their own. For example, Ken and Daria Dolan, America's first family of finance, have recommended *Homemade Money* from time to time as being the best book in its field, and I've also had extra mentions on ABC-TV's *Home* show, which gave me my first major television exposure.

This visibility came not because I aggressively sought it, but because I happened to be in the right place at the right time. The show's producer caught my monthly column in *Crafts* and called to see if I could recommend anyone to be a guest on the show for a week-long home-business segment they were planning. "You bet," I said. "Me!" I offered not only to contribute material for the show's writers, but said I could provide a list of successful home-business owners who would make interesting guests.

Thus, when Hollywood called, I was able to take two of my subscribers with me, and we had a terrific, all-expenses-paid week doing the show and seeing the sights. As the "guest expert" on the daily "Homemade Money" segment (about 7 minutes long), I had perhaps two minutes of talk time each day, and at the beginning of each segment, my book was flashed on screen for maybe five seconds. A few months later I learned firsthand the value of such publicity. As near as my publisher and I could determine, more than 10,000 books were purchased in bookstores as a direct result of this exposure.

If you think it's easy to be a Hollywood star, think again. We had to get up at 3:30 A.M. to get in and out of "hair and makeup" before the big stars came in, reminding me once again of why I like to work for myself. None of us got more than four hours of sleep a night the whole week, but thanks to *Home*'s great makeup artists, the blue under our eyes didn't show. It was a kick to be in makeup in the company of such notables as Steve Allen and John Davidson, who told me he had a homebased game board business. "Half of California has a cottage industry in the garage," he quipped.

It's been several years since I appeared on this show, but I still receive letters from people who mention that they remember seeing me on the *Home* show. The major lesson I've learned from my considerable PR experience to date is that each national mention I've received has added to my credibility as an expert in my field while also increasing the degree of confidence people have in my advice. Even when listeners or readers cannot reach me directly, they are often motivated to look for my books in their library or bookstore. And if they've read about me in a magazine before they receive one of my mail pieces, they are much more likely to place an order because I'm no longer a stranger to them. Likewise, your prospective customers and clients will be more interested in ordering from you or hiring your services if they perceive your business to be successful—and that's precisely what publicity does best.

Magazine and Newsletter Publicity

While radio and television exposure adds to your credibility as a homebased businessperson, boosts your ego and generates sales at the retail level, unless you offer a toll-free order number it seldom produces a profitable *direct response*. This does not mean you should not seek such publicity—because it often works for you in other ways—only that you should place maximum effort on getting print publicity if your time and budget for promotions is limited.

Some types of print publicity are more valuable than others. While newspaper publicity is great for the ego, and occasionally

Tell 'Em Where You Live!

When being interviewed, sneak in your hometown. Subtly tell the audience where you're located, in case the host doesn't give out your ordering info over the air. Say something like this: 'In Coral Gables, Florida, where I live, parents are so fed up with the public school that . . .' This way, members of the audience can get your number from Coral Gables directory assistance (if you're listed).

—Bill Harrison, publisher of
Radio-TV Interview Report

Merchandise Your Publicity

Get added mileage from your publicity mentions by having your clips reprinted as a promotional flyer. Paste articles to an 8½″ × 11″ sheet of white paper, include the name of the periodical in which it appeared, and have copies made as needed.

A great "promo clipping" can be used to advantage in a press kit designed to get publicity in other magazines. Or promotional reprints can be made for handout to your customers or clients (not to mention friends and neighbors), many of whom will be mightily impressed to see your business profiled in a major magazine.

Leila Albala, author of *Easy Halloween Costumes for Children*, received far too many publicity mentions to have each reprinted individually. If you, like Leila, reach the point where you have so many clippings you don't know what to do, arrange them in collage fashion on a large art board, then have your printer reduce the image to fit an 8½″ × 11″ sheet. (See collage illustration on page 286.)

profitable, reporters have an amazing tendency to misquote people and state facts incorrectly. Often, it's just as well that an article dies overnight. When the information is correct, however, one at least ends up with a useful media clip. If you are fortunate enough to be quoted or featured in a syndicated column, you may find the publicity continuing for months as different papers pick up on it.

Publicity opportunities abound in newsletters and in small-circulation periodicals. Often they will generate more business than larger magazines whose circulation is too broad for your particular publicity purposes. Publicity in newsletters expires about as quickly as newspaper publicity, but magazine publicity can pull for years. One reason is because they tend to live on in doctor's offices, beauty shops, libraries and home collections. Some professional and special-interest periodicals may pull for a long time, too, because people tend to trade or share such publications with others in their field.

Magazine publicity is easier to get than publicity on radio or television because editors are conditioned to receiving and using the thousands of press releases that cross their desks each year. It's their *job* to print the information in them so long as it benefits their readers. Publicity sometimes comes not through press releases, but through special letters to the editor or to a particular columnist or department editor. In using this approach, carefully study each magazine in which you would like publicity, then try to relate what you're doing to the individual departments and columns in that publication. If other people are receiving publicity in them, you may be able to get it, too. In contacting such columnists or writers, don't say, "I would like some publicity in the magazine." Instead, stress that the information you can contribute for use in the publication "would be of value to the magazine's readers because . . ." and that you would be glad to share information in an interview or by sending a useful package of information in exchange for having your name and address included with your tips or advice.

Although you should try to get publicity in major consumer magazines, it can be difficult to obtain since so many people are clamoring for mentions. Hope for it, but don't expect it. Where publicity is concerned, there are no guarantees. Publicity is a *gift* people in the media give to newsworthy individuals, businesses or organizations. Even if one were to hire an expensive PR agency to write and mail press releases, publicity could not be guaranteed.

Publicity novices are much more likely to get publicity in special-interest periodicals, newsletters, professional journals and trade magazines. Make it a point to obtain and read at least one issue of every trade or professional magazine related to your field. Study every section of each magazine to find the names of the special editors or departments that obviously are giving publicity. Most trade magazines have *New Product* departments that invite submissions. You will increase your chances here if you send a press photo with a good caption.

"Many people tend to think of publicity as newspaper or magazine articles only," writes designer Pamela Noel. "They do not realize that New Product review articles are not paid advertisements, nor do they know how to submit their products for such columns. This has been our major source of publicity, and until one of our items came out in a major trade magazine, my partner and I did not believe they would print this unless we paid them for it."

A press release for a trade publication should include technical information that will be of interest to readers in that trade. One product publicist recommends the use of an accompanying fact sheet that includes such pertinent information as engineering design, efficiency of operation, model sizes available, prices, distribution information, weight and any other specific information buyers will want to know. When considering which publications to add to your PR list, look not only at trade magazines that directly relate to your new product and its obvious uses, but other publications that *indirectly* relate to it. When you find them, write a different press release that presents your product from a new viewpoint and in a way that will appeal to the new audience of readers.

Writing Promotional Articles

One of the best ways to get publicity in special-interest consumer magazines and business periodicals is to write promotional articles that include your special tips, advice or know-how. For a long time, I couldn't find the time to write promotional articles. When I finally did, I was amazed at how welcome they were to editors in my field. Dozens of my articles have since been published; each one of them has contained my blurb at the end that tells readers how to order whichever book I'm promoting with the article. These articles not only increase the flow of daily inquiries and book orders, but also stimulate sales at the bookstore level.

Although you won't receive payment for promotional articles, you may receive free ad space if you request it, and you can write your own how-to-order information at the end of the article. Master marketer Jeffrey Lant calls this the "resource box" and in return for the free articles he offers the business community, he asks that his resource box be published exactly as written.

Lant regularly sends editors a lengthy list of the many articles currently available, a strategy that has made him the most widely read small business expert in the industry. In *The*

Unabashed Self-Promoter's Guide, he says, "You must produce articles at regular intervals to continue to keep your name and services before the proper public and underscore the fact of your indispensability." To keep time spent on article writing to a minimum, Lant suggests you master three basic types of article formats, which he calls "The Problem-Solving Process Article," "The Sentinel" and "The White Knight." (You'll have to read his book to get the nitty-gritty details.)

Michelle West, a self-publisher in Canada, has discovered the value of writing to sell her pattern booklets. "I'm not a profes-

In 1992, Leila Albala was named one of the top newsmakers in Canada by *Direct Marketing News.* Through the years, her unrelenting publicity efforts have sold thousands of copies of her self-published books, including *Catalogue of Canadian Catalogs* and *Easy Halloween Costumes for Children,* the title featured in above "PR Collage." (It has sold over 74,000 copies to date, thanks largely to Leila's publicity efforts.)

With more than 300 PR clips in file, Leila created her first clippings collage as a matter of convenience. "I had too many write-ups and couldn't send all those photocopies to editors," says Leila. "I decided that what was important was to show which publications have featured a book previously and show just glimpses of text. Now I have a collage for each book, and it's a history of what I have done so far. I send these to radio stations and editors who want to know more about me, offering copies of complete articles if they want them.

When I have a new title with no previous write-ups, the collages of my previous books are useful to show editors that I have been featured several times over the years and consequently have earned a certain reputation. Somehow my collage seems to impress and intrigue editors even more than a thick stack of complete write-ups. I also use the collage to get advance orders for new books yet to be published. My mass of clippings validates me in my readers' eyes and makes them trust me."

sional writer," she says, "but this should not be a problem if you present yourself properly. I have discovered that you need only three things to get published: You need to be able to write reasonably well; you need to learn the skills necessary to market what you produce (how to write a great query letter); and you need the self-confidence and courage to go after what you want. Nobody is going to come to you."

Larger magazines, of course, may not only pay you for your writing, but give you valuable sales plugs as well. For example, model ship builder Eugene L. Larson used press releases with considerable success when he first introduced his half-hull ship model kit line. He also provided a product review when he introduced his wood thickness sander for model builders, dollhouse furniture makers and fine woodworkers. "I have had 100 percent success in having most or all of the information and a photo published in model and craft magazines," he said. "In fact, some of the publications have given me more than a half page for the free product review."

Later, Eugene hit on something even better than free advertising. "I submitted an article on my sander to one of the model magazines with worldwide distribution," he said. "It was contained in two issues of the magazine, running nine pages in total, and they paid me their standard per-page rate for an author in addition to giving me a strong plug for my sander and half-hull line."

Folk artists Clark and Ronnie Pearson, who carve and paint primitive Santas and other country items, have been featured in several of the best country magazines. How did they do it? Says Ronnie, "We began by first writing detailed descriptions of each of our products, along with a background story about our business and how it evolved. Then we gave this information to business friends skilled in photography, graphic design, copywriting and publicity. They developed a color catalog, professional background article, press release and presentation folder suitable for mailing to magazine editors. Each press kit included photographs and color transparencies designed to make it easy for editors to create a story with little effort on their part."

This crafts couple stresses the importance of targeting press releases to appropriate editors, adding, "Different handcrafts lend themselves to different types of consumer magazines, and the inclusion of photos can make all the difference between a brief mention and a feature story."

Getting Publicity: Just Like Shooting Pool

I have a special fondness for pool because it was one of the first games my husband taught me after we were married. We don't play that game anymore, but in my mind I can still hear the

Become an Interview Source

Author Tana Fletcher says more business owners can become an interview source—one of the experts whom journalists call when they're researching stories—simply by letting the media know you're available.

"First, spend a little time preparing a list of topics you'd be willing to discuss, such as 'Running a Home Business,' 'Buying Residential Real Estate,' 'Selling by Mail' or 'Inside Advice on Interior Decorating'—any interesting topic that related to your business.

"Next, write to various publications, radio programs and television talk shows suggesting those topics you think might be of interest to that particular audience, and offer yourself as an interview subject. Add pizzazz to your pitch by including two or three of the most unusual, funniest or most dangerous situations you've encountered in your profession.

"Such mailings should include a complete package of information—press release, bio, article clips, etc. Media acceptance and credibility must be built slowly, but the rewards are worth the time it takes," says Tana.

How Publicity Pays

Here's a small idea of the kind of response certain publicity mentions have brought certain businesses in my network:

- When Sharon Holmlund's business, Shoebox to Showcase, was profiled in *Home Office Computing*, she received 433 inquiries from people who wanted her package of information on how to start a similar business. Fifteen percent of those who received this information ultimately joined this multilevel program through Sharon.

- When Sharon Olson received a plug in my "Selling What You Make" column in *Crafts*, over 930 readers ordered her $5 crafts directory.

- When book publisher Carol O'Hare got a mention in *Modern Maturity* for *Starting a Mini-Business—A Guidebook for Seniors*, she received over 4,000 mail orders and quickly had to order a second printing.

- When Janice Guthrie's business, The Health Resource, received a mention in an article in *Reader's Digest*, she reported 740 calls almost immediately, and 37 percent of these people ultimately ordered medical research reports (at $100+each) from her. Ah, yes, publicity pays!

- When *Home Office Computing* recommended my periodical, *National Home Business Report*, as "one of the best in the field," only 121 readers ordered a sample issue. But when it was mentioned in *Focus on the Family*, a Christian newsletter with a large readership of mothers, over 2,000 women ordered a sample.

- A mention of *Homemade Money* (with its postage-paid price) in *Parade* (newspaper supplement) generated over 500 orders and pulled for several weeks.

delicious *click* the pool balls made as I broke them with that first thrust of the stick. It's rather like the "good vibes" I get now when I put new press releases into the mail. "*Click, click, click*," they go, as they land on editors' desks across the country.

In pool, if you're good, your first shot will knock a few balls into pockets and position the rest near other holes for easy tapping in later. The same kind of thing can happen with a press release after it's mailed. For a moment, think of yourself as the pool stick, and the white cue ball as the press release. Let's imagine you have just sent a couple hundred copies of it to your publicity list (by first-class mail, of course), which may include local papers, a few major newspapers, regional and national magazines, special-interest publications, radio stations, organizations and so on.

One of your releases—let's relate it to the number three ball that just rolled into the center pocket—has landed on the local newspaper editor's desk. He decides what you are doing is worth at least a short article. On publication, it brings you to the attention of the president of a local organization (the number four ball), who asks you to speak at the next meeting. This will be an excellent publicity break for you. Hard to tell what opportunities await you here.

Meanwhile, you have other balls on the table—or, a lot of press releases still circulating—just waiting to be knocked into pockets. In pool, you often have to shoot two or three times to pocket a ball. The same thing is true when you shoot for publicity. Your first release may work beautifully, resulting in publicity in several publications, or it may just fizzle out. Or so you may think. What you may not realize is that your "publicity push," like those pool balls on the table, is in a state of limbo, waiting for yet another push from you. Maybe it's a follow-up telephone call, another press release, or some additional attention you are able to get for yourself. Often, these things work together to trigger other publicity you could not have received if the first publicity effort had not been made.

After reviewing Godfrey Harris's book, *Talk Is Cheap*, in my newsletter, I sent him a copy of the review and promptly received not just a thank-you note, but a couple of helpful tips I could publish in future issues. Godfrey is savvy enough to know that little fillers are just perfect for my quarterly—and for scores of other small business periodicals as well.

Throughout this chapter, I've given you examples of how publicity breeds publicity. You will recall that Eileen Heifner's first cable TV appearance led to a series of programs for another station. That first show also led to other appearances. "I was asked to donate some products for use on a Muscular Dystrophy Telethon, and then invited to appear on the show," Eileen told me. "Later the local PBS station invited me to donate products, which brought more favorable publicity."

After Janice Guthrie of The Health Resource wrote a short article for my periodical, it was read by journalist Brad McKee, who writes the "Managing Your Small Business" column for *Nation's Business*. He expanded on Janice's article for one of his columns on homebased businesses. Photographer Jim Bradshaw also reported on his experience. He was quoted in an issue of *Ebony Man* after I'd referred him to a reporter. "I then wrote a press release using the guidelines from *Homemade Money*. The release was picked up by a local paper and published in their business section. I now have two additional items to use in my press kits and presentation kits for prospective customers. More than that, I now have the realization that it's not hard to get into the media, provided you know and follow the rules."

I know better than most how publicity breeds and multiplies. There has not been a single month since 1979 that I have gone without national publicity of one kind or another, either for my books and various publications or for myself and my business. Yet, I have sent very few press releases to get this visibility. What I have done, and what you can do, too, is a lot of *networking* with people in a position to influence others. I sent letters, made telephone calls and mailed thousands of brochures to anyone and everyone who might conceivably be interested in what I was doing. In short, as a beginner in my field, I did a heck of a lot of hollering to get attention—and I got it. By being quoted in such prestigious publications as *Woman's Day*, *Family Circle*, *Time*, *Parade*, *New York Times*, *Inc*, *Entrepreneur* and *Money*, I first gained a reputation as an "authority," then "an expert." You may not feel like an expert now, but someday soon you may wake up and find that are *are* one.

"Experts 'happen' quickly," says *Writer's Digest* columnist Art Spikol. "One day you're an ordinary person who knows a lot of big things about something little or a lot of little things about something big. The next day you're quoted somewhere. Before the next 24 hours go by, you're an expert."

Click . . . Click . . . Click.

How to Develop Your Own PR List

You should have your own PR list even if you also plan occasionally to rent special media lists or use distribution services to print and mail press releases for you. Only with your own list can you be sure your message is reaching the individual editors and program directors most likely to respond to your press releases or media kits.

Developing and maintaining a PR list can be a never-ending job (1) because new opportunities for publicity are always presenting themselves, and (2) editors tend to move around a lot, which means constant corrections to your list. Depending on

How to Handle "Help Me" Calls

The minute you get publicity, the "wannabees" start calling, hoping you'll give them all your trade secrets so they can start a business with no effort on their part. Decide now how you will handle such calls when they come and accept the fact that you will often be wasting your time when you give free advice to such callers.

I know it's your nature to be helpful, but unless you can afford to work for nothing, your first responsibility is to your own business. To ease the guilt you may feel at saying no to someone who sincerely asks for help, try these suggestions:

1. Offer to consult with them on the telephone for a fee. ($50/hour is reasonable, payable in advance. They pay for the long-distance call, of course.)

2. Write a special report, booklet or how-to guide that shares general information but doesn't make it too easy for someone to start a competing business in your backyard.

3. Get your "help me!" callers off your back by referring them to books that answer their questions—like *Homemade Money*.

what you are promoting, your media list probably will be divided into basic categories, such as newspapers, radio and television contacts, consumer magazines, special-interest publications, small business newsletters, trade press and so on. Ideally, your mailing list will be computerized; if not, set up an efficient 3″×5″ card deck and type white paper masters that can be photocopied onto adhesive labels.

Build your media list in keeping with your business and publicity goals. If you are trying to reach the mass consumer market, concentrate on getting publicity in national consumer magazines, major newspapers, and radio and television stations across the country. If you're interested in reaching a specific segment of the consumer market, such as collectors, gardeners, new mothers, hobbyists, etc., first identify the periodicals these people normally read and learn about organizations to which they might belong. If you are a manufacturer trying to stir up interest in your newest product, you'll need to promote not only to the trade publications your dealers might read, but to the special-interest publications related to your field of business. And where do you find all these names and addresses?

Media lists can be rented from a variety of sources or meticulously compiled from telephone books, directories and periodicals. One of the niftiest directories I've seen is the *Gebbie Press All-in-One Directory*. It lists, in alphabetical order by category, the names and addresses of daily and weekly newspapers, AM-FM radio stations, television stations, general consumer magazines, business papers, trade press, black press, farm publications and news syndicates. With this directory (and others like it) you easily can zero in on a specific category of interest, be it art, babies, cooking, golf, travel or dozens of other special-interest areas. Listings include circulation information, type of readership served and more. (See chapter sixteen.)

In addition to standard media directories like this one, consider writer's publications, which are often-overlooked sources of media contacts. Many of my best names have come from *Writer's Digest* and *Writer*, magazines that regularly print market information and special market lists. (Once you know the kind of editorial material an editor wants, you also will know the kind of press releases most likely to attract attention.) *Writer's Digest* also publishes an excellent directory, *Writer's Market*, which is a tremendous source of information for anyone who wants contact with publishers in both the book and periodicals fields. (If you are trying to find a publisher for the book you have written, this is where you'll find the most up-to-date information on who wants to publish what.) For publicists and others who are building PR lists, this directory lists periodicals in dozens of categories within two general sections: consumer publications and trade/technical/professional journals.

Finally, keep your eyes open as you read the daily newspaper and your favorite magazines. Publicity from just one influential columnist could turn your business around overnight.

Publicity Humor

Humor is always in demand by the media, so if you can figure out how to write a humorous, yet tasteful, press release, you may triple your chances for publicity. (See related sidebar.)

For example, if you're a mother with six kids who's found a way to run a successful business at home, a humorous press release about your trials and tribulations—which also includes some solid tips on how to cope in such a situation—would surely bring results. Study the style of humorists such as Erma Bombeck for ideas.

Earlier editions of this book included sample releases by fiber artist Nancy Smeltzer, who for a while seemed to be getting publicity in every craft publication in the country. The sample headline earlier in this chapter—"Fiber Artist's Quilt Tours State of Maryland For Two Years"—was hers. Never at a loss for a peg on which to hang a release, Nancy was even able to get publicity when she had hand surgery. She titled that release "Fiber Artist, Nancy Smeltzer, Quilts Her Cast As She Recovers From Hand Surgery." It was accompanied by a photo of Nancy contemplating her quilted cast, and it was included in *The Crafts Report* along with her article, "How to Use Press Releases to Get Yourself Noticed." Said Nancy, "I thought the quilted cast would be a good angle since carpel tunnel syndrome is in the news a lot."

Nancy says the best compliment she ever received was from someone in her community who, upon meeting her for the first time, said that he had been hearing a lot about her, but thought she would be much older, considering all the publicity she had been getting.

"There's only one thing in the world worse than being talked about, and that is *not* being talked about," said Oscar Wilde. Publicity has certainly advanced my business, just as it will advance yours. I knew I was a success when a feature story finally appeared on me in the newspaper published in Paxton, Illinois, the town next to my hometown of Buckley, which is too small for a paper of its own. And I loved it when my sister, Mary Kaufmann, told a friend she ought to read my book, and her friend said, "You mean to say that *you* know Barbara Brabec?" (Since my sister is building a name for herself in her own field, I fully expect someday that someone will say to me, "Are you really Mary Kaufmann's sister?")

Of course I enjoy seeing my name in print, and with all the national visibility I receive, coupled with daily letters of praise from my readers, I sometimes get a bit heady from it all. Not to

Humorous Press Releases

Accessories designer Patricia Kutza produces one-of-a-kind neckwear positioned for career women. "I consider many of my pieces 'visual puns' since they incorporate most of the traditional components of mens' ties in unconventional ways," she says.

Patricia promotes her business, WhatKnot™, through speaking, offering such talks as "The Way We Wore," and "Fit to be Tied—Who's Who at the Zoo When Neckties Change Their Sex." Taking Barbara's advice to add a touch of humor to her releases, Patricia titled one, PICKPOCKETS™ ARE WELCOME (which promoted her retail/wholesale line of pockets with a fusible backing) and another:

FIT TO BE TIED . . .
knotted or just plain pinned! No matter which WHATKNOT™ from the neckwear collection of Patricia Kutza she chooses, she can be confident knowing her accessory will add polish to the rest of her outfit.
(. . . a paragraph of descriptive copy, then . . .)
To find out who's who at the zoo when neckties change their sex, send a self-addressed stamped envelope for the latest WHATKNOT™ catalog. . . .

Both releases were appreciated and used by editors.

worry. There's always Harry to keep my head on straight with his humorous putdowns. I'll never forget the day I told him there was once a saint who bore my name.

"Did you know that St. Barbara was patron saint to the artillery?" I asked in all seriousness. "No," he quipped, "but that explains why you think you're such a big shot."

To keep myself humble, I have a sign in my office that reads: "If at first you do succeed . . . try not to be insufferable."

DIVERSIFY AND MULTIPLY

12

YOU MAY NEVER MAKE A MILLION dollars from your homebased business, but once you get going, you certainly can increase your income through diversification. This chapter shows you how, and it's one you should return to from time to time as your business grows. Indeed, there is so much information in this book—so much tax and legal information, so many business management reminders and tips, so many new business ideas and so many marketing and publicity suggestions—that most readers will benefit from a periodic rereading of the entire book.

It's never too early to start thinking about how you can diversify a business. In fact, if you're still in the stages of trying to decide what business to start, the

Does a million-dollar business mean one million gross, one million net, or one million owed?
    —Kaye Wood, Kaye Wood Publishing Co.

Other Diversification Examples

• Nina Feldman expanded her word processing business not by subcontracting work, but by developing a network of over 150 other word processors, desktop publishers and computer support services who wanted business. She refers jobs to these businesses who, in turn, send her a check for 15 percent of the first job for each client, or 15 percent of all work in the first ninety days, whichever is greater. "My referral income now represents about 95 percent of my gross," says Nina.

• Judy Schramm opened Judy's Maternity Rental in 1988 to offer evening wear to pregnant women. Then she discovered a market niche as big as her fashions: an estimated 400,000 women in the DC area who wear a size sixteen or larger. "Now I rent an increasing number of dresses to women who are not pregnant, but who just wear larger sizes," she says.

• Joann and Bob Olstrom diversified Joann's Honey by adding honey-related food products such as ice cream toppings and Honey Stix™, then by adding the honey of other beekeepers to their line of honey.

(continues on page 295)

deciding factor in whether it's going to be profitable may lie in whether or not your idea has good diversification possibilities.

Why is diversification so important to the small business owner? Because often only a certain amount of profit can be realized from a particular endeavor, no matter how hard one works. Yet if that endeavor is tied to one or more closely related activities, one's profits may increase dramatically while overhead costs stay virtually the same.

In addition to being important to the financial success of a business, diversification also can be an antidote to business boredom. An interesting mix of activities not only adds spice to one's home-business life, but may be crucial to certain businesses; mail-order and seasonal operations, for example, which die down in certain months of the year. Clearly, something else must be done if income is to roll in regularly.

If your particular business does not lend itself to diversification into related products or services, you may need to start two or three separate businesses to bring in the dollars you desire. At the very least, strive for diversification in your product line if you happen to be in manufacturing or sales; if you make or sell only one type of product, your business might not survive if the bottom were suddenly to fall out of that product's market. Especially in product-related businesses, remember consumer interests change constantly and you may have to keep changing your product line, possibly your marketing methods as well, to keep up with their fickle buying habits.

Above all, don't overlook the economy, which can be a fierce foe or a staunch ally, depending on your particular business. Certain products and services may be in greater demand when the economy fluctuates, or not needed at all. It is never too early to start thinking about an "understudy" product or service—one that could go onstage should your star performer suddenly fail to perform. Thus, one formula for success in a homebased business is:

Diversification of Business = Multiplication of Dollars

Different people will use this formula in different ways. For example:

• People in service businesses often expand by adding related products to their line, which may then lead them into mail-order businesses. As they become known as experts in their field, they may be asked to speak about their business, which in turn may lead to consulting jobs or the writing of articles or books.

• People with product businesses may decide to diversify by adding other lines and possibly importing a line of supplies or finished merchandise. Others start their own party-plan businesses to move merchandise, and many end up in the mail-order business as well.

• Craft producers may begin by selling their wares to shops or at fairs, then go on to teach or write about their craft. Some get into self-publishing or kit manufacturing. Others go into show promoting or become sales representatives for other sellers.

• Designers often end up publishing their own pattern or design books, which leads them into the mail-order business. Then, to sell more of their books, they may begin to give workshops. Some eventually add supplies to their line.

• Authors tend to diversify into the seminar/consulting area and often end up writing and publishing their own books or newsletters. Many go on the speaker's circuit.

• Desktop publishers who buy a computer to do a newsletter may expand by producing newsletters for many different clients.

• Business owners in general may purchase a computer just to get their business life together, then accidentally discover one or more ways to make money simply because they now have technology in hand. (More about this in the next chapter.)

In brainstorming for ideas on how to diversify your business, try this recipe: Take your primary product or service and add to it a list of other products and services related to it. Stir in your knowledge about all of these things and mix well with the experience you have in all areas related to them. Add any business, professional or marketing contacts you may have and season with such intangible things as your personality and long-range business goals. The resulting mixture will lead you to an interesting discovery about what you might do to "diversify and multiply."

Diversification Ideas and Techniques

If you're the key individual in a business that is labor intensive, the real trick to growth and increased profits has to lie not in working harder, but in working smarter. By getting a handle on how you're spending your time, you can see what you must do to get more productivity from the same hours you've always worked; for example, computerizing your business to save time in one area that can more profitably be used in another.

Growth may also be achieved by getting control of business costs, making sure you're really charging enough for your products and services and seeking markets that might pay you more for the same work you've always done—topics we've already discussed at length.

Anyone who creates products for sale can easily come up with new designs for additional products. In addition to manufacturing more products, product sellers also can diversify by (1) offering custom design services; (2) becoming a sales representative or marketing agent for other product makers; (3) coordinating shows or sales; or (4) starting a marketing cooperative (an

Later expansions included beeswax candles/ornaments and honey cookbooks. They also sell supplies to other beekeepers, and Joann often speaks on the subject of bees.

• Jackie Iglehart, publisher of *The Penny Pincher* newsletter, diversified by publishing *The Penny Pincher's Calendar*, which offers a money-saving tip for each day of the year.

• Charlotte Wood diversified her custom-knitting business, Charda Classics, by selling Toyota knitting machines and teaching people how to use them. "It is rewarding to work with knitters, helping them to design anything from a set of placemats to a beaded evening dress," she says.

• Gift basket supplier, Judy Reilly, expanded her Dakota Baskets 'N More mail-order business by renting "showcase space" in a local gift shop to display various baskets and a collection of her woodenware. Basket buyers can create their own baskets, selecting from any item in the shop—a good example of cooperative marketing.

Sliding Into a New Market Area

Karen Hanover is a good example of how a business can slide into new market areas, which then suggest ideas for new products and services. While marketing insurance companies and HMOs, Karen acquired skill in getting through the bureaucracy of large organizations.

"I began spending so much time advising other people that I decided to start a side business of marketing and sales consulting called Trend Setters. Realizing that my greatest profits would be with major companies, I established relationships with both fast food companies and direct mail companies such as Carol Wright and Money Mailer."

Karen also established relationships with grocery chains and drugstores, then further diversified her business by creating a line of greeting cards to be marketed to these outlets.

organization that would represent the marketing needs of a diverse group of sellers).

If you buy goods for resale, it will be easy enough to find other products related to your line. If you are selling your own products, but have a limited line at the moment, a little searching will reveal many small companies who will work with you on a drop-ship basis (something I discussed in chapter four).

If you offer a service, refer to the business idea charts in chapter four for ideas on related services you might add. Think backward by first considering your market possibilities. Who needs what? What special problems are your clients having now? If your service is directed to consumers, could you modify it in some way to make it salable to the business community, or vice versa? For example, an organizational specialist might help families organize a home while also helping companies battle office chaos. A dressmaker might specialize in bridal gowns while designing uniforms or dressing gowns for the medical community at the same time.

Service businesses may also diversify by adding a retail product line. For instance, a calligrapher who does diplomas or scrolls might create a calendar, print quotes on parchment paper suitable for framing, or design a line of greeting cards. A wedding consultant might commission local artisans to create handmade garters or embroidered handkerchiefs to serve the "something blue" needs of brides, or perhaps offer handmade cake ornaments. Commercial items such as bride's books or paper products (napkins, nut cups, etc.) could also be purchased wholesale for resale to clients. A teacher might elect to sell books; a hairdresser, related hair care products; a computer consultant, software; and so on.

Interesting ideas for business diversification usually come as a result of stretching one's imagination and asking, "What if. . . ?" Do you recall the lady I talked about early in the book, the one who works all day on Saturdays to make bread she sells for 70 cents a loaf? In addition to selling bread on an occasional basis to a country store, the local restaurant, or a few neighbors, this bread baker could have diversified by adding:

• A "Bread Subscription Service," whereby regular Saturday deliveries would be made to homes, restaurants or stores in the community for a flat monthly fee—an echo of the golden days of daily milk and bread deliveries.

• A "Bread-of-the-Month Club." What works for fruit might work with bread. The month's "special" could be delivered on the first Saturday of every month to buyers themselves, or to their friends and relatives who may be unable to bake their own bread.

• A Party Service. Ethnic or gourmet bread products for cocktail parties or holiday celebrations.

• A "Season's Greeting Gift Pak"—a unique bread assortment, beautifully packaged in a basket or box, which executives and local merchants could give to their best customers as a special thank-you at Christmas, Hanukkah or New Year's. (This package might include some of the products mentioned below.)

• A related product sideline such as homemade jams and jellies, handcrafted cookie trays, breadboards, baskets and tea cozies, all made by people in the community who need a marketing outlet for their products.

• A cookbook—a published collection of holiday or fancy bread recipes, in booklet form suitable for sale in local shops, by mail order, or for use as a fund-raising product for local organizations.

• Speaking engagements. She could talk to local groups about the history and lore of bread or the art and craft of bread baking itself. (Speaking is an excellent way to promote any business.)

• Classes in bread baking. There always will be people who want to "do it themselves"; smart entrepreneurs tell them how, for a fee. Such students often become regular customers for other products and services.

You don't have to sell bread or other edibles to apply the kind of logic suggested here. Just put on your "thinking cap" and start looking at your product or service from a new angle.

An Outstanding Diversification Example

Sandra Manning is a perfect example of how the business diversification process works and how naturally it often occurs as people go about their day-to-day business activities.

In 1990, Sandra started Kaleidoscope Connections, Inc., a home day care and preschool operation geared toward encouraging the development of children's creativity. "I was able to utilize an educational background, set up my own educational 'system,' and venture into the business world while also being at home with my three children," she says.

When she began, Sandra had no idea how each of her new ideas would blossom and flower into other business activities. Networking led her to begin speaking on the importance of encouraging the imaginative process in young children. Special Saturday classes for creative children soon led Sandra to offer her service to local resorts and businesses. When she approached a local resort complex with a proposal to offer services to families vacationing in the summer, they described a need for a children's program that would free parents to attend seminars, golf or shop. Later, she added another resort to her client list, one in need of a summer camp.

Building On an Invention

Emma Graham and her inventor-husband, Don, launched a business around a sewing tool Don invented for turning fabric tubes from wrong- to right-side out. Called *Fasturn®*, it quickly found a ready market in sewing and craft stores nationwide.

The Grahams expanded their business by modifying their invention to enable rug makers to make tubes of fabric for use in braided rugs—a parallel industry and a new niche market.

Further diversification of the business has come with the publication of a complete line of patterns showing sewers and rug makers how to use fabric tubes to make a variety of products from jewelry to decorative accessories. Then Don followed with yet another companion tool.

"We work eight to twelve hours a day and currently employ four people," says Emma, who at seventy seems a long way from retirement.

"I also set up the adult entertainment and children's activities for their Family Nights," she said. "Two other resorts then asked me to write recreational programs for them and provide training programs for their in-house staff."

All of the above led Sandra to begin producing monthly displays at a local educational supply store to promote creative activities for teachers. The response from teachers in need of more ideas led Sandra to offer yet another service: developing hands-on activities around any subject area needed, to be shared with educators.

When I last checked with Sandra, she was in the process of pursuing funding for a new "reachout program" she wanted to develop, one that would provide more support and networking for those in the child care field, as well as incentive toward recruitment of individuals interested in child care as a profession. She had also just begun a weekly radio program on child-related issues.

Many people have expressed interest in buying a book of Sandra's ideas, which as yet does not exist. "But I have kept a mailing list of their names," says Sandra, "and plan to start my writing career soon." There she goes . . . diversifying once again!

Do you recall what I told you in chapter four about how to brainstorm for new business ideas? As Sandra's story proves, the four-step concept I explained there also works when you're trying to brainstorm for ways to expand an existing business:

1. Read, listen and observe.
2. Find a need and fill it.
3. Do what you love.
4. Build on what you know and do best.

Sandra's story also adds weight to the special tip I gave you in this chapter: *Nothing stays the same. Remain flexible. Go with the flow.*

Writing and Self-Publishing

After a while, anyone who operates a business naturally acquires certain information and insights that would be beneficial to others. Some people elect to share this knowledge through consulting, teaching or lecturing, while others prefer to put it into written form and publish it as information sheets, special reports or booklets. Others decide to publish periodicals or directories. Still others write magazine articles or books.

Some writers, like myself, combine self-publishing with the writing of books that are published by trade publishers. Since I know how to publish and market books, people often ask me why I don't publish all my own books. The answer is simple: Writing and publishing a newsletter is a full-time job. So is book publishing. And so is marketing. One person cannot do everything, and as I grow older, I want to do the work I like best and leave the publishing of future books to those who specialize in this field. That does not mean I won't work hard to promote and sell all of my books, however.

Not everyone can write a book worth publishing, but almost everyone has information or knowledge worthy of publication in the form of a special report or booklet. That's what I want to concentrate on now. When you reach the point in your business where you think you know something that other people might want to know, or you have gathered hard-to-find information that others might pay to receive, you are ready to think about putting this material into written form. (Ideally, you already will have access to the market most likely to buy it.)

What kind of information will sell? Anything and everything. People are hungry for information of all kinds, the more specialized, the better. They are willing to pay for it, too. A lot of material from self-publishers crosses my desk every month, and it generally falls into one of the following categories:

Special Reports

Usually on topics related to business, special reports often take the form of loose $8\frac{1}{2}'' \times 11''$ sheets stapled together. Some are printed on $11'' \times 17''$ sheets and then folded to $8\frac{1}{2}'' \times 11''$. Number of pages may vary from perhaps 4 to 20, depending on the topic. Because such reports generally contain highly specialized information, prices are always based on the value of the information, not on how fancy the report looks in printed form. Prices of between $3 and $10 are common.

How-To Booklets

These generally are of two sizes, $5\frac{1}{2}'' \times 8''$ or $8\frac{1}{2}'' \times 11''$, and usually have white paper inside and a heavier, colored stock for a cover. The number of pages varies from 12 to 84 or more. Larger books may be spiral bound, soft bound or placed in special three-ring binders. Prices may vary from $2.95 to $29.95, depending on how much the publisher had to pay to get the work into print, and how valuable he or she believes the information happens to be. (Smaller, inexpensive booklets often make great promotional tools, as you may recall from chapter eleven.)

Directories

These publications usually are $5\frac{1}{2}'' \times 8''$ with white paper inside and a heavier, colored stock for a cover. They are either saddle stitched or spiral bound. All kinds of information lends itself to

Self-Publishing vs. Trade Publishing

Confused about the difference between self-publishing and being published by a trade publisher? If you write a book that is accepted for publication by a trade book publisher, your work will be almost finished by the time you have written the book and turned in the manuscript. Your next job will be to work with the content and copy editors, double-checking their suggested changes. You may or may not be involved in the preparation of the index. After that, you have no further responsibilities to the book, except to help publicize it whenever you can. You just sit back and wait for your royalty checks to roll in, which often takes a long time. It is the publisher's responsibility to pay the printer, send out press releases, place advertising, and handle distribution of the book. In all likelihood, you will have little or nothing to say about any of this, and if you're working with a large publishing house, your suggestions won't be welcomed. (The smaller the publishing company, the more likely you will be able to play a role in helping your book gain a market.)

Conversely, when you publish your own book, you are in control from start to finish, and you assume all financial responsibility for the book. You not only write it and see that it's typeset, proofread and prepared for printing, but you also pay the printer, get out the publicity, place advertising and figure out how to get the book distributed to the general public. This is not easy for even the most skilled person to do alone. But when it's done right, it's truly exciting, and often quite profitable. Fortunately, there are many excellent how-to guides for novices in this field.

publication in directory form, from collections of supplier names and addresses to listings of craft fairs and shows, sales reps, shops and stores, community events and special-interest periodicals, among other things. The common denominator, of course, is a listing of names and addresses that certain people desire either for business or personal reasons.

Warning: Never publish a directory of names and addresses without contacting everyone listed to make sure such publicity is desirable to them. It can be dangerous to pick up and print information "secondhand," not to mention it being a terrible disservice to one's readers to publish inaccurate listings.

"Little" directories seem to sell best if they're priced in the range of $3 to $10. Some directories are distributed free of charge, with the publisher's profit coming from advertising placed in the directory by listees. Naturally, when the publisher charges for ads, distribution must be sufficient to produce a satisfactory response for advertisers or they will not pay to be in future editions.

Newsletters

If you are an author, nationally known consultant or widely respected "expert" in a particular field, a sideline newsletter might be the perfect diversification tool for you. Having a built-in following at the start of a newsletter venture will help assure success, since at the heart of every newsletter publishing success story is a loyal "fan club" of readers who stick with a periodical because they respect an editor's advice or appreciate the sense of family they have each time they read an issue. (For greater detail, refer to chapter four.)

Freelance Articles

If you have the desire to write but not self-publish, you might be able to add to your income through the sale of articles to consumer or trade magazines. Professionals in all fields are well paid for articles that share inside information while also promoting themselves or their businesses. Authors, consultants, business service providers, attorneys and accountants are only a few of the many self-employed individuals who fall into this category. Craftspeople and designers often sell how-to projects to consumer magazines or write personal profile articles. Other business owners write regular columns for newspapers or magazines. There are dozens of excellent books on how to be a successful freelancer, and you can find them by visiting a library or by contacting *Writer's Digest*, which has a good book club (see chapter sixteen).

Like any other seller, a writer must be able to deliver the

kind of material that currently is in demand. Beginners usually are advised to write about what they know; however, there also has to be a need for information, or it won't sell. To be a successful writer, you must first be an avid reader, regularly reading writer's magazines in particular.

Note: Many professionals, particularly authors who are promoting trade books (available in bookstores), other product sellers, and business service providers who are scouting for clients they can work with by mail, write promotional articles for small business magazines and newsletters. The only payment they ask is an appropriate closing "blurb" that tells readers how to order some particular product or service by mail. Instead of trying to sell products or services directly, such writers will often make a special offer of a free brochure, catalog, tip sheet, newsletter or other promotional items like the ones mentioned in chapter eleven. My newsletter regularly included such articles from leading business writers and entrepreneurs in my network, and I continue to use this strategy myself to promote my books and assure constant exposure of my name and products to my market. Particularly receptive to such articles are hundreds of newsletter publishers in all fields.

Teaching/Workshops/Seminars

Anything you do well can be taught to others. This is an excellent way to diversify a home business and increase one's annual income. Organized people with enthusiasm, patience and the ability to communicate their knowledge to others make the best teachers. A college degree or teacher's certificate seldom is required, but it may help command higher prices. (So will experience. The more you have, and the better a teacher you become, the more you can charge.) You may elect to teach a skill (art, lace making, woodcarving), present a special-interest class (astrology, graphology, gardening), or share your business expertise (marketing, computers, taxes).

"Non-credit learning is not one mass market, but an almost endless number of tightly focused niche markets," say Bart Brodsky and Janet Geis, authors of *The Teaching Marketplace—Make Money With Freelance Teaching, Corporate Trainings, and on the Lecture Circuit.* "Identify your prospective students by vocation, hobby, special interest, geographic area and lifestyle," they advise. "You can turn almost any life experience into a rewarding career teaching freelance or part time. You can customize the length of a class, the price, location and number of participants. You don't even need to be affiliated with a school."

Many skilled artists and craftspeople get started in teaching

Video Tapes: Profitable Products!

Kaye Wood began her homebased business in 1978 by traveling throughout northern Michigan teaching machine embroidery and selling supplies. As the result of a class she taught in 1981, she developed a line of handmade quilted vests that she wholesaled for a while.

Kaye no longer sells handmade vests. Now she is a full corporation with a staff of seven. In addition to publishing her own books and designing special tools and accessory products for quilters, this popular quilt author and teacher has produced over a dozen thirteen-week quilting programs for PBS-TV. She has further diversified her product line by producing videotapes that teach people how to quilt like a pro.

"It cost $6,000 to produce my first three videos," Kaye reports. "We did all three in one day. They are each one hour long and retail for $29.95 (wholesale for $19.50). Each tape costs me $9.25, so that nets me more than $20 each—a lot more profitable than books."

Kaye has become known for a particular style of quilting known as "strip quilting." Once or twice a year she takes quilters on a quilting cruise, and her latest brochure clearly shows her sense of humor. It reads: "Come Cruise With Kaye, and Learn to Strip Like a Pro!"

by offering to teach a class at the local craft supply store. This will be of particular interest if your class is designed to sell more of their supplies, and a teaching relationship with a shop is a good way to open up a new market for special patterns or how-to books you may sell.

Adult education centers provide opportunities for everyone. "Many colleges, universities and community colleges offer programs in adult and continuing education in addition to their regular credit courses," says Tracy Brotherton, former coordinator of Adult and Continuing Education at Panhandle State University in Goodwell, Oklahoma. "As a program coordinator, I was constantly on the lookout for qualified teachers," she says. "At one time or another, the University has offered, or been interested in offering, courses in folk art, holiday package wrapping, calligraphy, cooking, sweatshirt painting, crochet rug making, color wardrobe, silk scarf painting, needlepunch, oil painting, wearable art and horticulture."

While arts and crafts classes are very popular with program directors, a broad range of business-related topics are also in demand, particularly by those who coordinate business conferences. (See also "Speaking Professionally" below.)

When H.A. "Buzz" Bezanson, a Canadian self-publisher, decided there was a market for courses in starting a homebased business, he sent course proposals to ten Continuing Education departments in his area. Seven of them eventually booked workshops. He later expanded his client list to twenty by adding seminars on mail-order, self-publishing and computer businesses.

"Be sure to get the name of the program coordinator before sending your proposal," advises Buzz. "Follow-up calls revealed that a number of program coordinators hadn't received my earlier information, so I hand-delivered them."

Image consultant Donna Cognac says every adult ed class she has taught has brought her additional business. "The exposure has made me more of a recognized authority on the subject, but my key motivation is that I have been able to share my knowledge with others." Donna has found teaching opportunities not only at adult education centers, but in community colleges, state colleges and public high schools. She was delighted when her first "pitch letters" netted a response from every school she had written to, but her delight turned to shock when she discovered how poorly some of these teaching jobs pay—as little as $9.50 per class hour or $25 for a two-hour class. Deciding, however, that such teaching experience would be beneficial in other, less monetary ways (such as increased credibility or respect), she began to teach and has never regretted it.

A low-paying teaching opportunity can be made more profitable by having something to sell to students for an optional fee, such as a book or materials kit. "But such items must be offered in a low-key way, and one should obtain permission in advance," says Donna. "Some schools may wish to build the cost of a sale item into the course fee and then pay you directly in addition to your salary. If product sales aren't possible, be content with the exposure you will get from school catalogs and the positive impression you make on your students. Let them know you are in business, but don't treat the class as a captive audience for a sales pitch. Use your class roster sheet to add student names to your mailing list, and send them a brochure later."

Whether you will be teaching at an institution or in your own home, set your per-student or per-day price according to what others are charging for similar classes. If no standards exist, set a price you feel is fair, based on what you might pay if someone else were giving the class. (So much depends on the area in which you live and the demand for your particular knowledge or skills.)

Payment for adult education courses varies across the country. One teacher tells me she receives $500 for a 15-hour course taken for credit, but she thinks this rate may be higher than average. Another teacher reports receiving $20 per contract hour for a "one-shot" class that may run from one to four hours in length. While some teachers in my network have told me they receive similar payment for courses, others work on a split of total income derived from a course. This is especially beneficial to teachers who can enlarge a workshop audience through PR efforts or use of their own mailing list. A 60/40 split seems to be common, with the teacher getting 40 percent. Thus, if a day-long course is offered for $29, and attracts 40 students, the teacher would get $11.60 per student times 40, or $464, a tidy profit indeed. The more students, the more money.

Many teachers work local areas only, but there are many opportunities for anyone who wants to travel. In setting a fee for a day's work, be sure to cover not only the time you spend on the actual day of the workshop or seminar, but your preparation and travel time as well. For such work, it is customary either to receive a daily fee (or honorarium, as it is sometimes called), plus all expenses, or a travel allowance and payment on a per-student basis.

During the 1980s, I presented dozens of day-long home-business workshops across the country, working mostly with community colleges or small business development centers who took care of all advertising and other arrangements. I charged a daily fee plus all expenses. Sometimes one of my books was a required text; other times, all of my books were offered as optional purchases at day's end. In the latter case, I generally sold books to at least 85 percent of my audience, making these workshops quite profitable. At each one of these events, I also gained invaluable perspective on the kind of people who are likely to

The Extra Benefits of Speaking

Silvana Clark, a recreation specialist who presents innovative business presentations in many locations in the United States and Canada, was delighted when she received an invitation to speak in Germany and learned the sponsor would pay the airfare for her daughter and husband to go along. An entertaining speaker, Silvana's gimmicks include costumes, various products and props, and small gifts taped under everyone's chair. "I also pass around a hat during my speeches," she says, "asking everyone to put in their business card. Then I hold a drawing and award several door prizes such as flowers or gourmet coffee—a small price to pay for getting the names and addresses of everyone in the room."

Silvana's special tip: "Begin and end your speech with an interesting story, a unique fact or a question. The worst opening is: 'This afternoon I'm going to talk to you about my homebased business.' "

Like most speakers, Silvana has diversified by publishing a book. *Taming the Recreational Jungle* is filled with her best tips for other recreational directors.

start, succeed or fail in a business enterprise.

Over the years, as I gradually raised my speaker's fee, I found $500/day to be the most this market could afford to pay. Although my higher speaking fee now keeps me out of the college market, it's just right for organizations who need a keynote speaker for a business conference, or someone to lead a workshop on marketing without money (my favorite business topic). Like many other speakers in my network, I "fell into speaking" as a natural result of my wide visibility as an author and industry leader. This visibility, coupled with word-of-mouth advertising, continues to generate all the speaking engagements I desire.

If you are interested in teaching but lack a reputation that will bring speaking engagements your way, start to build one now by offering to give a free talk at the library or to some local organization. To attract students to private classes in your home, try classified ads in the local paper, post notices on community bulletin boards, and print flyers for distribution throughout the area. If tutoring individual students is more to your liking, establish an hourly rate per student, keeping in mind that you are providing a special service that may be unavailable elsewhere. Charge accordingly.

Not everyone is thrilled about speaking, as this reader illustrates: "I find myself being encouraged by others to branch out into areas I don't feel comfortable in. My biggest business hurdle so far has been deciding how much speaking I'm willing to do, or how many classes I want to teach. Since I have your basic speaking-in-public-phobia, this has been difficult for me. I need to do it to further my business, but I do it with great reservation and raw fear."

I don't know who said it, but I know many of you will identify with it: "The human brain is a wonderful thing. It starts working the moment you are born and never stops until you stand up to speak in public." If you like the idea of teaching but are insecure about the idea of "speaking in public," don't think of it as "speaking" but as *sharing your enthusiasm for something you love and know others would enjoy.* The first time a student comes to you after class and thanks you profusely for all you've taught him or her, your fears will fall by the wayside, and you will have found a wonderful and profitable new niche for your talents.

Speaking Professionally

If you have the "gift of gab," you can promote your business, earn additional income as a speaker, or build a full-time speaking career talking on topics that relate to your business or personal interests.

"Talk may not be cheap, but it certainly pays," says Dottie Walters, publisher of *Sharing Ideas* (the leading speaker's newsmagazine) and author of many books, including *Speak and Grow Rich*. "Each year, more than a million paid speeches on every possible subject are presented at conferences, conventions, workshops, seminars and meetings of all kinds." says Dottie. "Being a professional speaker will lead you in many different exciting directions. As the world of professional speaking expands at an ever-rapid rate, opportunities for all kinds of speaking, training, teaching, writing and related products are accelerating."

Dottie is a study in diversification. Many years ago when she began her business career, she approached speaking as the solution to a marketing problem. "I discovered it was much easier to speak to a group of prospects than to try to see them one at a time," she said. "So I made up a talk for business owners titled 'What Do Your Customers Want?' That talk helped me develop my advertising business into over two hundred cities and four thousand continuous contract advertising accounts."

Dottie's first $50 speaking engagement soon led to many more throughout the United States, and later, the world. Over the years, she has constantly expanded and diversified her speaking business by writing and publishing books and cassette albums and by offering cooperative advertising opportunities to other speakers. When speaking clients asked her to recommend speakers for other occasions, she diversified once again by starting the Walters International Speakers Bureau, which she operates jointly with her daughter, Lilly, who also coauthored *Speak and Grow Rich*. Today their agency books over 20,000 speakers who present every topic under the sun. Many of them earn $5,000 or more (plus expenses) for a keynote address.

Says Dottie, "A grandmother may speak on 'Getting Liberated'; another speaker teaches executives 'Good Etiquette for Business Meals.' Some speak on strategy, negotiation or implementation; time management, communication, sales or humor. Many are authors of books on these subjects. We often book characters from history who appear in costume, including Ben Franklin, George and Martha Washington and General George Patton. A galaxy of famous personalities are alive and well and appearing on the platforms of the world as professional speakers. Even Mahatma Gandhi can speak for your convention."

Other corporate speaking opportunities abound for business professionals, and the pay is good. One home-business owner told me she was receiving $350 for her one-hour training seminars on day care. Another reported fees of up to $1,500 for her three-hour corporate seminars on such topics as self-management and paper management. "Six hundred dollars for a one-hour seminar is not an unreasonable figure these days," she adds. Of course, one cannot command prices like these without top-notch speaking skills and expertise. It also requires good marketing skills to get such jobs in the first place.

Speaking on Cruise Ships

Want to earn a free cruise? Many speakers are featured on cruise ships today, and these luxury liners may feature five or six different seminars during a trip. Speakers are not usually paid for such jobs, but they trade their program for a cruise and often receive a free ticket for a spouse or friend. Additional information about this topic will be found in *Sharing Ideas* newsmagazine, which includes an annual cruise ship issue.

Sliding Toward Expertise

"An expert is someone who doesn't know more than most people, but has it better organized and runs a slide show," says the weekly journal of Denmark's civil engineers.

—as noted in the
Chicago Sun Times

Consulting

If you have developed special expertise in a given field and are currently looking at consulting as a possible sideline for an existing business, you may find it an easy thing to market. You may already have customers or clients who would welcome this additional service.

You will know when it's time to make this move because people will start coming to you, asking questions about how to do this or that. And as soon as they start asking for advice, you had better start charging for it. Every hour you give to someone else is one hour you cannot devote to your own business.

All of us who work at home need to share our knowledge and experiences with others in our industry if we hope to make gains and stay abreast of our competition. But the busier we become in our own businesses, the more selective we must be about the time we give to others. It's one thing to network with other business people, and quite another to freely give to a curious beginner (who may become a competitor in short order) all the information it has taken you years to acquire on your own. At least charge that person for the privilege of picking your brain.

I have always believed in sharing what I know, as this book proves, but the demands of my business now make it impossible for me to help people on a one-to-one basis unless they pay for my time as a consultant. The more successful you become in your own business, the more you will be asked for help and advice from others who would follow in your footsteps. Sooner or later you, too, will have to draw the line between how much you can share gratis, and how much you offer for a fee, through writing, teaching, speaking or acting as a private business consultant.

In the end, the determining factor probably will be whether you are working for love or with the idea of becoming, and staying, a profitable and self-supporting business. Time is your most precious possession. If you give it away, you will find it difficult to succeed in business. As a part-time paid consultant, you will be helping your business to succeed while also helping others.

Diversification Through Marketing

Sometimes a product business diversifies its operation merely by changing its marketing methods—moving from direct selling to consumers, to wholesaling to shops, or establishing a mail-order catalog division. Like product sellers, many service businesses can expand by offering a special service by mail, and everyone can diversify a business simply by concentrating on a new niche market. Still others may multiply profits by using an 800 or 900 number to take telephone orders, attract a new audience of prospects, or sell information through a hotline service.

Mail-Order Marketing

As explained earlier, mail order is not a kind of business per se, but merely a good way to market products and services.

Many product makers who have been concentrating on marketing to retail outlets through fairs or sales reps may find a much larger market when they move into mail order, either through a catalog of their own or through someone else's. If your products are handcrafts or other gift items, however, I would advise you *not* to start a consumer gifts catalog, as the competition from major catalog marketers is simply too great. Instead, concentrate on trying to break into one of these major catalogs as a supplier, offering a popular product with a high profit margin.

Your own catalog (or other appropriate package—letter, color flyers, price list) targeted to wholesale buyers is another thing entirely, and a great way to expand a handcrafts business that has previously done all its selling in shows or fairs. Ed and Pat Endicott, who launched their House of Threads & Wood in 1983 by selling at craft fairs, still exhibit in over twenty major shows per year, but now they also wholesale by mail. Their product hang tags will be found on items for sale in Disneyland, Silver Dollar City, and as far away as Hong Kong and New Zealand. Each year, they sell over 10,000 of their most popular item, a "potpourri trivet," string-quilted squares that, when placed under a warm dish, release a sweet-smelling aroma. (See sidebar.)

You need not have a whole line of products in order to diversify into mail-order. If you have just one suitable mail-order product with a good profit margin, create a one-page flyer that includes an order form with a blank space so other sellers can insert their name and address in that space and help you sell the product. Look for mail-order sellers who offer products similar to yours, and ask if they can work with you on a drop-ship basis (discussed in chapter four). Many small mail-order sellers are happy to include flyers from other product sellers in all their outgoing packages since they may lack sufficient products of their own to generate the bounce-back sales that are so important to success in mail-order selling.

Expanding Into Niche Markets

A corporate dropout in 1988 when she started her homebased business, Errands and More, Darlene Graczyk was burned out after spending almost twenty years as a graphic designer for State Farm Insurance Company. Although initially determined not to do anything with graphics arts at all, she ultimately used her experience in this area to diversify her errands business, originally intended to serve individuals only.

"I had a good working relationship with local printers

Doing Business by Ear

House of Threads & Wood does business with its ear, say owners Ed and Pat Endicott. "By listening to what our clients have to say, products are changed, new designs created and policies revised. Today, more and more companies are finding out that to compete is to provide outstanding service.

"We actively solicit ideas from our wholesale buyers by asking what their customers *didn't find*. Are they items we could offer? I ask about trends in their area. Why do they think an item is hot in one part of the country but not in another? Consumer buyers also provide us with product diversification ideas. After receiving our catalog of string-quilted placemats, coasters and potpourri trivets, someone asked whether they could have a table runner to tie it all together. And so a new product was born."

900 Numbers

Rohn Engh, who lives on a one-hundred-acre farm in the hinterlands of western Wisconsin, runs a diversified, high-tech publishing business. As the author of marketing books and reports for photographers and publisher of four newsletters—including *The Photoletter*—Rohn uses two 900 numbers. "Rather than write a letter, my subscribers may call at a cost of $.89/minute to make suggestions, complaints or give compliments," he says. "My other 900 number is a line on which I record hot monthly photo needs important to subscribers."

Rohn has four fax machines in his hundred-year-old barn-office and does most of his newsletter delivery not via U.S. mail, but by fax. He also uses several online services to broadcast the photo needs of photo editors at magazine and book publishers. Subscribers phone a central data-bank daily and are able to download information and listings into their files.

(continues on page 309)

because of my projects with State Farm," says Darlene. "When I did a direct-mail campaign, I naturally included some of those names on my mailing list. I was, of course, thinking of them as individual personal clients as opposed to their businesses being clients.

"Then one of the sales managers called wondering if I would consider delivering proofs and artwork to their clients when their salespeople couldn't. I was a better candidate than regular delivery people because I could explain everything to their clients and answer questions.

"My sudden discovery of this niche market prompted me to expand on this idea to include other printers and communication/marketing firms. I've done everything from taking photos to St. Louis and waiting for color separations, to working with stock photo houses to locate stock photos for a project, to being a production assistant for photo shots, to being a clipping service for a public relations firm."

During the recession of 1991, these new business clients kept Darlene's errands business stable, illustrating the importance of diversification of one's business as protection against economic instability. Darlene has since added many other small businesses to her client list.

800 Numbers

If you market by mail, you may find that you can diversify and expand your business merely by adding an 800 number to your business. This will move you into the area of high-tech marketing and make it much easier for people to respond.

Once you have merchant credit card status, the use of an 800 number people can call to place orders will automatically increase sales. And if you are able to publicize your business on radio or television, this could make all the difference in whether such appearances are profitable or merely ego-boosting.

900 Numbers

A 900 number is an information service people can dial from anywhere in the United States for either so much a minute or a flat rate fee. (Rates generally fall somewhere between one to three dollars per minute.) Although this industry has its share of rip-off artists who are pushing credit cards, job openings, "free" travel opportunities, sex numbers and worthless horoscope advice from "live experts," many helpful 900 number information services are now being offered by companies of all sizes and descriptions. Used properly, a 900 number can be a great marketing and business expansion tool.

If you think 900 numbers are only for the big guys, you're

wrong. An increasing number of smaller enterprises and entrepreneurs are making use of 900 numbers for specific "information on demand" applications, and an explosion of independent service bureaus has enabled people to set up an operation without the need to purchase expensive equipment. In selecting a service bureau, however, research carefully to make sure it will be there to service your number six months down the road. After publisher John Cali leased a 900 number to promote his small business publications and printed 10,000 catalogs listing that number, his service bureau simply discontinued the 900 number he was using. (See sidebar.)

Ron Hanus, a Naperville, Illinois, entrepreneur who leases 900 numbers and has written a report on this topic, suggests brainstorming for a profitable 900 concept by making a list of your customers' most common, irksome and frustrating problems. "Then consider which of these problems are the most important or urgent, but are most easily and simply solved with the right know-how," he says, "know-how that is not common knowledge and is not readily available. If your business is oriented more to products or services that enrich people's lives rather than ones which solve their problems, then focus specifically on what kinds of unique information or entertainment you could offer that would be of greatest benefit to your customers."

Business authorities in any field could offer changing monthly messages on what's happening in their particular industry, including tax and legal tips, market leads, latest information resources, trends, etc. For example, a literary agent could offer tips on which publishers were looking for certain books, or general guidelines on how to properly submit book ideas to publishers, with a note about books of particular interest to his or her agency; a consultant specializing in government grants could announce new money sources with tips on how to successfully apply for a grant, while subtly promoting the consulting service; or a show promoter could announce new exhibiting opportunities for sellers and pitch a newsletter or annual directory of such information.

Do your homework before entering the 900 industry. Read the books and reports that explain the ins and outs and watch business magazines, which often run articles on how other small business owners are currently using 900 numbers.

Franchising

Although franchising is a good diversification option for large businesses, in my opinion, few—if any—homebased business owners should consider it. Although the following information is discouraging, it may prevent you from making an expensive mistake—one of the most important goals of this book.

Subscribers to GEnie (electronic database) can get a free look at *The Photoletter* on the service's bulletin board.

John Cali, who used a 900 number for a while, says it wasn't hard to get people to call his number. "My calls averaged around $10 each, and my net was $7, less $2.50 for fulfillment (I offered a free book), or $4.50 per call profit."

John updated his "hotline message" every weekend, and with a small amount of advertising—mostly through his catalog/newsletter—he was soon generating between $300-$400 a month. "An important goal is to get people to call back more than once," says John, "which means you have to have information you can change or update regularly. I had a weekly small business tips hotline, and the incentive for calling was a free book."

Understand from the beginning that franchising is a time-consuming and expensive process that could cost as much as $100,000 to launch if you use a franchising consultant. While you might be able to save a small fortune by doing all the work yourself (including the complicated franchising documentation), some important questions to be answered here are these:

1. Does your business have a profitable track record?
2. Have you found a good niche market?
3. Will your service idea work anywhere?
4. How much competition is there?
5. Do you really have the time to devote to this separate business enterprise?
6. Are your marketing skills such that you could successfully market your franchise once it was ready to roll?

In my many years of communicating with homebased entrepreneurs, I have encountered only one individual who opted to franchise her service business. While she appeared to be a sharp businessperson, had an impressive franchise package and got a fair amount of publicity in business magazines, she didn't make it. I was going to use her as a success story for this edition of the book, but when I called to interview her, the phone had been disconnected.

I learned more about franchise pitfalls from Bob Johansmeyer, a former franchise consultant who switched to tax consulting when he became disenchanted with the industry as a whole. "Few small business owners have enough cash to do the job right," he says. "If your goal is to franchise on a shoestring, you're doomed to failure. A franchise operation is a long-term investment with a payoff far down the road—probably five years or more. Most people don't realize that starting a franchise means starting a whole new business, and anyone who is already busy is going to find it almost impossible to do the job right."

Even if you do get the franchise up and running before you run out of money, you will be heavily restricted by federal and state laws on what you can say to prospective franchisees, according to Bob. "Because of these laws, most franchisors now skirt claims about how much money one might make," he says, "which only makes it more difficult to sell a franchise. While franchisees are protected by these laws, there is no protection for the prospective franchisor. Most of the 'franchising sharks' have been caged now, but the ones making the most money in this industry are often the ones who are selling franchise consulting services to would-be franchisors."

Bob cautions to "always question who's giving you advice," a point I will second. I may have said this elsewhere in this book, but it seems particularly appropriate here: *Trust least the advice of those who stand to profit most from giving you their advice.*

ADDING A COMPUTER TO YOUR LIFE

··

THE INFORMATION IN THIS CHAPTER is based on questionnaires sent to seventy-five computer users in my home-business network, who represent a wide range of product and service businesses. Like all the other chapters in this book, what you're getting here is not theory but fact based on years of experience. Most of the individuals quoted in this chapter have been in business for over a decade, and most have been using a computer in their homebased business for at least eight years—some as long as fourteen years.

Their comments are not only timely, but have historical value since they clearly show how computers are impacting the personal and business lives of users in the 1990s. Computer novices will

13

Any Fool Can Do It

If you're concerned about being able to learn how to use new software, or simply how to use a computer system to begin with, remember Herman Holtz's advice:

"We all have to learn new things and, as a professor said about learning calculus, don't be afraid of it: What one fool has learned another fool can learn."

find great encouragement here, while experienced computer users will do a lot of smiling and head-nodding as they read the remarks of others who have had experiences similar to their own. Beginners and pros alike will relate to most embarrassing, expensive and funny computer experiences some people have had. (No other home-business book can boast such interesting copy!)

Why Some Businesses Aren't Computerized Yet

A survey of my readers in 1987 revealed four reasons why users had delayed their purchase of a computer, in this order: (1) they didn't think they could afford exactly what they wanted; (2) they were not convinced a computer would do that much for them; (3) they didn't think they had enough time to learn to use a computer because their business kept them so busy; and (4) they were concerned about their ability to learn to use a computer.

Today, most people in business realize they need computer technology, and those who are about to enter the computer age aren't as concerned about price or their ability to learn as much as they are concerned about being able to find the *time* to learn. I won't kid you here—it can take a hundred hours or more to master some complicated software programs, and even then, you may be utilizing only 25 percent of the software's total capabilities. On the other hand, you don't spend these one hundred hours on one program all at once. Because today's computers and software programs are much easier to understand and use, most people now report they are "up and running" in a few hours or days, after which time the learning process becomes a natural and continuing part of their daily lives.

Each day at the computer keyboard teaches you a few more things about computers in general, and your favorite software in particular. After more than ten years of experience, I find I'm still learning how to do nifty little things with my database and word processing software, thanks to information gleaned from books on my reference shelf and monthly computer magazines. What I know about computer technology wouldn't fill a teacup, *but I don't have to understand technology to benefit from it*. Unlike "computer techies," I have no interest in messing around inside my CPU—I figure that's what computer service centers are for. I don't have to be an expert on computers to get my machine to perform its tricks—all I have to do is follow the step-by-step instructions that can be found in dozens of manuals, books and magazines.

While many computers users agree with me when I say the secret to learning is to read, read, read, I realize this just isn't the answer for some people. "What everyone needs is someone to answer questions," says Judy Schramm. "Reading computer magazines and manuals does nothing for me." Tammie Vitale agrees. "Computer novices should forget reading and get 'hands-on' experience. Once you start playing, what you then read will make more sense. Being on line [modem] was helpful because I met people willing to come to my house, for free, and help me over the bumps."

"I would like one-on-one training," says a mail-order marketer who keeps putting off her computer purchase. "I feel overwhelmed by all a computer can do, and I don't know how to focus." A class would definitely help this person. Florence Feldman-Wood took six sessions in WordPerfect 5.1 before she bought her computer or software. "It was like learning to drive without a car on which to practice," she says, "but it was intellectually stimulating, and I was 'ripe' for this experience." Jacqueline Herter, who began by doing lots of reading, stresses the importance of working with one computer service person so you can get to know him or her well and can call with quick questions.

That's excellent advice. I got a lot of information and moral support from the dealer who sold me my first computer. Bit by bit, as I would telephone with different questions, I learned how to use my system efficiently. On two occasions when my hard disk "crashed," my special service person got me through the experience with a minimum of stress.

Support from a local dealer isn't as important as it once was, however, because help is now available from so many other quarters. How-to books, magazines, computer classes and user networks abound. Most hardware and software manufacturers offer technical support on a toll-free number, and there are also inexpensive computer videotapes available to help one learn and master computer basics or the intricacy of a particular software program.

Realize at the beginning that, no matter where you stand on the topic of computers, *you are not alone*. You may feel stupid about computers now, but so have most other computer users at one time or another. You may be frightened—or merely overwhelmed—by computer technology and technical jargon, but so are a lot of others. If you have not yet joined the computer generation, this chapter will get you started. I've included information about many of the things I once wondered about before I purchased my first computer—plus the research I did before purchasing a new state-of-the-art system in 1993. (See two-page chart, pages 330-331.) More than anything, however, this chapter shows how computers change and benefit both the personal and home-business lives of their owners.

If you're still on the fence, thinking you can "get along without a computer," think again. I turned out fabulous meals without a microwave oven until I was fifty-five years old, saying I neither wanted a microwave nor needed it. But when I finally got one

Who Uses Typewriters Anymore?

Computers haven't totally replaced the need for typewriters . . . but almost. Most computer users today use a typewriter only for things such as filling out forms and applications, typing occasional address labels and envelopes, doing postcards and notes, and preparing W-2 tax forms at year's end.

But don't get rid of your typewriter just yet. It can be a real boon when your hard disk crashes!

How Computers Are Being Used in Homebased Businesses

When asked for which specific jobs a computer was most often used, Barbara's respondents listed the following, in this order:

1. Word processing, correspondence and related office work
2. Desktop publishing, writing articles, newsletters or books
3. Processing orders, other database work or list management
4. Bookkeeping, accounting, invoicing or financial reports
5. Designing printed materials/mailers/forms
6. Business planning/marketing activities
7. Idea generation/business development
8. Online research
9. Graphic design
10. Networking/browsing bulletin boards
11. Computer programming
12. Games

for Christmas, and discovered how much it reduced my stress every time I got so busy in my business that I forgot to thaw meat or to put the casserole or baked potatoes in the oven in time for dinner at six, I wondered how I'd ever gotten along with it. The same thing is true with computers.

A "Computertalk" Networking Session

If I could have served as moderator, bringing together the many individuals who contributed to this chapter, we might have begun our discussion like this:

In looking back to life before the computer, who among you can imagine working without one now?

Patricia Katz: "Not me. My computer is my assistant—my right arm—my bookkeeper, secretary, clerk. I could not conduct my speaking and consulting business—at my current level of activity—without it. Adding fax-modem allowed me to send my weekly newspaper columns electronically, which saves half an hour a week in delivery time."

Elizabeth Bishop: "I never dreamed that word processing software could liberate me so much from the time-consuming writing and rewriting and editing process involved in pattern design. Pattern instructions now take half the time, and letters are a joy."

Eileen MacIntosh: "There's not a chance that I could live without my computer. As an artist used to dealing in graphic concepts, the idea of using a system based on logic—a foreign subject to me!—was intimidating. However, once I discovered that my computer could easily reduce my paperwork, streamline my correspondence, and generally minimize my tedious, overwhelming, administrative work . . . well, my life changed."

Before we discuss how a computer changes and benefits one's business life, I'd like to know how the computer has impacted your family's life.

Mary Ann Chasen: "Our family has benefitted because we've all become familiar with the computer, are at ease with it, and have a more-than-average focus on technology as a result."

Patricia Katz: "The kids now do their homework on computer, and we all play games on it, use it to reserve library books, send and receive e-mail. My first computer has now moved into my twelve-year-old daughter's bedroom."

Laura M. Rubin: "After my husband became interested in the computer, he began to manage our personal finances. He also enjoys playing solitaire."

Marshall G. Emm: "There are occasional fights in our family over who gets to use the computer—but schoolwork takes precedence over letter writing or games."

Sally Geier: "Time is a problem at our house, too. I use the computer during the day; my daughter, a junior in high school, uses it in the early evenings, and my husband, VP of Engineering at a structural steel company, uses it the rest of the evening and sometimes into the wee hours of the morning."

Nancy Malvin: "My husband has become more active in monitoring finances since we enter data together."

Dan Carlson: "My problem is that there is always more to learn, and the things that have to be daily done on the computer can take time away from the family."

Tim Long: "That's true . . . but one can't—or shouldn't—stay glued to the screen for 24 hours at a time when you get this machine. It's not good for your health, marriage or family life. It's a *machine*. It does what you tell it to do. It's not magic."

Some people love playing with the computer so much they actually become addicted to it, spending so much time at the keyboard that their family life suffers. Has anyone had this experience?

Laura M. Rubin: "Computer addiction is not the problem here, but rather *work addiction*. Because my work involves computers, I live at my computer. I enjoy learning the nitty-gritty of my programs and will spend hours with them."

Maryn Wynne: "I love my computer and spend a lot of time just playing around with it. When I'm working too hard, I find game-playing, such as Solitaire, to be a valuable stress reduction tool."

Jim Bradshaw: "I don't use the machine for games, but computer addiction is a problem with me. I sometimes find myself getting caught up in the mechanics of the software rather than focusing on the application of that program to the task at hand."

June and Loring Windblad: "We have a slight addiction to computer games. And with our first job we got in the habit of going all out all day long—the entire waking day—on the computer. We lived for the job we were doing, about 20 hours a day for 6 weeks, and 50 hours a week for the next 3 months. With the purchase of our second computer, we tended to gravitate to the computer room for our entire waking day—from work to play. Our leisure activities outside the home are virtually limited to church on Sundays. This, however, is changing. We are cutting back the 'on computer' time to much less, and taking time for an occasional movie and an outing out of the house at least once a week."

Sylvia Landman: "My husband, Philip, has definitely become an addict. He had no other hobbies before we got our computer. Now he spends every possible second in front of it or reading manuals and magazines. (He was a nonreader before as

Take Control of Your Life!

In her newsletter, Wendy Priesnitz reported on her computer system and what she learned during her learning period:

"After a week of days and nights spent almost nonstop in front of my new toy, I remembered one of the most important facts of life in the home office: The computer has an *off* switch.

"Home-business owners are in a unique position in that we increasingly have at our fingertips technology that is ready to work at any hour of the night or day. But can we push ourselves as hard as we can push machines? *And should we?*

"Let's not forget that one of the reasons most of us started our own businesses was to gain control over our lives. I've just discovered that the ultimate control is to turn off the computer."

Have You Named Your Computer?

Most of those questioned said they hadn't named their computer. Several said things such as "The names I call it aren't fit to print." One dubbed her machine "Buster," as in "Listen, Buster!" An IBM was called Bufford. "He has a definite personality, and has grown people talking silly to him," said this computer owner.

well.) As a writer/designer, I must share computer time with Philip, but the flip side is that he learns all the new programs and teaches me, lowering my learning curve."

Marlene Kouba: "I get so involved I lose track of time and forget to prepare meals. I love the computer . . . but some days I could throw it out the window when new programs have me baffled."

Marlene, your comment illustrates the love-hate relationship that sometimes exists with computer ownership. Will anyone else comment on this?

Susan Anderson: "I love my computer system, but it is rather like the love a mother has for a child who has been wayward at times and lovable at other times. I believe that you love the things you invest the most time in. I have invested enough time in my computer system that I have to love it a lot, like a child I've raised who has both good and bad traits. Some days it behaves and works well with me; other days it is all headaches and problems. As with a child, it takes a lot of time and maintenance for it to become worthwhile to have around. A new computer user should not begin with the idea that a computer will do all the giving. The computer takes a lot before it ever gives, and then requires a lot of loving care besides."

How long did it take for you to get your system fully operational?

Susan Anderson: "I did not have an appreciation for how many hours it would take to get our computer to the point where it became a workhorse for me instead of me being a nursing mother for it. During the first six months of computer ownership, I spent many, many nights working through computer problems, installing new software, restoring destroyed data, learning new computer programs, investigating breakdowns and just plain getting acquainted enough with the computer and operating system to be able to really control it. I also found the computer needed more hours of maintenance than I originally thought it would—backups, updating programs, etc."

Carol Moore: "Susan's experience must be unique because my husband and I use three programs to handle our correspondence, filing and bookkeeping needs, and I did not spend more than two days studying my manuals and learning the programs. When questions did arise, I simply called IBM's support system for help in solving the problem."

Newer computer systems are less complicated than the one Susan learned on, and some software programs are easier to learn than others. In addition, Susan's involvement from the beginning was much more than that of

"computer operator." She was fascinated by her ability to comprehend the solutions to difficult programming problems, and decided early on to become a computer programmer and all-around expert. In just a few months, she mastered at least ten programs.

Julie Ann Allender, Ed.D.: "Even if you don't decide to become an expert, it takes hours to fully master any computer system. On average, it took me 20 hours to learn the basics of any new program such as WordStar, WordPerfect, Lotus or dBase, but this was only the tip of the iceberg. By the end of my first six months, I had put in at least 200 hours' learning time. I no longer felt threatened by the computer, and it no longer took me 20 hours to replace my hard disk after I accidentally wiped it out. By then, I could do it in two."

Jeannie M. Spears: "I can certainly relate to that. When I brought my computer home, it was like being dropped in a foreign country without knowing the language. But I did learn it, and it was worth it, and every day I learn a little bit more."

The kind of business one operates clearly has a direct bearing on one's approach to a computer, as well as the amount of time it may take to input data and learn the number of software programs that may be needed for business efficiency. The more complicated and high-tech the business, the more complicated the software is likely to be, and the longer it's going to take to learn what one needs to know.

June and Loring Windblad: "Right! We are in computer graphics and presentations, and coincidentally in desktop publishing as an adjunct. We didn't decide to 'use a computer in our business,' Windy Dawn Marketing, but decided to 'have a business on the computer.' These are two vastly different and mutually incompatible concepts. Experience gave us new direction for our business. The entire world of computer creativity in graphics, presentations and desktop publishing was opened up to us.

"When we purchased our first computer system, we got the benefit of a private dealer to help design a system to meet our perceived computer needs. We took the best information available to us at the time, our best plans on personal direction, and ran with it. Unfortunately, we did not know enough about computers to begin with, and the decision was made on short notice, without sufficient knowledge or planning to really get our act together. Although we thought ourselves to be 'computer semi-literate' when we started, two and a half years later we still are learning. There are always new programs to consider, new versions of old programs, new techniques, new challenges with almost every job. For the new people coming into the business, our advice is not only to read, read, read, but talk *in depth* to as

Drawn in CorelDRAW! 2.0 by Loring Windblad of Windy Dawn Marketing.

Desktop Publishing: A Brief Look at an Amazing Phenomenon

The term "desktop publishing" (DTP) was coined by Paul Brainerd, founder of Aldus Corporation, maker of software for the DTP industry.

Thanks to DTP software, computer owners everywhere are publishing newsletters, newspapers, books, directories, special reports and other profitable publications. The quality of all this printed material ranges from absolutely dazzling to utterly awful. As one writer puts it, even the best desktop publishing software and a laser printer cannot make up for an individual's lack of graphic design skill.

"State of the art" used to mean owning an Apple Macintosh computer and LaserWriter. Today, both Macintosh computers and PCs can do a terrific job. Now your primary concern is likely to be with the speed of computer hardware, the amount of memory it includes, size of hard disk and type of monitor. (See chart, pages 330-331.)

Depending on your DTP needs, amount of money and learning time available, you may elect to buy a page make-up program such as Adobe PageMaker or Ventura Publisher, or begin with less expensive word processing software such as Word-Perfect or WordStar, which offers many of the same benefits with an easier learning curve.

widely varied a group of computer experts as you can gain access to; then practice new things on your computer with every spare moment."

In studying the questionnaires all of you completed, I can see we have some disagreement on the topic of whether a computer saves time or not. Who will comment on this?

Tom Ellison: "You're likely to be disappointed if you really expect your computer to save you a lot of time. Any time saved will automatically go into new tasks you hadn't realized you needed to attend to before getting your computer. The net result is that you improve your control of the business and probably increase your chances of succeeding at it, but you won't save any time that you'll notice."

Jim Bradshaw: "I agree. The computer has not saved me time, only enabled me to use the same amount of time to accomplish a tremendous amount of work. Not to mention the fact that previously tedious and boring jobs become almost fun on a computer. I now do my taxes with Taxcut for Windows, and it's so much more pleasant than those boring forms."

Do Computers Save Time?

Time out! What Tom and Jim are saying is that the time-saving aspects of a computer are something of a Catch 22: Any time one saves is automatically gobbled up by more work. I agree, but the topic of computers and time goes much deeper than that. Here's the way I see it.

If I hadn't computerized my business in 1986, I'd be out of business today. I launched my present publishing and mail-order business in 1981 with nothing more than an IBM Selectric typewriter, a secretarial desk and a comfortable chair. By 1984, with a mailing list of 20,000 names and a 24-page newsletter being produced entirely on typewriter, my business was wildly out of control and I was making myself a nervous wreck trying to get all this work done while also generating the unending supply of printed materials needed to sell my publications. Yet, lacking $5,000 a computer system cost in those days and being reluctant to go into debt, I struggled along for another two years, at which time prices finally dropped to where I could afford to buy. It took only a few days for me to realize that buying a computer was the smartest move I'd ever made—and the dumbest move I'd made to that point was in waiting so long.

Without computer technology, I could not have continued to manage my ever-growing mailing lists, expand my direct-mail efforts, continue publishing my newsletter, stay on top of my bookkeeping, tax and financial records, develop and maintain the growing number of database and word processing files necessary to the advancement of my business, create all the printed promotional materials needed to market my business, or write new books.

Because I knew I had to get in control of my mail list first, I purchased the most powerful database software then available—dBaseIII+. The simple word processing software that came with the computer made my newsletter and other writing jobs a breeze, but when I finally moved up to WordPerfect software, font programs and a laser printer, I suddenly gained the power to improve my professional image while also saving great chunks of money and time.

While it's true that most of the jobs businesses are doing today were once done without benefit of computer technology, just think how much longer it took, and how many employees such work required! To me, the real wonder of a computer is that it enables the average individual to successfully operate a business *single-handedly*, doing a job that years ago might have required half a dozen employees or, in my case, several outside services. In this light, then, a computer daily saves the average business owner enough time to do twice or three times the amount of work that once was done without such technology.

"Maybe the best way to summarize this topic is to say that a computer doesn't necessarily give one more free time; it merely allows one to make different use of the time he or she has," says Eileen MacIntosh. "In my case, the computer has freed up enough time that I've been able to write not just articles, but novels. And the computer makes work so much fun that I find myself wanting to work more hours."

While on one hand computers have put a lot of people out of work, they also have put a lot of people into business for themselves, giving them the kind of power that earlier generations of entrepreneurs couldn't have imagined. That's why I feel that all businesses, even the smallest, should embrace computer technology immediately.

One of the things the computer does best, of course, is speed up routine jobs. "In the press of a key I can find out how this month's sales compare with the same month last year," says Charlene Anderson-Shea, who uses her computer to manage a weaving business. "It is also a snap to find out what percentage of the budget I have spent on advertising, for example. In short, it has freed up my time to devote to designing or weaving, not paperwork. It did require a substantial investment of both time and money, but I feel it was worth it."

Eileen MacIntosh enthusiastically agrees. "In retrospect," she says, "I should have had a computer from the moment I went into business. I'm certain that the customers I lost, or didn't get in the first place, were far more expensive than what the computer cost me. The work overload is what keeps many homebased

Changing Technology

In 1951, Remington Rand's UNIVAC computer performed fewer than 1,900 calculations per second, weighed ten tons, and occupied 4,000 square feet of space.

In 1991, Hewlett Packard introduced its Palmtop Computer (fits in the palm of your hand) which weighed only eleven ounces and had the ability to process 2.7 million calculations per second.

In 1987, Cray Computers (which then cost about $5 million) were capable of performing 100 million operations in a second—a feat that can be likened to reading *Gone With the Wind* in the blink of an eye.

A news item on television in mid-1993 stated that the new Cray "Super Computer" can perform *two billion* operations per second, and soon there will be a computer five times as fast.

What mere mortal can comprehend this?

businesses small. The computer can handle that, and enable a one-person business to be much larger than before. My computer handles all the things I hate (bookkeeping, mailing lists, form letters, general files and paperwork). This leaves me the time (and peace of mind) to focus on the more creative aspects of my business. I hate the busywork but I love the money—and the computer cuts down on the busywork, lets me get more done in my workday, so I can make more money. I like that."

The Business Benefits of a Computer

Before we get back to our networking session, let me also share other information gleaned from my computer questionnaires. Of thirty home-business owners questioned about the benefits of computer technology,

80 percent said the computer saved them time;

80 percent said it improved office efficiency;

67 percent said it enabled them to accomplish things heretofore impossible;

63 percent said it improved their business image;

60 percent said it enabled them to create better sales and promotional materials, thus increasing profits;

57 percent said it enabled them to expand their products or services;

57 percent said it enabled them to improve their bookkeeping system and do better tax and financial records.

Curiously, only 33 percent of my respondents said they felt the computer helped them stay in control of their business—which doesn't make sense based on the above replies. A "better handle" on all of the above things automatically translates to better control of a business. If some people still have mixed feelings about whether computers save time, most agree that a computer increases efficiency and productivity. Book packager-agent-writer Elyse Sommer says the computer has not only saved her time, but cut down on expenses for typing, copy editing, manuscript styling and indexing. "My computer has also provided some unanticipated benefits: I was able to use my word processor to make illustrative charts for a crafts book (a tremendous aid for my illustrator). By hooking a modem to my computer, I've also been able to instantly transmit material, do research without leaving home, and make business contacts via electronic bulletin boards."

Most computer users can point to something a computer has enabled them to do that they couldn't do before. For example, Kathleen Satterfield, owner of Baby Signs, says her product, astrological charts for children, wouldn't be affordable without the computer because the time involved in doing a chart manually is just too expensive. Nina Feldman of Nina Feldman Connections,

How Barbara Uses Word Processing Software

Good word processing software, coupled with a font program and laser printer, gives one a lot of power and control over the many printed documents needed in the operation of any business. To give you ideas on how to get the most out of word processing software, here's a brief rundown on how I currently use WordPerfect software, a variety of font programs and a LaserJet printer to turn out hundreds of good-looking business documents and printed materials each year.

Newsletters, Articles, Speeches.
Because of its graphic capabilities, WordPerfect 6.0 is an ideal program for a periodical publisher, but even the most generic word processing program will make the job of writing easier. Standard formats and style sheets can be developed and saved, making future jobs of a similar nature all the easier. Previously written magazine articles and speeches may now be revised for use in other ways without losing the original document.

Books.
When I regained the publishing rights to one of my books, I completely revised it in the process of putting it on computer, doing page layout design as I went along. Once the pages were printed for the printer's boards, the book was transferred to floppy disks for permanent storage, except for the resource chapter, which is now updated each time it is reprinted. It's a simple matter to change prices, addresses, etc. and print out new pages for the printer. I now have the resource chapters of all my books on computer, to make updates easier in the future. (Today's publishers greatly appreciate the author who can deliver text on a computer disk.)

Reports and Resource Lists.
I currently sell a line of special reports and resource lists that are maintained on computer and laser-printed as needed. Some of these publications contain data that frequently need revising, and having the material on computer makes the job easy.

Brochures, Catalogs and Other Printed Materials.
It used to take me a week to create a simple brochure, what with figuring out a typesetting order, cutting and pasting and then having to reorder to replace type that was either too large or too small. Now I can do the same job in a day. I also use my WordPerfect software to create press releases, promotional postcards, subscription renewal notices, flyers, workshop handouts, workshop presentation packages and a variety of other promotional documents.

Business Reports/Documents.
Word processing software makes it easy to create a variety of business records and reports important to the management of a business, from sales reports and cash flow projections to income tax worksheets and annual profit and loss statements, balance sheets, etc. More important, once this vital business information has been transferred to computer, it can then be put on backup floppy disks (or other backup medium) and stored in a safety deposit box for maximum protection.

Correspondence.
Some people do all their correspondence on computer, especially because of the spell-check capabilities of their word processing programs, but I still prefer my electronic typewriter for all the little notes and memos I send each week. Whenever I want a file copy, however, I use the computer.

General Office Forms.
I have made mail handling infinitely easier with the creation of a couple dozen little notes that answer the most commonly asked questions I receive each week. I have also created dozens of other items, from stationery, notepaper and invoices to price lists and discount coupons.

Ideas.
How convenient it is to have a place where I can file all the ideas I keep getting but have no time to do anything about. It takes only a minute to bring up a file, jot a note and go back to whatever I was doing at the time. Periodically, as I begin new projects, I scan these invaluable idea files for inspiration.

Writer's Reference Files.
I have a growing number of files that contain copy that can be used for future columns, articles and new books. Because WordPerfect has a wonderful "search key," you can literally dump material into a file and then later find it merely by typing in a key word or phrase—anything you remember.

This return address label was designed by Nina Feldman using WordPerfect and DrawPerfect software.

Nina Feldman Connections
Word Processing and
Computer Support
Referrals
6407 Irwin Court
Oakland. California 94609

a word processing referrals business, says she couldn't keep track of her referrals or the qualifications of her contractors without a computer. "Now that I have a laser printer, I can make more attractive, more readable and more eye-catching flyers."

Sylvia Landman, who with husband Philip runs Self Employment Consultants, says she expected to get a lot from her computer, but she never anticipated designing needlework on it. "Also, the outline feature in WordPerfect has greatly facilitated my doing business plans for clients. More important, without a computer we never could have increased our business or been able to keep up with the financial/bookkeeping trail that is necessary to know what the business is doing."

"Owning a microcomputer has tremendously increased my productivity and has allowed me to take on jobs that were once too time-consuming to be profitable," adds Janet Attard, home-based writer and editor. "Additionally, since I am a fast but sloppy typist, having the computer has greatly enhanced my professional image by allowing me to turn in attractive-looking finished copy to my clients."

Patricia Katz, speaker, columnist, consultant and owner of The Organizers, says the computer allows her to tailor presentation materials and handouts to various clients—a requirement for premium pricing. Crafts consultant and designer Cindy Groom Harry would agree. "The better your image, the more you can command. Being able to typeset project sheets automatically doubled the value of my design work."

Marty Hughes, owner of Accu-Pro Data Management, says a computer helps businesses—no matter how small or large—communicate on paper in a professional manner. "A good portion of my business is for clients who either do not have a computer, the software, expertise or the time to do projects. I can't imagine trying to get my message across to clients and potential clients without a computer for my marketing."

To me, one of the greatest benefits of my computer system is the ability to quickly generate professional-looking printed materials. My stress level used to shoot to the moon every time I had to order typesetting and spend two or three days designing yet another brochure, self-mailer or catalog. Now, work that once took days can be accomplished in hours, and my printing costs are lower because there are no typesetting charges. In fact, a computer almost always leads to cost savings while also increasing the professional image of a business, as crafts business owner Johnnie Kearney confirms.

"The computer enabled us to make up a small catalog for our customers," she says. "The cost is minimal, yet it looks neat and businesslike and can be produced quickly. If items or prices change, it's easy to make corrections and print the necessary sheets. Putting our financial information in the computer also makes tax time easier. Records are more accurate, saving time for the accountant and automatically lessening the size of our bill."

Laura M. Rubin, of Executive Business Specialists, cautions that business image enhancement is not an absolute result of using a computer to design business materials. "The use of a computer is only as good as the computer user's capabilities. The computer provides the operator with the necessary tools for image enhancement, but the operator must carry through with the task (i.e., typestyle selection, layout design, document content, etc.). If these areas are not handled properly, even a computer will not improve your business image."

More Ways a Computer Helps a Business

Let's reopen our networking session with other comments on how a computer helps a business.

Marty Hughes: "A computer makes a big, *big* difference. A number of times people have voiced their surprise to find out that my business—desktop publishing, word processing and résumé writing—is a one-person business, and this has been because of my company literature and advertisements."

Herman Holtz: "The computer has vastly improved the quality of my work, as well as my productivity. It encourages rewriting and revision in many ways. I now do far more rewriting than ever, and that is nearly 100 percent of the secret of quality writing for most professional writers. Talent helps and an 'ear for language' is a great asset, but it is almost impossible to write well; most of us *rewrite* well."

Sylvia Landman: "I was surprised by how much I've learned from the software, Rightwriter, which improved my grammar and editing time. My rate of pay for magazine articles has risen markedly as they require less editing time from the publisher, thus, higher pay for me."

Mary Ann Chasen: "In my typing business, I find I am now producing more work with less effort. Until I had a computer, I never realized how much repetitive work it would save. Now I'm getting paid for work previously completed—sometimes from previous years. I find, too, that I can compete on a professional level with 'storefront' businesses. I can offer more services than I could if I had only a word processor or a typewriter."

Darlene Graczyk: "I figured that record keeping would be the most use I'd have for a computer in my Errands and More business. Now I find myself doing correspondence on it and keeping client sheets and records of work done for specific clients. I do a lot of consumer research for clients and give them the results. They invariably will misplace it and by having it on the computer, I can get to it quickly."

A promotional handout measuring 3½" × 8½", printed black ink on white card stock. Created by Nancy Malvin using WordPerfect software.

A collection of promotional materials designed by Marty Hughes, Accu-Pro Data Management.

Priority Sheet

Date _____

To Call

1. _____
2. _____
3. _____
4. _____
5. _____
6. _____
7. _____
8. _____

To Write

1. _____
2. _____
3. _____
4. _____
5. _____
6. _____

To Do

1. _____
2. _____
3. _____
4. _____
5. _____
6. _____
7. _____
8. _____
9. _____
10. _____
11. _____

Accu-Pro • 510/582-8211 FAX/881-1625
Desktop Publishing • Typesetting • Word Processing
advertisements • brochures • flyers • newsletters • forms • charts & graphs • presentations • letters • reports

WANTED

For providing creative, appealing & economical computer graphic designs that are effective, & within client's budget & time frame!!!

☞ Provides desktop publishing & word processing services!
☞ Works by the hour or by the project!
☞ Helps clients put their best look forward!
☞ Creates documents that will get attention & be read!
☞ Welcomes rush orders and one-time projects!

ACCU-PRO
510/582-8211
FAX 881-1625

Laser Typesetting
LARGE Variety of Typestyles
Thousands of Clipart Images
Fax Service

Advertisements
Announcements
Award Certificates
Brochures
Business Cards
Cards
Catalogs
Contracts
Coupons
Direct Mail Pieces
Directories
Flyers
Form Letters

Graphic Scanning
Invitations
Labels
Leases
Letterhead
Letters
Mailers
Manuals
Memo Pads
Menus
Name Badges
Newsletters
Overheads

Post Cards
Presentations
Press Releases
Price Lists
Programs
Proposals
Repetitive Letters
Reports
Résumés
Slides
Stationery
Tape Transcription
Tickets

From the desk of...
Marty Hughes

Dear Barbara,

This is a sample of the half note sheets I use for my business notes. They are a perfect size and help me to keep up my professional image. As a thank you gift to my clients, I design theses note sheets for them, using their logo, which I've already scanned.

I can change the font and font size to meet my needs.
I can easily change the font—or the size!
I can easily change the font—or the size!
I can easily change the font.
𝔍 can easily change the font.
I can easily change the font.
I can easily change the font.
I CAN EASILY CHANGE THE FONT.

Best Wishes
Marty Hughes

Accu-Pro Data Management • 510/582-8211
desktop publishing • typesetting • word processing

ACCU-PRO DATA MANAGEMENT
Computer Design & Layout
Helping you put your best look forward!

Marty Hughes
510/582-8211
FAX/881-1625

desktop publishing • typesetting • word processing

Enjoy Sophisticated "Hi-Tech" Professional Office Staff And Equipment...

On An "As Needed" Basis!

ACCU-PRO DATA MANAGEMENT
Computer Based Services

510/582-8211

A MEMBER OF
THE NATIONAL ASSOCIATION SECRETARIAL SERVICES
NASS

USE OUR
DESKTOP PUBLISHING
SERVICE

Computerized Design, Layout, And
Typesetting Of Your:

• Advertisements
• Business Forms
• Proposals
• Reports
• Brochures
• Flyers
• Newsletters
• Price Sheets

ACCU-PRO DATA MANAGEMENT
Computer Based Services

510/582-8211

A MEMBER OF
THE NATIONAL ASSOCIATION SECRETARIAL SERVICES
NASS

All of these printed items were created with Microsoft Word for Windows and Corel-DRAW! software. The illustrations are clip art. (CorelDRAW! offers thousands of pieces of clip art on a CD-ROM.)

How has the computer led to profitable sideline ventures?

Debbie Robus: "As a graphic artist, I didn't realize how the computer would enable me to develop an entire business creating business cards, letterheads, menus, newsletters, etc. This sideline business enabled us to pay for our computer equipment. While I no longer do this type work outside of our periodical, *Workamper News*, the work is there, and I get calls often. I never dreamed such a business potential existed."

Judy Schramm: "In my maternity wear rental business, I just use the computer to manage the business efficiently, do financials and planning. But I'm starting a new business now, doing international market research, and for that, the entire business will be run on computer."

Marlene Kouba: "My computer has opened new doors for me, too, while decreasing the amount of paper in my life. Writing is faster, more accurate and I love being able to throw away my eraser. I have written hundreds of news articles and features, plus I am working on a couple of books. A name tag kit has opened a new business for me in our rural area."

Karen Kari: "As an organizational consultant, I thought I'd use the computer only for my own administrative tasks, bills, etc. I've changed my way of thinking, however, and now It's Done! Inc. is solving client problems by organizing *their* information and records."

Darlene Ells: "As owner of D's Word Processing and Computer Services, I found a new niche when one of my clients asked me to do a mailing list of over 10,000 names in less than a month. To do the job, I purchased a full-page scanner and OmniPage Professional software. Once I had scanner capabilities, I added fax capabilities using the scanner. Together, this technology has enabled me to extend services to my present customers while also attracting a new client base."

I know many of you agree the computer is a great organizational tool that improves office efficiency, but there's more to this than meets the eye, right?

Laura M. Rubin: "Right! There's no question about the computer being a useful tool, but the person utilizing the computer must *use it properly* to increase efficiency. For example, there are numerous ways to improve efficiency (mailing lists, databases, standardized letters and forms, etc.), but if the computer user does not understand how to use his or her system fully, efficiency will not result. Only efficient use of *software programs* will result in efficiency."

A growing number of creative individuals in the art, crafts, needlework and design industries now use computers to manage their business or aid them in their design work.

Software: What's Available? What Do You Need?

These are the two big questions of all computer beginners. Your first job must be to list all the specific things you'd like a computer to do for you—and this includes far more than the basic business tasks described in this chapter. With the right software, a computer can—among other things—write music, talk back to you and link you with the entire world. Because there is such an overwhelming variety of programs, you must either do a lot of self-study to find out what you should buy, or work with a knowledgeable computer consultant who is familiar with currently available software.

The most common *types* of business software are: word processing, accounting, desktop publishing, database, spreadsheets and templates, time management and organizational software and utility programs (computer maintenance and operation). Many different companies are creating programs in each of these categories, and within each category will be found low-end programs (low cost, easy to learn) and high-end programs (more expensive, more difficult to learn, but more powerful and flexible).

When Barbara asked thirty computer users which software they absolutely couldn't work without, few of them named the same programs, and to list them here would be futile. The one software package named most, however, was WordPerfect (word processing software).

Computer-Generated Order Forms
With a computer, even the most compli-cated order forms can be revised in minutes.

A. Telephone order form used by Greg and Debbie Robus, Workamper News, de-signed with Aldus (now Adobe) Page-Maker software.

B. Order form used by Sally Geier, who used a Scanman scanner to add her logo to the printed piece.

C. Order form used by Sharon and Roger Davis, created on their Macintosh computer.

D. Order form from one of Barbara's catalogs, designed with WordPerfect soft-ware, clip art and fonts.

A

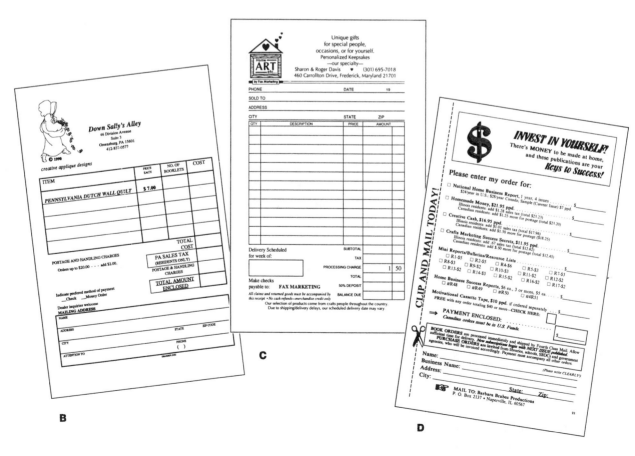

B

C

D

A 1993 survey of eighty craft businesses in my network revealed that 60 percent were using computers, and most of the rest were planning to buy one soon. What's the greatest benefit of a computer to a small crafts business?

Tim Long: "Connie and I didn't realize how valuable the computer would be to North Star Toys for inventory control, nor did we understand the huge potential of database management until we had hands-on experience."

Dan Carlson: "I know what Tim means about inventory control. It's essential to our growing business. With it, we have a better chance for having the right product at the right time for our customers. My wife Maureen and I own Wee Folk Creations. Maureen is clay artist, designer and teacher, and I do all the computer work. Four programs I've found absolutely essential are a word processing program, desktop publishing package, an accounting/mail-order program, and a diagnostic/compress program. Using our desktop publishing software, I designed a professional package for a new product which distributors have picked up. I also use the computer for labeling and invoicing, which gives us a better and quicker turnaround when customers order our products—a selling point for us."

Eileen Heifner: "I've operated Create An Heirloom Doll Kit Company since 1983, and the computer is a staple in my life. I can see how my computer knowledge has given me the edge over many of my competitors. I use it to produce our catalog, maintain a mailing list and do invoices. I find it especially helpful in keeping reference note files."

Isn't it true that, with computer skills under your belt, some of you have naturally expanded into writing or publishing?

Florence Feldman-Wood: "Yes! After getting WordPerfect software, I was surprised and pleased to learn I could also do graphics with it. The day I created a logo for The Textile Detective and showed it to my teenage son, I felt like a kid bringing home a picture from kindergarten! Now I'm publishing *The Spinning Wheel Sleuth* newsletter, a new product that would have been impossible without a computer."

Elizabeth Bishop: "I'm a needleworker, and before the computer, I sold only patterns or actual projects. Now I'm selling articles about various aspects of designing."

Who has a modem and can comment on its value to a business?

Janet Attard: "My modem is indispensable. Now, instead of having to print out and deliver ad copy, newsletters and the like to some of my business clients, I send finished copy over the telephone lines directly to their computers. With the modem, I've

Shareware vs. Public Domain Software

Free and low-cost shareware and public domain software saves money while offering useful, valuable programs.

Both public domain and shareware programs can be shared with others, but there are some differences between them.

Shareware usually means copyrighted, full-featured software with on-disk manuals and documentation. Using the honor system, if you like the program and use it, you send a registration fee to the developer. Depending on the offer, you'll receive support, printed documentation, extra features, updates, newsletters or whatever.

Public domain programs are not copyrighted and can be altered, modified and used without obligation. There are no strings. These authors resist going commercial. They either cannot afford heavy promotion and packaging, or feel their product speaks for itself. Many prefer the personal contact with registered users and the feeling of being appreciated.

Both kinds of software are available on computer bulletin boards and by mail. To find shareware and public domain catalogs, look in the back of any computer magazine. Ads may say "free disks" or "software: just $2.50 per program." "Free" means they merely charge a copying fee or they offer a free disk or program for every so many disks you order.

Once you see what you can get for next to nothing, you are apt to become a software junkie. Join the club!

—by Evelyn Mayfield, reprinted from National Home Business Report

It's silly . . . but in the beginning I was afraid of the computer . . . as if there was this little guy laughing at my stupidity before I learned to use it."

—Leila Albala,
ALPEL Publishing

Did you ever experience the feeling when you learned a new skill, that you felt real good about yourself except you knew there was a great possibility that you might really screw things up and you knew that possibility was just . . . right there . . . somewhere . . . but you weren't sure where . . . and one mistake could really be devastating . . . yet you really did have "a handle" on the situation? Short of a little insecurity about the next key punch or the next mouse drag.

—Tim Long, North Star Toys

also been able to tap into commercial networks and local bulletin boards to gather information for some of the articles I write."

Herman Holtz: "A modem opened a new dimension for me. Through computer-to-computer communication via my modem and telephone, I can now do research without leaving my desk. Like Janet, I am in regular touch with others via electronic bulletin boards."

How Computers Change the Personal Lives of Users

Now I'd like to bring attention to some additional, less obvious personal benefits of computer ownership. My first computer questionnaire brought back great evidence of how the computer affects one's feelings of self-worth and confidence. Marion Boyer said it especially well: "I have this feeling that I am hedging against the aging process. I think one way to feel like you are not growing old is to keep up with current technology. I have two sons, one in middle school. When he talks ROM and RAM, I at least know they aren't obscure mythical beasts in the *Odyssey* that I have forgotten. In fact, I have conquered my own mythical beast by learning how to use this machine to do me some good, and that is a major confidence-builder for me. It means the brain cells will still accept new concepts and skills, and that's pretty exciting for an entrepreneurial housewife."

Elyse Sommer said the computer had cured her of a lifetime sense of inadequacy regarding machines and anything too mathematical. "It took only the initial leap of faith to make me realize that a computer is only as smart as what I put into it," she explained. "And it took only a smidgeon longer to realize that one tames a computer with logic and not math skills. Naturally, fine-tuning your logical skills to solve computer problems carries over to everything else you do in life."

Another strong testimonial for the computer came from Susan Anderson, who said she never realized how much she could teach herself and how proficient she could become in a subject all on her own. "In just two years, I moved from being 'just a housewife' to someone who converses with university-trained programmers and systems people who are amazed by how much I've been able to do and learn. If anyone had told me I could do all this without going back to college, I would have thought them crazy. I did this because I just had to. The computer at my husband's office wasn't working, and someone had to figure out why. I just read, studied, experimented, tried, failed and eventually succeeded."

There is no question that computer usage encourages personal growth while unlocking creativity and new ideas. Liz DeCleene said that when she took typing in school, she was barely able to get a grade of D. "My mind and fingers just didn't seem to function at the same speed. Add terrible spelling to that and you have a real writing problem. I didn't realize, until after I got the computer, that all sorts of ideas were waiting to emerge on paper, but my typing problem had been keeping them locked in. The word processor thus was the key to my writing. Now I can design catalogs, write newsletters and compose columns. My new problem is that I can't find the time to write all the things I want."

Janet Hansen wanted to be an artist when she was young, but due to her family's financial situation, she wasn't able to pursue this. In operating a mail-order business and playing around with her Macintosh computer, Janet not only discovered her creative streak but released her sense of humor by publishing a book of business cartoons drawn on the Mac. "For years I had suffered through going to movies with other people who always laughed out loud at funny situations while I merely sat and smiled. Now, at movies, I find myself laughing along with the others."

Janet no longer sells her self-published cartoon book, but below is a sample from it.

Finally, one computer owner told me how her purchase had dramatically changed the whole household. Lynn Ocken agreed to give up her formal living room so the dining room could be moved into that position, thereby freeing up the old dining room space for a new office, computer and quiet room. "But what I didn't know at the time," says Lynn, "was that our original $3,000 computer would end up costing us almost $10,000 because of all the redecorating and furniture purchases prompted by this rearrangement of our home."

The Internet and World Wide Web

Since the fifth edition of *Homemade Money* was published in 1994, the Internet and World Wide Web have dramatically changed the lives and businesses of millions of computer users. It is beyond the scope of this book to discuss this topic at any length, but you will find helpful online resources listed in chapter sixteen. Also check the index listings for "Internet" to find some new sidebar copy on this topic.

Basic Computer Terms and General Buyer Guidelines

Computer technology has moved way beyond this author's ability to understand it, let alone give advice about it, but the following information may prove helpful to beginners. This "crash course in computertalk" is a quick reference list of what to look for and ask questions about when you shop for a computer. At the rate technology is advancing, however, my information could be out of date in a few months. You must accept responsibility for reading the latest computer magazines to stay informed about what's new, then ask a *lot* of questions before you buy.

CPU.

The CPU is the Central Processing Unit—the heart of a computer. The "microprocessor" is its brain. First generation IBM-compatible PCs contained an "Intel 8088 processor." This dinosaur has since been replaced with new generations of computers that are identified both by name and number. For example, Macintosh computers have names such as Macintosh Apple, Classic II and PowerBook, while the IBM-PC and IBM-compatibles are identified both by brand and model names, plus numbers that describe the speed or type of the CPU's microprocessor.

The 8088 generation of computers was soon followed by faster microprocessors numbered 80286, 80386, 80386SX, 80486, 80486SX and 80486DX. In writing about these computers, the first two numbers are dropped, leaving us with 286, 386 and 486, etc. The higher the number, the faster a computer operates. (Don't ask me why a "DX" is faster than an "SX," however, because there is no alphabetical logic here.) The 286-computers became obsolete when faster 386s hit the market and, by 1994, 486s were the microprocessor of choice. Businesses that need maximum power and speed are now buying higher-priced Pentium processors.

What to buy . . . bottom line? If your budget is severely limited, you can probably find a used 486 for a few hundred dollars, and it offers more speed, power and disk space than most homebased businesses will ever need. Yet if you plan to use several powerful software programs, a scanner and several other peripherals (see page 331), you may need a Pentium now. The wonderful thing about technology is, as computers have become faster and more powerful, prices have *decreased.* Thus, computers that seem expensive today will seem inexpensive tomorrow. (Many computer users now trade in their computers every year or two, just as they trade in their automobiles.)

MHz.

A computer's speed is measured in terms of MHz (megahertz), and the higher the MHz rating, the faster a computer operates. For comparison's sake, first generation computers crawled along at speeds of between 4.77 and 12 MHz, while 386 and 486 CPUs have speeds of 33 or 66 MHz. Pentium processors currently feature speeds of 100-166 MHz.

RAM.

Stands for "Random Access Memory." (Volatile user memory in the computer.) The more RAM, the better; the more RAM, the more expensive the computer. Early computers typically had 64k of RAM, followed by 640k which was the standard in the 80s. By the mid-90s, the standard was 8MB (megabytes; sometimes indicated as "Meg"). Now, if one is using the latest Windows software or surfing the Internet, a minimum of 16-24 RAM is recommended.

When purchasing RAM, also ask about RAM speed, which is measured in terms of *nanoseconds.* The lower the nanosecond rating (ns) rating, the faster the RAM. The faster the RAM, the faster you can get your work done so you can squeeze more work into your schedule.

Cache RAM.

Newer machines are designed to work with "cache RAM," which is "memory set aside for quick access to oft-needed information." Currently, computer experts suggest getting at least a 256K cache that is expandable to 1MB.

ROM.

Stands for "Read Only Memory." (Nonvolatile memory containing programs related to computer's operation.) ROM makes no demands on us; it's just there.

Disk Drives.

They come in two sizes: 3.5-inch (1.44MB) and 5.25-inch (1.2MB). There are "low-density drives" (older computers) and "high-density drives." Low density drives use DSDD (double-sided, double-density) floppy disks, which hold 360k, or approximately 145 typewritten pages with 250 words per page. High density drives use DSHD (double-sided, high density) floppy disks, which hold 1.2MB, or approx. 486 typewritten pages. Newer machines generally include only a 3.5-inch floppy drive. (Note that the 3.5-inch floppy disks are contained in hard plastic sleeves to keep them from flexing.)

While a high-density drive (newer computers) can read a low-density disk (older computers), a low-density drive cannot read a high-density disk. If you are buying a new computer with a high density drive, and wondering about data on floppy disks that are no longer on your present computer's hard disk, rest assured that you can retrieve all the material on those disks through the new high-density drive and store it to your new hard disk before backing up once again to new high-density disks or a tape backup system. (Do not continue to use low-density floppies for anything except short-term storage, however, since data copied this way will not long remain stable, according to the author's contact at 3M.)

In addition to the disk drive of your choice, you may want a CD-ROM drive and an external drive bay for tape backup or other peripherals.

Hard Disk.

First generation computers had floppy disk drives only; then we were offered 5MB and thought we had it all . . . until 20MB disks came along, followed by 40, 100, 250MB and so on. Now many computers have hard disk drives of 1.2 to 2.0GB (gigabytes), not because people need this much space for their files, but because just one of today's powerful software programs may require 50-70MB of disk space. You could store all the information in an entire set of encyclopedias in just 40MB of space, but if you plan to install several software programs or games, you'll need a lot of hard disk space.

In your purchase of a hard disk, speed is also a consideration. Just because a hard disk is big doesn't mean it's fast. The time it takes, on average, to locate and retrieve data is referred to as *access time,* and it's measured in *milliseconds* (ms). So far in this discussion, the measures have been "the higher the better." Here, it's "the lower the better." A couple of years ago, the recommended access time was between 18-28ms. I've lost track of what newer computers now offer.

Peripherals and Ports.

Peripherals are computer hardware devices such as keyboards, hard disk drives, display terminals, printers, etc.

while *ports* are what peripherals are connected to. Ports have *serial* and *parallel* interfaces that connect peripheral devices to the computer. Today's computers may include a mouse port, two serial and one parallel port. This may, or may not, be enough to attach all the peripherals you want to use. Check it out.

Cards or Boards.

These are electronic circuit boards inside the computer which can alter or increase a computer's flexibility or capabilities. A *Video Card*, for example, speeds up graphic applications, and some are better and more expensive than others. For best results, a video card must be compatible with the type and size of monitor you select.

Modem.

Modems may be external or internal. Currently, the speed of the most common modem is 28.8 kilobits (Kbps) per second, but 33.6 Kbps is on the horizon. The slower your modem, the longer it will take to download files, so if you plan to spend a lot of time online, opt for at least a 28.8 modem.

Monitor.

Older computers had 7″×9″ monochrome monitors until 14″ became the standard. Now 15″, 17″ and 21″ color monitors are standard. The quality of a monitor—its "resolution"—is measured in terms of *pixels*, the more, the better. The better the resolution, the less flicker and the easier viewing will be on your eyes. The standard for good resolution used to be 640 by 480, then 800 by 600 pixels, or "dpi." Now the standard is 1,024 by 768 dpi, but ultra-fine 21″ monitors may offer resolutions as high as 1,800 by 1,440dpi (favored by graphic artists). The sharpness of a monitor's image is also determined by a "dot pitch" measurement. Generally, the smaller the dot pitch, the sharper the image. Currently, computer authorities recommend getting a dot pitch of 0.25 -0.28mm. Also check out the refresh rate of the monitor, which should be a minimum of 71Hz. (The lower the number, the more eyestrain.)

Solutions to VDT-Related Health Problems From Barbara's Readers

Wrist or Arm Pain. Avoid arching your wrists as your work. Use a padded wrist rest for your keyboard. If you have wrist pain now, wear a support whenever you type. (There are right- and left-hand occupational supports that allow easy finger movement.) Frequently "shake loose" your wrists, and ask your doctor about special exercises you can do to help avoid carpal tunnel syndrome.

Eyestrain or Headaches. Look away from the screen periodically to increase your field of vision. Close your eyes once in a while to rest them; computer users traditionally blink less when staring at a monitor. Buy an extra pair of glasses to leave at the computer for the "computer distance" your reading glasses may not cover. Eye specialists say the middle of the computer screen should be about five to six inches below eye level, and the screen itself should be sixteen to thirty inches from your eyes. Hard copy (source documents) should be about as far from the eyes as the computer screen. See your eye doctor regularly.

Backaches or Shoulder Problems. Buy a height-adjustable chair or, if you already have one, experiment with different heights. Or buy a kneeling chair and try switching between that and your regular office chair. Also try a footrest. Get up and walk around from time to time, swinging your arms and rotating your shoulders to release tension. Pay careful attention to your posture. Make sure your keyboard is at the proper height. (Even with your elbows.)

Mistakes and Miscalculations

One of my questionnaire questions was "What mistakes—or miscalculations—did you make in buying your present system that others could avoid?" Some answers were:

• "I regret not taking more time researching prior to purchasing my font cartridge. I now wish that I had purchased soft fonts instead of the cartridge I've installed. The soft fonts offer a larger variety of typestyles at the same price. As a result of this poor purchase, I'm now looking into purchasing a soft font package, and I feel as though I wasted my money on the cartridge."—Laura M. Rubin

• "The graphics program and scanner I bought proved to be inadequate for my design needs, but being green at the onset, I took advice from a nonartist."—Elizabeth Bishop

• "My system is not big enough, but it was one of the best at the time. I should have read more about kinds of software before I had them installed with purchase of computer."—Marlene Kouba

• "My mistake was in thinking I could learn many software packages almost immediately. If I had it to do over, I'd buy a word processing program, then a bookkeeping one, then spreadsheet, then database management. I bought them all and ripped most of my hair out in the first six months."—Karen Kari

• "I'm happy except . . . I bought a keyboard which makes a loud clicking noise. I chose that purposely because I like the satisfying 'feel/sound,' but now I find that I can't take notes surreptitiously while I'm talking to clients/contractors on the phone the way I used to."—Nina Feldman

• "We went to a private computer seller (homebased business) for our first computer, and had a long, heart-to-heart discussion in designing the computer which best met our needs. The fact that this computer didn't meet all those needs, and that we had to add a second hard drive after three months, then a second computer with twice the hard drive after sixteen months, had no bearing on the ultimate wisdom of our first decision."—June and Loring Windblad

When asked what they would look for if they were buying a new system, almost everyone said (1) more speed; (2) bigger hard disk; (3) more RAM; (4) better or larger monitor. Marty Hughes added she would buy a large monitor and CD-ROM. "The recent upgrade for my favorite software program, CorelDRAW!, contained wonderful new art and fonts—on CD disk—so unless you have a CD-ROM, you are out of luck."

The Curse of the Computer Age

Here I go again, giving you bad news. While you are going to love what a computer does for you, your family and your homebased business, you may end up hating what it does to you physically . . . unless you take steps early on to prevent or forestall the problems millions of computer users are now reporting.

There is no doubt too much time spent in front of a computer can be harmful to your physical well-being. More than half the computer users I've questioned report physical problems as a result of prolonged periods at the computer—everything from eyestrain and backaches to pain in the shoulders, elbows, hands, fingers and especially the wrists.

After thirty-five carefree years of pounding a typewriter, I thought I might be immune to such problems, but after only a few years of life with a computer, I've "joined the club" with occasional backaches, headaches, and particularly wrist and finger pain. The finger pain occurs primarily in the fourth and fifth fingers of my right hand whenever I'm keyboarding intensely for a few hours. It seems impossible to prevent because these fingers carry a much heavier typing load, handling the return key, + key, page-up, page-down and several arrow keys. The only solution I've found so far is to type less for several days in a row, or to slow my typing down to a crawl and clumsily use the second and third fingers on these keys. Since I plan to write as long as I live, I'm naturally concerned about this problem.

It's not surprising that our wrists and fingers are suffering. Today, our computers enable us to make an estimated 40 percent more keystrokes with fewer breaks of the kind we experienced at a typewriter—not only a slower machine, but one that required a greater range of hand, eye and body motion. Because we have become so productive at our computers and love our work so much, some of us hate to stop at day's end, and these long hours may lead to backaches and eyestrain.

Exercise helps my back, breaks away from the screen rest my eyes, and when I finally began to use a wrist rest on my keyboard, it made all the difference in controlling my wrist pain. Until then, I had no idea how many hundreds of times a day my wrists were dropping (bending) at the keyboard's edge. If you're not using a wrist rest now, *get one immediately* since it may prevent, or delay for years, the dreaded carpal tunnel syndrome, now viewed as the industrial disease of the information age. The National Institute of Occupational Safety and Health believes half of today's work force may be vulnerable to repetitive-strain injuries (RSI).

When Nina Feldman began to experience neck and shoulder pain while running her word processing business, she solved the worst of her problems by changing the nature of her business, starting a referrals business instead of doing all the typing herself. She still sees a bodywork/massage therapist every two weeks, however.

Florence Feldman-Wood eased her problems by buying a

How to Preserve Your Computer's Life

"Consumers spend many prepurchase hours shopping for the perfect computer, yet spend little or no time learning the basics of preserving the life of the machine," says Steve Solomon, General Manager of the computer products division of Fuji Photo Film, U.S.A., Inc. Here are his tips on how to make your computer live longer:

- Turn off the monitor when it's not being used. This will prevent "image burn-in," a light shadowing caused by images left too long on the screen.

- Keep floppy disks in file box holders to protect them from dust and other particles that can damage a computer's fragile disk drive.

- Buy a good antivirus program to prevent the loss of information on your hard disk or operating system.

- Keep your keyboard clean. Protect it with a cover and/or occasionally turn the keyboard upside down to gently shake out the dirt.

- Invest in a surge protector to prevent damage from fluctuations in electrical current.

- Cover the entire system when not in use. Dust and other materials, particularly pet hair, can get into the system, keyboard and fan, decreasing performance over time.

- Keep food and drinks away from the system.

- If your computer is brand new, you may want to "burn in" the system (keep it running for a specified length of time—consult your operating system manual) to uncover any weak components that will generally fail when first used. (Check with your manufacturer to see if such a test was already performed.)

Don't Trust Your Computer's Memory

Loss of data due to failure to back up files remains the greatest error most beginners make. It's not a matter of *if* your computer's hard disk is going to "crash," but *when*. The reasons are too numerous and varied to discuss here, but your insurance against a crash is backup disks or tapes.

There are different types of backup systems available, and you will need to explore your options here. In the beginning, while the amount of data you may be protecting is small, regular backup to floppy disks may suffice. The problem so many beginners encounter, however, is getting in the habit of backing up regularly. If you have to back up data on floppy disks, make yourself a chart of all the files you need to protect, and each time you change any of these files, note the date. Don't let more than a couple of days go by before making backup copies, and whenever you make major changes to a file, back it up at day's end.

Make copies of *everything*, particularly important operating system files like config.sys and autoexec.bat files—and store all back up copies in a location away from your home office, such as in a safety deposit box.

Surge Protectors. The average office or household receives 100

(continues on page 335)

computer cart that has a feature important to her needs: a slanted shelf between the keyboard and the monitor on which material can be rested for copying. "It's called 'O'Sullivan Mobile Oak Computer Cart,' and its great benefit is you don't have to keep twisting your neck to read while you type," says Florence. "It retails for between $60-$100, depending on where you buy it."

Vision problems are now so common among computer users that the malady has been given a name: Computer Vision Syndrome (CVS). In 1992, a survey of 5,000 American optometrists revealed they were seeing over 8 million video display terminal (VDT) related eyestrain cases per year. By 1993, the figure had risen to 10 million. The three top problems reported are eyestrain, headaches and blurred vision. Screen glare is the predominant environmental factor—a problem home-business owners can fix by (1) repositioning the computer so it's at right angles to any windows; or (2) changing the room's lighting; or (3) using a quality, glass antiglare filter; or (4) buying a new monitor with better screen resolution.

If you don't suffer from any of the above-mentioned physical problems but do find yourself irritated after a day's work at the computer, it may be the computer's fault. The high-frequency, barely audible squeal from video display terminals gives some women headaches, say two researchers who have linked such noise with stress symptoms in women (who hear high-frequency sounds better than men). It may help to switch to a high-definition monitor, or use foam earplugs to relieve the intensity of the noise without affecting normal conversation.

Many computer users combat VDT-related problems with antiinflammatory drugs and pain-killers, physical therapy, massage and long, hot baths or hot-tub sessions. A couple of days away from the computer keyboard now and then may be the best therapy of all.

The irony of all this is that it's not enough that we must be concerned about *our* health; we must also monitor our *computer's* health. Like all machines, a computer requires maintenance, and in sidebar copy on page 333, you'll find tips on how to preserve your computer's life.

Most Embarrassing/Most Costly/ Funniest Experience

Let's get back to our networking session. As time passes, it becomes easier to laugh about the dumb things we've done in our lives. So 'fess up folks . . . what's the dumbest, most embarrassing or most expensive computer goof you've ever made?

Sally L. Geier: "My dumbest mistake happened years ago

when we first bought the Commadore. I inserted the Demo disk into the drive and promptly erased the entire thing. My husband had to go and plead with the store manager to beg, buy or steal him a replacement."

Jacqueline Herter: "Don't feel bad . . . I once deleted two of the most important files on a computer: my config.sys and autoexec.bat files—with no backup."

June Windblad: "That's nothing . . . I once used Delete (*.*) on the Church computer, costing a whole twelve-hour day to 'fix' things back up. And Loring's dumbest thing was creating a lot of new files in WordPerfect with a .COM (for communications) extension, then accidentally erasing all of them with a DEL *.COM command and losing the system. Worse, he did this while I was in restructuring the church computer!"

Nancy Malvin: "During my first year of owning a computer, I learned an expensive lesson. The day the hard drive on my machine started sounding like a vacuum cleaner that had thrown a belt, I thought I'd fix it by hitting it . . . like you would any other machine that rattles. It died a premature death!"

Roger Davis: "I've crashed the system numerous times, but the most ridiculous thing I've done is drop a paper clip into the keyboard. It got under the keys and caused some problems."

Laura M. Rubin: "The dumbest—and most expensive—thing I ever did was work on a customer's project for a long period of time and never back it up. Of course, my system crashed and I lost everything. Losing this document not only wasted my time but also money; having to start from scratch was not very efficient. I can't stress enough how important it is to back up your documents on a regular basis. Don't learn the hard way like I did."

Marshall G. Emm: "Backing up isn't always the solution. I once backed up (semiautomatically) files containing errors, thus overwriting the needed files. (This was also my most expensive mistake.)"

Cindy Groom Harry: "Once, when I didn't have a backup disk on a project sheet layout, someone in my office inadvertently 'dumped' it. Now we have at least two backups for everything."

Marlene Kouba: "Before I learned how to save my information, I lost about a thousand names and addresses on database, plus parts of two books I was writing. I had somebody (an expert) help me install some programs and a menu and they lost it after supposedly saving it for me."

Judy Schramm: "Occasionally I forget to save files before I leave the room—big mistake. I have small children, one of whom will see the computer on and decide to play; the other gets a kick out of turning the machine off and on."

Dan Carlson: "My most expensive mistake was having a gut feeling that I should back up my data—but not doing it. I lost

power surges of as much as 1,000 volts each month. These may be caused by nearby electrical storms or merely by the on-and-off switching of air conditioners, refrigerators and other equipment. Such sudden increases in voltage can internally damage or destroy computers, fax machines, telephones, TVs, VCRs, stereos and microwave ovens unless they're protected by a surge protector.

The less voltage that gets through a surge protector, the more effective the protection. Current Underwriters Laboratories standard is 400 volts or less (getting through). When buying a new surge protector, look for one that offers a manufacturer's warranty that includes not only replacement of damaged surge protectors, but of damaged hardware caused by a power surge. (If you have a modem, make sure your surge protector includes an outlet for the modem.)

Don't count on a surge protector to save your computer in the event of a direct lightning strike. To dramatically cut your chances of loss, avoid using your computer during storms and unplug the system until the lightning stops. Although your backup tapes may be current, it could take you a couple of weeks to replace a damaged computer system and get back to work, so what's a couple of hours' down-time during a storm?

Computer-Generated Publications
Left: This 12-page newsletter was created by Nancy Malvin using WordPerfect software, an Adobe PostScript font cartridge and a LaserJet printer. (Nancy ceased publication in 1996.)

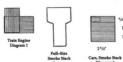

Above: A center-page spread from an issue of the author's newsletter, created with WordPerfect software, fonts and clip art.

Left: A computer-generated crafts project sheet designed by Cindy Groom Harry. Pencil drawings were scanned into the computer, and layout of the finished piece was done with Aldus (now Adobe) Page-Maker software.

two days trying to recover. Moral: Listen to your gut and *always back up!*"

Darlene Graczyk: "I've learned not to trust spellcheck. I once sent out a letter to clients with a whopper of a mistake I should have caught."

Cindy Groom Harry: "I was embarrassed the day I called a repair person to fix the computer . . . and all he did was replace the depleted paper supply."

Maryn Wynne: "Talk about being embarrassed . . . once, on a friend's computer, I was showing her all the neat things you could do in the Windows desktop to include changing the color palette. The day after, she booted her computer and a whole bunch of things in Windows were missing. After a frustrating week and a visit from a computer expert, it was discovered that I had changed the color of the type to the same color of background. Her files were still there. . . . they just couldn't be seen!"

Now I know what Woody Allen meant when he said in one of his movies that "Comedy is tragedy plus time." The more time that elapses after a tragedy—such as losing all the data on your computer—the easier it becomes to laugh about it. Does anyone have a computer story that was funny at the time it happened?

Marty Hughes: "When a good friend and client of mine was going through a divorce, we were looking at my cartoon clipart manual, and let me tell you . . . we really came up with some good cartoons about her soon-to-be-ex. We laughed a lot that day. In fact, I did one up for her to frame in her new home."

Marshall G. Emm: "This is often reported by others, but it actually happened to me. A user called to say he couldn't find the "any" key, which the screen was telling him to press."

Leila Albala: "Nothing funny has happened to me yet . . . can't wait!"

Barbara's Experiences

It's not fair of me to ask others to "bare their souls" without doing the same. The day I began to use my computer, I opened a diary file in my word processing software that included every dumb question and experience I had during the first few weeks—and there were a lot of them. I learned early on that software manual writers assume too much knowledge on the part of the user, and one of the smartest things I did was throw away the manual that came with my dBaseIII+ software and buy three books by capable writers who spoke language I could understand. These writers got me through the learning process of this complicated software. When I acquired WordPerfect 5.1 and later upgraded to 6.0, I did the same thing—even though this software has an excellent manual of its own.

Parallel or Serial?

Here's a chuckle from *WordPerfect Report*. In one issue, they shared a sampling of the variety of calls they answer daily, from users in the White House to Stephen King to a woman in San Francisco who called because her computer wouldn't boot up after it had fallen off her desk during an earthquake.

Then there was the lady who replied, when asked if her printer was parallel or serial, "Well, I think it must be parallel because it's sitting right next to my computer."

Computer Viruses

In mid-1992, when many computer users were being warned about the danger of computer viruses (ask your dealer about software to control this problem), *PC/Computing* magazine challenged its readers to send their own satiric virus jokes just for fun. They received more than a thousand entries, and four of the published entries Barbara appreciated most were:

- **Oprah Winfrey Virus.** Your 200MB hard drive suddenly shrinks to 80MB, and then slowly expands back to 200MB. (David Lustig)
- **Adam and Eve Virus.** Takes a couple of bytes out of your Apple. (Robert J. LaConte)
- **Jimmy Hoffa Virus.** Nobody can find it. (John S. Barker)
- **Dan Quayle Virus.** Their is sumthing rong with yor compueter, ewe just can't figyour out watt. (Gregory S. Shaffer)

The dumbest thing I did in the beginning was ignore advice that explained how to set up directory files on the computer. I didn't understand this and just dumped everything in my computer's "root directory." I finally hired someone from the computer service center to come in for an hour and explain the basics of DOS (disk operating system) and straighten up the mess I'd made of things.

"Now show me how to format a disk," I said, and he did. The next day I couldn't do even this simple thing. What the fellow forgot to tell me was that I had to be in the DOS directory to do this job. It was a long time before I figured out how to properly organize my hard disk, add "path messages," and change my configuration system and "autoexec.bat." files—things you will learn in due time.

My biggest fright came a few weeks after I'd learned how to use my database software. I had finally gotten my entire subscription list into the computer and just in time, too, as I had a newsletter about ready to mail. All I needed was to print the labels. But I couldn't do it. It was easy to get information into the computer, but I was having a heck of a time trying to get it out. The books didn't explain how to make or print labels in a way that I could understand. No one at the computer store was versed in dBase software, and I worried myself sick for a week trying to figure out the solution to this problem. I finally found someone who gave me the secret to setting up a label, plus the magic command to type at the dot prompt that would release the names and addresses to labels in the printer. Talk about "Open Sesame!" From that point on, I began to understand the logic that is part of mastering the computer.

Another dumb thing I did happened several years after I'd been using a computer. I was trying to erase database files from a disk so I could use it to back up word processing files. I put the floppy into the A drive and, being tired, forgot to type the command that would put *me* into the A drive. So, while still in the DOS directory, I typed *.* (which means delete everything in a file or directory). The computer asked, *Are you sure?* and I said yes . . . and promptly erased my DOS software—only the most important program in the computer. Fortunately, I had a backup floppy of the software and could just reinstall it, but I sure felt stupid that day. It was a good lesson, though. I think many of the most expensive mistakes computer users make are during times of extreme tiredness or when they are feeling overly stressed by the demands of their business. Whenever the computer gives us an "Are you sure?" message, we should stop for a few seconds and be *really* sure we know where we are on that hard disk, and exactly what we're doing.

Another of the smartest things I did during my learning process—which got me out of a lot of pickles in the beginning and still helps me today—was to write my own computer manual as I went along. I set up a word processing file with a chapter for each software program, and especially for DOS. Every time I learned a new command or solved a problem, I put it in my manual *in language I could understand*. Later, I supplemented my computer manual with a three-ring notebook of how-to articles gleaned from computer magazines—little tricks and techniques I knew I'd want to try later when time allowed. The important thing to remember here is that *memory alone will not serve where computers are concerned*. The more you learn, the more there is to remember . . . and the more there is to forget. Software reference manuals, how-to books, and monthly computer magazines are great, but your own computer manual will give you a sense of control you cannot obtain in any other way.

One more story. Along about the end of my first week of playing with the computer, I decided to give myself a treat by playing with the computer for an hour before going to bed. Sat down, entered my word processing program, pulled up my diary file, began to page down to the end of my notes . . . and got the message, "error on drive C, fix, then press any key."

Fix? How? At 11 P.M. with no one to call? The escape key didn't get me out; the help key got me nowhere, and as I began to press other keys, the message kept changing, getting worse, as in "disk error . . . fix, etc." I got out the manual and at its suggestion pressed the "retry" and "abort" keys to no avail. Finally the screen flashed "general disk failure"! Oh boy, I thought . . . there go the two articles in this thing, and I haven't even learned how to make backup copies yet. I tried everything and nothing worked. Finally, near panic, I remembered the advice of a friend who said, "when all else fails, hit the reboot/reset button." So I did. That took me back to the C prompt, and I just shut off the machine and fell into bed, worried and exhausted by the experience. (Everything worked OK when I booted up the next morning. I never figured out what I did wrong.) I guess that's why I found this story from Tim Long so amusing:

It was about 3 A.M. I was bound and determined to get this thing going and figure out how it worked. I was afraid I was going to ruin something and fry the machine. I was doing a printer check, and the printer began printing madly using all the fonts. (This was a normal check.) Since our office is in the bedroom, Connie jumped up from a deep sleep asking, "What's wrong?" "I don't know," I said, "this thing is going crazy!" Even though this was routine and everything was normal, in my exhausted, frustrated, sleepy state—hearing this printer moving and printing like a hyperactive little dog—I couldn't take it. I just pulled the plug, made myself a cup of hot milk and went to bed.

Tim and I—and all the other computer users quoted in this chapter—not only survived the "agony of beginning," but went on to master our machines. Or at least feel we're in control of them. I hope the lighthearted material above has convinced you that there is absolutely nothing to be afraid of where computers are concerned. No matter what you do as a nervous beginner, someone else has already done it, and worse. Just buy that computer, start playing with it, read, learn, talk to others and see what happens. As one beginner says, "Each day gives me more confidence and I no longer panic when a prompt comes up telling me that it can't find a file or something. I just keep on trying until I convince the computer I know what I'm doing. And I feel like such a winner when I'm right!"

MAINTAINING CONTROL

14

AT FIRST GLANCE, YOU MIGHT THINK this to be a depressing chapter. After all, it's filled with a discussion of negative aspects of working at home, such as trying to work efficiently around children and within the limited workspace the average home provides; making difficult decisions; managing stress; fighting burnout; staying motivated; and ceasing a business. Many of you haven't even started yet, and here I am, telling you how to quit. What kind of home-business leader am I, anyway?

An honest one. *A realistic one.*

Remember what I said earlier in the book, about using *Homemade Money* as a guide throughout the life of your homebased business? You may not yet need the information this chapter

The great advantage of a hotel is that it's a refuge from a home-based business.
—Beverly Neuer Feldman

Quick! The Chocolate Chips!!

In a telephone conversation with Silvana Clark, we were talking about how some mothers manage young children when they're on the telephone, and I said I'd read somewhere about a woman who tosses her child a jelly bean to keep him quiet each time the phone rings.

"I can top that," says Silvana. "I was on the phone in the kitchen when my two-year old toddled into the room, mouth open, all set to vocalize. I quickly grabbed a nearby package of chocolate chips and threw a handful on the floor. Entranced, my daughter began to pick them up, eating them one by one. And I kept on throwing handfuls of chips until I was able to complete the important contractual agreement I was then negotiating."

provides, but when you do, it's here for you. Don't wait till then to read it, however, because I've included some home-business humor in this chapter to make the medicine go down, and an extra laugh today will be good for you.

Actually, I think you will find this chapter not only encouraging, but motivational. What home-business beginners fear most is the unknown, so the more you know about what *might* happen in the months and years ahead, the better prepared you will be to deal with it when it does. Isn't it wonderful to know someone else has already figured out a solution to a problem you haven't even thought of yet? When you do begin to think about it, half your worry will be removed simply by knowing how others have solved the problem. All you have to do is follow their lead.

The success strategies shared in this chapter—indeed, the whole book—are mostly from individuals who used earlier editions of *Homemade Money* to launch a business or increase the profitability of a going endeavor. They wrote to thank me for the book, told me about their business plans, and then continued to share their successes with me. Like Susan Brown who said, "It was *Homemade Money* that started me on my venture, and without it I would probably still be on square one." You'll meet Susan later in this chapter. I think of her—and all the other business owners and professionals quoted in this book—as part of my home-business family and special support network. The information they have shared with me over the years has been passed along to thousands of others in my various newsletters, reports, columns and books.

Working Around—and With—Your Children

Some will say it can't be done—building a successful business at home with kids under foot—but don't you believe it! It's true certain types of professional service businesses can't be run with young children causing a ruckus, but dozens of other homebased businesses seem to function quite well when structured around the needs of a family. This section includes insight on how some couples have encouraged their children to contribute to their business and fostered entrepreneurial spirit in the process. And there are some special tips for parents who need guidance on how to train their children to respect their business needs.

Do you recall what I said about the tax benefits of paying your children a small salary for helping you with your business? "Your willingness to involve your children in your work allows them to discover their own values for entrepreneurship," says Donata Glassmeyer, founder of H.O.P.E. (Homeworkers Organization for Productive Enterprise) in Tallahassee, Florida. "If they are put on the payroll with simple, age-appropriate tasks, children begin to truly understand the value of work. If they know you are generally happy and satisfied with your job, they'll likely internalize similar work ethics." Donata adds that helping young children develop a healthy respect for your homebased endeavor comes not from scolding or nagging, but from example.

Eileen Anderson, who owns Word Enterprises, agrees: "My children have occasionally helped with various tasks. My daughter, catching the entrepreneurial enthusiasm, made up brochures outlining her expertise in babysitting, distributed them to the neighborhood children along with the candy at Halloween, and since then has had more babysitting jobs than she can handle. It's exciting to see others catch the vision for what they can accomplish with a dash of creativity."

Years ago when she was just starting in business, Dottie Walters said her children added to her stress by yelling and making noise while she tried to work. "They felt left out of the business," she said, "so I gave each child a title. Made little business cards for them on the copy machine. Paid them for their work in the company. My husband told the oldest, our son, that when he figured out a way to do a job faster and better, he would get a raise. The boy had an improvement for our business and his work within a week. He learned to use not only his hands but his brain. We were amazed when each of the younger children also thought of a better way to do their job. They got raises too. We praised and rewarded them constantly, and listed them on our letterhead."

If you let your children answer the telephone, teach them to do the job right. Dottie taught her children how to answer with an uptone in their voice, using a musical instrument to illustrate. "I taught them to smile as they spoke. To take care of the customer. We practiced. All of my children learned how to please our customers and take wonderful messages. Our customers said, 'Your kids are better on the phone than our adult employees! How do you do it?' My answer was: 'We practice, we include, we value their suggestions, we pay them. It is not *my* business—it is *our* business.'"

By involving her children in her business, Dottie gave them a tremendous platform on which to build their own professional lives. The son mentioned above is now an attorney. Daughter Lilly is in charge of Walters International Speakers Bureau. Another daughter is a speech and communication teacher. And grandson Michael is the advertising manager of Dottie's newsmagazine, *Sharing Ideas*.

"The media are perplexed by the idea of working at home without babysitters," says writer Jan Fletcher, who published a home-business newsletter for several years before going on to more profitable endeavors with husband Charlie. "It seems that one must be isolated in order to be creative and manage a home business. Nonsense! Your brains don't shrivel after childbirth. I

A *Stop* Sign and Three-Minute Timer

Purewater dealer Victoria Turner says you have to learn to manage your interruptions. Her "telephone trick" is a sign she hangs on her office door. "The youngest toddler can learn that green means go and red means stop," she says. Using this logic, she made a sign for her door, one side a picture of a red traffic signal, the other green. "When anticipating an important call, I turn the sign to red. Even the neighbor children know this means stop, and they won't enter except for an emergency."

Victoria also has a great three-minute timer trick other mothers may want to try. "I keep the timer on my desk. The reason I'm at home is to enjoy my family. When I say I'll come and play in a minute, my three-year-old turns over the timer. When it is time, I go out to be with her. Conversely, on the occasions when I say I can only be with her for a few minutes, she turns over the timer to know when it's time for me to go back to work. The impartial timer means no tears and no letting time sneak away—for me or her."

How Children Can Help

won't postpone my creative instincts until my children are adults. I've simply changed my perception of work, altered my view of distractions and interruptions, and adjusted my work schedule to accommodate the needs of my children. Of course, we choose our clients carefully, and that makes it work. We think about the kinds of jobs we can handle and those we can't."

When Shirley Sigmund and her husband were operating Marrakech Express Printing out of their home, Shirley had to deal with having a young child around the house. "Except for my desk and files, everything in the house was made accessible to our child," she says. "All breakable, fine or dangerous items were put away or out of reach so I didn't always have to be saying 'no, don't touch.' Because Dana was free to touch and play with everything she could reach—except the papers on my desk— she learned to respect this at a very young age. Also, I gave her her own little desk, toy typewriter, an old, defunct telephone and lots of blank paper, pens, pencils, crayons, paints and colored markers."

When Dana began to walk, Shirley used mother's helpers of various ages to play with her while she worked. By the time she was four, she was extremely bright and artistic, confident and secure, Shirley says, "owing greatly, I feel, to the fact that I was always with her during her formative years. I cannot stress enough that trying to understand and respect one's child from infancy on is much more important than trying to achieve outer 'control' and 'discipline.' "

Author Kate Kelly says many at-home, working mothers eventually resort to hiring a babysitter for a certain period each week so they know they will have the time to get their work done. "If your child will be at home under someone else's care during your uninterrupted time, choose for your workspace an area of the house where you aren't in sight. At the appointed hour, close the door and try not to listen. (It gets easier with practice.) In almost all cases, your sitter should be given the authority to handle whatever comes up. If you teach your child that certain disturbances will bring you out, you can be guaranteed of a lot of them. Give your child a chance to forget you."

Kate adds that, with time, your uninterrupted time will be increasingly productive. "While there will be difficult days when you feel pulled in too many directions (like the day your child is running a high fever and your biggest client is expecting a delivery), you'll probably still find the effort is worth it. When it's time to return to the children, you will feel all the better for the time you had for your own interests."

Do you recall Cindy Groom Harry, the crafts consultant you met in chapter four—the woman whose business now employs a dozen people? Cindy's two daughters grew up knowing a ringing telephone meant the TV or stereo or most recent fight over a toy or article of clothing *went off immediately.* "They learned hand signals early on," she said. "One signal indicated business (when they were expected to disappear into another part of the house); another indicated they could play nearby quietly."

Cindy's children also monitored the door when she was on the phone, informing the most recent visitor that silence was expected. Even grandmas and grandpas had to comply.

"I've always been a real bear about this because it is such a source of irritation to me and indicates such a lack of professionalism. Children's ages have nothing to do with their ability to know when to be quiet and when to resume watching Big Bird, or to continue the fight. I love my daughters tremendously, and I have always expected them to love me back enough to respect my demand for silence when it was required."

Cindy's P.S. on this letter said, "I'm still trying to get my husband to catch on. At any moment he's apt to come in saying—at the top of his lungs—'Hi, honey, what's happening now?' "

That was in 1983. Now the girls attend trade shows, teach classes and assist with sales work. Cindy's husband has taken a major role in the company. Ironically, now he and the girls silence Cindy with, "Please, not so loud! I was talking with a client on the telephone."

Blending Business Into Your Lifestyle

One of the first problems facing the typical home-business owner is where to set up shop, do the work involved and store related merchandise, supplies or files. It's not so bad if you have a four-bedroom home, but it takes real skill and ingenuity to run a business out of a small apartment, house trailer or recreational vehicle—something more and more people are doing these days. Initially, a business may be confined to one room or area of one's home but, like weeds that creep into a garden, it soon consumes all unoccupied space. "Ours is the only home in the neighborhood with three toll-free telephones in the living room," says one diversified business owner. "Actually, we don't run the business out of our home—we run the home out of our business."

Even when there is plenty of space in which to work, a complete separation of business from one's private life is an impossibility for most of us. Thus we never have the sense of quitting at five to go home. After a while, this can have a disturbing psychological effect. That's why people devise all kinds of little tricks to help them mentally "quit work and go home." One woman says she carries her purse into the office in the morning, and takes it with her when she leaves at night. Another says she dresses in business clothes while she's in the office, and changes to jeans when her work day is done. A fellow says when he's through for the day, he goes out into the garage, comes in, slams the door

Office Hours of Small Business Owners

Open most days about 9 or 10,
occasionally as early as 7,
but some days as late as 12 or 1.

We close about 5:30 or 6,
sometimes as late as 11 or 12.
Some days or afternoons,
we aren't here at all.

Lately I've been here
just about all the time,
except when I'm someplace else,
but I should be here then, too.
—Author unknown

and hollers, "Hi, honey, I'm home."

Even when you've mentally quit for the day, your customers or clients may intrude on your privacy unless you make plans to control such interruptions. Some home-business owners assume that, because they are working late in the evenings or on weekends, everyone else is, too. And people who telephone the offices of home-business owners often have little regard for regular business hours or time-zone differences. I am sometimes still in bed when a caller forgets it's only 7 A.M. in Illinois; or it's 5:30 P.M. and I'm trying to fix dinner; or it's 9 P.M. and I'm in the middle of a marvelous mystery. That's why I now turn the answering machine on at five and leave it on until the next morning.

Once your business gets rolling and your work load increases, it may become difficult to successfully manage both your personal and home-business lives. Brenda Batykefer, who works with husband Bob on their part-time Chevrolet Specialties business, says it's important to set aside time for children's activities. "We keep four calendars in the house so everyone has a clear view of what is happening each day. Ball games, practices, meetings and appointments are not missed as a result."

Although it may be impossible to make a complete physical and mental separation of business from your home life, strive to attain some kind of psychological separation from time to time. Although vacations may seem a luxury you don't have time for, or can't afford, some time away from the place where all the work is waiting is essential to your mental and physical well-being. Remember: The more important you are to the continuity of your business, the more important it is for you to put your own health (mental as well as physical) first. Otherwise you may not be able to run your business at all.

After several years of working at home, Susan Brown's rubber stamp business, Wood Cellar Graphics, suddenly took an upward turn. "My husband had to quit his job and join me to keep up with all the orders," Susan told me. "We continued at home for another year and just about lost our minds. We continued to grow and grow, and pretty soon we had the house full, and also a two-car garage. We were overflowing the space that we had, with nowhere to turn. After muddling our way through the summer months, with our kids helping us fill orders, we made the decision to move our business into a shop/warehouse. We needed to hire help, but had nowhere to have them work."

Sometimes one's home can be remodeled or enlarged to accommodate a growing business. Sometimes one can move to a larger house. Sometimes the business simply has to go. Yet another example of how nothing stays the same, why you should remain flexible and always be prepared to go with the flow.

Growth—or Status Quo?

Although we all want to realize a substantial profit from the time we spend on our businesses, we don't all want to be major corporations when we grow up. Most of us don't want employees running about our homes, invading our privacy. And most of us don't want a business to grow so large it requires us to move the business outside the home. Thus, the longer one is in business, and the more successful a business becomes, the harder it is to stay in control. The real challenge for many of us is to constantly increase the business income and profits while keeping the volume of work at a level that can be handled alone, or by family members or outside contractors.

That's precisely why some home business owners—particularly mothers who work at home because they want to be there for their family—set a limit on the number of hours they will work and the level of income they wish to make. When they reach their income goal, they simply quit striving for more because to grow would only create problems they don't want to face. One of my readers put it well when she wrote: "I'm not interested in getting any bigger or more spread out than I can handle myself. Maybe it's because I'm not supporting myself or anyone else, so what I earn is sort of play money. But it is very gratifying to feel that people like my products well enough to buy them. It is the sort of ego boost that many women my age need desperately. My four grown kids are quite impressed with the fact that their mom is paid $200 a day to daub paint on a board. I need this respect."

Many others, however—particularly those individuals who originally entered the home-business field with total self-employment in mind—look at their growing business and make a conscious decision to keep growing, even if it means hiring employees—a thought that bothers a lot of small business owners. Publisher Diane Wolverton explains: "Small business owners know their trade, but few of them are ready to take on the responsibility of leading and developing people. That's why it's so hard to make the decision to bring people into the business. We hesitate because we just don't know what to do."

When Diane and her husband Bob purchased the Bridger Valley *Pioneer* in 1988, they envisioned their new roles as romantic and exciting. "We saw ourselves, just the two of us, covering town meetings, writing compelling editorials, snapping award-winning photographs and spending the weekends camping in the nearby mountains," she says. "What we didn't see was who was going to do all the typesetting, sell the ads and drive the 120-mile round trip to take the finished product to press. And if we were camping on weekends, who would cover the dedication of the new town hall on Saturday? It took about one week and several all-nighters in a row for us to realize we couldn't do it all

The Scented Workplace

Researchers in the field of smell report we may work more efficiently if we add fragrance to the office atmosphere. Stressed? Try the relaxing scent of Lily of the Valley. Lavender wakes up our metabolism, while peppermint stimulates the brain's electrical activity and fights drowsiness.

Since we're all working up a sweat in our home offices, a little perfume couldn't hurt.

Whoops!

"You know you're pushing too hard when you put the raw corn on the table and microwave the salad," says one of my readers, adding that a friend of hers actually did this . . . the same day she dropped her bank deposit in the mailbox instead of at the bank.

alone. I decided I could either invest in employees, or invest in my own burial plot. Frankly, the fear of death overpowered my fear of the unknown. Within a few weeks we hired a proofreader, salesperson and typesetter, and I became a people manager."

Diane, who later diversified the business with the publication of a home-office newsletter, says it's easy to make excuses about not wanting employees because of the red tape and paperwork, but that the tradeoff is worth it. "I now know that a business is limited only by the vision of the owner. If you see your business as a small, one-person operation, that's what it will be. If you see your business as a growing, thriving business that provides good income to you as well as to others, then that's what it will become."

As your business grows and takes more and more space in your home, the thought of moving to outside quarters may begin to sound appealing. As one entrepreneur put it in a newspaper interview, "Now that the business has begun to grow so quickly, I'm feeling overwhelmed about how much space it occupies. There's a delicate line as to when it's ideal to be home and when it's time to move out," she said.

Theresa Strumpf, who ran TLS Tax Service out of her home for several years, told me why she finally relocated her business to an outside office. "It was hard to work at home with the family," she said. "My daughter's friends were always coming in and out. There were stairways coming into my home office, making it difficult for many of my older clients. More important, my business had grown to the point where I had to have help. I could no longer do all the work, and there wasn't enough room in our home for an employee work station."

Theresa says it is a great relief to have help at last. "It's worth the extra money," she adds, "and with extra help and my new location, my tax services are now being used not only by individuals, but by the business community."

Susan Brown, the rubber stamp entrepreneur, said the hardest part of growth was letting go . . . delegating responsibilities. "You get so used to doing it all yourself for so long, and then when you let someone else do it, it's hard."

Now, with three employees and a completely organized business, things look very promising, Susan says. "What a boost for the old self-esteem—to create something, work your buns off for it, and then see it succeed. There's nothing better!"

Coping With Stress

It's not hard for me to imagine the extra stress Susan and every other business owner mentioned in this book has had to cope with as they pursued their various endeavors. But have these people been harmed by stress?

We all have stress. It plagues our daily lives as we try not to lose our patience with a slow salesclerk or an overbooked doctor who keeps us waiting for an hour or more. We feel stressed when we are rushing about to accomplish a long list of errands, are interrupted in the middle of a project, are criticized or forced to listen to noise we can't control. In truth, stress is essential for life. Its absence is death, says Dr. Hans Selye, one of the world's leading authorities on this topic. While *distress* (negative stress) can play havoc with your mind and body, *eustress* (positive stress) is energizing. For example, if you challenge yourself by setting a worthwhile goal and then work very hard to achieve that goal, this can be healthful stress—especially if you enjoy what you're doing.

Dr. Selye has said that all the talk about the dangers of overwork and excessive striving is exaggerated, and only arouses unnecessary anxiety. He maintains that each of us gradually develops an instinctive feel that tells us whether we are running above or below the stress level that suits us best. His recipe for the best antidote to the stresses of ordinary life is first to decide if you are a racehorse or a turtle (do you want to run fast or slow?). Then choose your own goals (don't let others impose their goals on you). Finally, Dr. Selye suggests the practice of "altruistic egoism"—which is looking out for yourself by being necessary to others. Nothing in life is as stressful as a feeling of purposelessness, he maintains.

I am not always in control of my business activities or my reaction to the various stresses of life. But I've learned how to regain control on those occasions when things get out of hand. Like every other successful business owner I know, I've developed certain bounce-back strategies and escape mechanisms to keep both my mind and body healthy.

On that morning back in 1984 when I was trying to finish the first edition of this book, I was under enormous stress. At that time, I had exactly ten days in which to meet my publisher's tight schedule, and I had to do an out-of-town workshop during the same period. In addition, we were then receiving hundreds of letters a day in response to a terrific publicity mention in *Family Circle*. So, what happened? I complicated the situation by injuring myself.

I had taken a quick run to the shopping center the day before to buy a new pair of shoes for my upcoming workshop. I put them on to break them in and promptly fell down. Hard. The combination of haste, a slick floor and the slippery soles of my new shoes resulted in an embarrassing, face-forward fall that bruised my ego, banged up both kneecaps, sprained my left ankle and hurt one of my best typing fingers. I spent the remainder of that day in bed with ice packs on various parts of my body, feeling sorry for myself and upset because I was losing time away from

Lessons Learned

After reading an earlier edition of this book, a reader said *Homemade Money* had literally saved her sanity. "I'm finding out firsthand how the unexpected can interfere with family, creativity and mental state in general," said Sheila Dillon, Shooting Star Designs. "Here's what I learned about myself as a businessperson after two particularly stressful days:

- Friends are not always the best ones to explain and understand business problems; we need people who are in business (a network).
- A positive mental attitude is important. My "major problems" have now become "inconveniences."
- I've learned I can handle two tasks at one time as long as only one of them is an inconvenience.
- If one person or organization can't help, remember to ask if they know of another that can.
- Always write down your short- and long-term goals. When things get frustrating, look at your goals list to see how much you really have accomplished."

Networking

Get involved in a network! Home-based workers often feel a sense of isolation that in itself can be depressing and thus stressful. But contact of any kind with others who understand what you are going through—and are there to lend help when needed—can make all the difference in the world.

If a local network doesn't exist, start one yourself with an announcement in the paper. Join some organizations related to your field, and don't just read their newsletters, but attend meetings once in a while. As a member of the Society of Craft Designers says, "I regularly attend an annual educational seminar (held in a different city each year). Although this is an expensive trip, it always has been worth the cost because I come away feeling totally refreshed and newly inspired. And this is after four days of around-the-clock meetings and networking. Here I meet old and new business friends, trade ideas with writers, editors and publishers and catch up on the latest information relative to a special field of interest. Meetings like this are actually restful for me because they break the daily routine of business and allow me to get away from it all."

the typewriter and this book. Meanwhile, Harry was trying to cope with 350 pieces of mail, give me sympathy and get dinner on the table.

The next morning, however, I was back at my desk, swollen ankle propped on a pillow. It was business as usual. It *had* to be. Deadlines had to be met. Work had to be finished. And the stress of it all had to be dealt with. Such are the realities of a home business, which insists on being run even when you don't feel like running it.

Little has changed for me over the years. The reasons are different, of course, but I'm still working under stress. Which brings me to my point: After you have been working for yourself for a while, you either get good at maintaining control and dealing with stress, or you simply cave in. I have become pretty good at it. Harry and I have been married more than thirty-five years now, and our life together has never been ordinary. Although happy, it has been loaded with stress, much of it of our own making. For instance, Harry's work, in conjunction with his restless spirit, has necessitated fourteen changes of residence in our married life. Seven of those moves have occurred during the time we have been operating a home business. It's not easy to meet publishing deadlines and keep a mail-oriented business running smoothly when you're forced to move about this often, but somehow we've always done it. Not without stress and special coping techniques, however.

These days, when I find myself pushing too hard, or see that my husband's patience with my driving ambition is about to break, I organize my work so we can get away for a few days to one of our favorite out-of-state motels with a hot tub and lots of good restaurants nearby. We take good music and books with us, perhaps some puzzles, games or hobby projects, and put business totally out of our mind for as many days as possible. To relieve my stress at other times, I allow myself a whole day from time to time to do something I love—pursue a favorite hobby, play the piano, work a jigsaw puzzle, or read a nice relaxing psychological thriller or murder mystery. (Even here, my subconscious mind must be on business because I keep finding great quotes to use in my writing. For example, in Lawrence Sanders's *Timothy's Game*, I found this: "Always expect calamity. Then when a mere misfortune arrives, it's good news." I know a lot of home-business owners who can relate to that one.)

Bob Riemke, publisher of *The Real Entrepreneur*, says there have been many times when he has felt overwhelmed by his business, and times when he wanted to throw up his hands in utter despair and call it quits. "When I reach that point," he says, "I know it's time for some R&R (rest and relaxation). I just shut up the house, take off to nowhere in particular and completely put everything out of my mind, except having a good time, and relaxing. When I return to the office, nothing has really changed—except me."

Some of my readers have told me an exercise program has been very helpful to them in relieving stress. I keep telling myself I'm going to start an exercise program soon . . . as soon as I find time. I really hate to stop doing something I love—which is working—to do something I hate—which is exercising—and am I ever good at finding reasons not to exercise. Actually, I get a lot of exercise every day in my homebased business. The only trouble is it doesn't burn enough calories. I'm talking about:

- *Stretching* to reach new heights . . .
- *Leaping* to grasp opportunity . . .
- *Running* to meet deadlines . . .
- *Hopping* from one project to another . . .
- *Struggling* with responsibility . . .
- *Beating the bushes* for new business . . .
- *Jumping* to conclusions . . .
- *Flying* off the handle . . .
- *Pulling* myself together, and
- *Pushing my luck!*

Making Lists

Another way to reduce stress is to become better organized, a topic discussed in chapter seven. I chuckled when I read a cartoon in *The Crafts Report* that showed a woman sitting in a messy work room. The caption said, "The advantage to being disorganized is that if a burglar breaks in, he won't be able to find anything either."

One trick all good organizers use is list-making. There is great satisfaction in starting the day with a long list and crossing items off, one by one.

Once, after Harry and I had relocated to Missouri, I received a timely letter from a friend. "The trouble with moving," said Sarah, "is that it realigns your priorities whether you want it to or not. Getting your house/life in order takes precedence over a lot of things that you need to be doing to keep your business running. If you should feel an anxiety attack coming on, and you feel guilty and inadequate because you can't do everything fast and efficiently, just remember that you are demanding too much of yourself. Say to yourself, I am one person. What needs to be done . . . will get done. Now, what needs to be done *today*?"

Sarah's letter arrived shortly after the moving van, and as I read it, half of me was concerned about where I had put the frying pan so I could get a quick meal on the table; the other half was trying to figure out how to set up a temporary office to handle the mail that had piled up since we had packed the office. Sarah's

How to Stay Motivated

One secret is to read uplifting publications. Another is to associate with inspiring and enthusiastic people, in person and by mail. Don't listen to discouraging talk. Keep a diary of your accomplishments and reread it periodically for encouragement. Consider all setbacks merely a profitable learning experience. Ask for help when you need it.

advice brought a smile to my face. "Ask yourself what needs to be done before Friday of this week, then make a list. Go through this process and set reachable goals for the month, three months and one year. Just making the list will relieve a lot of pressure."

She was right, of course. I had made just such a list before leaving our old residence, and although it took a whole day to plan my last month's work in that area, it was as if a giant weight had been lifted from my shoulders when my day-to-day schedule was completed. I knew then that I had to worry only about what was on each day's list of things to do. Try it. You will be amazed at how much it helps when you feel you can't cope with all the work ahead of you.

Making lists of the work to be done is one good way to stay in control of things even when you don't feel overwhelmed by the weight of your responsibilities. But, no matter how many lists I make, something unexpected always seems to happen to upset my work schedule. Like the morning I went to the freezer to take out meat for dinner. To my dismay, I discovered the door I had last opened the morning before had not closed because a package had shifted and jammed against it. Now the ice cream was dripping through the shelves, berry juice was streaming down the inside of the door, and all the green beans and peppers I had worked so hard to freeze the month before had thawed, along with about thirty pounds of meat and a lot of specialty foods we had brought from Chicago on our last shopping trip.

At first, I was close to tears. Then I got angry at myself for being so careless. The office work I had planned to do clearly was second on my list of priorities for this day. After I spent another five minutes feeling sorry for myself, the part of me that always welcomes a challenge came to life. An unsympathetic Harry helped me carry everything to the kitchen, where I made a list of the thawed ingredients, got out my recipe box, and went to work. While stewing about the fine mess I'd gotten myself into, I cooked, baked and boiled my way out of it. Eight hours later, I had more meals in the freezer than I could count. All in all, it wasn't a bad experience. In fact, those prepared meals turned out to be a great time saver in the busy weeks to follow, and the experience was good for at least one laugh. One evening when Harry complimented me on one of the stews resulting from this fiasco and asked me how I made it, I said, "Well, first you let the freezer thaw. . . ."

Talking to Yourself

Many people get through life, I'm convinced, simply because they have a sense of humor. And when you work for yourself at home, it's essential for survival. I consider my sense of humor one of the greatest gifts received from my parents. They instilled in me and my sisters the belief that, no matter how bad things might get, they could always be worse; and we should always look for whatever good we could find in a situation and try to laugh our troubles away. I guess that's why, when the freezer thawed, I thought how lucky we were that we had not just put in half a beef. And the green peppers were still growing, so I could replace them. The beans? In spite of warnings not to refreeze food, I refroze them anyway, and although they were a little mushy, they tasted fine. And when I fell in the shopping mall that day, my first reaction was to feel sorry for myself because I didn't need that kind of complication then. But on the way home, I realized it could have been worse. I might have broken my wrist or a couple of fingers and been unable to work at all.

And you know what? As that next day wore on, I began to tell myself my ankle didn't feel all that bad, even though it was twice its usual size. By tomorrow, I told myself, it will feel better and so will I. Actually, what I was doing was having a private conversation with myself, during which time I came to the conclusion there was no real problem. Result? The stress I felt was soon relieved.

Throughout my life, I have tried to maintain a positive attitude about everything, and it has never failed to benefit me. Some people look at a partially filled bottle and say, "It's half gone," but I say, "There's still half a bottle left." I try to apply the same kind of thinking to the daily happenings of my life and business. When things go wrong or get out of control, I may not be able to do anything about the situation at that particular moment, but I *can* do something for myself immediately, and I do. I find something positive to think about. You must learn to do the same.

In the end, each of us has a choice about how we perceive our experiences in life, and how our bodies will react to them. You have heard about the power of positive thinking and what it can do for you; where stress is concerned, positive thinking can make all the difference in the world. When you think negatively about anything, your body also responds negatively because the power of suggestion definitely affects the nervous system. But if you force yourself to think in positive terms, your body will respond accordingly.

Remember: Your subconscious mind has the ability to accept as real any impression that reaches it, whether positive or negative, constructive or destructive. That's why it is vital to your mental and physical well-being to protect your mind from undesirable influences and suggestions that can bring you down.

The next time you find yourself thinking negative thoughts that begin with "I can't," go to the mirror and give yourself a pep talk. Look yourself in the eye and say "I *can!*" You will then be sending a clear signal to your subconscious mind and planting a seed that will grow in strength and eventually help you find the

Stress Reduction Techniques

- Get out of the house, away from everything that reminds you of business. If you have no place to go, just take a walk. Commune with nature. Think good thoughts about yourself.

- Pour out your feelings in a letter to a confidant, or write in your private journal. It can be a great emotional release to put your thoughts in writing even if you're the only one who will ever read them.

- Call a friend who understands your situation. A few words of encouragement from someone who cares about you can do wonders for your morale.

- Read an inspirational book or listen to a motivational tape.

Quick Fix

"Take some time off and go to the park or the beach," says Betsy Hatch. "Your mind will naturally start spinning back to business problems, but use the Scarlett O'Hara approach and keep telling yourself, 'I'll think about that tomorrow; today is for me to relax.' The more relaxed you are, the more equipped you will be for facing tasks at hand."

answer to the "how" part of your problem.

I was delighted the day I received a review copy of a book titled *What to Say When You Talk to Yourself* by Shad Helmstetter (Grindle Press). On reading it, I was even more delighted to learn I had been saying all the right things to myself. This book confirms what I've been telling my readers for years: Our minds are like computers that accept all the information we and others pour into it, good and bad alike. If we don't like what we're getting back, we simply have to change the programming.

"Imagine what you could do if you could override the programs in your subconscious mind, those that still work against you, and replace them with a refreshing new program of absolute belief?" Helmstetter states in his book. "How successful you will be at anything is inexorably tied to the words and beliefs about yourself that you have stored in your subconscious mind. You will become what you think about most; your success or failure in anything, large or small, will depend on your programming—what you accept from others, and what you say when you talk to yourself."

Positive Workaholism

In a survey of 450 entrepreneurs, a Boston university professor learned that most of them believed total immersion in their work was necessary for success, and that personal and family sacrifice was almost universal. Although most of the entrepreneurs in this particular survey could afford to take vacations, few of them did, preferring instead to work.

A lot of people believe that so-called A-type personalities like these are prone to heart attacks, high blood pressure, ulcers and a number of other health problems. Some of them—those who cannot deal with stress—probably are. But a lot of hardworking people, myself included, tend to agree with author Dennis E. Hensley, who claims it isn't stress that kills, but boredom. Dennis believes the answer to all problems is hard work that a person enjoys. He urges ambitious entrepreneurs to work as hard as they want, because the satisfaction they realize from productive work probably will do more to combat the ordinary stresses of life than anything else.

There must be something to this theory. I have felt terribly stressed all my adult life, yet I am neither unhappy nor unhealthy. My blood pressure is on the low side of normal, I don't have ulcers, and my attitude remains positive. I do suffer occasionally from insomnia, not because of stress, but because I have an overactive mind and always want to accomplish more in one day than hours will allow. I think I try to steal time by not sleeping. Or, as John Steinbeck wrote in *Journal of a Novel*, "Last night I hardly slept at all. It was one of those good thinking nights."

Dennis, who has written several books and hundreds of articles, coined the term "positive workaholic" in 1976, and he is living testament of his own positive workaholic systems. He says he never sleeps more than six hours a night and is at his most productive from 10 P.M. to 2 A.M., the time when he does most of his writing. Although Dennis is active as a lecturer, teacher, publicist, businessman, church deacon, husband and father, this has not kept him from realizing his dream of becoming a professional writer. His philosophy is that success is obtainable to everyone who desires it and is willing to work for it, and he cites four common denominators among positive workaholics:

- A winning attitude
- High levels of energy
- Fierce independence
- A "mystical sense of destiny"

In summary, don't fret if you find you're always having to defend your work habits to others who keep telling you you're going to kill yourself by working so hard. It could be that working hard on your own business is the most healthful thing you could be doing.

Fighting Burnout

One stress expert says burnout is the total depletion of one's physical and mental resources, and it's caused either by trying to reach unattainable goals or as a result of things that get in your way over which you have no control.

In the home-business community, burnout most often occurs when individuals

1. Experience so many personal life stresses—death in the family, divorce, job loss, problems with children, etc.—that they can no longer cope with the added stress of a business;
2. Live with too high a level of stress for too long a time without seeing any positive results; or
3. Become so excited about their possibilities that they take on more than they can handle.

Because home-business beginners often lack clear-cut goals or fail to monitor their progress in the right way, they begin to feel their expectations are not being met, and before long, they may begin to feel like a failure. In addition, many people receive absolutely no positive feedback from family or friends, and one cannot long work in such a vacuum without a mental or emotional collapse.

"People who work at home successfully learn to crack their own whips and to pat their own backs, sometimes all in one day," said one entrepreneur in an interview. She is right. As a

When you reach the end of your rope tie a knot in it & hang on!

Illustration by Joyce Goad, used by permission.

Found by Barbara: A New Source of Strength

I've learned something important about self-sufficiency since the fifth edition of this book was published in 1994.

When my mother—my greatest motivator—died in mid-1992, I felt as though a part of me had died, too. The following summer, I learned I had breast cancer. Caught early, I took it in stride, but the experience (which I viewed as a wake-up call from God) took a lot out of me. I made some changes to reduce my business stress, but my spirits continued to sag until the fall of 1994 when I admitted for the first time in my life that I lacked confidence and direction. I was tired, restless, insecure and totally burned out, a woman whose previous ambition and spirit had fled.

So what do you do when you realize you've used the last ounce of your personal strength resources and don't know how to replenish them? In discussing this with a good friend, she said, "Have you tried praying? To get help, you must *ask* for it."

In thinking about this, I saw that I had always taken great pride in the fact that I could "do it myself." I've always been so self-sufficient I've never asked anyone for help, even when I needed it. Certainly I'd never thought of asking God for help for He was surely too busy with the important things of the world to be concerned about my little problems.

One night, however, unable to sleep because of all my cares and worries, I got down on my knees and ardently prayed for the first time in thirty years. I said, "Lord, I really need some help here!" Then I told Him in detail what was bothering me and

(continues on page 357)

self-employed individual, you may be the only person from whom you can draw the strength you need on any given day, and you may also be the only one around who's going to pat you on the back and say, "Well done!"

Burnout affects men and women alike, but if my reader mail is any indication, more women than men working at home suffer its consequences. In all the great success stories of men in business, have you ever noticed the direct link between their success and their degree of commitment to their work? It's usually not that difficult for a married man to make a serious, full-time commitment to a homebased business, for he can generally assume that his wife not only will take care of things on the home front but perhaps assist him in business as well. If there is no wife at all, it's a piece of cake. Married women—especially those with children—seldom get that kind of break. Oh! The times I have wished for the equal of a wife like myself who would take care of things on the home front so I could attend to important business matters.

If any one theme runs rampant through the mail I receive from women who run businesses from home, it's guilt. "Guilt is an easy trap, especially for the self-employed," says a psychology professor in an article I read. "It is anger turned inward; it produces a growing sense of failure, dwindling self-esteem, and a gnawing questioning of our ability." In reaching for their dreams, most married women have to sacrifice something, whether it's time with their children or spouses, or attention to homemaking details such as housecleaning, laundry, meal planning and grocery shopping. While they're busily succeeding in business, they secretly begin to see themselves as failures in other areas of life, simply because they can't figure out how to do it all, like some kind of superwoman.

If such women do not take steps to control the way they are spending their lives—trying to mix too many activities at once—they may eventually suffer burnout symptoms. Sometimes the cure is as simple as taking a vacation; other times, they must cease something altogether in order to avoid serious health problems or destructive influences on their personal life. Sometimes it's the marriage, rather than the business, that ends up on the chopping block.

Being a superwoman was never one of my goals, and being perfect isn't important either. *Doing the best job I can under the circumstances is what matters most to me.* I think that if more women would look at their lives from this viewpoint, there would be less guilt and lower blood pressure readings all around.

The psychologist I mentioned earlier says it's dangerous for anyone to compare himself or herself to others, because everyone brings to a career or business a unique set of personality variables, family, financial and health factors—not to mention a differing ability to cope with stress. Therefore, it's impossible for one person to tell another how to successfully balance his or her life. Each of us must learn the hard way to do this ourselves, trying first one strategy, then another, until we find one we and our loved ones can live with.

Reviewing the Situation

Whether you plan to keep your business small and controlled or are shooting for the moon—and ready to handle all the stress that comes your way—you need to sit back and carefully rethink your grand plan from time to time. You may have to make certain modifications, perhaps even decide if you are on the right track after all. Or, as Fagin sang in the Broadway musical, *Oliver*:

I'm reviewing the situation . . .

I think I'd better think it out again.

The harder you work on your business, the more likely you are to have ambivalent feelings like these, expressed by another of my readers: "I've run into so many problems that I wonder if it is as worthwhile as I once thought. I feel I'm at a crossroads. I can choose to continue to work extremely hard and possibly overcome my problems, or let my fears get the best of me and stop the ball from rolling any farther. One part of me wants to scream and say, 'Hang in there, your rewards are coming,' while the other part argues back, 'You're only deceiving yourself.' "

As a home-business owner, you must expect feelings like these and learn to cope with them. *They come with the territory.* One day you can be on a terrific "high" because of some new achievement, a big order or some publicity that boosts your business; the next day you may feel totally overwhelmed by the weight of too many responsibilities, too little time and not enough money. A fight with one's spouse or even a minor family problem often can seem like the last straw. At times like these, you may feel like a salmon swimming upstream. Although you feel compelled to keep going, you no longer are sure you can make it. What seemed like a little swim at first has now become a fierce struggle to survive. In retrospect, you may discover, like so many others before you, that beginning was easy. It's *continuing* that is hard.

Although each new upstream swim gets easier, the decisions to be made only get harder. To grow, or not to grow? To take a risk, or not to take a risk? To stay at home, or move the business out? Is this the right business after all? What's all this doing to the family?

I think I'd better think it out again.

After reviewing the situation, some people throw in the towel, others slow down, still others change directions

asked Him to give me strength, courage and guidance.

My prayer was answered the next night in a way that to me was both miraculous and glorious. Since this is a business book, I'll spare you the details of what happened, but don't be surprised if I write a book about it someday. I'll say this, however: My whole life began to change in exciting ways as soon as I plugged myself into God's power.

I now see we can go a long way under our own steam and much farther when others are behind us offering motivational support and encouragement. But sooner or later, with or without emotional and motivational support, we're all going to run out of ourselves someday. The problem today is there are so many books and so many humanists out there saying "You can do it! All you have to do is believe in yourself."

As many before me have learned, that's not enough. There is a limit to the number of times you will be able to pull yourself up by the bootstraps. Unless you plug into a source of power greater than yourself, one day you may discover as I did that, without God, you're as dead and useless as a light bulb without electricity.

So remember to thank God for the talents and abilities He has given you, and don't hesitate to lean on the LORD when you need help or encouragement in either your personal or home-business life. From experience I have learned that if we will simply open ourselves to God's spirit, He will lead us in surprising new directions and reveal wondrous things we never could have discovered on our own. As the Bible confirms, "Commit to the LORD whatever you do, and your plans will succeed."

(Proverbs 16.3 NIV)

Being Your Own Motivator

One of the things I find difficult in being a small business owner is that I have to be my own personal motivator. I don't have any time clock to punch, any time to be docked, or anyone to fire me if I don't get the work done. I must motivate myself whether I'm sick, exhausted, pregnant or whatever. If I'm not there to do the work, it won't get done unless I have figured out some other system that will work for itself, such as a secretary, a robot, a salesperson, etc.

What is worse is that if I don't find the energy to motivate myself, the money won't come in and then I panic. If I get to this state of panic, hopefully I jolt myself awake and get back on the right track. If not, most likely my business will go down the tubes, and being a small business it might not even pay to file Chapter 11. How depressing!

On the cheerier side . . . every accomplishment, all the money and the future I create is mine. There is power and good feelings in knowing this. It's like finding a pot of gold at the end of the rainbow.

—Julie Ann Allender, Ed.D., licensed psychologist

completely, and a certain percentage forge ahead in the original direction, pushing all the harder. Driven by some force even they do not understand, they work with unceasing fervor, supremely confident the success they dream of one day will be theirs.

Like salmon, some home-business owners make it, some don't. There are no sure bets in this game, but one thing is certain: It *is* a game worth playing. Even those who fail as business people will succeed as individuals. It takes gumption and guts to start and operate a business of any kind, and anyone who does it, even for a little while, is a winner in my book.

Etiquette for Going Out of Business

"Any damn fool can start a love affair, but ending one successfully takes a real genius," said George Bernard Shaw. That applies to starting and ending a business, too.

As one who may be on the brink of success with many exciting years of good business ahead, it may seem ridiculous to think now about how you're going to get out of the business you're currently working so hard to build. But take it from one who's been there: It's a kind of insurance to know where the exit is. Remember my business motto: "Hope for the best . . . prepare for the worst . . . and always leave yourself an escape route."

There will always be new people ready to jump on the home-business bandwagon, but many who merely anticipate an exciting ride will get off quickly when they learn they have to do the driving and it isn't as easy as they thought.

You may have heard the joke about the pig and the chicken who were discussing the fact that they're the most popular items on the breakfast table. "Yeah," says the pig. "But you're only *involved* in breakfast. Me? I'm *committed*." The day may come when you find yourself asking if you're really committed to the idea of business, or just taking an interesting sidetrip on the road of life.

Home businesses come and home businesses go. I once surveyed a group of my expired subscribers to see why they had let their subscriptions lapse. Most said they simply weren't in business any longer. Some readers told me they had found it necessary to take outside jobs. "My homebased business could not provide the money that working for others can," said one. "The economy of our small town is in considerable distress," said another, "and I must apply to the basic needs." Still others said their activities were more hobby than business. A mother who recently had her third child said the children had "cramped her style for home business." A widow said she now had other interests to occupy her remaining years.

Being able to make yourself work when you'd rather not is, in my opinion, a determining factor in whether you will succeed as a self-employed individual. It is no easy job to stay motivated when you are tired from overwork, challenged by marketing problems, concerned about your cash-flow situation or pressured because of time restraints or family responsibilities. Until recently, the hardest time of the year for me was December. While other women were baking cookies, decorating their homes and trees for Christmas, and shopping for gifts, I was always rushing to get my newsletter to the printer before the holiday. That has changed, however. (See sidebar at right.)

I think the second law of thermodynamics applies to home-based business owners at year's end. It holds that "all organized systems tend to slide slowly into chaos and disorder, while energy tends to run down, and the universe heads into darkness." (Would you believe I found this tidbit in a John MacDonald novel?)

A sole proprietorship is a double-edged sword in that one usually has little money with which to start, and even less if the business must cease because of lack of profit. Two kinds of businesses suffer most: publishing and mail order. That's because the mail never stops coming, especially if you've done a good job with your advertising and publicity. People will continue to send you money for your products and publications for years after you've ceased business. There will also be letters of inquiry from people who still want your brochure, catalog or whatever else you may have been advertising. You have a professional obligation to respond in some way.

Some people who want to escape a business and its obligations will simply move or close their post office box without leaving a forwarding address. This, at least, will get the mail returned to senders. It's also the coward's way out, and it doesn't work if you've been using your street address as your business address. If you have nothing else to sell and can't afford to respond to your mail, order a rubber stamp that says, "Refused/Out of Business— Return to Sender." You will incur no extra postage costs, and interested people who send you money will get their checks back or know why you aren't sending the information they requested.

Don't be like the publisher who was listed in an earlier edition of this book and continued to accept four-dollar checks for sample issues of his periodical long after it had ceased publication. When a reader brought this situation to my attention, I contacted the publisher, who told me, "Don't worry, we're not cashing the checks. Just tell people to look at their bank statement." How unprofessional! Besides, it's not my job to tell people that some of the businesses I've publicized in earlier editions of my book or periodical are no longer in business.

If you should ever find yourself on the verge of bankruptcy, or just ready to quit, try to exit gracefully, professionally. Look for other businesses like yours who might be able to fulfill your

Knowing When to Quit

Early in 1994, I finally admitted to myself that I was burned out on publishing a 28-page quarterly periodical. With each passing calendar quarter, I had found it more difficult to find the 80-hour block of time I needed to create each new issue. After doing this four times a year for ten years, I simply couldn't bring myself to do it anymore.

Rather than stop publishing I renamed my newsletter for the third time and went back to the 8-page format and bimonthly publishing schedule I had begun with in 1981. Although it now took me less time to create each issue, the deadlines were closer together and, by mid-1995, I felt burned out again. And now I had a contract for a new book whose deadline seemed too close for comfort.

Just before Christmas, an inner voice said "If you're ever going to find time to write all those books you're dreaming about, you must cease publication of your newsletter *now*. On the spur of the moment, I picked up the phone and asked a fellow publisher if she would fulfill my subscriber obligations. My last issue in the Spring of 1996 marked the end of my fifteenth year of publication, and quitting when I did was the smartest move I've made in years. At long last have the time I need to write new books.

The hard thing about making a big change in your business is that you can't be sure you've done the right thing until after you've made the change. All you can do is trust your instincts. This worked for me; I think it will work for you, too.

Many things look bleakest at their moment of occurrence . . . but at least we ain't got locusts.

—Old Oriental philosophy once expressed by Jack Soo on the *Barney Miller Show*

orders or inquiries with substitute products or publications. If you have previously solicited publicity, you should also notify important media contacts that publicity is no longer wanted. Remember, you might want to start a new business someday, and if you ruin your reputation the first time around, few will give you a second chance.

Dreams die hard for some. For others, giving up a home business is easy when boredom sets in, major lifestyle changes necessitate the ending of a business or burnout occurs, often because business income is not commensurate with effort expended. My reader mail confirms that every year a certain number of home-business owners also disband their business simply to preserve their sanity or to keep peace in the family. If and when your business does cease, do not for a minute let yourself feel that you have failed. What you will have learned from your entrepreneurial experience will benefit you for the rest of your life, in ways you cannot yet imagine.

I firmly believe it is better to have bossed and lost than never to have bossed at all.

EPILOGUE

....

"LIFE IS SHORT, AND LIFE WITHOUT books is much too small," says Garrison Keillor. "Books are what change our lives, and a person has to feel sorry for people who say they don't have time to read. It's like not having time to dream."

I see books as natural beginnings to all kinds of wonderful things. It was a book, after all, that led me to start my first small home business. That book, *You Can Whittle and Carve*, released a stream of creativity in me that has yet to cease. I never made much money selling my wood-carvings, but oh, what I learned in the process.

A few years later, another book, *On Writing Well*, by William Zinsser, changed my life because it changed the way I thought about myself. It convinced me I

The toughest thing about success is that you've got to keep on being a success.
—Irving Berlin

could be a professional writer if I chose to be one. Many other books have taught me additional things and propelled me in exciting new directions, as I hope this book will do for you.

In the process of writing it, I learned something about dreams and goals that I want to share with you. After I finished my first book, I told myself I was going to write another one. Someday. When I had more time. I dreamed about that book for five years. For a long time, I used the excuse that I was overwhelmed by work and couldn't possibly find time to write another book. In time, I came to realize that part of my reluctance to start a new book was I was afraid I would not be able to write a second book that would measure up to my first. (I think a lot of one-book authors must feel this way. You have done it once . . . but can you do it again?)

Thanks to a publisher who kept nudging me, I finally stopped dreaming about this book and made plans to write it. Believe me, there is nothing like a written contract with a firm deadline to spur one onward! Curiously, while the dream of a second book had seemed an impossibility for five years, the book—as a clearly defined goal—suddenly seemed achievable. There can be no doubt about it. We do not make gains by dreaming about things. We must set firm goals and then work like the dickens to achieve them, else they will remain dreams forever.

When I finished the first edition of this book in 1984, I thought, "Whew! What a big job. Am I glad it's finished." I did not realize then that I had written what would soon become a classic in its field, not to mention a book that had to be updated often if new readers were to be well served. Nor did I realize these updates would take hundreds of additional hours of my time, actually preventing me from writing other books. But with each new edition, I felt a special kind of satisfaction in knowing I had done what was necessary at the time. My books are like children to me, and like children they require my care and attention as they mature.

When *Homemade Money* was acquired by a new publisher in 1992, I was asked once again to deliver a new edition. For a book to be considered a new edition, at least one-third of it must be changed or updated. While I had been limited in the changes I could make to earlier editions, this time I was given a free hand. When I first wrote the book, I did it on a typewriter, and anyone with a computer and word processing software knows how much better one can write when one has the capability of being able to edit, rewrite and move material from one place to another. So with computer power this time around, I took a hard, cold look at this book and decided it was time for "baby" to grow up. So much had changed in a decade. I had learned so much more about business, about my industry, about the people in it, about myself, about success and failure, about life.

Instead of taking the easy way out—changing only one-third of the book—I decided to completely rewrite it with an eye to the future. In so doing, I've invested nearly a thousand hours more into a product many said was already the best of its kind. Still more time has gone into the latest reprinting of this book, which includes a totally updated text and resource chapter. My husband doesn't understand why I can't leave well enough alone, but Norman Vincent Peale explained it when he said, "We are self-made victims of mediocrity. We make ourselves content. But no one should ever be satisfied with a performance less than the best. Every human being has top quality built in. We are born to be achievers."

Age has taught me there is always room for improvement, even in the best products and services, and we must never become lazy and think we can rest on our laurels. ("If you rest on your laurels, all you'll end up with is a leafy design on your behind," say authors Esther Blumenfeld and Lynne Alpern.) As you, too, may already have learned, there is enormous satisfaction from having done the job right.

It will be that way for you, too. The hard work and extra hours you put into a business, now or in the future, is going to cause problems or work pile-ups in your day-to-day life. It definitely will add to your stress level, and it positively will exhaust you time and again. But, oh, the exhilaration of it all! There is nothing quite so satisfying as the achievement of a goal that's important to you.

That's why I urge you to stop dreaming about the things you want to do, and start making plans to *do them* before another season passes. Set firm, written goals and then get to work. It's absolutely amazing what you can accomplish when you believe you can do it. This book is proof positive.

Remember the rhyme: Believable . . . Conceivable . . . Achievable. It really works.

Do It Now!

While life lasts, it's good to remember that death is coming, and it's good that we don't know when. It keeps us alert, reminds us to live while we have the chance. Somebody should tell us, right at the start of our lives, that we are dying. Then we might live life to the limit, every minute of every day. Do it! I say whatever you want to do, do it now! There are only so many tomorrows.

—Michael Landon, in an interview for *Life* shortly before his death

U.S. AND CANADIAN RESOURCES

16

Don't merely be a passive receptacle for information. Understand that information is a commodity and the more you have about your industry, the better off you'll be. In spite of the avalanche of printed information available, much helpful information does not come from printed sources. Much is only available from the horse's mouth. So get to know the horse.

—Jeffrey Lant, one of America's most well-known business authorities

"THE ONLY THINGS WORTH LEARNing are the things you learn after you know it all," said Harry S. Truman. Although I have crammed this book with detailed how-to advice on every topic related to the selection, start-up, management, marketing and expansion of a homebased business, you undoubtedly have several "niche interest areas" that will require additional research on your part.

While this chapter provides a mind-boggling checklist of more than 300 information resources—books, periodicals, organizations, government agencies and other information providers—it represents only a small part of all the small business information available to you. If you hunger for more, request the mail-order book catalogs at the end of this section.

Books will always be one of your best sources for reliable business information, and never before has there been such a wealth of how-to titles on every aspect of business. Nearly 50,000 books are published every year even as countless others go out of print, some only a year or two after publication. Whether a book lives or dies depends not only on the value of its content, but on how hard a publisher or author works to promote it. Even when good books go out of print, however, they often survive on library shelves, so always look there when you're searching for a title you can't find in a bookstore. In trying to wade through the many titles of interest to you, always consider the author's experience and background, and trust most the advice of authors who do for a living the thing they are writing about.

Although dozens (if not hundreds) of home-business how-to guides have been published in the past few years, I am recommending here only selected titles I feel contain special information or perspective not found in *Homemade Money*. (At this point you don't need a beginner's start-up guide or a rehash of standard business information.) In other categories, no attempt has been made to list all books in print on a particular topic. Instead, I've generally referenced recently published or long-established books by leading authors or business experts whose knowledge I respect. Note that many recommended titles have gone into new or revised editions (indicated by the abbreviation "rev. ed." or the number of the current edition), a signal not only of a book's sales popularity, but an indication of its quality of content. A book that survives into a second or later edition is often on its way to becoming a classic in its field (if not already there).

To learn about *all* books in your field (current, new and forthcoming), you must get acquainted with the *Books in Print* directories in the library. Even branch libraries carry this reference, which is updated annually and supplemented with periodic editions of *Guide to Forthcoming Books*. Look under subject categories of interest to turn up new book titles and pertinent information regarding each book's publisher, publication date, price and so forth.

In the listings that follow, addresses are not given for well-known publishers since it is assumed their books are available in bookstores or libraries. In a few instances, however, I've included a publisher's address if a book may be available only by mail or is unlikely to have wide bookstore distribution.

Theoretically, all good books, particularly new ones, will be found in bookstores. In truth, many self-publishers do not seek bookstore distribution, and it can take months for new trade books to become established in the marketplace to the point where bookstores will stock them on their shelves; even then, stock purchases may be limited to two or three copies of a title. In many cases, you will have to ask a bookstore to place a special order for you. Another option is to order from a mail-order catalog, and at the end of the "Books" section, you will find a list of catalogs that feature small business books. Most of the titles I've recommended will be found in one or more of these catalogs.

Note: The information in any kind of resource directory begins to go out of date as soon as it is compiled because businesses are always moving, books come and go, periodicals cease publication or change names and organizations collapse. If your mail to any address in this chapter is returned, visit the library and check the latest edition of a directory related to that resource. Publishers, organizations and businesses of any size make it a point to be listed in as many directories as possible, and many of them can be found in your library. (See Section III.) If you live miles from a library, note that you can always telephone the reference department of a library for assistance. (My local library tells me they answer more than 225,000 reference questions each year.)

Finally, if you wish to telephone a business or organization listed in this resource directory, obtain the telephone number by dialing the area code of the city you want to reach, then 555-1212. Large companies may have a toll-free number. To find out, dial (800) 555-1212.

Section I: Books   368

Homebased Business and Entrepreneurship—General
How-To Business Start-Up Guides
Planning and Management
Legal and Financial
Marketing and Publicity
Mail-Order Book Sources

Section II: Periodicals   375

Home Business/Entrepreneurial/Opportunity Publications
Marketing Periodicals
Special-Interest Business Periodicals

Section III: Organizations   378
and Directories

Selected Business and Trade Organizations
Key Library Resources and Privately Published Directories
Online Services

Section IV: Government and   382
Small Business Agencies

U.S. Government Agencies
Selected Canadian Government and Economic Development
Resources

Section V: Other Resources   384

SECTION I: BOOKS

Homebased Business and Entrepreneurship—General

☐ *101 Best Weekend Businesses* by Dan Ramsey. 1996, Career Press.

☐ *The Best Home Businesses for the 90s* by Paul & Sarah Edwards. 1991, Jeremy P. Tarcher, Inc.

☐ *The Best Home-Based Franchises* by Gregory Matusky. 1992, Doubleday.

☐ *Bringing It Home: A Home Business Start-Up Guide for You and Your Family* by Wendy Priesnitz. 1995, The Alternate Press (Canada).

☐ *The Closet Entrepreneur—377 Ways to Start Your Successful Business With Little Or No Money* by Neil Balter. 1994, Career Press.

☐ *The Complete Work-At-Home Companion* by Herman Holtz. 1994, 2nd ed., Prima Publishing.

☐ *Fast Cash for Kids—101 Money-Making Projects for Young Entrepreneurs.* 1991, Career Press.

☐ *Finding Your Perfect Work: The New Career Guide to Making a Living, Creating a Life* by Paul and Sarah Edwards. 1996, Jeremy Tarcher.

☐ *Home-Based Business Manual* by Barbara Mowat. 1990, Province of B.C., Ministry of Regional & Economic Development (Victoria).

☐ *The Home Business Bible* by David R. Eyler. 1994, John Wiley & Sons.

☐ *The Home Office and Small Business Answer Book* by Janet Attard. 1992, Henry Holt.

☐ *How to Raise a Family and a Career Under One Roof* by Lisa M. Roberts. 1996, Bookhaven Press.

☐ *How to Succeed on Your Own* by Karin Abarbanel. 1994, Henry Holt.

☐ *How to Start a Business Without Quitting Your Job: The Moonlight Entrepreneur's Guide* by Philip Holland. 1992, Ten Speed Press.

☐ *The Joy of Working From Home—Making a Life While Making a Living* by Jeff Berner. 1994, Berrett-Koehler Publishers.

☐ *A Kid's Guide to Starting a Business at Home* by Wendy Priesnitz. 1995, The Alternate Press (Canada).

☐ *Making It On Your Own: Surviving and Thriving on the Ups and Downs of Being Self Employed* by Paul & Sarah Edwards. 1991, Jeremy P. Tarcher, Inc.

☐ *Mid-Career Entrepreneur—How to Start a Business and Be Your Own Boss* by Joseph R. Mancuso. 1993, Dearborn Trade.

☐ *900 Know-How: How to Succeed With Your Own 900 Number Business* by Robert Mastin. 1996, 3rd ed., Aegis Publishing Group.

☐ *Scams, Swindles and Rip-Offs— Personal Stories, Power Lessons* by Graham M. Mott. 1994, 2nd edition. (Available from Golden Shadows Press, 4343 West Ponds Circle, Littleton, CO 80123.)

☐ *Small Time Operator—How to Start Your Own Business, Keep Your Books, Pay Your Taxes, and Stay Out of Trouble* by Bernard Kamoroff, CPA. Revised annually. Bell Springs Publishing.

☐ *Starting a Successful Business in Canada* by Jack James. 1995, 13th ed., Self-Counsel Press.

☐ *Working From Home—Everything You Need to Know About Living and Working*

Under the Same Roof by Paul & Sarah Edwards. 1994, 4th ed., Jeremy P. Tarcher, Inc.

☐ *Working Solo: The Real Guide to Freedom & Financial Success With Your Own Business* by Terri Lonier. 1994, Portico Press.

☐ *Working Solo Sourcebook: Essential Resources for Independent Entrepreneurs* by Terri Lonier. 1995, Portico Press.

How-To Business Start-Up Guides (Alphabetically by title)

☐ *The Agri-preneur's Prosperity Manual—How to Survive and Profit in the New Economy and Rediscover the Joy of Rural Living* by Peter Reese. 1995. (Available from Catalyst, P.O. Box 28, New Market, MN 55054-0028.)

☐ *Building a Mail Order Business: A Complete Manual for Success* by William Cohen. 1991, 3rd ed., John Wiley & Sons.

☐ *The Business of Sewing* by Barbara Wright Sykes. 1994. Collins Publications, 3233 Grand Ave., Chino Hills, CA 91709.

☐ *Catering: Start and Run a Money-Making Business* by Judy Richards. 1994, TAB Books.

☐ *Cleaning Up For a Living* by Don Aslett & Mark Browning. 1991, 2nd ed., Betterway Books.

☐ *The Complete Guide to Self-Publishing— Everything You Need to Know to Write, Publish, Promote, and Sell Your Own Book* by Marilyn & Tom Ross. 1994, 3rd ed., Writer's Digest Books.

☐ *Computer Consulting on Your Home-Based PC* by Herman Holtz. 1994, McGraw-Hill.

☐ *Crafting as a Business—The Do-It-Yourself Guide to a Successful Crafts Business* by Wendy Rosen. 1996, Chilton Book Co.

☐ *Crafting for Dollars—How to Establish & Profit from a Career in Crafts* by Sylvia Landman. 1996, Prima.

☐ *Creative Cash—How to Sell Your Crafts, Needlework, Designs & Know-How* by Barbara Brabec. 1995, revised 5th ed. (Available from Barbara Brabec Productions, P.O. Box 2137, Naperville, IL 60567.)

☐ *Flowers for Sale: Growing and Marketing Cut Flowers Backyard to Small Acreage; A Bootstrap Guide* by Lee Sturdivant. 1992. (Available from San Juan Naturals, P.O. Box 642, Friday Harbor, WA 98250.)

☐ *From Kitchen to Market: Selling Your Gourmet Food Specialty* by Stephen F. Hall. 1996, 2nd ed., Upstart Pub. Co.

☐ *Getting Started as a Freelance Illustrator or Designer* by Michael Fleischman. 1990, North Light Books.

☐ *The Greenhouse and Nursery Handbook—A Complete Guide to Growing and Selling Ornamental Plants* by F.X. Jorwik. 1992, Andmar Press.

☐ *Health Service Businesses on Your Home-Based PC* by Rick Benzel. 1993, Windcrest/McGraw-Hill.

☐ *How to Be a Weekend Entrepreneur Making Money at Craft Fairs & Trade Shows* by Susan Ratliff. 1991, Marketing Methods Press.

☐ *How to Get Happily Published—A Complete and Candid Guide* by Judith Appelbaum. 1997, 5th ed., HarperCollins.

☐ *How to Get Started Selling Your Art* by Carole Katchen. 1996, North Light Books.

☐ *How to Make At Least $100,000 Every Year As a Successful Consultant In Your Own Field* by Jeffrey Lant. 1992 rev. ed., JLA Publications.

☐ *How to Make a Whole Lot More Than $1,000,000 Writing, Commissioning, Publishing and Selling "How-To"*

☐ *Information* by Jeffrey Lant. 1990, JLA Publications.

☐ *How to Make Big Profits Publishing City & Regional Books* by Marilyn & Tom Ross. 1987, Communication Creativity.

☐ *How to Make Money Growing Plants, Trees and Flowers* by F.X. Jorwik. 1992, Andmar Press.

☐ *How to Sell Your Photographs and Illustrations* by Elliott & Barbara Gordon. 1990, North Light Books.

☐ *How to Start a Bed & Breakfast Home* by Jan Stankus. July, 1997, 5th ed., Globe Pequot Press.

☐ *How to Start a Bed & Breakfast* by Jan Stankus, 1996, 4th ed., Globe Pequot Press.

☐ *How to Start a Home-Based Catering Business* by Denise Vivaldo. 1996, 2nd ed., Globe Pequot Press.

☐ *How to Start a Home-Based Day-Care Business* by Shari Steelsmith. 1996, Globe Pequot Press.

☐ *How to Start a Home-Based Mail Order Business* by Georganne Fiumara. 1996, Globe Pequot Press.

☐ *How to Start and Operate a Mail Order Business* by Julian L. Simon. 1993, 5th ed., McGraw-Hill.

☐ *How to Start and Run a Writing & Editing Business* by Herman Holtz. 1992, John Wiley & Sons.

☐ *How to Start a Home-Based Landscaping Business* by Owen E. Dell. 1996, 2nd. ed., Globe Pequot Press.

☐ *How to Start a Home-Based Secretarial Services Business* by Jan Melnik. 1996, 2nd ed., Globe Pequot Press.

☐ *How to Succeed as an Independent Consultant* by Herman Holtz. 1993, 3rd ed., John Wiley & Sons.

☐ *How to Succeed on Your Own—Overcoming the Emotional Roadblocks on the Way From Corporation to Cottage, From Employee to Entrepreneur* by Karin Abarbanel. 1994, Henry Holt.

☐ *The Information Broker's Handbook* by Sue Rugge & Alfred Glossbrenner, 1995.

☐ *Information for Sale* by Everett & Crowe. 1994, 2nd ed., Windcrest/McGraw-Hill.

☐ *The Inventor's Handbook: How to Develop, Protect and Market Your Invention* by Robert Park. 1996, 2nd ed., Betterway Books.

☐ *Legal & Paralegal Services on Your Home-Based PC* by Katherine Sheehy Hussey & Rick Benzel. 1994, Windcrest/McGraw-Hill.

☐ *Mail Order Moonlighting* by Cecil C. Hoge, Sr. 1988, 2nd. ed., Ten Speed Press.

☐ *Make Money Reading Books—How to Start and Operate Your Own Home-Based Freelance Reading Service* by Bruce Fife. 1993, Picadilly Books.

☐ *Making Money Making Music (No Matter Where You Live)* by James Dearing. 1990, rev. ed., Writer's Digest Books.

☐ *Making Money Typing at Home Everything You Need to Start, Run and Succeed in Your Own Typing Business at Home* by Peggy Glenn. 1990 rev. ed., Aames-Allen.

☐ *Money Talks: The Complete Guide to Creating a Profitable Workshop or Seminar in Any Field* by Jeffrey Lant. 1992 rev. ed., JLA Publications.

☐ *Newsletters From the Desktop: Designing Effective Publications With Your Computer* by Roger C. Parker. 1990, Ventana Press.

☐ *Newsletter Sourcebook* by Mark Beach. 1993, North Light Books.

☐ *Open Your Own Bed & Breakfast* by Barbara Notarius. 1992, 2nd ed., John Wiley & Sons.

☐ *Owning and Managing a Newsletter Business* by Lisa Rogak. 1995, Upstart Pub. Co.

☐ *Publishing Newsletters—A Complete Guide* by Howard Penn Hudson (publisher of *The Newsletter on Newsletters*, listed in Section II). 2nd ed., Scribner's.

☐ *The Self-Publishing Manual: How to Write, Print and Sell Your Own Book* by Dan Poynter. 1993, 7th ed., Para Publishing.

☐ *Self-Publishing to Tightly-Targeted Markets* by Gordon Burgett. 1989, Communication Unlimited.

☐ *Sell and Resell Your Photos* by Rohn Engh. 1997 4th. ed., Writer's Digest Books.

☐ *Sew Up A Storm: All the Way to the Bank How to Succeed in a Sewing-Related Business* by Karen L. Maslowski. 1995, SewStorm Publishing.

☐ *Start Your Own At-Home Child Care Business* by Patricia Gallagher. 1996, rev. ed., Mosby Lifeline.

☐ *Success in Newsletter Publishing—A Practical Guide* by Frederick D. Goss. Newsletter Publisher's Association (see Section III).

☐ *Talk Your Way to a Successful Career* by James A. Fisher. 1996, Avant Pub. Co.

☐ *The Teaching Marketplace—Make Money With Freelance Teaching, Corporate Trainings, and on the Lecture Circuit* by Bart Brodsky & Janet Geis. 1991, Community Resource Institute Press.

☐ *Word Processing Profits at Home: A Complete Business Plan* by Peggy Glenn. 1992, 2nd ed., Aames-Allen.

Planning and Management

☐ *The Business Plan Guide for Independent Consultants* by Herman Holtz. 1994, John Wiley & Sons.

☐ *The Business Planning Guide: Creating a Plan for Success in Your Own Business* by David H. Bangs, Jr. 1995, 7th ed., Upstart Pub. Co.

☐ *The Entrepreneur's Guide to Growing Up—Taking Your Small Company to the Next Level* by Edna Sheedy. 1993, Self-Counsel Press.

☐ *Fresh Ideas in Letterhead & Business Card Design* by Diana Martin & Mary Cropper. 1993, North Light Books.

☐ *Getting Organized* by Stephanie Winston. 1991 rev. ed., Warner Books.

☐ *The Home Office and Small Business Answer Book* by Janet Attard. 1993, Henry Holt.

☐ *How to Design Trademarks & Logos* by John Murphy & Michael Rowe. 1988, North Light Books.

☐ *How to Get Organized When You Don't Have the Time* by Stephanie Culp. 1986, Betterway Books.

☐ *Letterhead & Logo Design 4* by the editors at Rockport Publishers. 1996, North Light Books.

☐ *101 Home Office Secrets* by Lisa Kanarek. 1994, Career Press.

☐ *101 Simple Things to Grow Your Business* by Dottie Walters and Lilly Walters. 1995, Crisp Pub.

☐ *Organizing Your Home Office for Success—Expert Strategies That Can Work For You* by Lisa Kanarek. 1993, NAL/Dutton (Plume).

☐ *Running a One Person Business* by Claude Whitmyer, Salli Rasberry & Michael Phillips. 1994, rev. ed., Ten Speed Press.

☐ *WorkTips: Organizing Strategies for a Productive Worklife* by Patricia Katz. 1996, Leader Post Carrier Foundation (Canada).

Legal and Financial

☐ *The Business Agreements Kit—How to Legally Protect Your Business with More than 110 Contracts, Letters, Agreements and Forms* by Ted Nicholas. 1996, 2nd ed., Upstart Pub. Co.

☐ *The Complete Book of Small Business Legal Forms* by Daniel Sitarz, Attorney-at-Law. 1996, 2nd ed., Nova Publishing Co.

☐ *The Complete Guide to Consulting Contracts* by Herman Holtz. 1997, 2nd ed., Dearborn.

☐ *The Copyright Handbook: How to Protect and Use Written Works* by Stephen Fishman, 3rd ed., 1996, Nolo Press.

☐ *The Corporate Forms Kit: Contains the Documents You Need to Simplify Procedure and Protect Your Corporate Status* by Ted Nicholas. 1996, 2nd ed. Upstart Pub. Co.

☐ *Everybody's Guide to Small Claims Court* by Attorney Ralph Warner. 1995, 6th ed., Nolo Press.

☐ *Financial Savvy for the Self-Employed* by Grace W. Weinstein. 1995, Henry Holt.

☐ *Government Giveaways for Entrepreneurs II* by Matthew Lesko. 1994, 3rd ed., Information USA.

☐ *Guerilla Financing: Alternative Techniques to Finance Any Small Business* by Bruce Blechman & Jay Conrad Levinson. 1992, Houghton Miflin.

☐ *How to Form Your Own Corporation Without a Lawyer for Under $75* by Ted Nicholas. 1996, 3rd ed., Dearborn Trade.

☐ *How to Profit by Forming Your Own Limited Liability Company* by Scott Friedman. 1995, Upstart Pub. Co.

☐ *Importing to Canada—A Practical Guide to An Exciting and Rewarding Business* by Anne Curran & Glen Mullet. 1995, 5th ed., Self-Counsel Press.

☐ *Incorporate Your Business: The National Corporation Kit* by Daniel Sitarz, Attorney-at-Law. 1996, 2nd ed., Nova Publishing Co.

☐ *Incorporation and Business Guide for British Columbia* by Jack D. James. 1995, 19th ed., Self-Counsel Press.

☐ *INC Yourself—How to Profit by Setting Up Your Own Corporation* by Judith H. McQuown. 1995, 8th ed., Harper Business.

☐ *The Legal Guide to Starting & Running a Small Business* by Fred Steingold. 1995, 2nd ed., Nolo Press.

☐ *Patent, Copyright & Trademark—A Desk Reference to Intellectual Property Law* by Attorney Stephen Elias. 1995, Nolo Press.

☐ *Patent It Yourself* by Attorney David Pressman. 1995, 4th ed., Nolo Press.

☐ *Patent Your Own Invention in Canada—A Complete Step-by-Step Guide* by Sheldon Burshtein. 1991, Self-Counsel Press.

☐ *Smart Tax Write-offs: Hundreds of tax deduction ideas for home-based businesses, independent contractors, all entrepreneurs* by Norm Ray, CPA. 1996, Rayve Productions.

☐ *Stand Up to the IRS: Defend Yourself in an Audit* by Tax Attorney Frederick W. Daily. 1996, Nolo Press.

☐ *Tax Planning and Preparation Made Easy for the Self-Employed* by G. Dent & J. Johnson. 1996, John Wiley & Sons.

☐ *Trademark: How to Name Your Business and Product* by Kate McGarth & Stephen Elias. 1996, 2nd ed., Nolo Press.

Marketing and Publicity

- [ ] *Advertising Manager's Handbook* by Robert W. Bly. 1993, Prentice Hall.

- [ ] *Big Ideas for Small Service Businesses: How to Successfully Advertise, Publicize, and Maximize Your Business or Professional Practice* by Marilyn and Tom Ross. 1993, 2nd ed., Communication Creativity.

- [ ] *Book Publishing Resource Guide* by Marie Kiefer. 1997 ed. Ad-Lib Publications.

- [ ] *Cash Copy—How to Offer Your Products and Services So Your Prospects Buy Them . . . Now* by Jeffrey Lant. 1992, 2nd ed., JLA Publications.

- [ ] *The Complete Direct Marketing Sourcebook* by John Kremer. 1992, John Wiley & Sons.

- [ ] *Finding Your Niche—Marketing Your Professional Service* by Bart Brodsky & Janet Geis. 1992, Community Resource Institute Press.

- [ ] *Getting Business to Come to You* by Paul & Sarah Edwards & Laura Clampitt Douglas. 1991, Jeremy P. Tarcher, Inc.

- [ ] *Getting Publicity—A Do-It-Yourself Guide for Small Business and Non-Profit Groups* by Tana Fletcher & Julia Rockler. 1995, 2nd ed., Self-Counsel Press.

- [ ] *Great Connections—Small Talk and Networking for Businesspeople* by Anne Baber & Lynne Waymon. 1992, 2nd ed., Waymon & Associates.

- [ ] *Guerrilla Marketing for the Home-Based Business* by Jay Levinson & Seth Godin. 1995, Houghton Mifflin.

- [ ] *Guerilla Marketing—How to Make Big Profits in Your Small Business* by Jay Conrad Levinson. 1985, Houghton Mifflin.

- [ ] *Handmade for Profit—Hundreds of Secrets to Success in Selling Arts & Crafts* by Barbara Brabec. 1996, M. Evans and Co.

- [ ] *Keeping Clients Satisfied—Make Your Service Business More Successful and Profitable* by Robert W. Bly. 1993, Prentice Hall.

- [ ] *Let Your Customers Do the Talking: 301+ Word-of-Mouth Marketing Tactics Guaranteed to Boost Profits* by Michael Cafferky. 1995, Dearborn.

- [ ] *Making $$$ At Home—Over 1,000 Editors Who Want Your Ideas, Know-How & Experience* by Darla Sims. 1996, Sunstar Publishing.

- [ ] *Marketing Online Low-Cost, High-Yield Strategies for Small Businesses & Professionals* by Marcia Yudkin. 1996, Plume.

- [ ] *Marketing Your Home-Based Business* by Jeffrey P. Davidson. 1990, Bob Adams.

- [ ] *Marketing With Newsletters—How to boost sales, add members & raise funds with a printed, faxed or Web-site newsletter* by Elaine Floyd. 1997, 2nd ed., Newsletter Resources.

- [ ] *Marketing Without Advertising—Creative Strategies for Small Business Success* by Michael Phillips & Salli Rasberry. 1989, Nolo Press.

- [ ] *The Market Planning Guide—Gaining and Maintaining the Competitive Edge* by David H. Bangs, Jr. 1995, 4th ed., Upstart Pub. Co.

- [ ] *Money Making Marketing—Finding the People Who Need What You're Selling and Making Sure They Buy It* by Jeffrey Lant. 1991 rev. ed., JLA Publications.

- [ ] *Multi-Level Money: The Complete Guide to Generating, Closing & Working with All The Prospects You Need to Make Real Money Every Month In Network Marketing* by Jeffrey Lant. 1994, JLA Publications.

- [ ] *Niche Marketing For Writers, Speakers and Entrepreneurs—How to Make Yourself Indispensable, Slightly Immortal,*

☐ *and Lifelong Rich in 18 Months* by Gordon Burgett. 1993, Communication Unlimited.

☐ *No More Cold Calls—The Complete Guide to Generating and Closing All the Prospects You Need to Become a Multi-Millionaire by Selling Your Service* by Jeffrey Lant. 1992, JLA Publications.

☐ *1001 Ways to Market Your Books* by John Kremer. 1997, 5th ed., Ad-Lib Publications.

☐ *Persuading on Paper: The Complete Guide to Writing Copy That Pulls in Business* by Marcia Yudkin. Plume, 1996.

☐ *Point & Click Business Builder—How to Get Online and Make Your Small Business or Home Business Muscular* by Seth Godin. 1996, Upstart Pub. Co.

☐ *Priced to Sell: The Complete Guide to More Profitable Pricing* by Herman Holtz. 1996, Upstart Pub. Co.

☐ *The Publicity Manual* by Kate Kelly. 1996, rev. ed., Visibility Enterprises, 11 Rockwood Drive, Larchmont, NY 10538.

☐ *Selling to Uncle Sam: How to Win Choice Government Contracts For Your Business* by Clinton L. Crownover & Mark Henricks. 1993, McGraw-Hill.

☐ *Selling Your Services—Proven Strategies for Getting Clients to Hire You (or Your Firm)* by Robert W. Bly. 1991, Henry Holt & Co.

☐ *Talk is Cheap—Promoting Your Business Through Word of Mouth Advertising* by Godfrey Harris. 1991, The Americas Group.

☐ *That's a Great Idea—How to Get, Evaluate, Protect, Develop, and Sell New Product Ideas* by Tony Husch & Linda Foust. 1990, Ten Speed Press.

☐ *Turning Your Great Idea Into a Great Success* by Judy Ryder. 1995, Peterson's, 1995.

☐ *The Unabashed Self-Promoter's Guide: What Every Man, Woman, Child and Organization in America Needs to Know About Getting Ahead by Exploiting the Media* by Jeffrey Lant. 1992, 2nd. ed., JLA Publications.

☐ *Web Wealth—How to Turn the World Wide Web Into a Cash Hose For You and Your Business* by Jeffrey Lant. 1996. JLA Publications.

☐ *The Woodworker's Guide to Pricing Your Work* by Dan Ramsey. 1995, Betterway Books.

Mail-Order Book Sources

☐ *Barbara Brabec's Books & Reports.* For information about the author's other home-business books and reports, write to Barbara Brabec/HMM5, P.O. Box 2137, Naperville, IL 60567.

☐ *Directory Marketplace.* Source for business books and directories of all kinds. Todd Publications, P.O. Box 635, Nyack, NY 10960.

☐ *Maverick Mail Order Bookstore.* Books and directories of interest to writers, speakers, desktop publishers, book publishers, marketers and consultants, including titles by publishing consultants Marilyn and Tom Ross. Free from Communication Creativity Corp., P.O. Box 909-BB, Buena Vista, CO 81211.

☐ *Be Your Own Boss Catalog.* Start-up manuals on 200 types of businesses, free from *Entrepreneur Magazine*, (800) 421-2300.

☐ *Self-Counsel Press Catalog.* Start-and-run guides, including titles on direct mail, exporting, franchising, accounting, advertising and marketing. Free from Self-Counsel Press, 1704 N. State St., Bellingham, WA 98225.

☐ *Sure-Fire Business Success Catalog.* Hundreds of books, reports and tapes of interest to entrepreneurs, including those published by Jeffrey Lant on topics of marketing, publicity, consulting and self-publishing. Free from Jeffrey Lant Associates, Inc., 50 Follen St., Suite 507, Cambridge, MA 02138.

☐ *Upstart Catalog.* A line of business books featuring titles by author David H. Bangs, Jr. Free from Upstart Pub. Co., Inc., 155 N. Wacker Dr., Chicago, IL 60606.

☐ *The Whole Work Catalog.* One of the largest and best selections of career/entrepreneurial books available by mail; $1 from New Careers Center, Box 2193, Boulder, CO 80306.

☐ *Writer's Digest Catalog* and *North Light Books Catalog.* The first catalog will be of interest to writers, songwriters and photographers; the second includes titles for artists, and desktop publishers. Free from Writer's Digest/North Light Books, 1507 Dana Ave., Cincinnati, OH 45207.

SECTION II: PERIODICALS

Home Business/Entrepreneurial/ Opportunity Publications

For content information of these periodicals, request subscription information or price of a sample copy. (Note many of these publishers now have a presence on the World Wide Web.)

☐ *The Business Woman's Advantage*, 921 Gregory Lane, Schaumburg, IL 60193. Business newsletter published by Mershon Shrigley.

☐ *Eagle News—Tips, Tactics and Thoughts for Those Who Would Soar!*, 2005 Shore Rd., Ocean View, NJ 08230. Motivational newsletter published by Walter Boomsma.

☐ *Entrepreneur: The Small Business Authority.* A monthly magazine available on newsstands.

☐ *Home Business Report*, 2949 Ash St., Abbotsford, British Columbia. V2S 4G5 Canada. Alison Gardner, associate editor. This quarterly magazine serves readers nationally.

☐ *Home Office Computing.* A monthly magazine available on newsstands.

☐ *Homeworking Mothers*, P.O. Box 423, East Meadow, NY 11554. Quarterly newsletter of the Mothers Home Business Network, published by Georganne Fiumara.

☐ *Income Opportunities—America's #1 Source of Money-Making Ideas.* A monthly magazine available on newsstands.

☐ *New Business Opportunities—The Business Start-Up Magazine.* A monthly magazine available on newsstands.

☐ *Opportunity Evaluation Newsletter*, G.C. Associates, P.O. Box 28521, Bellingham, WA 98228. A bimonthly newsletter published by George Czerlinski.

☐ *Publishing Entrepreneur—Profit Strategies for the Information and Publishing Industry*, 121 E. Front St., Suite 401, Traverse City, MI 49684. Mardi Link, editor.

☐ *The Real Entrepreneur*, 806 Kings Row, Cohutta, GA 30710. A monthly newsletter of money-making opportunities published by Bob Reimke.

☐ *Rolling Ventures*, P.O. Box 2190, Pahrump, NV 89041. A money-making newsletter published by Gary Stewart for RVers.

☐ *Roman Reports*, 12600 Rockside Rd., Suite 107, Garfield Heights, OH 44125. This bimonthly, published by Dave Roman, evaluates "get-rich ads" and "opportunities."

☐ *Svoboda's Home & Small Business,* 1440 W. Pratt Blvd., #1, Chicago, IL 60626-4277. Monthly newspaper for Chicago's independent professionals. Jill Cleary, editor.

Marketing Periodicals

☐ *Classified Communication,* Agnes Franz Advertising, P.O. Box 4177, Prescott, AZ 86302. This newsletter, published by Agnes Franz, illustrates how to cut ad costs by tightening copy, which words pull best, etc.

☐ *Direct Marketing,* 224 Seventh St., Garden City, NY 11530. A trade magazine for direct marketers with good articles on how to write better ad copy and get better results from direct response advertising.

☐ *The Direct Response Specialist,* Direct Response Specialist, P.O. Box 1075, Tarpon Springs, FL 34688. A monthly how-to newsletter published by Galen Stilson for professional mail marketers, with emphasis on effective response/profit techniques.

☐ *Info Marketing Report,* P.O. Box 2038, Vancouver, WA 98668. This monthly from Jerry Buchanan is targeted to everyone interested in creating and selling informational packages of any kind.

☐ *Radio-TV Interview Report,* Bradley Communications Corp., 135 E. Plumstead Ave., #102, Lansdowne, PA 19050. This twice-monthly ad medium published by Bill Harrison reaches 3,800 talk show hosts, producers and program directors.

☐ *Yearbook of Experts, Authorities & Spokespersons,* Broadcast Interview Source, 2233 Wisconsin Ave. N.W., Washington, DC 20007. A major newsroom and talk show reference published annually. (Request listing form.)

Special-Interest Business Periodicals

☐ *Advantage Digest—Your Only Source for the Latest in Network Marketing &*

☐ *Business Opportunities,* 7 Broadway #642, New York, NY 10004. Published bimonthly by Kevin N. Lee.

☐ *Apparel Industry Magazine & Sourcebook,* 180 Allen Rd., Suite 300, Atlanta, GA 30328. A trade magazine available by subscription only.

☐ *Book Marketing Update,* Open Horizons Publishing Co., P.O. Box 205, Fairfield, IA 52556-0205. A bimonthly newsletter published by John Kremer for book publishers and other businesses looking for media opportunities.

☐ *The Business of Herbs,* 439 Ponderosa Way, Jemez Springs, NM 87025. A bimonthly trade journal published by Paula Oliver for herb-related businesses.

☐ *Consulting Opportunities Journal,* Consultant's National Resource Center, Box 430, Clear Springs, MD 21722. Bimonthly newsletter from consultant Steve Lanning.

☐ *Craft Marketing News,* The Front Room Publishers, P.O. Box 1541, Clifton, NJ 07015. Adele Patti publishes this monthly newsletter for professional crafters in search of new marketing outlets.

☐ *The Crafts Report—The Business Journal for the Crafts Industry,* P.O. Box 1992, Wilmington, DE 19899. This monthly magazine focuses on marketing, management and money. Bernadette S. Finnerty, editor.

☐ *Craft Supply Magazine—The Independent Journal for the Professional Crafter,* 225 Gordons Corner Plaza, Box 420, Manalapan, NJ 07726. Good source for information on wholesale suppliers and trade shows. Maria Nerius, editor.

☐ *The Dream Merchant—How to Make Money From Good Ideas,* 2309 Torrance Blvd., Suite 201, Torrance, CA 90501. A bimonthly magazine for inventors and others interested in profiting from their creativity. Mike Foley, editor.

☐ *Flash—The Premier Journal of Desktop Printing*, BlackLightning Publishing, Inc., Riddle Pond Rd., West Topsham, VT 05086. This informative bimonthly is published by Walter Vose Jeffries.

☐ *Gift Basket News*, 9655 Chimneyville Lane, Suite 1036, Dallas, TX 75243. Newsletter of business, marketing and product information for gift basket retailers.

☐ *Gift Basket Review—The Magazine of the Gift Basket Industry*, 815 Haines St., Jacksonville, FL 32206. A quarterly connection to suppliers in the industry, marketing insight, trade show news, etc. Kathy Horak, editor.

☐ *Image Networker*, P.O. Box 62465, Colorado Springs, CO 80962. Quarterly networking newsletter for professionals in the image or corporate consulting business.

☐ *Interior Design* magazine and related *Buyers Guide* are published by Cahners Publications, 249 West 17th St., New York, NY 10011.

☐ *MarketWave*, P.O. Box 27587, Fresno, CA 93729. Leonard W. Clements publishes this business analysis newsletter focusing on the MLM industry.

☐ *MT Monthly—The Monthly Newsletter for Medical Transcriptionists*, Computer Systems Management, 1633 N.E. Rosewood Dr., Gladstone, MO 64118. The first and only monthly for the nation's 120,000 medical language specialists. Jennifer Martin, editor.

☐ *Neighbors and Friends—The Art & Crafts Market Guide*, 3410 Black Champ Rd., Midlothian, TX 76065. This monthly magazine for professional crafters is published by Renee Chase.

☐ *The Newsletter on Newsletters*, The Newsletter Clearinghouse, P.O. Box 311, Rhinebeck, NY 12572. Editor Howard Penn Hudson reviews new newsletters and brings readers information about the latest developments in the industry.

☐ *Photo Stock Notes*, PhotoSource, Int'l., 1910 35th Rd., Dept. 10, Pine Lake Farm, Osceola, WI 54020. Published monthly by Rohn Engh, this marketing newsletter pairs picture buyers with the collections of photographers.

☐ *The Professional Quilter*, 104 Bramblewood Lane, Lewisberry, PA 17339. A quarterly magazine published by Morna McEver Golletz.

☐ *Sew Up A Storm*, SewStorm Publishing, 944 Sutton Rd., Cincinnati, OH 45230-3581. A quarterly newsletter for sewing entrepreneurs published by Karen L. Maslowski.

☐ *Sharing Ideas*, Royal Publishing, Inc., P.O. Box 1120, Glendora, CA 91740. Bimonthly networking and marketing newsmagazine published by Dottie Walters for professional speakers, meeting planners, agents, consultants, trainers and seminar leaders worldwide.

☐ *Shifting Gears—Working At Home For a Quality Life*, P.O. Box 194, Bryn Mawr, PA 19010. A quarterly newsletter published by Lynn Kerrigan.

☐ *Sunshine Artist—America's Premier Show and Festival Publication*, 2600 Temple Dr., Winter Park, FL 32789. Monthly magazine published by David F. Cook.

☐ *Tips for Multi-Level Mailers*, P.O. Box 86036, Madeira Beach, FL 33738. Charles G. Possick publishes this newsletter and other publications for MLMers who recruit by mail.

☐ *Winning Ways News*, P.O. Box 39412, Minneapolis, MN 55439. This motivational bimonthly newsletter is published by Barbara J. Winter for self-employed individuals.

☐ *Workamper News*, 201 Hiram Rd., Heber Springs, AR 72543-8747. A bimonthly newsletter published by Greg & Debbie Robus for individuals interested in working-while-camping.

SECTION III: ORGANIZATIONS AND DIRECTORIES

Selected Business and Trade Organizations

This is just a small sampling of organizations likely to be of interest to homebased entrepreneurs. To find others (or to find a new address if mail is returned), check library directories such as *National Trade and Professional Associations of the United States & Canada* (Columbia Books) or *Encyclopedia of Associations* (Gale Research Co.).

The benefits of membership in a business or trade organization are numerous, including:

- group insurance programs
- discounts on business products and services
- merchant card service (VISA/MasterCard)
- annual buyer or supplier guides
- access to membership directories (helpful for marketing purposes), special reports, books or industry guidelines
- a subscription to the organization's trade magazine or newsletter
- professional certification programs
- educational or business conferences, workshops and trade shows

For complete information about specific membership benefits of any organization listed below, request a free brochure.

☐ The American Association of Home-Based Businesses, P.O. Box 10023, Rockville, MD 20849.

☐ American Craft Enterprises (trade arm of the American Crafts Council, listed below), 21 S. Elting Corners Rd., Highland, NY 12528.

☐ American Crafts Council, 72 Spring St., New York, NY 10012.

☐ American Institute of Professional Bookkeepers, 6001 Montrose Rd., Suite 207, Rockville, MD 20852.

☐ American Society of Indexers, P.O. Box 386, Port Aransas, TX 78373.

☐ American Society of Interior Designers, 608 Massachusetts Ave., N.E., Washington, DC 20002.

☐ American Woman's Economic Development Corporation, 71 Vanderbuilt Ave., Suite 320, New York, NY 10169.

☐ Artists Equity Association, Inc., P.O. Box 28068, Washington, DC 20038.

☐ Association of Part-Time Professionals, Inc., 7700 Leesburg Pike, Suite 216, Falls Church, VA 22043.

☐ Canadian Association for Home-Based Business, 1200E Prince of Wales Drive, Ottawa, Ontario, K2C 1M9 Canada.

☐ Canadian Direct Marketing Association, 1 Concorde Gate, Suite 401, Toronto, Ontario M3C 3N6 Canada.

☐ Council of Better Business Bureaus, Inc., 4200 Wilson Blvd., Suite 800, Arlington, VA 22203.

☐ The Direct Marketing Association, 1120 Avenue of the Americas, New York, NY 10036.

☐ The Freelance Editorial Association, Box 380835, Cambridge, MA 02238.

☐ Graphic Artists Guild, 11 W. 20 St., 8th Fl., New York, NY 10011-3704.

☐ Hobby Industry Association of America, 319 E. 54th St., Elmwood Park, NJ 07407.

☐ Home Business Institute, Inc., P.O. Box 301, White Plains, NY 10605-0301.

☐ The Home Office and Business Opportunities Association, 92 Corporate Park, Suite C-250, Irvine, CA 92714.

☐ Home Office Association of America, 909 Third Ave., Suite 9909, New York, NY 10022.

☐ International Franchise Association, 1350 New York Ave., N.W., Washington, DC 20005.

☐ Inventors Workshop International, 1029 Castillo St., Santa Barbara, CA 93101.

☐ Museum Store Association, 501 S. Cherry St., #460, Denver, CO 80222.

☐ National Association for the Self-Employed, P.O. Box 612067, Dallas, TX 75261-2067.

☐ National Association for the Specialty Food Trade, Inc., 120 Wall Street, 27th Fl., New York, NY 10005.

☐ National Association of Desktop Publishers, 462 Old Boston Rd., Topsfield, MA 01983.

☐ The National Association of Fine Artists, P.O. Box 4189, Ft. Lauderdale, FL 33338.

☐ National Association of Secretarial Services, 3637 4th St. N., Suite 330, St. Petersburg, FL 33704.

☐ The National Business Association, 5151 Belt Line Rd., #1150, Dallas, TX 75240.

☐ National Federation of Independent Business, 600 Maryland Ave. S.W., Suite 700, Washington, DC 20024.

☐ National Mail Order Association, 2807 Polk St., Minneapolis, MN 55418.

☐ The National Needlework Association, Inc., P.O. Box 2188, Zanesville, OH 43702.

☐ The National Writers Club, 1450 South Havana, Suite 424, Aurora, CO 80012.

☐ Newsletter Publisher's Association, 1401 Wilson Blvd., Suite 207, Arlington, VA 22209.

☐ Ontario Crafts Council, Craft Resource Centre, 35 McCaul St., Toronto, Ontario M5T 1V7 Canada.

☐ Professional Secretaries International, Box 20404, Kansas City, MO 64195.

☐ Small Publishers Association of North America, P.O. Box 1306, Buena Vista, CO 81211-1306.

☐ Society of Craft Designers, P.O. Box 2188, Zanesville, OH 43702.

☐ SOHO America, 10800 Lyndale Ave., Suite 200, Minneapolis, MN 55420.

☐ Support Services Alliance, Inc., P.O. Box 130, Schoharie, NY 12157-0130.

☐ Toy Manufacturers of America, 200 Fifth Ave., New York, NY 10010.

☐ Volunteer Lawyers for the Arts, One E. 53rd St., 6th Fl., New York, NY 10022.

Key Library Resources and Privately Published Directories

Directories are one of your most important marketing tools. Use them to gain a general understanding of the size of the field or industry in which you are interested or involved, to find a particular address or telephone number, or to compile targeted mailing lists for press releases or special marketing projects.

Following are key directories available in libraries and bookstores, along with lesser-known, privately published reference guides available only by mail (for which a contact address has been provided). Prices have not been included since they are always subject to change. Generally however, directories range in price from $20-$250. Request more information from the publisher.

☐ *Artist's & Graphic Designer's Market* (Writer's Digest Books). This annual

☐ directory lists 2,500 buyers of all types of commercial artwork, including magazine and book publishers, ad agencies, greeting card companies and more.

☐ Artist's Marketing Directories. *Artworld Hotline Newsletter* and four related directories galleries, artist exhibition spaces, corporate art collectors and art publishers are published by Art Network, P.O. Box 1268, Penn Valley, CA 95946.

☐ *Ayer Directory of Newspapers & Periodicals.* Lists newspapers, magazines and periodicals published in the United States and Canada, with circulation and rate info, maps and market data.

☐ *Bacon's Publicity Checker.* Revised annually, this is a two-volume directory, one listing media contacts at over 8,000 business, trade, consumer and farm magazines in the United States and Canada; the other listing 1,700 U.S. and Canadian daily newspapers and over 8,000 U.S. weekly newspapers.

☐ *Books In Print* and *Forthcoming Books* (R.R. Bowker). Your complete guide to all books still in print and new ones scheduled for publication.

☐ *Chase's Annual Events* (Contemporary Books). Published annually in November, this is a useful PR tool for publicity seekers who want to tie their business news into major events, anniversaries and special occasions in the United States.

☐ *Directory of Printers* by Marie Kiefer. The 1997 edition lists nearly 800 printers (books, catalogs, magazines and other bound publications) you can work with by mail. From Ad-Lib Publications, 51-1/2 W. Adams, Fairfield, IA 52556.

☐ *Directory of Directory Publishers.* Lists some 9,000 directory publishers worldwide and the titles they publish. From Directory Marketplace (which also publishes a related newsletter and sells by mail many of the directories mentioned on this list), Box 301, W. Nyack, NY 10994.

☐ *Dun & Bradstreet Directories.* The "who, what and where" of commercial and industrial activity around the world. Several volumes list companies by annual dollar volume; within each directory, companies are listed alphabetically, geographically and by product classifications.

☐ *Encyclopedia of Associations* (Gale Research Co.). A complete guide to organizations and associations in all fields: trade, business, commercial, environmental, legal, technological, hobby, etc.

☐ *Gebbie Press All-in-One Directory* (Gebbie Press). Revised annually, this guide includes every daily and weekly newspaper, radio and TV stations, plus consumer and trade magazines.

☐ *The Gift & Decorative Accessory Buyer's Guide* is an annual directory (companion to trade magazine of the same name) that lists some 30,000 manufacturers, importers and distributors serving the gift industry; with sources for manufacturing and assembling materials, show and shop display cases, classifications of trade names, listings of trade shows and more. Gifts & Decorative Accessories, 51 Madison Ave., New York, NY 10010.

☐ *Hudson's Subscription Newsletter Directory.* Published annually, this is a useful marketing tool because it indicates which newsletters buy freelance material and invite press releases. Available from The Newsletter Clearinghouse. (See related *Newsletter on Newsletters* listed in Section II).

☐ *Literary Market Place* (R.R. Bowker). Includes addresses for trade book publishers, wholesalers and distributors, plus book reviewers for radio, television, magazines, newspapers and syndicates; printers, art and design services; direct mail promotion services, and more.

☐ *Matthews Media Directory.* Published three times a year; Canadian dailies, magazines, radio and TV contacts. Available from Canadian Corporate News, 1 Financial Pl., #500, 25 Adelaide St. East, Toronto, Ontario, M5C 3A1 Canada.

☐ *Directory of Business Incubators.* Will help you find an incubator (special center to help businesses in their early stages). Published annually by National Business Incubation Association, One President St., Athens, OH 45701.

☐ *National Directory of Catalogs* (Oxbridge Communications). Describes the products carried by over 4,000 U.S. and Canadian catalogs, with contact names, list rental data and production information for each.

☐ *National Trade and Professional Associations of the U.S.* (Columbia Books). Includes over 7,000 associations listed alphabetically and geographically.

☐ *Oxbridge Directory of Newsletters* (Oxbridge Communications). Lists more than 15,000 newsletters with information on subscription lists available for rental.

☐ *Photographer's Market.* (Writer's Digest Books). Updated annually, it lists 2,500 international photo buyers periodicals, ad agency, book publishers, galleries and stock photo agencies.

☐ *Power Media Selects.* This annual directory, compiled by Alan Caruba, profiles only the most influential U.S. print and broadcast media contacts, including leading newswires and syndicates, the top 50 dailies, major radio-TV networks and talk shows, city and regional business publications and the most influential columnists and newsletter editors. For more info, and a free *PowerSources* newsletter, mention this book when you write to Broadcast Interview Source, 2233 Wisconsin Ave., N.W., Washington, DC 20007.

☐ *Small Press Record of Books in Print.* This annual directory, now available only on CD-ROM, is used as an ordering tool by libraries, bookstores, teachers and individual readers interested in finding books by the independent press. To get your books listed in the next edition, send for free listing form from Dustbooks, P.O. Box 100, Paradise, CA 95969.

☐ *The Standard Periodical Directory* (Oxbridge Communications). The largest authoritative annual guide to U.S. and Canadian periodicals consumer magazines, trade journals, newsletters, government publications, house organs, directories, yearbooks, literary and social group publications, etc.

☐ *Standard Rate and Data Service (SRCS)* directories list business, trade and technical publications categorized by markets served; includes marketing demographics, information about mailing lists, and special distribution programs for marketers.

☐ *Thomas Register of American Manufacturers.* Its 23 volumes profile over 152,000 companies, with a description of over 50,000 individual product and service headings, and 112,000 trade and brand names. Helpful when you're trying to locate raw material suppliers, wholesale supply sources or the owners of brand names and trademarks.

☐ *Ulrich's International Periodicals Directory* (R.R. Bowker). Published annually and updated quarterly, this directory lists some 65,000 periodicals published around the world.

☐ *Writer's Market* (Writer's Digest Books). This annual directory lists 4,000 book and magazine markets, syndicates, contests and awards, writer's workshops and agents.

Online Services

☐ CompuServe Information Service, P.O. Box 20212, Columbus, OH 43220. Includes the *Working from Home Forum*, the *International Entrepreneur's Network* and the *Consultants Forum*. (800) 848-8199.

☐ GEnie (GE Network for Information Exchange), 401 North Washington St., Mail Stop MC5A, Rockville, MD 20850. Offers a wide range of business and computer support groups, including the *Home-Office/Small Business Roundtable.* (800) 638-9636.

☐ Prodigy Interactive Personal Service, Prodigy Services Co., 445 Hamilton Ave., White Plains, NY 10601. Offers some home-business advice and computer software reviews. (800) PRODIGY.

SECTION IV: GOVERNMENT AND SMALL BUSINESS AGENCIES

U.S. Government Agencies

Your tax dollars are paying for the thousands of small business publications offered by your federal government, so be sure to take advantage of this help when you start a business. Free information is available by mail from any of these agencies. If you are online, also look for the government information site on the Internet and World Wide Web.

☐ Bureau of Consumer Protection, Division of Special Statutes, 6th & Pennsylvania Ave. N.W., Washington, DC 20580. Your source for information on labels required on wool garments or textile products of any kind.

☐ Bureau of the Census, Customer Services, Data User Services Div., Washington, DC 20233. Demographic and economic statistics for marketing purposes. The Bureau also publishes a number of guides, catalogs and indexes.

☐ Consumer Information Center, P.O. Box 100, Pueblo, CO 81002. Send for the free *Consumer Information Catalog*, which describes free and low-cost federal publications of consumer interest including useful booklets on money management and small business. If you're interested in patent information, *General Information Concerning Patents* is available for $2 from this address.

☐ Consumer Products Safety Commission Bureau of Compliance, 5401 Westbard Ave., Bethesda, MD 20207. Various free booklets from this government agency explain consumer safety laws and regulations you may need to know about. In particular ask about: *The Federal Hazardous Substances Act; The Consumer Product Safety Act of 1972*; and *The Flammable Fabrics Act.* To hear various recorded messages from this office, call this toll-free number: (800) 638-2772.

☐ Cooperative Extension Service. Extension services are a part of the U.S. Department of Agriculture and the Land Grant University of each state. A national office in Washington oversees state programs, and each state has an office with subject matter specialists in many different areas. These specialists train and work with county extension home economists, among others, who in turn work with the general public. Home business owners and others who want to start businesses should connect with their county extension office by calling the county seat.

☐ The Copyright Office, Register of Copyrights, Library of Congress, Washington, DC 20559. If you have created an original work of any kind, and want to protect it from theft by others who would profit from your creativity, request all free publications available, including: *The Nuts and Bolts of Copyright* (Circular R1); and *Trademarks* (Circular R13).

☐ Department of Commerce, Office of Consumer Affairs, Washington, DC 20233. If you're interested in importing/exporting, start with this government agency for information. For information about the use of endorsements and testimonials, or warranties and guarantees, ask for these free booklets: *Advertising, Packaging & Labeling* and *Product Warranties and Servicing.*

- [ ] Department of Labor. For information relating to your status as an employer or an independent contractor, contact your local Labor Department, Wage & Hour Division. Look in the telephone book under "U.S. Government."

- [ ] Federal Trade Commission, Div. of Legal & Public Records, 6th St. & Pennsylvania Ave. N.W., Washington, DC 20580. The FTC is especially concerned with truth in advertising and the mail order industry (information about which is contained in the booklets available from the Department of Commerce). They also enforce trade practice rules and labeling requirements applicable to certain industries and offer such free booklets as *Guide for the Jewelry Industry*; *The Hand Knitting Yarn Industry*; and *Catalog Jewelry and Giftware Industry.*

- [ ] Food and Drug Administration, 5600 Fishers Lane, Rockville, MD 20857. Will provide information on federal, state and local requirements governing packaging and labeling of food-related products.

- [ ] Internal Revenue Service. Your local IRS can always provide information on request. Some publications of interest to new business owners are: *Your Business Tax Kit*; *Business Use of Your Home*; *Determining Whether a Worker is an Employee*; and *Tax Information for Direct Sellers.*

- [ ] Patent & Trademark Office, U.S. Department of Commerce, Washington, DC 20231. This office will send you free information about patents and trademarks. Or, if you'd like to hear informative prerecorded messages on the telephone, you may call this toll-free number: (800) 786-9199.

- [ ] U.S. Small Business Administration (SBA) and SCORE (Service Corps of Retired Executives). The SBA's mission is to help people get into business and stay there. Help is available from local district offices of the SBA in the form of free business counseling and training from more than 8,000 SCORE volunteers nationwide. (See your local telephone directory under SCORE, U.S. Government or Small Business Administration.)

  The SBA office in Washington has a special Women's Business Enterprise section that provides free information on loans, tax deductions and other financial matters. District offices offer special training programs in management, marketing and accounting.

  To receive a listing of all the low-cost management and assistance publications and bibliographies available from the SBA, write to: SBA Publications, P.O. Box 30, Denver, CO 80201-0030. Ask for *SBA Form 115A.*

  Finally, there is a toll-free SBA information line offering a variety of prerecorded messages and a connection to your nearest SBA or SCORE office. Call (800) U-ASK-SBA. (800) 827-5722.

Selected Canadian Government and Economic Development Resources

- [ ] Alberta Ministry of Economic Development, 12th Fl., Sterling Place, 9940 - 106 St., Edmonton, Alberta T5K 2P6 Canada. Offers booklets on small business.

- [ ] B.C. Business Information Center, 601 West Cordova St., Vancouver, British Columbia V6B 1G1 Canada. This is the main source of business information for the province. Canadians may call toll-free: (800) 972-3900.

- [ ] Canadian Council of Better Business Bureaus, 2180 Steeles Ave. West, #219, Concord, Ontario L4K 2Z5 Canada. Offers brochure on work-at-home schemes.

☐ "Enquiry B.C." This Provincial toll-free telephone information service will refer you to the appropriate ministry, branch or department of government you may need to contact. Call (800) 663-7867 from 7 A.M. to 7 P.M. Monday-Friday.

☐ Federal Business Development Bank, Business Information Centre, 601 W. Hastings, 7th Fl., Vancouver, British Columbia V6B 5G9 Canada. Local FBDB offices offer counselling service assistance to small enterprises and information, including booklet, *Assistance to Business in Canada.*

☐ Ministry of Consumer and Commercial Relations, Upholstered and Stuffed Articles Branch, 3300 Bloor Street West, 3rd Fl., Toronto, Ontario M8X 2X4 Canada. Information on labeling and license requirements for makers of products that contain stuffing of any kind.

☐ Ministry of Small Business, Tourism & Culture, 1405 Douglas St., Victoria, British Columbia V8W 3C1 Canada. Source for general business information.

☐ "Reference Canada." When you don't know who else to ask, call this toll-free number for answers and referrals to information sources throughout Canada: (800) 667-3355.

☐ Revenue Canada Taxation Information Services, 123 Slater St., Ottawa, Ontario K1A 0L8 Canada. Ask for *Business and Professional Income Tax Guide* and information on goods and service tax (GST) applicable to all businesses in Canada grossing $30,000 or more.

☐ Tourism Saskatechewan, 500-1900 Albert St., Regina, Saskatchewan, S4P 4L9 Canada. Offers information on a wide variety of business topics, including all government programs relevant to business; and booklet, *Starting a Small Business in Saskatchewan.*

SECTION V: OTHER RESOURCES

Again, the previous listings represent only a fraction of the publications and organizations that are out there for the homebased business entrepreneur. As you dig further into your chosen field, you are bound to discover a multitude of other resources that will help you along your way as well. You can record them in the space that follows.

INDEX

Earlier editions of this book carried a note on this page asking readers to write to me about their businesses. They did, and many of those individuals are quoted in this edition of *Homemade Money*. I look forward to hearing from you someday, too.

While it's impossible for me to correspond personally with readers (unless I'm working with them in regard to publishing some of their information), I value reader mail nonetheless. It is my daily mail that gives me inspiration and encouragement to continue my work.

If you write to me for any reason, your name will be placed on my mailing list to receive information about all my home-business books and reports. Please use the specially coded address below, which automatically tells me you've read this book.

You may be interested to know that *Homemade Money* has been recognized as one of the most comprehensive books of its kind. Upon publication of the fifth edition in 1994, it was a selection of three book clubs. Now with over 100,000 copies sold, it continues to serve the needs of an ever-growing audience of individuals interested in starting a business at home.

In addition to having a huge fan club of personal readers, *Homemade Money* is recommended by SBA and SCORE advisers, Cooperative Extension specialists, directors of small business development centers and business editors and book reviewers across the country. In addition, many colleges, universities and seminar leaders use this book as a text in their courses on small business and entrepreneurship.

I trust this latest edition of *Homemade Money* will prove beneficial to your business, and if so, I hope you'll recommend it to others. Thanks for your interest . . . and do write when you can find the time.

Barbara Brabec
HMM5 Feedback
P.O. Box 2137
Naperville IL 60567-2137